BIM Content
Development

BIM Content Development

Standards, Strategies, and Best Practices

Robert S. Weygant,
CSI, CDT, SCIP

Developed with the cooperation and support of the
Construction Specifications Institute

WILEY

John Wiley & Sons, Inc.

Library of Congress Cataloging-in-Publication Data:
Weygant, Robert S., 1973-
  BIM content development : standards, strategies, and best practices / Robert S. Weygant.
      p. cm.
  Includes index.
  ISBN 978-0-470-58357-9 (pbk.); 978-0-470-95133-0 (ebk); 978-0-470-95152-1 (ebk); 978-1-118-03045-5 (ebk); 978-1-118-03046-2 (ebk); 978-1-118-03047-9 (ebk)   1. Building information modeling. I. Title.
  TH437.W49   2011
  690.0285—dc22

                                                                          2010047226

Printed in the United States of America
10 9 8 7 6 5 4 3 2 1

Contents

Introduction: Using this Book

UNDERSTANDING BUILDING INFORMATION MODELING

What is BIM? Whether we are talking about building information modeling or building information management, BIM is a technology that has improved the way structures are designed and built. Just as CAD (computer-aided design) improved upon hand drafting, BIM is improving upon CAD. The difference is that BIM involves so many more project participants than just the architect. Building information modeling allows the architect to design and detail, the specifier to document, and the contractor to develop far more quickly than previous methods. The owner and facility manager also see tremendous benefits in forecasting and budgeting.

Initially, BIM was viewed as a tool to design in three dimensions and use components rather than lines. In the time that it has evolved, it has grown tremendously, to a tool that is used for model analysis, clash detection, product selection, and whole project conceptualization. Just as the aerospace and automotive industries develop digital prototypes of vehicles, the Architectural, Engineering and Construction (AEC) disciplines are now able to provide a digital representation of a building well before the first dollar is spent or the first shovel hits the ground.

BIM is by no means the panacea for all that ails the AEC communities—it's simply a better tool for the job. There is no expectation that every component will be accurate to the last screw or that colors will match identically. BIM provides a level of detail necessary to design and construct a specific project under specific conditions, analyze the design for its merits, and determine specific courses of action based on a greater level of detail than was previously available. Until recently, the components used within a BIM project were generic and simple in nature, more like a symbol for a component that is to be used than an exact replica of a specific product. As hardware and software technology improves and the number of involved manufacturers increases, the level of detail and amount of information improve as well.

Manufacturers are becoming more and more involved in BIM because industry trends dictate the necessity of BIM on certain projects. This increases the accuracy of the product information, in turn increasing the accuracy of the project. Some of the greatest benefits of BIM are the ability to analyze the benefits of a specific product when used in conjunction with others, perform space planning based on different sizes of actually available components, and, in many cases, conceptualize exactly what the space will look like once completed.

BASIC DEFINITIONS AS THEY APPLY TO BIM

- *Building*: Any structure, project, system, or space.
- *Information*: Knowledge of specific events or topics gathered or received by communication.
- *Modeling*: Creation of a schematic description of a system, theory, or design that accounts for its known or inferred properties for further study of its characteristics.
- *Management*: The organization and control of something.
- *Building information*: Knowledge applicable to a given project, system, or element.
- *Building modeling*: Description of a structure, project, system, or space by way of visual and graphic representation.
- *Information modeling*: A description of the attributes of a design for further study of its characteristics.
- *Building information modeling (BIM)*: A technology that allows relevant graphical and topical information related to the built environment to be stored in a relational database for access and management.
- *Building information management (BIM)*: The collection, organization, analysis, and distribution of attributed data contained within a building project.

WHO SHOULD READ THIS BOOK

Design professionals in the AEC (Architectural Engineering and Construction) communities can leverage the information in this book to implement best practices in their BIM strategy. Since every firm works a bit differently and every project has its own requirements, AEC professionals can develop a set of internal standards that are based on widely accepted formats and principles in use today. By developing new BIM standards based on current standards, the learning curve is made shallower, and interoperability between offices becomes easier.

The AEC communities have the responsibility of actually creating, placing, and managing the content from inception, so the more effort that is put into content creation up front, the less effort is required over time. A well-built window object can last as long as the software, needing little more than periodic modifications to options and underlying product and performance data. Managing the data is the cumbersome part for many, as the data must be kept organized and consistent between specifications, technical data sheets, CAD details, websites, and now BIM objects.

One must consider how this information is to be managed over time. If there is not a singularly qualified individual on staff who can maintain the information, then sourcing or acquisition of BIM content through a hosting agency such as ARCAT.com or Sweets can be a practical approach. These agencies organize multiple manufacturers in multiple product categories so they can be located and downloaded from a single source, rather than our going from website to website searching for specific components when time is short. When downloading BIM content from a manufacturer or content library, it is important to consider important points such as how it was created, the size and quality of the graphics, the amount and accuracy of the information and how dynamic the models are.

Not all content is created equal. Most readily accessible models are lacking a great deal of the product information and formatting necessary to sort and filter the model after it has been created. Regardless of whether the model is created in-house, outsourced, or downloaded for free, without consistent development strategies in place, the ability to provide accurate quantity takeoffs and schedules is diminished considerably. Geometry and graphics are the visible aspect of most any BIM component, but are not necessarily the most important. While the graphics of the model as a whole are critical, certain products need not have accurate graphics, as they are selected and specified based on their performance, not their appearance. This is typical of most mechanical and structural elements and many other architectural elements as well. The type of graphics and the level of information are determined by the individual firm working on a specific project, which has its own requirements and merits. Not all projects require the creation of a true as-built model "digital owner's manual," but in terms of content, it is always better to have the detail and data and never use them than to need them and not have them. Contractors are a driving force behind the growth of building information modeling. Some of BIM's greatest improvements to the construction industry as a whole are felt by the contractors, subcontractors, estimators, and supply-chain personnel. It is not uncommon to see a general contractor take a set of two-dimensional drawings and create a model prior to construction in order to affirm the constructability of the structure and analyze the model for phasing and estimation purposes.

BIM software has the ability to perform interference checking or "clash detection," which determines when the locations of two elements are in conflict with each other. In the case where a drain pipe runs across a floor for any length, it will slope downward to allow water to flow. If the pipe does not clear a structural member as it attempts to pass below it or if it interferes with the structural member, a "clash" is detected and the user is notified. This type of design conflict is difficult to spot and easily missed when dealing with several two-dimensional drawings. Determining these types of clashes saves contractors and owners millions of dollars and countless hours annually versus traditional design methods.

Phasing a model is a functionality that allows the contractor to record progress digitally and plan logistics accordingly. When products are to be brought on site, they need storage facilities that can accommodate them until they are installed. As they are installed, designing a specific workflow pattern ensures that subcontractors are not on top of each other. Phasing a project within a BIM model allows the contractor to find the closest and most appropriate storage locations and workflow patterns to minimize excess hours and fatigue associated with effort to move equipment and materials.

BIM data can be used by contractors to simplify estimation by automating quantity takeoffs, perform clash-detection studies to confirm that the design is buildable, and ultimately minimize errors and change orders.Building products are the building blocks of every construction project and, thus, the building blocks of a BIM project. Not only does BIM provide a new conduit through which products can be marketed and sold, it can simplify the processes by which supply-chain and sales personnel handle product ordering and distribution. Conceptualizations allow actual products to be placed in a model to determine size and aesthetic considerations, and, as products are placed within a project, they are quantified and organized in neat schedules. The details that differentiate the products are listed and the links to additional data and contact information are embedded within the model for reference.

BIM is different from CAD in terms of its function and purpose. While CAD drawings for manufacturers' products show every last detail, BIM is designed for the benefit of the architect and those implementing the product. This drastically limits the graphic representation of the product to only that information necessary to the architect for design and implementation. As product models are created, it's important to realize that they are not typically exact replicas of the product, but more of a symbol to represent the overall space the component takes up. The major appearance details are shown graphically, while the minor details are shown in terms of data in the model or omitted altogether where deemed unnecessary. Think of the component in terms of its scale in relation to the overall project. A general rule of thumb is to model the graphic elements that are visible when viewed from 10 to 15 feet away in their installed position.

Data drive the success or failure of BIM for manufacturers. While graphics are important within the model, a manufacturer wants to see his product specified and ultimately installed in the project. If we can't count the number of components used or even determine their names, providing the models in a BIM format is no different than using a symbol that comes with the software right out of the box. The identification information surrounding the actual products, using actual materials with actual sizes, is only the entry point for a good BIM component. Throughout this book, we will discuss the types of additional information necessary, how it can be used, and why it should be associated with the model.

I caution manufacturers against adding cost information into a model, as prices fluctuate constantly and it may be several months or even years from the time the model is created until the project is actually ready for construction. Adding cost information to an individual component can (and usually will) lead to headaches. It also cannot take into consideration the installation or labor costs associated with the project, so this value is best left to an estimator who may be leveraging the model for cost forecasting. Another pitfall with cost information is that without all components in the project tagged with cost information, the overall valuation will be inaccurate. The best method for costing within a BIM is still to perform square foot cost based on the assemblies used within a project. Organizing the components with their appropriate Uniformat and MasterFormat codes allows cost information to be easily derived from the model. Owners and facility managers can be provided with a "digital owner's manual" of a facility, providing them with the ability to schedule maintenance, forecast and budget for replacements, and track various usage throughout the lifecycle of the facility. Imagine a user interface that would allow us to point and click on a specific light fixture and turn it on or off, or find the camera nearest to a fire alarm that has just sounded. It all starts with a solid BIM that has been developed using actual components with the appropriate amount of information.

Regardless of the software used or the amount of information contained within the model, any BIM will be able to provide size, shape, and location information for components found within the project. At bare minimum, square footage and unit counts are available to analyze. Adding the attributed information about which specific components were used on the project allows for more detailed analysis and a more accurate basis from which to derive cost and replacement information. Basically, the more information that is put into the model, the more detailed is the analysis that can be performed.

WHAT TO EXPECT FROM THIS BOOK

BIM Content Development—Standards, Strategies, and Best Practices has been written to consider all members of a BIM-based project. The concepts within this book are meant to assist all parties—architects, specifiers, contractors, facilities managers, and owners—in developing and leveraging appropriate BIM content. Each member of the project has a different role and requires different information to perform his task. While the architect or design team is ultimately responsible for creating the model, the downstream users of the information contained in the model are of equal importance. Creating tools that allow the architect to pass information through the model to the downstream users of the model integrates everyone associated with the project into a singular team in which all benefit from BIM technology. The figure shows a typical hierarchy of information as it is passed from person to person during the project cycle.

This book is not meant to be a how-to guide for specific software platforms, but a ready reference guide on best practices and principles that apply to all BIM software. Each type of software has advantages and limitations, so from the practices and principles contained within this book, we can extend

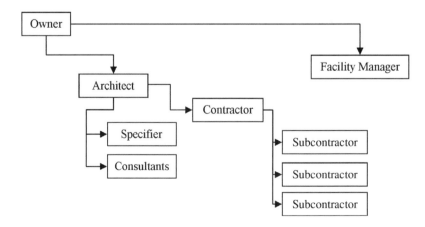

Project information flow

the knowledge to our software of choice and implement the portions that apply to a given situation.

Every firm and every project is different, so it is unlikely that anyone will use every part of this book on a single project or in a single practice. The level of information and detail necessary for a given situation will vary, and since implementation of practices from the book is very much à la carte, specifics of content development for the different categories are organized in a ready-reference format in Part III. Basic concepts of content development are approached from an angle that balances functionality and accuracy to provide the most effective BIM solutions for every member of a project. Content types are viewed with considerations of developing the materials used, the graphics or geometry that are drawn, the types of data and information necessary for a given category of an element, and potential ways to leverage the element effectively.

Management and organization of content is an essential aspect of creating BIM components. Once the components are created, they are reusable, so long as the information about the products remains current. Every time a product or a system's performance values change, or every time a product or option is added or eliminated from a manufacturer's offering, the models must change accordingly. Maintaining this type of information is no easy task, so keeping a clear and simple organizational structure of the product information is critical to the long-term functionality of the components.

Industry standards and formats for information management exist for many organizations. For the construction industry, CSI MasterFormat and Uniformat are the most widely accepted formats. They organize construction information based on the work results and types of construction elements within a structure. In terms of BIM, standards and formats such as these provide ready access filters with which to sort and organize large amounts of information quickly and easily. These formats organize the information that is necessary to determine *what* product was selected, but cannot qualify *why* and *how* a product was chosen over another. This type of information is necessary in determining which products to use for a specific set of conditions, so additional formats are both available and being developed to manage this type of information. *BIM Content Development—Standards, Strategies, and Best Practices* gives an in-depth look at the different standards available, how and where to implement them in BIM content, and how to leverage the information once the standards are added to BIM projects.

Throughout the book, you'll find TIPS, which will help you make decisions about what to put in a component, how to think about its development, and, in some cases, whether or not it's actually necessary.

FUTURE OF BIM

Building information models are driven by the components or *content* used to build them. A BIM project is best described as a digital representation or prototype of what is to be built. The use of real-world products allows us to analyze the performance and aesthetics of a building before it is built in order to confirm design intent. The ability to perform this type of analysis is controlled mainly by the level of detail and accuracy that goes into the content. This, among other things discussed in the book, is what differentiates a BIM project from a traditional CAD-based project.

The wall, floor, ceiling, and roof are primary components that make up the core and shell of a building. These elements carry the information necessary to determine and outline spaces within a structure, and the overall form the building will take. In addition to their graphical aspects, these components have the ability to carry the information about their individual compositions or makeup, from limitations of their usage to the performance aspects that help us determine why a specific configuration was selected.

Mechanical, electrical, and plumbing components are used to develop entire systems within a building, which allows powerful analysis to be performed from HVAC load calculations to balancing a circuit panel, to laying out the most effective domestic water and fire protection systems. Every component used from the longest pipe to the smallest fitting can be accounted for, which simplifies the estimation process considerably. All of this analysis, though, is dependent on properly created and formatted content.

Beyond the core and shell of a building and the systems contained within are the components that amass to form the building. Products such as doors and windows, fixtures and fittings, furnishings and equipment, and lighting provide a conceptualization of the actual building and the information used to select the products. Openings such as windows and doors are selected and specified based on specific performance criteria and affect the overall energy performance of a building based on such criteria. Embedding performance data into a model allows the designer to actively specify and analyze the model based on the actual product used. This simplifies product selection and specification by allowing a designer to test the use of a various products to see how each will perform.

Ultimately, BIM is a technology that allows us not only to create visual simulations of a project, but to provide a digital prototype of a building prior to construction. Just as no jet aircraft would roll off of the assembly line before it is fully tested, BIM allows a building to be built and tested before the first pile is driven into the ground. Without appropriate content to use for model analysis, a bottleneck is formed. Currently, a great deal of the content available is limited in the amount of actual performance information available to leverage. Throughout the book, you will find tips, tricks, and best practices for adding information into the models to enhance its functionality without overburdening the overall project.

PART I

Getting Started

CHAPTER 1

The Mental Transition to Building Information Modeling

BIM—A WHOLE-BUILDING APPROACH TO DESIGN

Building information modeling changes the way architects, engineers, and contractors work today. It promotes collaboration among all members of a project team, and opens the door for additional members to add relevant information to the design before considerable development has occurred. In traditional two-dimensional drawing, the design and documentation are disjointed in that there is no real relationship between a window and a wall, a wall and a roof, or the roof and the outdoors. BIM allows the design to be looked at as a whole, rather than as individual components that show up on some schedule that was manually created.

The design process no longer consists of lines that represent and enclose spaces and symbols that represent building components. Rather than drawing a series of lines that represent the location of a wall, we can draw the wall itself as a single unit, carrying all of the components and layers associated with it. Floors, ceilings, and roofs are drawn as the areas in which they exist, with the ability to add a specific slope, thickness, and type, as well as identify every component of the assembly. Rather than symbols being used to represent building components in a project, such as windows, doors, fixtures, and fittings, a graphic representation of the component is placed at its appropriate location. These components may be trained to understand how they are to be placed within the project, what they are, and how they relate to adjacent elements in the project.

Openings such as windows and doors are elements placed in a wall to allow the passage of light, traffic, and, in some cases, air. As a window or door is placed into a project, it is trained to remove a specific volume from the wall based on its determined rough opening. Since the window or door is typically not as thick as the wall itself, it allows the user to look at or through the opening from different three-dimensional views, providing a realistic perspective of the building. As components are placed into a model, and volume is removed from the host component, in this case a wall, the information is stored within the software so it may be retrieved later. The type and counts of each component are noted, as well as their dimensions, areas, and locations. Above and beyond visualization and conceptualization of a project, this type of information may be leveraged for square foot cost estimation early in the project, and more accurate quantity takeoffs during bidding. Figure 1.1 depicts the relationships between two-dimensional linework and three-dimensional modeling.

During the early stages of a project, the most important elements used in a project are the walls, floors, roofs, and openings. These elements determine

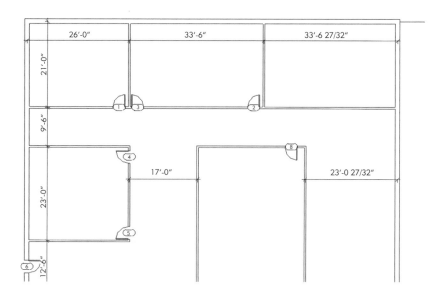

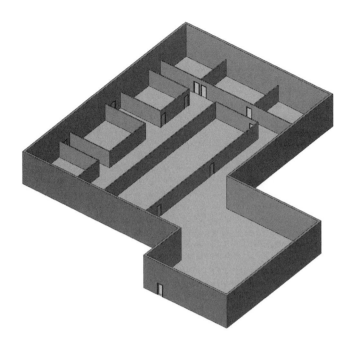

FIGURE 1.1 2D linework and 3D modeling

how spaces are enclosed, how those spaces are accessed, where natural light and visibility exists, and why their locations may be beneficial or detrimental. Before the addition of a considerable number of components that complete the overall design, these core elements are added to the model for analysis of the preliminary or schematic design. In many cases, interior walls may not even be created at this point, as locations of HVAC (heating, ventilating, and air conditioning) components, plumbing, and electrical wiring often take precedence over the location of interior partitions. The design process of every project is different, as every project has a different intended purpose, a different set of design criteria, and a different construction style. Building information modeling gives architects and engineers the flexibility to design in the same way they usually do, but to have a more robust set of tools to work with, a more intelligent design platform, and the ability to analyze the design on the fly.

The most notable difference between computer-aided design (CAD) and building information modeling is the aspect of working in three dimensions. As we transition to working in three dimensions, the brain must be rewired to think in three dimensions. For some this is an uphill climb, while for others, it is second nature. Ultimately, the finished plans submitted to the contractor for construction are two-dimensional, and on paper; however, during the design process the model created may be viewed at any angle, from any location. This allows owners and designers the ability to see exactly what is being built prior to construction, as well as to determine spatial relationships and make determinations of how much area is necessary for a given room or space. Three-dimensional conceptualizations and high-resolution, photorealistic renderings become a function of the design model. These high-definition deliverables allow the industry to digitally prototype a construction project, affirming design intent and visually confirming that design expectations are being met.

As noted, a model created can be viewed at any angle necessary. All of these views are a function of the model as it is being created, and automatically update themselves based on what happens in the design. If we place a window in plan view, it will show up in its corresponding location when viewed in an elevation view. If we place a lighting fixture from within a 3D view, it shows up in its appropriate location when viewed in plan view. This eliminates the need to manually create an entire series of views as with traditional CAD software. Views may also be created that consider only specific components, allowing quick creation of trade-specific drawing sheets, which may apply to structural, electrical, plumbing, or other work to be performed on the project. This drastically reduces the amount of time necessary to create drawing sheets, maximizing the amount of time available for the architect to think through the actual design. The expertise of an architect lies in his ability to create beauty and maximize the aesthetic. Putting pen to paper so to speak, only documents and visualizes the architect's ideas so that others may construct what he has created, so it seems only natural to minimize the amount of effort necessary to convey the design.

Once the modeling of the project is complete, two-dimensional detailing occurs in order to create exact depictions of transitions, terminations, penetrations, and junctions throughout the project. Where a roof meets a wall or a wall meets the floor, there are countless ways in which construction could occur, based on project circumstances that are not known by the software. Since the software is not intuitive enough to understand different design criteria and construction methods, we rely on two-dimensional detailing to convey this information. Typically, either this line work is drawn in manually or additional detail objects are dropped in for repetitive types of detailing. The section view of dimensional lumber or a concrete block is the same throughout the project, so rather than redrawing the line work every time, a two-dimensional detail object may be dropped in to represent the cut view.

Another component of two-dimensional views is the annotations or callouts that are used to point to various materials and components shown. With building information modeling, information about components and materials can be generated automatically by adding specifically designed annotations to call out that material or component.

While there is nothing wrong with the way the design, construction, and procurement teams work today, building information modeling forces the industry to rethink how projects are delivered. In a traditional project delivery method, there is little collaboration among the parties. *The owner works with the architect. The owner works with the contractor. The architect works with the contractor. The contractor works with the subcontractor. The project is designed and built.* Linguistically, the last four sentences are disjointed, and while there is nothing wrong with each sentence independently, when read together, they do not flow. The same is true of any type of project; the more collaboration that occurs, the better the flow, and the faster it happens. In a collaborative environment, we may read something like this: *The owner, architect, contractor, and subcontractors collaborate, and the project is designed and built.* These are the fundamental concepts of Integrated Project Delivery or IPD.

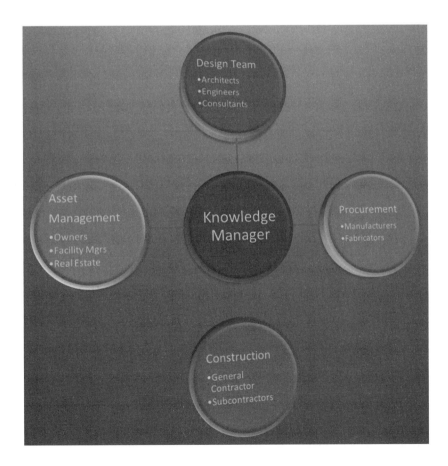

FIGURE 1.2

The collaborative approach to design and construction

CAD VS. BIM

Building information modeling offers many advancements over traditional two-dimensional and even three-dimensional computer-aided design technology. The original concept of CAD was to be able to draw simple lines quickly and easily without having to rethink and erase large parts of a drawing on paper. This was a tremendous advancement over hand drawing and considerably cuts down the amount of time necessary to document a design. As CAD technology grew, it allowed us to separate different line types and categorize the different lines into various layers based on what was necessary in given views, and ultimately entered the world of three-dimensional design. When architecture moved from designing using two-dimensional lines to using three-dimensional solids, the game had changed forever; enter building information modeling.

The technology shift from CAD to BIM gave the design community the ability to look at not just what an element within the project looks like, but what it is. A wall that was previously represented as a series of lines in different views is now a component in and of itself. It carries information about each component that makes up the assembly, how the assembly performs as a whole, and even what the assembly is in terms of adjacent components. The wall intuitively determines how it connects to other components, and how other components connect to it. When placing a window within a wall, the wall understands that it must create an opening, and the window understands that it can only be placed in a vertical application such as a wall.

Building information modeling opened the door for assigning attributes to each component created within the model. Whether it is a dimension, a material, or a nongraphical piece of information regarding the performance of the component, the information may be contained within the component for access, manipulation, and retrieval. As simple as it may sound, this advancement created one of the largest cost benefits that the design and construction communities have ever experienced. This parametric technology allows us to reuse components and line work over and over, rather than needing to redraw them on each project. Instead of having to draw a different door for each size, material, or style, attributes are assigned to the various dimensions, materials, and styles. These attributes can be assigned values, which can allow a single door component to represent a countless number of combinations of size, material, and style to suit a project.

Outside of graphics, building information modeling has advanced architecture's ability to manage information effectively. Each component within a project has the ability to carry as much or as little information as is necessary to suit the needs of the owner, design team, specifier, or contractor. In most cases little or no information above and beyond dimensions and basic graphic information is added to these components, as the information is generally related to a specific manufacturer's product. Architects are not in the business of creating product information for manufacturers, so the responsibility for providing models that contain exact information about a product lies in the hands of the manufacturer. When specific attributes regarding the performance, usage, installation, and lifecycle of the product are added, architects may leverage this information in several different ways: a model may be queried to extract the information for creating construction documents and the project manual; a series of schedules can be created to represent each and every component of the model; contractors can sort through the model to find the required performance for the work they are responsible for. The software itself has the potential to leverage information that is placed in the model for criteria analysis. Attributes related to energy consumption may be analyzed, as well as the structural performance of the individual component in the building as a whole, thermal performance, and code compliance, and a host of other studies may be performed. Third-party software plug-ins are allowing better and more accurate analysis of models as the technology advances, but still rely on the basic information associated with individual components. The more information we add to the components and the project as a whole, the more analysis we may perform as time moves forward.

During construction it is not uncommon to find instances where two elements interfere or "clash" with each other because the design did not take into consideration exact locations. When a design is created using two-dimensional means, the various views used to represent the project are disjointed, so when dealing with components, such as ductwork and pipe, it is difficult to accurately depict their elevation and slope such that they do not interfere with structural members. This "clash detection" technology, shown in Figure 1-3, allows more accurate design prior to construction, minimizing and in some cases eliminating costly change orders that occur in the field.

Building information modeling is by no means the panacea for all that ails the architecture and construction professions and is not without its downsides and pitfalls. As with all new technologies, there is a learning curve associated with understanding new methods for performing tasks and becoming skilled in using different software. Seasoned professionals who have been using computer-aided design technology for most or all of their career may find themselves resistant to this change until they understand all of the benefits associated with switching. Just as architects who drew by hand were resistant to designing with CAD, many architects drawing with CAD

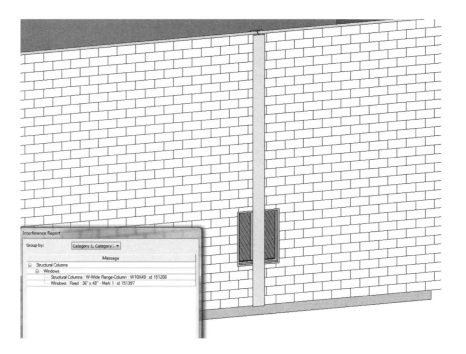

FIGURE 1.3
Clash detection analysis

are resistant to BIM. Outside forces such as government agencies and code bodies are causing some professionals to switch by requiring the use of BIM on specific projects or in certain locations. Over the past couple of years, building information modeling has experienced exponential growth. Prior to that, there was a chicken and egg scenario where architects were hesitant to switch until more manufacturers made their products available, and manufacturers were hesitant to make their models available until more architects were using it. A relatively slow growth pattern ensued until critical mass was reached, where enough architects and enough manufacturers were involved to make it a viable mainstream option. Since then, manufacturers have seen the benefits of making components available, and architects have found themselves saving considerable amounts of time between the new technology and the abundance of content available for modeling.

CAD + SPECS = BIM

To put it simply, CAD + specifications = BIM. Without the attributed data associated with components, we might as well be using traditional CAD software. By definition, CAD is computer-aided design, regardless of whether it is performed in two dimensions or three dimensions. BIM is building information modeling, with emphasis on the "I", which is what differentiates the two technologies. CAD can be defined as both computer-aided design and computer-aided drafting, but both cases emphasize the "computer-aided" aspect of the proposition. BIM can be defined as both building information modeling and building information management, and, similarly, the "building information" aspect is emphasized.

The real value proposition of building information modeling lies in the ability to analyze data. Any cheap CAD software can provide conceptualizations and visualizations of a project and work in multiple views based on a singular model. This is nothing new. Better CAD software provides robust professional tools that are more intuitive and are based on the needs of the design team. Neither of these technologies has the ability to understand the difference between a floor and a roof, as they do not have the embedded information that defines the differences between the two.

For all practical intents and purposes, CAD carries only graphic information. There are rudimentary ways of organizing the different line types to create a minor definition for them, but CAD does not have the ability to understand their relationships to other components, only to their place in space. If we take three-dimensional CAD technology and merge it with the information found in a project manual, we have the ability to assign as well as limit the associations we create. We can create a series of paints and coatings, and limit them based on the VOC (volatile organic compound) requirements of the project. We can create a series of walls, and limit them based on their thermal performance. This allows project templates to be created that may be reused over and over and that carry specific requirements. Schools, for instance, may not be allowed to use products that contain VOCs. A template may be created that carries only products that apply, or that is designed specifically to show the VOC amounts for all components in the project. Other components may be required to attain specific performance values and the design team may have preferred manufacturers for certain component types. Embedding this type of information into a model allows us to "digitally prototype" a project well before construction, analyze it for its merits and miscalculations, and correct or improve upon design elements before the first shovel hits the dirt.

The graphics of BIM outline what a component looks like. The specifications carry information regarding what a product is and why it was selected. There are justified reasons for using certain products in certain applications. Whether it is sizing an HVAC system based on the size of the project or using specific types of metals for roof flashings based on its proximity to the ocean, there is intent behind each decision the architect, engineer, specifier, or contractor makes. While we would like to think that all of these parties are collaborating on every project they perform together, this is not the case. Information can be disjointed, so to assist in information exchange, creating a single point of reference from which information may be sourced allows everybody to have the correct facts without actually being in the same office or even working on the project at the same time. The building information model is the logical point of reference, as it has the ability to carry both graphic and nongraphic information regarding every aspect of the project, from general requirements all the way through facility management. The earlier this information is embedded into the project, the more accurate and useful it may be throughout the project lifecycle.

In building projects today, the design begins with the owner and the architect. An owner may hire an architect to design a building based on his needs and requirements. Early in the project lifecycle, very few decisions are made regarding specific components and exact details. Using building information modeling to create a preliminary design of the building based on its walls, floors, roofs, and openings gives both the architect and owner a rough idea of the project scope. Generally, no information is contained within the components used for this schematic design; but what if there were? If we look at a project as linear rather than a series of steps or phases, it makes more sense to embed attributes into these components but omit values until such a time as decisions are made. This streamlines the design process by minimizing the amount of component swapping that is necessary throughout design development. Rather than create five versions of the same component to represent five different levels of detail or project phases, it is far more effective to create a single component that can evolve based on the amount of information known about it. A window, for instance, might morph from opening, to window, to aluminum window, to aluminum casement window, to a specific manufacturer's product as decisions are made regarding that specific component. This allows information to be added in a rolling fashion rather than during specific phases, or even all at once.

Component selection can be tricky and is often based on the knowledge of other related products. Specific types of roof insulation may be necessary based on the type of roof membrane used and how it is attached based on the type of substrate beneath it. The type of roof membrane used may be dependent on the location of the project and the needs of the owner. We don't have to know all of these pieces of information to make decisions, but if there are hard-line project requirements that can be built into the model early on, product decisions that are based on those requirements may be made to narrow the field to only products that are suitable.

When researching products for their suitability in certain circumstances, architects and specifiers often must search high and low to find information that helps them make decisions. By embedding additional resource information into the components in the form of Web links, the design team has a powerful tool to find the information necessary to determine and affirm whether a product is suitable for their design. Early in a project, the requirements for the glazing in a building may be unclear. Embedding links to more information from either specific manufacturers or trade industry organizations can assist in appropriate specification with the least amount of effort. Similar information may be embedded regarding the installation procedures, procurement, code restrictions, and maintenance requirements of the product.

CONCLUSION

As we transition from computer-aided design to building information modeling, we need to understand that it is a long-term transition that benefits not only the design team but the world as a whole. BIM allows us to digitally prototype projects the same way the automotive and aerospace industries have done for years. If we look at the improvements seen by the automotive industry from leveraging digital prototyping, we will see that today we have much safer cars that are designed to last much longer, perform better, and get better fuel economy. If we translate that to building design and construction, it will ultimately equate to better structural integrity of buildings capable of withstanding seismic activity, weather events, and even terrorist attacks.

By analyzing information in the model, we can create buildings that use less electricity, have more efficient and effective heating and cooling systems, and protect their occupants from harm. Whether we want to improve indoor air quality, minimize the amount of artificial light in a building, create efficient traffic patterns throughout a building, or plan for means of egress in the event of an emergency, building information modeling is a powerful analytical tool. It takes what we know of design and construction and hands it to a computer that returns results that we may analyze and use in making decisions.

To err is human, but to truly botch a task requires a computer. It is important to understand that BIM is little more than a better tool for the job. It does not replace the knowledge and understanding of a seasoned specifier who is expert in selecting products, nor does it replace an architect capable of designing magnificent structures. Engineers are still required to design structural, HVAC, plumbing, and electrical systems. Building information modeling takes much of the legwork out of the design by creating tools that automate mundane tasks. Software does not understand the physics of force, electricity, hydrology, or strength of materials, but can only manipulate the information supplied by competent individuals who are expert in the design and implementation of a given product.

BIM should not be thought of as a decision engine or "configurator" that will select the right product for project, or a tool that will automatically generate our specifications based on the products. These are noble concepts, and one day artificial intelligence may allow building information modeling to learn from its mistakes and assist in product selection. I would caution us to be careful what we wish for, though, as that type of technology would put the entire design team on notice.

CHAPTER 2

Content Hierarchy

UNDERSTANDING MATERIALS, OBJECTS, ASSEMBLIES, AND PROJECTS

Before developing content, it is important to understand how materials, objects, assemblies, and projects interrelate. This is the backbone of the BIM. Having a clear understanding of each component will allow us to create a stronger model that is more organized and will allow for intelligent access to the data.

The two most common types of content are objects and assemblies. Objects are stand-alone components, such as windows and doors, and assemblies are a series of components that work together to create a single element. Walls, floors, roofs, and ceilings are the most common examples of assemblies, but assemblies can extend further into stairs, railings, piping, ductwork, and wiring as well. There are substantial differences between the two in how they are created, managed, and implemented in a project, but they share the common element of the materials from which they are created.

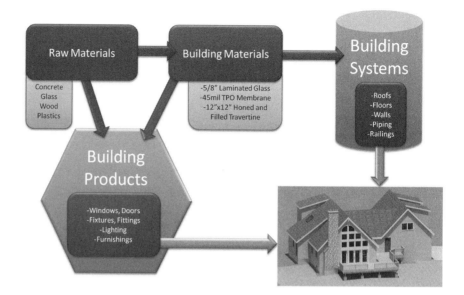

FIGURE 2.1 How materials, objects, and assembles interrelate

Materials are the baseline from which all graphics are derived. They carry information about the composition, physical performance, and appearance of each solid used in the component. Whether it is structural steel, glass, wood, concrete, or paint, each is its own material with its own unique properties. In a real-world project, steel, wood, glass, and concrete are not actual materials. They each have more specific descriptive properties, such as compressive strength, tensile strength, shading coefficient, or species, and may have specific finishes, such as primed, stained with semi-gloss polyurethane, bronze tinted, or broom finish. Materials that carry the information that pertains to their appearance and performance can be analyzed and selected based on their individual merits. This is crucial when dealing with wall, floor, ceiling, and roof assemblies, which are made up of multiple materials, each with performance aspects unrelated to the assembly as a whole. Figure 2.1 shows us how materials are entered into objects and assemblies, acting as the basis of the BIM hierarchy.

WHAT IS A BIM OBJECT?

Objects are stand-alone components that work on their own inside a BIM project and don't rely on adjacent components to be understood. Objects usually carry information about their identity, appearance, performance, and usage and should carry all of the information necessary to design, locate, specify, and analyze a given product. In addition, the information about the materials and components that make up the object is added. For a window the added information might include the handing or operation, glass type and color, grids, weather stripping and hardware, and any other components that may be relevant to the appearance or functionality of a window.

Certain objects can only be placed in specific orientations or locations. Windows and doors are always placed in walls, recessed lights are always placed on ceilings, and a skylight is always mounted in a roof. Thinking of objects in terms of their real-world applications and constraints can aid in developing components that will do only what they are capable of doing and limit the user's ability to inadvertently place a component incorrectly. In Figure 2.2, common window and door objects might be configured as single or double swinging, or have multiple units affixed to each other. In order for objects to accurately represent real-world applications, we must think of them not just based upon what they look like, but on how they are used, designed with, and installed.

Use caution when using location or orientation limitations on certain objects, as there may be unique situations where they do not apply. For instance, much of the time a ceiling fan is located in a ceiling, but, in some cases, it could be placed on an exposed structural member beneath the ridge of a roof. An object that relies on a surface or "face" allows the fan to be placed on either a ceiling or a structural member.

FIGURE 2.2 Common window and door objects

WHAT IS A BIM ASSEMBLY?

Assemblies are made up of several materials and components to provide an easy-to-use element that is created or "instantiated" by drawing a line or series of joined lines to enclose an area. When a line is drawn, for practical purposes, it is one dimensional. The information inserted in the data set for a given assembly will provide the second, third, and even fourth dimensions. Assemblies carry dimensional and attributed information about the different components that make up the assembly, such as the thickness and type of every component involved, from the interior to the exterior surface, or from end to end.

Individual components and materials carry their own information, which not only drives the assembly but allows them to be created once and reused an infinite number of times. A very simple example of an assembly is a peanut butter and jelly sandwich. A PB&J sandwich is made up of bread, peanut butter, and jelly. Peanut butter, jelly, and bread would all be created as materials and carry all of the information that applies to them individually. When assembled, the same components will carry the information that pertains to them collectively.

Any change to the assembly, no matter how small, will result in a different assembly. If we have four bread options of white, wheat, rye, or potato bread, two options of creamy or chunky peanut butter, and three options of grape, strawberry, or raspberry jelly, we could multiply out to 24 possible peanut butter and jelly combinations. If we add the possibility of an open-faced sandwich, we'd have 48 combinations, and if the peanut butter were on the top instead of the bottom, there would be 96 combinations.

Now that the combinations are created, there is the aspect of information that applies to the *sandwich* as well as the components that make it up. Different combinations will have different values based on the components used. In some cases they are additive. If we want to know the total calorie count or grams of sugar in the sandwich, we can add the sugar and calorie count from each component to provide a total for the sandwich itself. In other cases, information is subjective and cannot be quantified by totaling values from included components. For instance, shelf life is not determined by a sum of the shelf life of sandwich materials. It is a function of the sandwich as a whole, so becomes an attribute of the sandwich. Figure 2.3 shows us section views which detail the thickness and appearance of each material in the assembly.

Later in the book, we will discuss specific attributes and considerations for the different types of assemblies.

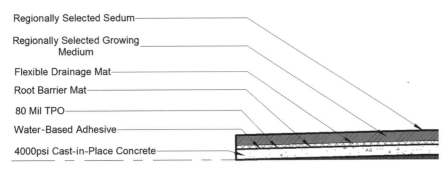

Regionally Selected Sedum
Regionally Selected Growing Medium
Flexible Drainage Mat
Root Barrier Mat
80 Mil TPO
Water-Based Adhesive
4000psi Cast-in-Place Concrete

Typical Roof Assembly

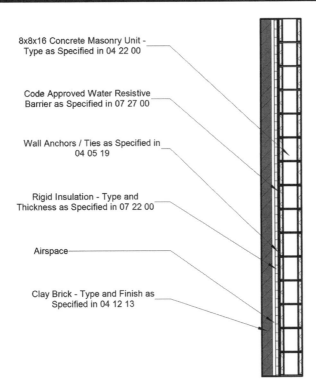

8x8x16 Concrete Masonry Unit - Type as Specified in 04 22 00

Code Approved Water Resistive Barrier as Specified in 07 27 00

Wall Anchors / Ties as Specified in 04 05 19

Rigid Insulation - Type and Thickness as Specified in 07 22 00

Airspace

Clay Brick - Type and Finish as Specified in 04 12 13

Typical Wall Assembly

FIGURE 2.3 Typical roof and wall assemblies

WHAT GOES INTO OBJECTS AND ASSEMBLIES?

Graphics

An assembly is mainly driven by where the user places it and how large it is. The graphical aspect of an assembly is primarily determined by the thickness of each component layer, colors and finishes on interior and exterior faces, and the hatch pattern used in section views. Little more than these items is associated with the graphics.

Objects are much more graphically oriented. Objects have several pieces of geometry that are combined to create the shape and appearance. How detailed these components are is determined by many factors, including the type of component, location in the project (is it visible?), and overall size. Specifics on geometry and component types are discussed in Part III of this book.

Data and Product Information

An object or assembly should carry enough information to accurately specify an actual product. It should provide the architect or specifier with the ability to determine not just what a product is, but why it was selected, how it performs, who is responsible for it, where it may be installed, when it should be installed, how it is maintained, and when it should be replaced. This is a "cradle-to-cradle" approach to building products, which looks at them from design through replacement.

Product data can be either hard-coded into the components or linked to a website, depending on the information in question. It does not always need to be in the model. With technology allowing us access to information from anywhere, linking information is often a more practical method of maintaining the data. Data that are used by the software for analysis purposes always needs to be directly in the model, but it is often better to provide a link for more referential information. This allows the data to be updated in one location, and the model can access that location when requested.

There are several types of product data associated with a given component, which are easily categorized as follows:

- Identification—*What is the product?*
- Performance—*How well does the product work?*
- Installation—*How is the product installed?*
- Appearance—*What does the product look like?*
- Lifecycle/sustainability—*How is this product maintained?*

There are other categories of product data, but for the most part, these are the most common, and are a good high-level starting point for structuring product information. Throughout the book, we'll see examples of different product types and the types of product data associated with them.

Product information in a BIM is what differentiates a graphic depiction of a component and a digital representation of what the materials, objects, and assemblies are. Information should be limited to technical information and that which is necessary to select, design, install, or maintain the specific component.

Tip

Before adding data to the component, ask, "Who needs this information?"

WHAT IS A BIM PROJECT?

The BIM project is the culmination of all assemblies and components used in the actual project. The components used in the project are not necessarily modeled if the scope of the design project does not dictate their necessity. For instance, on a commercial interiors project, we may not see anything on the shell of the building, and in an exterior remodel, we may not find any interior components. The level of detail associated with a project is determined by the design team, and the ultimate intent and use of the BIM.

BIM projects can be used for everything from massing studies and basic schematic design, to cost estimating and scheduling, to facility management and project analysis. What we can get out of a BIM is based entirely on what we put into it. This is where the level of detail contained in the materials, objects, and systems is critical. These details compose the data used to analyze the model, so if this information is missing or incorrect, analysis cannot be performed.

A BIM project is searchable the same way a database is. Actually, a BIM is little more than a database with a graphic user interface. Most software also provides an environment where we can view all of the data without ever looking at the graphics. This allows for quick and easy management of the data within a project by persons who may or may not be familiar with how to use BIM software.

Within any given project, virtually any piece of information can be located regarding a specific component; we can find out what color it is, what floor is it on, who manufactured it, when it will need replacing, how many of them are there on the entire project, and so on. The amount of information is limited only by what is put into the model, so developing a quality library of components that can be used over and over, similar to an office master, is critical to streamlining the efforts of the design team. If each component is developed with the attributes necessary to perform the model analysis desired on a specific project, periodic maintenance is all that is necessary to develop projects quickly and easily.

Materials carry information relevant to objects and assemblies, and objects and assemblies carry information relevant to projects. This is the basic hierarchy of BIM. Organizing and maintaining this information can become very confusing, so it is essential to put together a strategy for managing the information and to employ standards and formats that are commonly recognized in order to allow the model to be useful above and beyond the internal development team. The Construction Specifications Institute (CSI) maintains a series of standards and formats recognized by the architectural and construction communities that are the most effective methods of cataloging information within a BIM.

CHAPTER 3

Understanding Parameters, Attributes, and Constraints

PARAMETERS

What Are Parameters and Attributes?

The dictionary defines a parameter as a set of physical properties whose values determine the characteristics or behavior of something. In terms of building information modeling (BIM), parameters and attributes are a series of pairs that carry an attribute or title, and a value associated with the title. The primary benefit of organizing information with parametrics is the ability to input, access, modify, and extract the information quickly and easily, without having to look at the actual graphics. Parameters can control more than dimensions, though, having the ability to control materials, colors, and actual attributed specification and performance data.

The difference between traditional computer-aided design (CAD)-based software and BIM is the ability to assign values to dimensions, text values, and other pieces of information that may be beneficial inside a project. Parameters allow us the ability to research products while we're inside a BIM project.

Think about being able to look at a door or window and quickly determine which one to use based on the U-factor, solar heat gain coefficient, available color options, or performance values. Graphics can now contain powerful information that helps us determine not just what is in the model but why it was selected. This information can flow from the design, into specification, through construction, and into facility management. If information is placed in a model early, it can assist in making educated decisions about which products to use to meet the design criteria of the project.

The most commonly used type of parameter is a length or dimension parameter. This is used to simplify BIM object creation and management. A window or door, for instance, may be available in hundreds of different sizes, but a single object can represent all of them, using parametrics. By creating a dimension and giving it a name, as shown in Figure 3.1, one can assign one or more values to the dimension. Generally, a BIM object will have several dimensional parameters, all of which may be slightly different for a given version or type. If we have a dimension called width and another called height, the parameters created can all be given independent values, but clustered together to create versions of a BIM object.

With the development of BIM objects, we're dealing with real-world products in real-world situations, so it is also important to take into consideration what the product is made of. Geometric solids can have material parameters attached to them that allow classification of each component of an object based on actual materials. The materials used in products often determine where and why they are used, so they are essential aspects of content. Rarely is it enough to simply call out a color for component, as a door that is red gives no indication of whether it is made of wood, steel, or some composite material.

Here is a very basic example of both materials and dimensions used as parameters to determine the construction of something. Let's say we're creating an object that is a simple ball. To make the ball dynamic we would add a few parameters to allow it to be adjusted as necessary to suit the needs of the user. We could add a parameter for the diameter, the color, and the material of the ball. If we assigned 2 inches to the diameter, red to the color, and rubber to the material, we have created a 2-inch-diameter red rubber ball. Because the object is parametric we could quickly and easily switch it to a 1-inch-diameter mill-finish steel ball, or a 12-inch-diameter blue plastic ball.

Several different types of attributes and parameters may be used inside a BIM, and we will discuss these later on, but the most commonly used are those of dimension and material, as they determine the overall appearance

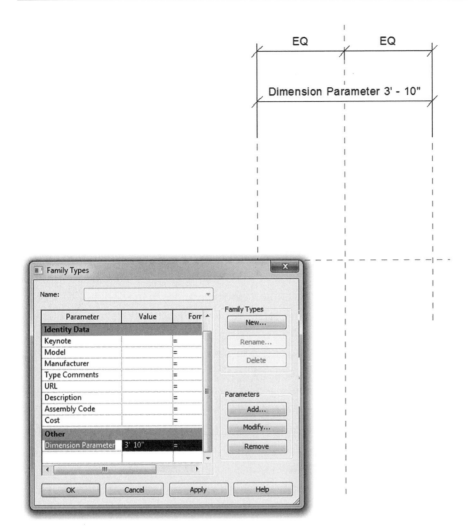

FIGURE 3.1 Dimension parameter

of the component that is being developed. Depending on whom we ask, parameters and attributes can be considered essentially the same thing. I prefer to differentiate them by considering parameters to be values of a graphic or visual nature, and attributes to be values of informational nature that do not directly affect the appearance. *Length* is a parameter, since it changes the appearance of the model, and *weight* is an attribute, since it changes the data but is a nongraphical value.

Types of Parameters and Attributes

Different types of parameters are used for different purposes and, depending on which software we are using, are managed differently and have different limitations. There are several other parameter types that consider industry-specific items for engineering communities and specialty and calculated information, such as hyperlinks, area, and volume, but most content developed uses the following parameter types as a minimum.

- *Length*: As we discussed, dimensional parameters such as length allow us to assign a name to a dimension, rather than just a value. An additional benefit of this is the ability to translate between units automatically. The software can programmatically convert between SI and metric units, so if an object is developed in feet and inches and loaded into a project that is working in metric, it automatically converts to the appropriate metric notation.

- *Area*: The area parameter is essential for performing quantity takeoffs and estimation within a model. In many cases it is automatically determined, but in other cases a user may develop a calculation to automatically determine a specific area based on dimensions made parametric. For instance, for a window to meet egress code it is required to have a specific clear opening area. The software cannot intuitively define the opening area without input from the user creating the object. By creating parameters for clear opening width and clear opening height, the clear opening area can be determined programmatically using simple arithmetic.

- *Angle*: Angle and slope parameters allow us to create a dimension that can either identify a slope or an angle, or change the orientation of an object relative to its surroundings. It is commonly used in roof slopes, but also found in several other locations from lighting to piping and ductwork, stairs, and railings.

- *Text*: The text parameter is sort of the catchall to parametrics. It allows us to assign any value to any attribute. It's most beneficial when dealing with informational properties, identification, and attributes that are not used by the software for analysis. Everything from a product name and description, to the ASTM performance aspects can be listed as a text-based attribute.

- *Boolean (yes/no)*: Yes/no parameters or checkboxes are mainly used to turn graphics on and off or to note whether a component does or does not have a specific accessory. It is an easy way to change graphic appearances without tremendously increasing file size. Rather than embedding different types of graphics, often times we can turn on and off geometry to perform the same task.

- *Number*: Number parameters allow an attribute to be categorized using a specific number of decimal places, and in many cases can be rounded to suit the needs of the project.

- *Integer*: Whole-number attributes are often used in arrays or to count the overall number of a specific component. These differ from a number attribute in that they can only be whole numbers, so we must be careful using this type of attribute when dealing with calculations, as division of two integers may result in a fraction or decimal.
- *Hyperlinks*: Hyperlink parameters allow the user to add a dynamic link to the model that allows the software to automatically open a specific URL using the default browser. This is a tremendous benefit when attempting to add attributed information that might change frequently. Attributes that are not used by the software to analyze the model are usually better linked rather than embedded.

There are other types of parameters that are more specific to performance values or physical properties associated with certain types of components. Structural components may have force, mass, load, or stress parameters added. Lighting components may carry lumens, candela, wattage, or color temperature. Many of these types of parameters are specific to the software that's being used, but all use a uniform unit of measure that applies to the specific parameter category. This allows models to be developed in a uniform sense, which gives the user the ability to qualify the components used in their project based on performance or usage criteria in the basis of design. Unless the model is using the data from these parameters for analysis, it's often impractical to use them and is easier to simply use a text parameter to convey the information.

Using Parametrics to Speed up the Design Process

The biggest benefit to the design process gained by using parametrics is that values can be assigned to distances, rather than fixed dimensions. When decisions have yet to be made about a specific size, material, or location of a component, making the choice parametric allows the user to set an arbitrary value and quickly change it later, after choices have been made. It also allows the user to limit the choices that may be made to a specific set. If there are a finite set of flooring options for project, the user can limit those choices, and select from them once a decision has been made. Generally speaking, the design will start by creating a mass, or overall shape of the building to be built. Once this mass is generated, walls, floors, roofs, and ceilings are the first components to be added to the model. From here, the openings are added, such as doors and windows. The sizes of each of these openings may not be known right away, so adding windows and doors that can be easily changed allows selections to be made on the fly, without the extra work of changing the shape of the wall that they are placed in.

Once wall assemblies are placed, the user can determine which walls can or cannot be moved, and lock in mobile walls accordingly. Downstream, this will help the user determine what can and cannot be changed to suit the needs of the project as additional components are added. Interior load-bearing walls and wet walls are great example of this. Structural components, plumbing, and ductwork may need to be placed in certain locations based on the structural and mechanical design of the building, which will require walls to be placed to consider or encapsulate these elements.

The type or size of a window or door used in a given location may change based on the usage of the room in which they are located, the local building code, the amount of natural light desired in a space, or simply owner preference. These decisions may not be known early on in the design process, so developing the window and door components such that they can be quickly changed gives the user the ability to compare the appearance and performance of different sizes quickly. Above and beyond size, the aesthetic qualities of the window should also be parametric so that the color and configuration of the window can be swapped out to ensure that a window not only meets the performance requirements but achieves the desired design intent.

After openings are placed in a space, fixtures and fittings may be added to complete the model. Components such as cabinetry, casework, furnishings, fixtures, and fittings are added to fill the spaces with desired components. As these components are added, additional decisions are made regarding size, shape, and location. These decisions may affect other decisions regarding placement of walls and openings, so the benefit of parametrics is further compounded by limiting possible solutions. By understanding which walls can and cannot move, we can easily make decisions regarding component and opening locations.

Once all the components are added to a model, a schedule can be created that lists all the components in a given category, or all the components in the project, for that matter. Since the attributes of each component are parametric, the information can be viewed, manipulated, and updated quickly and easily in a tabular form, instead of our having to hunt and peck to change the material of each cabinet or the type of glass in each window. Traditionally, schedules have been used only for certain component categories, such as doors or door hardware, finishes, fixtures, and windows. With BIM technology, anything and everything can be scheduled as shown in Figure 3.2, allowing quantity takeoffs to be performed on every component added into the model. Whether we're

Count	Identification			Dimensions			Performance	
	Model	Manufacturer	Description	Height	Width	Jamb Depth	U Factor	SHGC
3x33 Circlehead								
	33x33 Circlehead	Pella	Proline Circletop - 33" Radius	2' - 0"	3' - 0"	0' - 6 9/16"	.31	.30
	33x33 Circlehead	Pella	Proline Circletop - 33" Radius	2' - 0"	3' - 0"	0' - 6 9/16"	.31	.30
341								
	2341	Pella	Proline Casement - 23"x41"	4' - 0"	2' - 0 1/8"	0' - 6 9/16"	.31	.30
	2341	Pella	Proline Casement - 23"x41"	4' - 0"	2' - 0 1/8"	0' - 6 9/16"	.31	.30
	2341	Pella	Proline Casement - 23"x41"	4' - 0"	2' - 0 1/8"	0' - 6 9/16"	.31	.30
	2341	Pella	Proline Casement - 23"x41"	4' - 0"	2' - 0 1/8"	0' - 6 9/16"	.31	.30
347L_2347R								
	2347L_2347R	Pella	Proline Casement - (2) 23"x47"	4' - 0"	4' - 8 1/2"	0' - 6 9/16"	.31	.30
	2347L_2347R	Pella	Proline Casement - (2) 23"x47"	4' - 0"	4' - 8 1/2"	0' - 6 9/16"	.31	.30
	2347L_2347R	Pella	Proline Casement - (2) 23"x47"	4' - 0"	4' - 8 1/2"	0' - 6 9/16"	.31	.30
335								
	2535	Pella	Vinyl Casement - Single Sash - 25"x35"	2' - 4 3/8"	2' - 0 1/8"	0' - 6 9/16"	.45	.36
347								
	2947	Pella	Proline Casement - 29"x47"	4' - 0"	2' - 4 3/8"	0' - 6 9/16"	.31	.30
	2947	Pella	Proline Casement - 29"x47"	4' - 0"	2' - 4 3/8"	0' - 6 9/16"	.31	.30
347L_2947R								
	2947L_2947R	Pella	Proline Casement - (2) 29"x47"	4' - 0"	4' - 0"	0' - 6 9/16"	.31	.30
	2947L_2947R	Pella	Proline Casement - (2) 29"x47"	4' - 0"	4' - 0"	0' - 6 9/16"	.31	.30
321								
	3521	Pella	Proline Awning 35"x21"	1' - 4"	2' - 0"	0' - 6 9/16"	.33	.30
	3521	Pella	Proline Awning 35"x21"	1' - 4"	2' - 0"	0' - 6 9/16"	.33	.30
	3521	Pella	Proline Awning 35"x21"	1' - 4"	2' - 0"	0' - 6 9/16"	.33	.30
335								
	3535	Pella	Proline Casement - 25"x35"	4' - 0"	2' - 8"	0' - 6 9/16"	.31	.30
	3535	Pella	Proline Casement - 25"x35"	3' - 0"	3' - 0"	0' - 6 9/16"	.31	.30
	3535	Pella	Proline Casement - 25"x35"	3' - 0"	3' - 0"	0' - 6 9/16"	.31	.30
	3535	Pella	Proline Casement - 25"x35"	3' - 0"	3' - 0"	0' - 6 9/16"	.31	.30
	3535	Pella	Proline Casement - 25"x35"	3' - 0"	3' - 0"	0' - 6 9/16"	.31	.30
	3535	Pella	Proline Casement - 25"x35"	3' - 0"	3' - 0"	0' - 6 9/16"	.31	.30
	3535	Pella	Proline Casement - 25"x35"	3' - 0"	3' - 0"	0' - 6 9/16"	.31	.30
	3535	Pella	Proline Casement - 25"x35"	3' - 0"	3' - 0"	0' - 6 9/16"	.31	.30
341L_3541R								
	3541L_3541R	Pella	Proline Casement - (2) 35"x41"	3' - 4 13/16"	6' - 0"	0' - 6 9/16"	.31	.30
rchitect 3681								
	Architect 3681	Pella	Architect Series 36"x81" Sidelight	6' - 7 1/2"	3' - 0 1/8"	0' - 6 9/16"	.30	.30
	Architect 3681	Pella	Architect Series 36"x81" Sidelight	6' - 7 1/2"	3' - 0 1/8"	0' - 6 9/16"	.30	.30
	Architect 3681	Pella	Architect Series 36"x81" Sidelight	6' - 7 1/2"	3' - 0 1/8"	0' - 6 9/16"	.30	.30
rchitect 7281								
	Architect 7281	Pella	Architect Series 72"x81" Inswing Glass Door	6' - 7 1/2"	5' - 11 1/4"	0' - 6 9/16"	.30	.30
	Architect 7281	Pella	Architect Series 72"x81" Inswing Glass Door	6' - 7 1/2"	5' - 11 1/4"	0' - 6 9/16"	.30	.30
X2446								
	FX2446	Heavenscape	Fixed Skylight - 24"x46"	4' - 0"	2' - 0"	0' - 3 1/2"	.45	.55
	FX2446	Heavenscape	Fixed Skylight - 24"x46"	4' - 0"	2' - 0"	0' - 3 1/2"	.45	.55
	FX2446	Heavenscape	Fixed Skylight - 24"x46"	4' - 0"	2' - 0"	0' - 3 1/2"	.45	.55
	FX2446	Heavenscape	Fixed Skylight - 24"x46"	4' - 0"	2' - 0"	0' - 3 1/2"	.45	.55
X4746								
	FX4746	Heavenscape	Fixed Skylight - 47"x46"	3' - 10"	3' - 8"	0' - 3 1/2"	.45	.55

FIGURE 3.2 Typical component schedule

counting units, square footage, or lineal footage, using parametrics simplifies the estimation process by showing how many of what components have been added into the project.

Product Attributes for Model Analysis and Leveraging of the Model

Ultimately, it is the design team that is responsible for adding attributes into the model, as they are the ones that place each component individually. After the model is created, the model may be used by the specifier, engineer, contractor, subcontractor, facility manager, or owner. Since a BIM project has such an important downstream potential, adding attributes for model analysis is critical. The design team should consider not just the attributes important to them but perhaps the attributes important to the other individuals or teams that may leverage the model in the future.

While it may or may not be the responsibility of the architect or design team to provide this level of information, it is nevertheless important and in some cases crucial. This is where manufacturers come in. Manufacturers generally know more about their products than the design team that is implementing them. Manufacturers who provide accurate depictions of their products for use by the design team do a service not only to themselves but to all members of the project involved with the BIM. When the manufacturer has the attributed data about performance and lifecycle assessment of the product, the design team can select the appropriate product for the project conditions, the specifier the salient points necessary to develop a specification, the contractor the relevant points of installing the product, and the facility manager or owner the appropriate information necessary to maintain the product through its lifecycle.

If we look at a window in a project, the design team may need little more than the width and height dimensions to properly locate the window in the drawings. BIM is more than drawings, though; it considers not just appearance in plan or elevation views but what the product actually is. To convey this type of information, at bare minimum the materials and performance information should be added alongside the identification properties necessary to determine not just what the product is but why it was selected. Depending on where in the world the project is it may need to have specific thermal properties, such as U-factor, R-value, or solar heat gain coefficient, or physical performance values, such as air infiltration, water penetration, or structural test pressure. These are usually determined based on the local code or energy requirements, but this type of information can also be used to analyze the model in determining cost-benefit of different components.

Each component category has its own set of attributes that are needed to determine why it was selected. Later on in the book we will dive into each category and look at the attributes that are commonly used to design, specify, and implement the different components.

Using Attributes in Construction Documentation

There is a hope that one day the information contained within a BIM project will automatically create the construction documents based on what was actually placed in the model. Developing a system that will do this is no small task, and while I have seen several software vendors attempt to do this, I have yet to see software that will pass information bidirectionally. Because the information in the drawings and specifications is supposed to be complementary, it is critical for changes to one to automatically affect the other. What this means is that if the BIM changes, the specification will change, and if the specifications change, the BIM will change. If it does not work in both directions there is a considerable risk for inaccurate information and confusion as to which is correct, the model or the specification.

As the level of information contained in a model increases, the types of documentation used will likely change as well. While there will be a need for a traditional construction project manual for the foreseeable future, it is far more effective to capture the information in a tabular form as well. This allows for quick updates and quick comparisons, and the ability to analyze the information whether manually or by software. The project manual is still an analog process, where a specifier needs to remove information from a model to create a specification. As applications that automate this process improve, we will likely see a diminished need for the role of the spec writer and an increased need for the role of the specifier. To clarify, a spec writer edits a document to suit the needs of a specific project, and a specifier has an extensive knowledge of the products, systems, and assemblies and can select the appropriate combinations for a specific project. Basically, a spec writer will tell us what, and the specifier will tell us why.

As attributes are added into components and placed into the model, the specifier can organize the information based on CSI MasterFormat®, and shake the information back out to quickly build specifications or specify products based on these performance criteria. Because the information is held within the model, during the bid review process, the design team can actually affirm the applicability of a specific manufacturer's product based on the specified values in apples-to-apples comparison. When different manufacturers' components are dragged and dropped into the model, the schedule can show the different values for each product within a component category and allow the architect to see line by line how each product stacks up against the others. Once a determination is made as to which product should be used, the others can be easily swapped out, and the unused components deleted. The information remaining in the model may be used to drive, or even create, parts of the text specification used in the architect's project manual. Figure 3.3 depicts a sample window graphic, corresponding data set, and possible specification text, which was generated by the model.

Later in this book we will take a closer look at the integration between BIM and specifications, but in the meantime we have a cursory understanding that there is no simple solution or easy way to link the two together at present. It is the goal of many specification providers, including this author, to create a specification interface that will allow information to seamlessly pass between a specification document and BIM software.

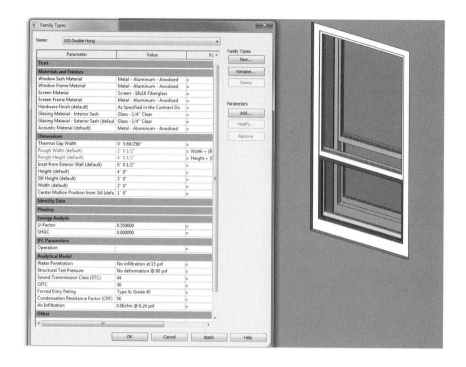

C. Aluminum Double-Hung Window
    1. Options:
        a. Impact/Blast/Hurricane (5 inch frame STC to 44) Exposure: B Wind Speed: Zone 3, 130 mph ASTM E 1886-02 and ASTM E 1996-02.
        b. Internal Venetian Blinds (6-1/2 inch frame STC to 49.
    2. Performance:
        a. AAMA/WDMA/CSA 101/I.S.2/A440-05:
            1) Rating: 920 H-C60 48 X 72.
        b. Operating Force: Less than 45.
        c. Air infiltration when tested at 1.57 psf (75 Pa) according to ASTM E 283.
            1) Model 920 H-C60 48 X 72: 0.06 cfm/ft2.
        d. Summer Water:
            1) Model 920 H-C60 48 X 72: 8 psf water.
        e. Winter Water:
            1) Model 920 H-C60 48 X 72: 12 psf water.
        f. Positive/negative structural test pressure without damage when tested according to ASTM E 330:
            1) Model 920 H-C60 48 X 72: Deflection 60, Structural plus 90 psf / minus 90 psf.
        g. Pass a forced entry resistance test of at least Grade 40 to meet requirements set forth in ASTM F 588.
        h. Air infiltration rate and/or the condensation resistance factor when tested in accordance with AAMA 1503-09:
            1) Model 920 H-C60 48 X 72:
                a) CRF Frame: 56.
                b) CRU Glass: 71.
        i. U factor when tested in accordance with AAMA 1503-09:
            1) Model 920 H-C60 48 X 72: 0.47.
        j. Acoustical: STC 40 to 56 as tested in accordance with ASTM E 90.

FIGURE 3.3 A BIM component data set aligned with a specification section

CONSTRAINTS AND CONDITIONS

What Are Constraints?

Constraints are used in a project to limit the possibilities to those that are actually available or possible. A wall can be constrained to a specific location such that it cannot be moved, a window can be located such that it is equidistant between two walls, or a door could be limited such that it is only available in red, white, or blue. Constraining objects can limit the possibility or potential of user error, but when too many constraints are added, a project can become computationally large, causing the software to slow down and efficiency to suffer. Every time a decision needs to be made within a project, the software needs to recompute each decision, so the more decisions, the more time is necessary for computation. For this reason constraints should be limited to those that are necessary for the design, and not used to limit manufacturers' product choices.

While BIM software can be used as a condition engine, and certainly can limit components to maximum heights or widths, often this is not practical as it makes the components slow to regenerate and slow to use. BIM should be thought of as a better toolset, rather than a decision engine that will limit users from creating impossible choices. While it is highly unlikely that we'll ever see a door that is 3 feet tall and 9 feet wide, creating minimum and maximum constraints on a door object is not practical. It should be up to the user's good judgment to develop the appropriate components for their project. Rather than constraining sizes, it is more appropriate to create a catalog of all available sizes, or where fully customizable, create a text notation which calls out the range in which the component may be created.

Although constraints should be used sparingly, they do have their place. There are times when constraints could be used, should be used, and definitely should not be used. Constraints are helpful in that they limit what can and cannot be done, but they're harmful in that they can confuse the user, inadvertently limit movement, and, in the worst cases, slow down the modeling speed to a crawl.

The most commonly used constraint is probably the equality constraint. This allows two or more distances to be made equal in relation to fixed points. If a hole is to be drilled through the center of a rectangular solid, the center point of the circle may be located such that it is equidistant from both length sides and both width sides. Additional reference points may be added in the case where multiple locations need to be aligned appropriately. Another form of the equality constraint is at the project level. A user can locate a component or components in specific places based on aesthetics and balance. If four windows are equally spaced in a wall, but the length of the wall is still undetermined, the user may enact equality constraints between each wall and each window such that they are always equally spaced regardless of how long the wall becomes.

Another way of constraining the component is to fix its location or alignment. One geometric solid may move with another, so locking the two components to one another allows them to move together. A good example of this is the glass in a window. Rather than showing the overall height and width of a piece of glass, the geometry can be locked to the frame so when the frame size changes, the glass size changes accordingly. Unless the overall size of the glass pane is necessary, it is not practical to add dimension parameters to the component. The driving dimensions of a window are generally the unit height and unit width. Secondary dimensions, such as rough opening sizes and a clear opening aperture, are typically derived from the driving dimensions, and, in some cases, do not need to be shown in the data set. Where these attributes are necessary, creating calculations to determine them is often more effective than having to change multiple dimensions and risk errors in the components.

In rare instances one may choose to limit sizes of a component by creating minimum and maximum values of highly customizable components. Many manufacturers offer windows in any size, down to a 16th or 32nd of an inch. Creating a catalog of every size is impractical, so the question arises: How do we limit the user's ability to select from a finite range? In most cases it's not practical to actually create minimums and maximums, but where absolutely necessary it can be done by creating minimum and maximum parameters and building a conditional statement that allows the creation of a component that is less than the minimum or greater than the maximum. While this slows modeling speed, it is often desirable to the manufacturer, as it limits the potential for improperly engineered components.

Figure 3.4 shows us how constraints can be used to limit everything from minimum and maximum dimensions or the equality of two dimensions, to complex equations that will either turn graphics on and off or return a specific text string to the data set. When a series of formulas is created, a parameter can reference one or more other parameters in an equation to change the behavior of the model. If the width is of a dimension greater than a specific value, graphics may be turned on and off. If users try to modify frame depth to a value less than what is available, the software can stop them. Constraining parameters can also lock down text attributes so they cannot be modified from within the project.

Parameter	Value	Formula
Constraints		
minframedepth	0' 4 1/2"	= if(FrameDepth < 0' 3", 0' 3", FrameDepth)
glzht	2' 7"	= Height - 0' 1"
dblraftrhz	☐	= Width > 3' 6"
Glzwdth	1' 9"	= Width - 0' 1"
GlzThk	0' 0 7/8"	= Outboard Pane Thickness + Inboard Pane Thickness + Spacer Thickness
CldgHt	0' 4"	= minframedepth - 0' 0 1/2"
Construction		
Text		
Materials and Finishes		
Dimensions		
Identity Data		
Phasing		
Structural Analysis		
Energy Analysis		
U_Factor	0.470000	=
SHGC	0.330000	=
ENERGYSTAR Qualified	N, N/C, S/C, S	= if(and(U_Factor < 0.601, SHGC < 1), "N, N/C, S/C, S", if(and(U_Factor < 0.601, SHGC < 0.401), "N/C and S/C", if(and(U_Factor < 0.7
IFC Parameters		
Other		
Manufacturer Website	http://www.arcat.com	=
Manufacturer Phone - Toll Fr		=
Manufacturer Phone	(203) 929-9444	= "(203) 929-9444"
Manufacturer Fax	(203) 929-2444	= "(203) 929-2444"
Manufacturer Email	bim@arcat.com	= "bim@arcat.com"
Manufacturer Address	1077 Bridgeport Ave, Shel	= "1077 Bridgeport Ave, Shelton, CT 06484"

FIGURE 3.4 Common types of constraints

Creating Conditional Statements

Conditional statements are created as a series of "IF" statements, which drive how the component appears or behaves. Typically, only dimension, integer, number, or Boolean (Yes/No) parameters may be controlled with a conditional statement. There are exceptions to this, but in most cases these are the only parameters that really need to be controlled in this way. Simple conditional statements may only contain one operator, while a more complex statement may have several operators and several statements embedded within it. Simple conditional statements may be used to control everything from this ability to minimum and maximum dimensions to performance values based on specific dimensions. A conditional statement can make a text notation regarding minimum and maximum size if it is outside of its appropriate range rather than actually stopping a user from creating that size. A conditional statement may also turn on specific graphics based on a dimension, return performance values of a window based on its size, or determine the number of components based on a length and spacing of components.

Complex equations can be generated that can control either data or graphics. In Figure 3.5, the equation calculates whether or not and where in the country a skylight meets the requirements to achieve an ENERGY STAR rating. It asks for the U-factor and SHGC attributes, which are built into the object, and references them against the criteria for the approval. This is only an example of

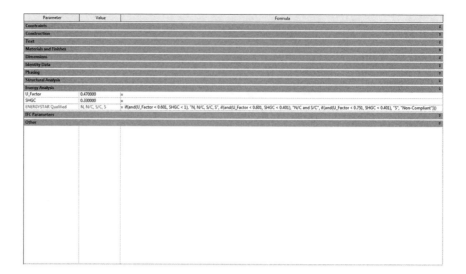

Parameter	Value	Formula
Constraints		
Construction		
Text		
Materials and Finishes		
Dimensions		
Identity Data		
Phasing		
Structural Analysis		
Energy Analysis		
U_Factor	0.470000	=
SHGC	0.330000	=
ENERGYSTAR Qualified	N, N/C, S/C, S	= if(and(U_Factor < 0.601, SHGC < 1), "N, N/C, S/C, S", if(and(U_Factor < 0.601, SHGC < 0.401), "N/C and S/C", if(and(U_Factor < 0.751, SHGC < 0.401), "S", "Non-Compliant")))
IFC Parameters		
Other		

FIGURE 3.5 Typical conditional statements

the type of calculations that can be developed to constrain an object. The values are only representative and do not reflect actual requirements for achieving any type of rating.

$$\text{if(and(U\_Factor} < 0.601, \text{SHGC} < 1), \text{"N, N/C, S/C, S",}$$
$$\text{if(and(U\_Factor} < 0.601, \text{SHGC} < 0.401), \text{"N/C and S/C",}$$
$$\text{if(and(U\_Factor} < 0.751, \text{SHGC} < 0.401), \text{"S", "Non-Compliant")))}$$

Conditional statements can do many things, but, just like constraints, they can slow down modeling speed, so they should be used only where necessary. Conditional statements allow a great deal of control within the model. When so much control is added, there is a tendency to micromanage the information, which can lead to considerably slower models. We must carefully select which aspects of a component we want to limit, as limiting them all will ultimately lead to slower models and heartache.

CHAPTER 4

Standards and Formats

THE PURPOSE OF STANDARDS AND FORMATS

Standardization of information is essential to proper leveraging of information within a building information modeling (BIM) project. It is not enough to just have the information in a model. Information must be universally understandable and accessible; otherwise, it is useful only to the individuals who inserted the information into the model originally. A standardized taxonomy of construction and design terms allows information to be exchanged freely without the possibility of errors in terminology.

Construction terms can be confusing, and may have multiple definitions which apply to the various disciplines. *Lavatory* and *beam* are two prime examples shown in Figure 4.1 and Figure 4.2. Depending on the context, a lavatory can be a bathroom sink, toilet, or an entire bathroom. A beam can refer to either a structural member or a lighting element. Because a database does not understand context, creating a set of accepted terms is necessary for information management within a building information model. From the

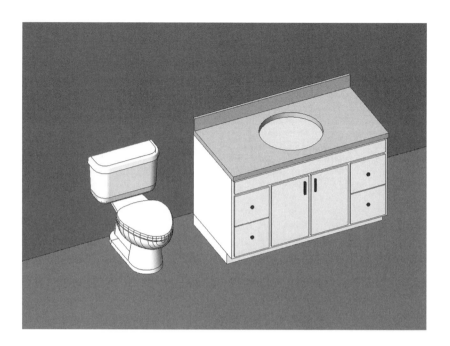

FIGURE 4.1 Multiple definitions for lavatory

accepted terms, a series of synonyms or alternate terms can be linked to consider colloquialisms and multiple terms.

Enumeration is another aspect of standardization that allows for easier cataloging and data access. Just as the Dewey Decimal System is an alphanumeric format that organizes books based on category, the Construction Specifications Institute (CSI) maintains the MasterFormat® and UniFormat™ formats, which organize construction information based on the type of work performed and the type of element being installed in a project. These alphanumeric formats allow a database to quickly and easily insert, organize, and extract information pertinent to specific disciplines. Hierarchical organization of information allows relevant data to be viewed based on the amount of information necessary at a given points in a project.

A logical hierarchy for windows might look like the following:

Level 1 – Opening
Level 2 – Opening – Window
Level 3 – Opening – Window – Aluminum
Level 4 – Opening – Window – Aluminum – Casement

Early in a project, a designer may know that an opening needs to be in a wall but not know whether it will be a window, door, curtain wall, storefront, or

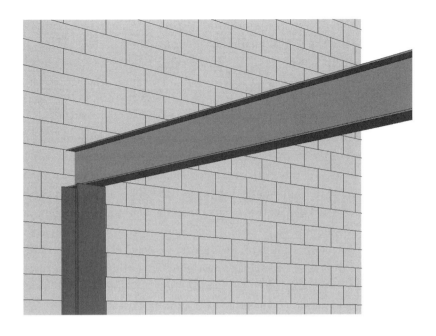

FIGURE 4.2 Multiple definitions for beam

some other form of opening. As the project progresses, a determination is made that a window will be installed. Further research determines that aluminum windows are the most effective for the given project. Eventually, the determination of how the window will operate is made and analysis and preference specify the use of an aluminum casement window.

There are further aspects of an element that determine how and why it is chosen, but the commonly accepted architectural standards do not drill down into the hierarchy. Standards such as OmniClass and IFC pick up where MasterFormat® and Uniformat™ leave off. The ability for interested parties to exchange information among themselves is reliant upon a strong set of standards and formats that allow information to be mapped from one user to the next. If I were using the six-digit MasterFormat® numbering system to organize my information, but the firm that needed to receive the information was working with the older five-digit numbering system, there would be a disconnect with our ability to organize information. By leveraging of series of accepted industry standards, we level the playing field and allow all of the data to exchange appropriately, regardless of what platform we are using.

Taxonomy and naming conventions are a critical aspect of standardization. To ensure that a computer reads information appropriately, without errors, a standardized taxonomy must be used. In many cases, enumeration of terms and terminology is a solution to the problem of standardization. A number is a number regardless of what language it is in, so assigning a number value to a specific category or attribute allows it to be read into a database with far less chance of error. Developing a syntax for numbering system is essential as well. People may realize that 08 55 00 is the same thing as 085500, but a database will read the spaces between the numbers and assume that the two numbers are different. Developing an industry-accepted syntax for titling and numbering will maintain a reasonable set of attributes that are understandable programmatically.

Currently there are a series of industry-accepted standards and formats in use by the design and construction communities. It takes into consideration the work that is being performed, the types of construction elements within the design and on the project, and even the individual products that are selected. Additional formats are being developed that lend themselves to use within building information modeling platforms. Most notably, MasterFormat®, UniFormat™, and OmniClass are series of formats and standardized tables that allow information to be captured and organized so it is both logical and readable. The level of detail associated with many of the OmniClass tables is more than the design and construction disciplines need to digest, but they set the stage for more effective information exchange and better collaboration among all parties associated with a project.

MASTERFORMAT®

For years, MasterFormat® has been recognized as the industry standard for the organization of construction information. As projects are developed, a series of paper documents is generated to archive the project design as well as provide an instruction manual for how the project is supposed to be assembled. MasterFormat® classifies information based on the various results of work performed on a project, not the products themselves, allowing all related efforts associated with the installation of an element to be documented together. Section 07 54 00 – *Thermoplastic Membrane Roofing,* for example, may contain all of the information that applies to the roof assembly as a whole, not just the roof membrane itself. This allows insulation, slip sheets or underlayment, fasteners, adhesives, stone ballast, flashings, and any other associated products or components to be listed alongside the membrane, and keeps the information together.

MasterFormat® follows a specific hierarchy to organize an architect's project manual in such a way that he will always know where to find the information he is looking for. The overall format itself is broken into two primary groups: the Procurement and Contracting Requirements Group, or Division 00, and the Specifications Group, which contains Division 01 through Division 49. Division 00 contains introductory information, procurement requirements, and contracting requirements that are related to the project as a whole, not to the individual component of a project. Because we're dealing with BIM content in this book, detailed information associated with Division 00 and Division 01 is being intentionally overlooked. Focusing on Divisions 02–49 will allow us to learn more about the structure that organizes, and the type of information that is used with, specifications and building information model components.

The specifications group is a series of 49 divisions that relate to work results. There are five subgroups that further organize information from a specification or building information model based on the type of work that is being performed. Division 01 – *General Requirements Subgroup* contains basic project, product, and administration requirements that apply to all work performed on the project. As noted previously, this type of information is best organized at the project level, and since we are discussing building information modeling components, details are intentionally omitted. Division 02–19 – *Facility Construction Subgroup* categorizes the components and work performed on a project related to the construction of a project, but not the facility services, such as plumbing, electrical, and heating, ventilating, and air conditioning (HVAC). Divisions 20–29 – *Facility Services Subgroup* classifies the work associated with the installation of all services within a project. This includes fire suppression, plumbing, HVAC, integrated automation, electrical and communications, and security. Divisions 30–39 – *Site and Infrastructure Subgroup* is a series of divisions that are related to site preparation improvements related to a project. This includes earthwork and excavation, exterior improvements, utilities, transportation, and marine construction. While much of the information associated with this subgroup is contained in models created prior to the architect's design, Division 32 – *Exterior Improvements* relates to a considerable number of BIM objects that are used on the exterior of the project. The last subgroup is Division 40–49 – *Process Equipment Subgroup,* which speaks more to processes and equipment than to building components, so little information is likely to be added into the model from this subgroup.

MasterFormat® Groups, Subgroups, and Divisions

Procurement and Contracting Requirements Group

    Division 00 – Procurement and Contracting Requirements

Specifications Group

    General Requirements Group

        Division 01 – General Requirements

    Facility Construction Subgroup

        Division 02 – Existing Conditions

        Division 03 – Concrete

        Division 04 – Masonry

        Division 05 – Metals

        Division 06 – Wood, Plastics, and Composites

        Division 07 – Thermal and Moisture Protection

        Division 08 – Openings

        Division 09 – Finishes

        Division 10 – Specialties

        Division 11 – Equipment

        Division 12 – Furnishings

        Division 13 – Special Construction

        Division 14 – Conveying Equipment

    Facility Services Subgroup

        Division 30 – Reserved for Future Expansion

Division 31 – Earthwork

Division 32 – Exterior Improvements

Division 33 – Utilities

Division 34 – Transportation

Division 35 – Waterway and Marine Construction

Division 36 – Reserved for Future Expansion

Division 37 – Reserved for Future Expansion

Division 38 – Reserved for Future Expansion

Division 39 – Reserved for Future Expansion

Site and Infrastructure Subgroup

Division 30 – Reserved for Future Expansion

Division 31 – Earthwork

Division 32 – Exterior Improvements

Division 33 – Utilities

Division 34 – Transportation

Division 35 – Waterway and Marine Construction

Division 36 – Reserved for Future Expansion

Division 37 – Reserved for Future Expansion

Division 38 – Reserved for Future Expansion

Division 39 – Reserved for Future Expansion

Process Equipment Subgroup

Division 40 – Process Integration

Division 41 – Material Processing and Handling Equipment

Division 42 – Process Heating, Cooling, and Drying Equipment

Division 43 – Process Gas and Liquid Handling, Purification, and Storage Equipment

Division 44 – Pollution Control Equipment

Division 45 – Industry-specific Manufacturing Equipment

Division 46 – Water and Wastewater Equipment

Division 47 – Reserved for Future Expansion

Division 48 – Electrical Power Generation

Division 49 – Reserved for Future Expansion

Within each of the MasterFormat® divisions is a series of sections that narrow the scope of work as they progress from level 1 numbering through levels 2, 3, and 4. Each pair of digits is associated with a level of detail contained within a specification section. Level 1, or the division, will contain only the very basic information that might apply to all work performed in the division. Rather than the specification becoming tremendously large in order to take into consideration all of the work within the division, it is best looked at as a high-level overview that contains only the information that is associated with all of the components; the general requirements for that division, if you will. Level 2 narrows the scope of the division to a slightly more specific "section," containing relevant information that applies to all work in a given category. Creating a specification section at this level allows a considerable amount of work to be placed in one location when the general requirements and installation aspects of the type of work allow. Creating specifications and managing building information modeling data at this level typically creates larger data sets and fewer specification sections and objects. At this level of detail, we may typically see representative modeling of BIM components, or graphically simplified objects used to represent multiple products that are similar in nature. This will be discussed later in the book throughout various chapters. Level 3 is an even narrower category, which points out detailed information about the scope of work:

> Level 1 – Section 07 00 00 – Thermal and Moisture Protection
>
> Level 2 – Section 07 31 00 – Shingles and Shakes
>
> Level 3 – Section 07 31 13 – Asphalt Shingles
>
> Level 4 – Section 07 31 13.13 – Fiberglass-reinforced Asphalt Shingles

Through the years, MasterFormat® has gone through several updates and changes, the most noticeable being in 2004 when a wholesale update was made that changed the numbering system from five digits to six digits and, in very specific instances, eight digits. The 2004 expansion also reorganized the entire structure, expanding the format from 16 to 49 top-level divisions. This allowed MasterFormat® to more accurately cover the various types of work found on a construction project. While many architects and specifiers still used the five-digit MasterFormat® numbering system, the Construction Specifications Institute (CSI) discontinued support of it in favor of the more practical six-digit system. More information on MasterFormat®, including a detailed listing and description of all of section numbers and titles, is available at masterformat.com or directly through the Construction Specifications Insuitute at csinet.org.

UNIFORMAT™

While MasterFormat® classifies information based on its work result, UniFormat™ classifies information based on elements within a project. An element is typically more than a single component or product, and more a series of components that work together. Walls, floors, ceilings, and roofs are the most common examples of elements. Each of these assemblies comprises several materials and several work results, none of which provides a finished component on their own. An interior partition wall may be made up of two layers of ½-inch drywall on one side, a 4-inch steel stud wall and another layer of ½-inch drywall on the other side, with primer and two coats of paint. This assembly has three clear work results and four unique products, but in terms of its purpose, it is a partition wall.

A window or door seems like a simple singular product, but secondary products are necessary for the installation of the window or door, such as flashing tape, fasteners, casing, extension jambs, and sealants. When we look at all of the products associated with the installation of the component we realize that there is more to the cost and the implementation of the window than just its price.

UniFormat™ is most commonly used for square-foot cost estimation, as it simplifies components into basic categories, allowing cost estimators to look at unit prices quickly without having to determine exact products that are being used. Early in a project, products are rarely determined, so for preliminary budgeting to be performed there needs to be a method by which the figures can be calculated without a tremendous amount of research. Organization of components based on UniFormat™ has been very successful historically. New purposes for UniFormat™ are beginning to unfold, such as preliminary project descriptions, or PPDs, which are used to outline the very basic information about a project during schematic design.

For building information modeling, UniFormat™ provides a second opportunity to organize information and cross-reference it against other formats, such as MasterFormat®. Model data may be extracted and organized by its UniFormat™ code at several points during the design to create a rolling cost estimation procedure. As the components in the model become more detailed, their UniFormat™ code changes to a more specific element. Assigning cost-estimation data to each element will allow the amounts of each element to be multiplied by the cost in order to automate the square-foot cost estimation of the project. There is no one-to-one relationship between UniFormat™ and MasterFormat®. While certain elements, such as windows and doors may have a direct relationship, others, such as walls, floors, and roofs, are entire assemblies, which may contain information from multiple MasterFormat® sections.

During the early stages of design, specific MasterFormat® sections are likely unknown, as specific elements have not been selected. UniFormat™ is better at categorizing information earlier in the project because it speaks to the evolutionary process of selecting an element. An interior partition wall becomes an interior fixed partition, and an interior fixed partition becomes an interior fixed partition with two layers of ⅝-inch gypsum on one side, metal studs, and one layer of ½-inch gypsum on the other side. Using both UniFormat™ and MasterFormat® within each BIM object will allow them to be cross-referenced in order to connect the informational dots from schematic design through facility management. Table 4.1 shows a sample evolution of a project element as it first relates to UniFormat™ and then also MasterFormat®.

UniFormat™ follows a hierarchy beginning with the elemental categories found within a given project. There are eight Level 1 categories, nine if we count the introduction, each with a specific set of elements contained within:

Introduction

A – Substructure

B – Shell

C – Interiors

D – Services

E – Equipment and Furnishings

F – Special Construction and Demolition

G – Building Sitework

Z – General

Table 4.1 UniFormat™ and MasterFormat® evolution

Phase	Element	UniFormat™ number	MasterFormat® number	Title
Preplanning	Building enclosure	B30	N/A	Exterior horizontal enclosures
Schematic design	Roof assembly	B3010	N/A	Roofing
Design development	Low-slope roof assembly	B3010.50	07 50 00	Low-slope roofing
Construction documents	TPO roof assembly	B3010.50	07 54 23	Thermoplastic polyolefin roofing

Within each category, there are Level 2, 3, 4, and 5 classifications, which separate out the Level 1 "parent" into more specific subcategories. Each subsequent level has a parent-child relationship with the previous level, making the information that much more specific as it drills into its lowest appropriate level for the project. More information on UniFormat™, including a detailed listing and description of all of the elements and titles, is available directly through the Construction Specifications Institute at csinet.org.

OMNICLASS

OmniClass is a series of tables that allows the information contained within a model to be organized to its simplest level and cross-referenced in a variety of ways. This allows information within the model to be shared among several members and easily be communicated to those not directly involved with the development of the project. Not all OmniClass tables will find their way into a building information model. Many of the tables are more of a higher-level project management information method rather than model data management formats. Following is a list of all of the OmniClass tables. The ones that have the most bearing on building information modeling are listed in **bold** type:

- Table 11 – Construction Entities by Function
- Table 12 – Construction Entities by Form
- Table 13 – Spaces by Function
- Table 14 – Spaces by Form
- **Table 21 – Elements**
- **Table 22 – Work Results**
- **Table 23 – Products**
- Table 31 – Phases
- Table 32 – Services
- Table 33 – Disciplines
- Table 34 – Organizational Roles
- Table 35 – Tools
- Table 36 – Information
- Table 41 – Materials
- **Table 49 – Properties**

While the ones in bold are not the only tables from OmniClass that may be used within a building information model, they're the ones that provide the most benefit in our day-to-day work. Depending on your discipline, you may find uses for some of the other tables; architects may choose to leverage Table 13 – Spaces by Function and Table 14 – Spaces by Form, whereas a general contractor may find a benefit to using Table 35 – Tools. Many of these tables may find their way into design, construction, and facility management data structures in the future, so it is important to understand what they are and how they work so that we may begin to build the data sets within BIM components so that they may be sorted, filtered, and leveraged through the use of these tables.

The following sections of this chapter offer a brief discussion of the different OmniClass tables to better acquaint you with their purpose. Once you understand how each table works and what it was designed for, you may find a purpose for it within your day-to-day operations.

Table 11 – Construction Entities by Function

The Construction Entities by Function table classifies an entire building based on its environment. It can be used to scope the project based on its surroundings or for project planning. Owners who are attempting to perform feasibility studies can look at an entire area, see all of the buildings of a given type, and determine whether it's practical to add a building of a similar type based on its proximity to others. For instance, suppose a fast-food chain is looking to open a franchise in a given area. Being able to look at an entire city and quickly locate each fast-food restaurant, regardless of its brand, allows for quick demographic study and determination of where there are opportunities for product placement. Construction entities by function is certainly a big-picture format, rather than a look at the individual components within a project. BIM is larger than the individual material, product, assembly, or project. It allows us to look at an entire area as a whole and analyze the information for city planning and area mapping. Just as a project relies on the information within its components, the future of city planning will rely on the information of its individual projects.

There is a real potential for future developments that will allow property owners and city planners the ability to quickly and easily study the surrounding regions to speculate about urban sprawl and future development. While this table will likely not find itself being used within a BIM software platform, it is still a powerful format when looking at the concept of building information management or, on a larger scale, city information management.

Example Table 11 – Construction Entities by Function

11-17 00 00 – Commercial Facilities

11-17 24 00 – Retail Commercial Facilities
    11-17 24 11 – Department Store
    11-17 24 14 – Specialty Store
    11-17 24 17 – Grocery Store

Table 12 – Construction Entities by Form

The Construction Entities by Form table looks at an overall project based on its shape, appearance, and overall form. Its highest level of information classifies construction entities based on whether they are buildings, structures, or physical forms within the earth. The most practical use will be found in the category "Buildings," which further categorizes them into low-rise mid-rise, and high-rise buildings. Each of these categories is further organized into basic types of buildings, to give a more defined and more accurate description of the type of construction entity that is being classified.

Example Table 12 – Construction Entities by Form

12-11 00 00 – Buildings
    12-11 17 00 – High-rise Buildings
        12-11 17 11 – High-rise Free-standing Buildings
            12-11 17 11 11 – High-rise Point Tower
            12-11 17 11 19 – High-rise Slab
            12-11 17 11 99 – Other High-rise Free-standing Buildings

Table 13 – Spaces by Function

Spaces by Function classifies areas or spaces within a project based on what they are used for. It considers not what it looks like in terms of its physical form, but what it is used for. Certain spaces are used for certain tasks, such as a bedroom for sleeping, a kitchen for cooking, and a dining room for eating. Classifying by way of this table may allow space planners to organize their information effectively and make determinations quickly and easily about how much area is used for what tasks. By organizing information with this table from within a building information modeling project, calculations of gross and net areas as well as percentages of the total can be derived and categorized.

Example Table 13 – Spaces by Function

13-55 00 00 – Commerce Activity Spaces
    13-55 11 00 – Office Spaces
        13-55 11 11 – Office Service

13-55 11 13 – Dedicated Enclosed Workstation
13-55 11 21 – Open Team Setting

Table 14 – Spaces by Form

As Table 13 classifies spaces based on what they are used for, Table 14 – Spaces by Form classifies spaces based on what they look like and what they are. It does not discuss the usage of an area or space, but whether it is open or enclosed, covered or uncovered, and the topography or legal definition of the space.

Example Table 14 – Spaces by Form

14-11 00 00 – Fully Enclosed Spaces
   14-11 11 00 – Rooms
      14-11 11 11 – Room
      14-11 11 14 – Lobby
      14-11 11 21 – Auditorium

Table 21 – Elements

Table 21 is also referred to as UniFormat™, which we discussed earlier in this chapter. It categorizes components within a construction project based on their elemental categories. In my opinion, it is the most intuitive formatting method used in the design and construction industry, as it groups construction components into logical categories that are based on their location rather than their purpose. The enumeration process differs between UniFormat™ and OmniClass Table 21. Table 21 uses a number prefix instead of a letter.

Example Table 21 – Elements

21-02 10 – Superstructure
   21-02 10 10 – Floor Construction
      21-02 10 10 10 – Floor Structural Frame
      21-02 10 10 20 – Floor Decks, Slabs, and Toppings
      21-02 10 10 30 – Balcony Floor Construction

Table 22 – Work Results

Table 22 – Work Results is also known as MasterFormat®. It is a classification of the resulting effort put into a project through construction. Rather than classifying the products that are used in a project, it is often far more relevant to think in terms of what was done, or the goal that was accomplished.

Windows and doors are related in that they are both openings in a wall and, thus, are located in the same top-level category: Division 8 – Openings. Roofing and siding are related in that they both provide the building with protection from the elements and are located in the same top-level category: Division 7 – Thermal and Waterproofing.

Example Table 22 – Work results

22-07 00 00 – Thermal and Moisture Protection
   22-07 46 00 – Siding
      22-07 46 16 – Aluminum Siding
      22-07 46 23 – Wood Siding
      22-07 46 63 – Fabricated Panel Assemblies with Siding

Table 23 – Products

Table 23 – Products is likely to become the latest and greatest standard added to building information models. It has already been adopted by some of the software platforms, allowing specific building materials and products to be categorized within the project. As MasterFormat® looks at the work result and UniFormat™ looks at the element classification, Table 23 looks at the product itself. This gives architects and contractors and increased ability to identify, sort, and count each product within a project. The operation of a window, whether it is a casement, double hung, or fixed, is not taken into consideration under the MasterFormat® numbering scheme, and the construction of the window, whether it is aluminum, wood, or vinyl, is not taken into consideration under the UniFormat™ numbering scheme. Using these two standards together will allow us to make determinations of the window, but rather than creating a cross-reference query within the model, the use of OmniClass Table 23 will provide a direct reference to both its operation and construction.

Example Table 23 – Products

23-17 00 00 – Openings, Passages, and Protection Products
   23-17 13 00 – Windows
      23-17 13 13 – Windows
         23-17 13 15 – Wood Windows
         23-17 13 15 11 – Wood Fixed Windows
         23-17 13 15 15 – Wood Single Hung Windows
         23-17 13 15 21 – Wood Awning Windows
         23-17 13 15 23 – Wood Casement Windows

Table 31 – Phases

The Phases table organizes time and activity along a building's lifecycle. It begins with the concept of developing the project and moves all the way through to decommissioning and demolition. It looks at not just the design and construction aspect of a project, but the overall scope of the building as a whole. This is an excellent tool for facilities management purposes, as well as being useful for project scheduling during design and construction. It is possible to set expectations for performance and completion at various phases throughout the project by assigning dates and levels of development to various tasks at different stages throughout the design and construction of the project. The most relevant sections of this table are the design stage, construction documents stage, and execution stage, as these are the points within a project where data from the building information models may require extraction and manipulation to perform an additional task. At different points in the design stage, different amounts of detail are necessary. Aligning the American Institute of Architects (AIA) level of development (LOD) concept with given phases from Table 31 can allow the information to be built-in and managed from within the model, rather than on a related spreadsheet or handwritten form.

Example Table 31 – Phases

31-20 00 00 – Design Stage
    31-20 20 00 – Design Development Phase
        31-20 20 11 – Detailed Design Phase
        31-20 20 24 – Product Selection Phase
        31-20 20 34 – Estimating Phase

Table 32 – Services

The OmniClass Services table refers to the various actions, tasks, and jobs that are associated with the lifecycle of a construction project. It considers more than the basic design disciplines and construction trades that are most notable on a project, and adds into the mix a series of related services associated with administration, financing, maintenance, and advisement of the project as a whole. If we look at a project in terms of not just designing and building it, but also its purpose for being built, we will see that many aspects of the project have not been considered. Let's suppose a new office building is being built by a property owner. The financier provides the money to build it, an attorney represents the owner for real estate matters, an architect designs the building, a series of contractors and subcontractors constructs the project, a sales and marketing team works to ensure that the offices are sold or leased, and a facility manager ensures that the building is properly maintained.

While much of this information may be outside of the scope of the building information model, it is nevertheless relevant to the overall lifecycle of the building. It allows the individual or team managing the overall project to consider not just design and construction but the tasks that need to be performed both before design and after construction.

Example Table 32 – Services

32-49 00 00 – Documentation Services

    32-49 11 00 – Modeling

        32-49 11 13 – Creating BIM Content

        32-49 11 23 – Creating BIM Schedules

        32-49 11 25 – Linking BIM/CAD Files

Table 33 – Disciplines

Whereas the services table organizes responsibilities based on the task at hand, Table 33 – Disciplines looks at them based on the individual or team responsible for the task. A certain level of expertise is expected of those performing tasks related to a construction project. This table looks at the task of the firm, not of the individuals performing those tasks. Carpentry, for instance, is a discipline whose task is to provide various types of framing and finish services on a project. The discipline is a high-level overview of what the responsible firm is supposed to do, the framing service that they have been contracted to provide.

Example Table 33 – Disciplines

33-41 00 00 – Construction

    33-41 11 14 – Subcontracting

        33-41 11 14 14 – Carpentry

        33-41 11 14 21 – Plumbing Subcontracting

        33-41 11 14 61 – Painting

Table 34 – Organizational Roles

The Organizational Roles table takes Table 33 – Disciplines, and expands upon it to add a level of information that applies to the individuals responsible for a given task. Regardless of the task, every role has a certain degree of skill or expertise associated with it. By assigning organizational roles to tasks or aspects of the project, there can be an expectation of the quality of work on the project.

The table can also be used within general contracting firms for time and resource budgeting in terms of manpower. Large contracting firms may have multiple projects working at once, so by assigning an organizational role to each employee, the firm can organize the data see how and where to use its resources most effectively.

Example Table 34 – Organizational Roles

34-35 00 00 – Execution Roles
    34-35 21 00 – Tradesperson
        34-35 21 14 – Laborer
            34-35 21 14 11 – Skilled Laborer
                34-35 21 14 11 11 – Master Craftsman
                34-35 21 14 11 11 – Journeyman
                34-35 21 14 11 11 – Apprentice

Table 35 – Tools

Table 35 – Tools organizes equipment resources that a project may require. It is not so much a method for use within a building information model software platform but an external database that may allow contractors to schedule their resources effectively. An excavator may own four backhoes and have five excavation projects going at the same time. He can look at his schedule information and cross-reference it against a table such as this to determine whether workers can move equipment from one location to another at various points in the project, or whether they will need to obtain additional resources. This table is more useful in managing the management than managing the project itself. Ensuring that the resources necessary for the project are available is an essential aspect of the success or failure of any business, so more than a construction information table, it is more of a business information table.

Example Table 35 – Tools

35-51 00 00 – Physical Tools
    35-51 11 00 – Construction Tools
        35-51 11 31 – Power Tools
            35-51 11 31 11 – Cutting Power Tools
                35-51 11 31 11 11 – Power Saws
                35-51 11 31 11 14 – Hand-held Power Drills
                35–51 11 31 11 24 – Jackhammers

Table 36 – Information

Table 36 – Information is a low- to high-level look at how we process data in the real world. In this day and age, there are several formats in which we can exchange information, and even more types of information. The classification of the different types of information, how they are exchanged, and the format that they are in may allow us to quickly parse through information to find what is relevant versus what is not on a given project. This table is more process based than project based in that is speaks to how information is exchanged and the type of information being exchanged, not how the information relates to the project or task at hand.

Example Table 36 – Information

36-71 00 00 – Project Information
    36-71 67 00 – Project Cost Information
        36-71 67 13 – Cost-estimate Information
            36-71 67 13 11 – Element-based Cost Estimates
            36-71 67 13 15 – Element Unit Prices
            36-71 67 13 17 – Material/Product Unit Prices

Table 41 – Materials

Table 41 – Materials classifies real-world materials, not building products, so it is useful when looking at building products and BIM components based on what their composition is. For instance, we can categorize building materials in terms of whether they are made of wood or concrete or solid or viscous, and get more specific about precisely what they're made of. This may be useful when attempting to query a model for the amount of Forest Stewardship Council (FSC) – certified lumber on a project, or the amount of recycled materials in order to perform Leadership in Energy Efficient Design (LEED) credit calculations.

The Materials table breaks down materials based on whether they are elements, or whether they are compounds made of solid, liquid, or gas. It drills in further to categorize materials based on logical categories: Is the solid in question from a rock or a plant or is it metallic? Is the liquid in question water-based, mineral based, or synthetic? While much of this categorization aggregates information past the point of relevance within a construction project, certain aspects of it are nevertheless valuable, such as the relationships between wall materials and building products. There are often requirements that limit specific amounts of chemicals and compounds that are considered volatile organic compounds (VOCs). In other cases there may be requirements that minimize or eliminate the use of polyvinyl chloride (PVC) on a project. If all materials used within the building information model are attached to Table 41, we can quickly recognize whether or not the project meets that aspect of the design criteria.

Example Table 41 – Materials

41-30 00 00 – Solid Compounds

    41-30 30 00 – Plant Materials

        41-30 30 14 – Materials From Trees

            41-30 30 14 11 – Timber

                41-30 30 14 11 11 – Softwood Timber

                    41-30 30 14 11 11 11 – Southern Yellow Pine

                    41-30 30 14 11 11 17 – Spruce–Pine–Fir

                    41-30 30 14 11 11 24 – Western Red Cedar

Table 49 – Properties

As mentioned earlier, a proper taxonomy is essential to the success of any data structure used in a project. Table 49 – Properties was updated in 2010 and released as a draft for comment. The development of a taxonomy requires input from a large cross section of the design, construction, facility management, building product manufacturing, and administration disciplines, at the very least. Rather than releasing a finalized table containing a series of attributes to be used for design and construction of projects, the Construction Specifications Institute felt that disseminating the information as a proposed (draft) standard rather than a defined format would allow a larger audience to comment on the information prior to judging its suitability for the industry.

Since many properties associated with building materials are industry specific, I emphasize the need for comments from the various trade organizations within the building product manufacturing community to ensure that not only the selected properties are correct but the definitions for those properties are clear. The overall number of properties associated with all of the building materials used in a given project could easily reach the tens of thousands, so Table 49 was developed first and foremost as a standard taxonomy for commonly used properties, but also as a starting point to allow for future development with the addition of more industry-specific information.

For more information about Table 49 – Properties, and to submit any questions or comments regarding the table, go to omniclass.org or csinet.

org. Appendix A at the end of the book lists all of the numbers and titles currently listed within the draft Table 49 – Properties table.

Example Table 49 – Properties

49-81 00 00 – Performance Properties
    49-81 31 00 – Strength Properties
        49-81 31 21 – Bond Strength
        49-81 31 43 – Flexural Strength
            49-81 31 43 11 – Flexural Strength, Parallel
            49-81 31 43 13 – Flexural Strength, Perpendicular

CHAPTER 5

Where to Begin

At this point you should have a basic understanding of what building information modeling (BIM) is, its purpose and intent, and why the development of content is essential to its advancement. A BIM project is only as good as the components that were used to create it, and its graphic accuracy drives how it will appear in model views, drawing sheets, and rendered views. The information contained in each component has a direct effect on how much analysis may be performed and how detailed schedules and exports can be. BIM components are the building blocks of all projects and usually have one or more levels of subcomponents. There is a hierarchy of graphic and data development that will allow information to be placed in its appropriate location and retrieved intuitively.

There are two ways to look at BIM content: based on what it is, and based on how it is implemented into a project. If we think about what it is, there are four core types of BIM components used within projects: materials, objects, assemblies, and details. When looking at how it is implemented, we can organize it into three main categories: primary, secondary, and tertiary. Determining how to approach development of a component is the first step: Is a roof a material or an assembly? Is a railing an assembly or an object? Is glass a material or an object? Much of this is determined based on the intent and usage of the component, when it is implemented into the project, which discipline is responsible for it, and how detailed the component needs to be. In some cases glass can simply be a material; in other cases it is more appropriate to model it as an independent component.

WHAT IS IT? MATERIALS, ASSEMBLIES, OBJECTS, AND DETAILS

Materials

Materials are the basis from which all other BIM components are developed, and are components in and of themselves. They are used to make up objects and assemblies, and often used independently as paints, coatings, and finishes. On its own, a material is nongraphic until it is used within a project. It is a series of attributes designed to control the outward appearance of whatever it is assigned to. It may be assigned a specific color and surface pattern, have a designated rendering appearance, and carry specific line work for two-dimensional detail views. Materials are also able to carry information regarding identity, physics, performance, and usage.

It is important to maintain a consistent level of detail among all materials, such that all model views look appropriate, materials that need a rendering appearance are designed accordingly, and the information contained within is consistent throughout. In many cases, materials need little more than a name and a description, especially if they are only used within components and not assemblies. Materials used within assemblies often are building products sold on their own and carry specific performance values necessary to determine why they were selected. When determining what and how much information to put into a material, make sure parameters that apply to one material apply to all materials. If you are not careful about this, you will get an exceptionally large data set with very few values actually assigned to individual materials.

Developing a naming convention that works for materials is essential to allow them to be found quickly and viewed without interruption. In many cases, the software limits the number of characters that can be viewed within the preview pane, so keep material names brief and on point, and use their descriptions to embellish them for callouts and further detail. Materials are often assigned to particular specification sections, so for individuals with a clear understanding of CSI MasterFormat®, using its six-digit number as a prefix can assist in organizing the materials logically. The chapter on creating and managing materials further discusses options for naming conventions.

The appearance of the material within the model view is probably its most important aspect. This is how the design team will view the model on a day-to-day basis, so avoiding colors that strain the eye and patterns that confuse the user can improve the software user's performance considerably. The exact accuracy of color is more important in rendered views than it is in model views, and there is no assumption that a color used during modeling is an actual color of the product. Where possible, pastels and muted colors are more soothing to the eye. Use surface patterns sparingly, and only where absolutely necessary. This is especially important on floors, as horizontal lines along the floor can confuse the user when attempting to place additional components in plain view. Figure 5.1 shows the material control interface of a widely used software platform. The materials information is highly detailed and neatly organized into intuitive tabs, which contain the relevant controls for appearance, identification, structural qualities, and how the information behaves in rendered views.

Materials are used on their own as finishes and coatings, as building products within assemblies, and to represent options within various objects. How a material is being used controls the graphic and informational level of detail necessary. Materials used on their own generally require a considerable amount

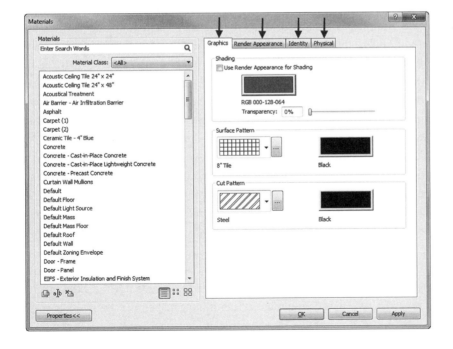

FIGURE 5.1 Typical materials controls

of information about graphics and attributes, as they are typically finished building materials, such as paints, coatings, or metals with unique ornamental finishes. With the exception of materials designed for the surface, those used within assemblies generally have less appearance properties and more informational properties, as they are rarely or never seen in three-dimensional or rendered views. When materials are placed within objects, they generally have few informational properties and considerable appearance properties. This is largely because an object that is a finished component is sold as a whole, so the properties of the materials lose relevance and the properties of the product as a whole are showcased.

Assemblies

Assemblies contain a series of layers, each of which is assigned material and thickness parameters that correspond to specific materials used within a project. These assemblies are essentially a sandwich of materials, and represent materials in terms of an entire area. In some cases this can create difficulty in understanding, as items such as framing, insulation, and fasteners do not always cover the entire surface of the assembly. Walls, floors, ceilings, and roofs are the four basic types of assemblies found on projects. They are used to enclose spaces, can be trained to understand whether they are structural or nonstructural, and relate themselves to adjacent assemblies so that they may be appropriately attached.

Because assemblies are the primary components used in a project and typically the first to be added, it is only logical to also consider them as hosts for additional components in the model. Windows and doors for instance, in most cases, may only be installed in a wall, so thinking of the wall as the host for these components allows them to be created such that they automatically remove volume when they are placed in the project. This type of low-level intuition built into the software minimizes the need to manually create openings in walls for each component.

Wall assemblies are unique in relation to the other assemblies in that the layers are arranged vertically, where floors, ceilings, and roofs are horizontal or sloped in nature. Walls arrange materials from the exterior to the interior, and allow for specific products to be noted at precise thicknesses. There are actually two ways to generate walls using BIM software. The first is as an assembly, which is based on a single line, and the second is as a curtain wall, which is based on a grid. Because much of the work within a project is done in plan view, the most common walls are drawn as a single line, and the information regarding the associated materials and their respective thickness is carried along based on a reference point within it. For each wall that is placed, we instruct it to start and end at specific heights, assign a structural value to it, and ultimately control its behavior with relation to other components.

Something to consider when developing wall assemblies is that not all wall components cover an entire layer of the assembly. For instance, wall studs are placed a specific distance apart, insulation is placed between the studs, and fasteners are affixed to the assembly as a designated spacing or density. It is impractical to expect anyone to place every insulation fastener or stud within a project for no other reason than to count them. Alternatively, we can add a material to the assembly called "fasteners," assign a specific fastening rate to it, and calculate the number of fasteners based on the areas in which the material is found. The materials may be joined together with a description added to represent layers of this nature as well. For instance, rather than having a material for insulation and a material for wall studs, create a single material called *4" metal studs – 16" O.C. w/ R-13 fiberglass batt insulation*. There is an upside and a downside to doing this, which we discuss further in the chapter on walls.

Walls that are drawn based on a grid allow for considerably more control, but also require considerably more work. These are known as curtain walls or panel walls. Using a grid, we can assign vertical and horizontal members as well as panels that are located between the grid lines. These were designed to create, and are most commonly used for, glazed curtain walls, panel walls, and rainscreens. The grid system also affords the user the ability to create additional types of components by adapting the features of software to suit the needs of the user. For instance, these tools can very easily create a simple framing system by assigning the panels to be insulation, the vertical grids to be studs, and the horizontal grids to be plates. The discussion on the use of the curtain wall tools to create adaptive components continues in the chapter on curtain walls.

Floors, roofs, and ceilings are assemblies with layers that are arranged horizontally. With the exception of controls that are specific to these assemblies' nature and usage, they are essentially the same thing. As shown in Figure 5.2, materials are arranged from bottom to top and allow specific materials to be used and their thicknesses to be controlled. Just as with walls, there are specific materials that are often placed within the same layer and may be combined to simplify the process, framing and insulation being the most noteworthy. Where walls are based on length and height and have their width controlled by the layers, horizontal assemblies are based on length and width and have their height controlled by the layers. Since most design work is performed in plan view, to represent horizontal assemblies, a series of lines are drawn to enclose an area, rather than a single line to represent

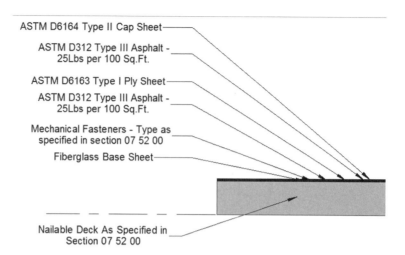

ASTM D6164 Type II Cap Sheet

ASTM D312 Type III Asphalt - 25Lbs per 100 Sq.Ft.

ASTM D6163 Type I Ply Sheet

ASTM D312 Type III Asphalt - 25Lbs per 100 Sq.Ft.

Mechanical Fasteners - Type as specified in section 07 52 00

Fiberglass Base Sheet

Nailable Deck As Specified in Section 07 52 00

FIGURE 5.2 Typical roof assembly

a length. As an area is drawn into the project, the slope, perimeter, area, thickness, and volume that have been created are returned to the data set for analysis and estimation purposes. As assemblies are created, they can be trained to relate themselves to areas within the project, such as specific rooms or spaces. They also relate themselves to a specific level that is defined within the project, or a distance from a given benchmark.

Objects

BIM objects are singular components that do not rely on the other components for their design. Assemblies are a series of material components that work together to create a single element, but rarely are those material components used on their own. Objects are autonomous and, wherever possible, are designed so they do not need to be coupled with additional objects to complete their design. Within every object are one or more geometric solids, each of which has a material parameter assigned to it. These parameters control the graphical aspects of the objects in both model and rendered views based on the designated material. More complex objects often contain sub-objects nested within them to simplify the creation of the object and allow for more control and selection of options. There are countless ways to streamline the creation of content, which we will discuss in depth based on the category of the component.

Components within a project that do not rely on either other components or post-assemblies are what I refer to as stand-alone components. These make up a lot of the fixtures and fittings used in projects, such as cabinets, lockers, plumbing fixtures, furniture, and a whole host of components that are mounted on host assemblies but not through them. While components that are designed to be mounted on walls may be created as wall-hosted components, in many cases this is not good practice as circumstances may dictate that the component be mounted on a vertical surface that is not a wall. In addition, components that are related to mechanics, electrics, and plumbing elements should not be host based, as, in many cases, the hosts are not added to these models.

Hosted objects must be installed on or through a base. The most commonly used hosted objects are windows, doors, and skylights. The primary reason for using hosted objects is twofold: to eliminate volume from the host that is taken up by the component, and to limit the placement of the component to only that host category. The elimination of host volume is critical when dealing with any type of glazed opening, as these openings allow the passage of light within the model. Limiting placement is not always necessary and, in many cases, can be a detriment. While usually walls are the host for a hand dryer, it could also be mounted on a column. If the hand dryer is created as a wall-based component, then the model will disallow its presence on the column. Because the hand dryer does not need to remove volume from the wall, and is also an electrical component, it is more effective to create it as a stand-alone object with controls that will align it to the placement surface.

When components become very complex or have several options that will change the graphic appearance of the model, it is often effective to embed subcomponents in order to maximize control and improve model performance. Using a door as an example in Figure 5.3, we can see that it is made up of several components, the most notable being the frame, panel, and, in some cases, glass. Usually the frame does not change except for its depth in relation to the thickness of the wall, and the material and finish associated with it. The panel is the most noticeable and decorative aspect of a door, often selected based on its aesthetic qualities. By creating the panel as a subcomponent of the door, it is much easier to control the appearance of the panel, and allow for several door panel options and still be able to recycle the graphics for the door over and over. If the panel is a function of the door the same way the width is, one door has the ability to represent both a single- and double-panel door.

There are series of system components that are something of a hybrid between autonomous BIM objects and assemblies. A series of specifically designed objects is created for an express purpose. Railings are a very visible example of this. Railings are made up of one or more horizontal rails, one or more balusters or infill panels, and one or more structural support posts. None of these components is ever used independently, and most railings typically cannot be created without all three. Curtain walls are another example of system components, where various types of extrusions line the perimeter and along

FIGURE 5.3 Typical door object

the gridlines, and panels fill in the spaces. There are many other types of system components; electrical wiring, piping, ductwork, and stairs all have multiple components that must work together to create a complete system.

When developing BIM components, sometimes we run into situations where an object becomes too large for its own good, even when it is not overly detailed. Often the number of options available for a component will increase the size of the file to the point where it is unmanageable. This is where the creation of a *constellation object* can be beneficial. The concept behind a constellation is that each subcomponent is autonomous in nature but works together with other components to create a complete element. I have had great success in creating doors as constellation objects, allowing for the independent management and control of the frame, panel, access hardware, threshold, closer, and even the weather stripping without ever exceeding 500 KB.

Details

Details are used to expand upon assemblies and, in some cases, objects to further explain how they are to be installed. Without a detail view, a vertical section view of a window within a wall will show us where the window sits in relation to the opening, in some cases the actual rough opening space, and some basic appearance information about the section view of the window and the wall. When we add a detail to a component that applies to the installation of the window within a specific type of wall, we can show exact fastener and flashing placement, as well as the appropriate sizes and locations of the structural supports. While it is possible to add this type of detailing to the window component itself, it is often based on the type of wall into which it is being installed.

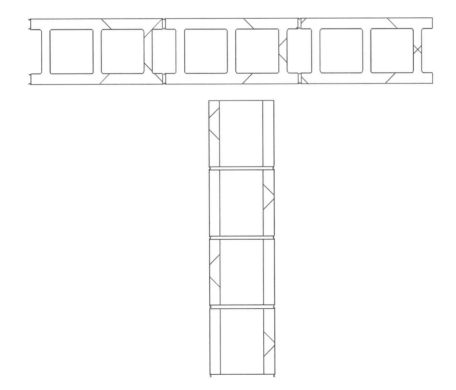

FIGURE 5.4 Typical detail—vertical and horizontal section views of a CMU

Brick cavity walls, as shown in Figure 5.3, have different requirements from wood-framed walls, and wood-framed walls differ from cast-in-place concrete walls. Rather than overburdening the window family with multiple details that apply to each construction, creating a series of detail components is more effective and allows the model to perform better.

IMPLEMENTING THE COMPONENT: PRIMARY, SECONDARY, AND TERTIARY

Components that are added to an architectural model can be categorized as primary, secondary, and tertiary. Exactly which category a specific component fits into depends largely on the individual or discipline. In addition to the architectural components, a series of structural, mechanical, and specialty components are used to further detail the model for design and analysis through specialty consultants and contractors. For architectural purposes, it is not always necessary to add each structural element, mechanical equipment, or specialty components unrelated to the design intent. In many cases, taking into consideration only basic dimensions and locations is acceptable to allow other contractors and consultants to design based on the spaces allotted. While this is a disjointed approach and in no way collaborative, it is not an uncommon practice and thus should be taken into consideration when thinking about how to organize the various types of components used in modeling.

Primary components are made up of the core elements used to enclose and access spaces: floors, walls, ceilings, roofs, and openings. These elements of the project are the first to be added, often during schematic design. They divide spaces, create layouts, and enclose the overall building. Walls are added into a project and used to enclose and divide spaces. It is important to maintain a consistent reference point within the walls so that they align properly. Because walls have several materials within them—from structural, to surfaces, to finishes—determining the reference point is often specific to the needs or type of project at hand. When creating exterior walls as we show in Figure 5.5, using the exterior edge of the structural member as the reference plane may be most effective, whereas when creating interior walls, the center line of the wall may be best. Using a consistent strategy for aligning walls minimizes the risk of errors through design development. In many cases the number of layers and thickness of materials within the wall is unknown until well after the original walls have been placed. A great deal of time is spent manipulating these elements such that they may become

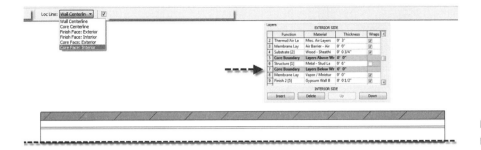

FIGURE 5.5 Reference points of assemblies

permanent as design development progresses. Once the design begins to consider secondary components, it is common for errors to occur should the primary components need to be moved or changed. Developing a strategy for creating, maintaining, and organizing wall assemblies will allow walls to be swapped out at any time without the risk of moving walls due to differing reference points.

As BIM technology improves, the number of components that may be defined as secondary is increasing. Before they were made readily available, components like toilet partitions and fixed furnishings were not always graphically modeled. This is largely due to the amount of effort required to create a graphic representation of a component. As more manufacturers make their components available, the number of designers wanting to place them in their model increases.

Secondary components are essential to the design but may remain largely unknown or undecided until later in design development. They rely on the dimensions and locations of the primary components for decision making and product selection, and are generally nonstructural in nature. The most common secondary components on projects are stairs and railings, fixtures and fittings, casework and cabinetry, specialty partitions, and certain types of fixed furnishings and storage. These types of components are essential to the understanding of spatial relationships and the conceptualization of many aspects of the project. It gives the owner an understanding of what the space is used for. The walls may define the boundary of a kitchen, but the cabinets determine what it is.

If we think about different components in relationship to the overall size of the project, we can make the determination of how graphically accurate they need to be. Secondary components are those that are integral to the design, but not integral to the structure. In most cases these types of components are selected based on their appearance as much as on their performance. When a component is selected partially or entirely based on its aesthetic, how it is represented within the model becomes more important. The frequency at which these components are placed in the model is also a consideration when determining the graphic accuracy. If a component is placed in the project only once but is selected solely based on its aesthetic, it is reasonable to put more effort into its graphic accuracy, as maintaining its performance and file size is not as relevant for a component such as a door, which may be placed hundreds of times throughout a single project.

Component size and location also come into play when considering the graphic accuracy of an object. A good rule of thumb is if you can't see it from 10 to 15 feet away in its installed position, don't spend a lot of time on it. This is the typical distance used for up-close rendering. Since the primary reason for making close representations of products is to improve the rendering aspect of the model, if it's not being rendered, it might as well be a cube. Many components in a project are actually very small. Whether it is a light switch, a drawer pull, or a window crank, deciding how accurate these components must be is an important undertaking. While every manufacturer wants to think that his components are the most important, we have to look at the model in terms of scale. Ask yourself how important a window crank is to a 1,000,000-ft.^{2} building, and what purpose it serves if it is not visible in rendered views. The answer lies in its ability to be quantified and qualified. If a component needs to be quantified or qualified, it can add value to the model. Let's go back to window hardware as an example and look at three possible scenarios: (1) If a manufacturer offers several hardware options, and the hardware will likely be visible in many rendered views, it should be added to the model graphically and have the ability to select options. (2) If a manufacturer offers several options for the type of hardware used, but it will not be seen in a rendered view, it is more effective to list the hardware as an attribute of the window without graphically modeling it. (3) If only one type of hardware is available from the manufacturer, is perfectly acceptable to omit it from both the graphics and the information contained in the project. If there are no choices to be made and the component is not commonly used for selection or specification purposes, then adding it to the model offers little value to the architect, specifier, or contractor.

Tip

If you can't see a component from 10 to 15 feet away in its installed position, don't spend a lot of time on it.

Tertiary components are those added during detailing, or not at all. While it is my belief that every component that is used on a project should be brought into the model in some way, shape, or form, that does not necessarily mean it should be done graphically. There are ways to embed information regarding components without actually placing them in the project, and there are ways to simplify how a tertiary component is placed in a model as well. Hopefully, this will minimize the number of tertiary components within a project and increase the number of secondary components. Over time this could translate into more accurate models and a greater demand for as-built models as a final deliverable to the owner.

A component such as door hardware is an essential element within a project, is found in hundreds of locations, and even has its own special schedule, yet it is arguably a tertiary component that is often overlooked or omitted. Most architects choose not to deal with door hardware for the amount of effort necessary versus the benefit received from placing it in the model. Components like this are often better represented in context. Door hardware is a function of a door and, as such, should be placed and controlled from within that door. Rather than attempting to place door hardware components at each location within the project, making door hardware a function of the door itself can allow it to be a graphic aspect of the model and carry the important information to its respective schedules.

Accessories, movable furnishings, and equipment are tertiary components. Because they may be relocated at any time and are more commonly used for conceptualization and space planning, these types of components are typically

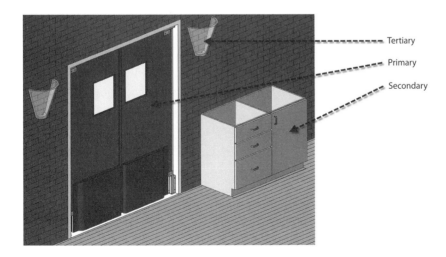

FIGURE 5.6 Graphic accuracy of primary, secondary, and tertiary components

not modeled. As a general rule, when the placement of a component is not integral to the structure or the design of a project, the component can be considered tertiary. Another way to look at it is if there is no specification section for the component within the project, it is probably a tertiary component.

DATA MANAGEMENT CONCEPTS

As we begin to develop content let's look at why we add data to the models. Information contained in various components and the project as a whole can be useful to the architect, specifier, contractor, and owner. This is not to say that the model will be passed to the owner upon completion, but this practice is becoming more and more common. If a BIM project is used only by the architect, and information or graphics will not be passed to any other parties, the value of adding information is considerably diminished and often unnecessary. The information contained in the model may be relevant to the architect in terms of product research and model analysis, but when information will be passed along, it can be used to perform additional functions such as quantifying and qualifying each component, developing facility management databases, and documenting the project by leveraging the information contained to create the project manual.

The earlier we add information to the model and its related components, the easier it is to make decisions. If we think about the project lifecycle as linear rather than a series of steps, each decision that is made moves us a little bit further along the line, rather than having requirements necessary to go from one step to the next. We may have a considerable amount of information regarding our windows but know nothing about our doors, yet we cannot move along to another phase of the project until we have that information. Conversely, if we have a considerable amount of information regarding our walls early in the design phase, then we can narrow the possibilities for different finishes and the types of windows that may be acceptable for the given wall types and even begin to consider how to detail certain areas of the project.

Related information links may be embedded in each component to simplify product research. A BIM object can be thought of as a singular point of reference from which all product information may be sourced. If we need a specification, we can click one link or for additional construction details, click another link; manufacturers' technical data sheets, material safety data sheets, and color charts could be other links to relevant information that will assist during the design, specification, and construction phases.

Very early in the design phase, there may be little or no information available regarding the exact components to be used. In cases such as this we may often add attributes to specific components, but list the values "As Specified" or not at all. This creates a placeholder for information to be added later. The earlier information is added, the easier it is to add and the more it may be leveraged. A series of schedules within the project allows information to be added in a spreadsheet format, which can simplify the process considerably as well as create visual cues where information may be missing. This is an open door for a specifier to begin working within the project maintaining this information without ever having to learn the graphic aspects of the software or manipulate the design of the model. At different points along the design timeline, the model may need to be queried to extract information for different purposes. If we look at the information that will be necessary later in the project, a series of queries may be written in the form of database exports and schedules, which, in most cases, can be recycled from project to project.

A considerable amount of information may be contained within a project. It is not necessary to place any information into the model that will not be used at some point downstream. While it is better to have the information and not need it than to need it and not have it, it is best to try to avoid information overload. Keeping models clear, concise, complete, correct, and consistent with other contract documents can speed up the project timeline, save all members of the project team time and effort, and ultimately provide a better project to the owner.

NAMING CONVENTIONS

Components that are used within a BIM project are different from traditional CAD files as their names must be visible from within the project. This creates a requirement of an intuitive naming convention, so we may find and retrieve the components we are looking for quickly and easily. As we name components, the method differs slightly, depending on the type of component we're dealing with—whether it is a material, an object, or an assembly. More detail will be given in respective chapters, but there are some basic guidelines to follow, regardless of the type of component being created.

Names should be descriptive but brief. BIM software often limits the number of characters that are easily visible on screen. Avoid conjunctions and truncate names and words wherever possible. The information is within a database, not on paper, so it is more important for the name to be understandable than intelligible. Just as the world has come to understand that "Ctrl" equates to the word "control," truncating the names of components does not mean that they need to become unrecognizable. The use of special characters and spaces within filenames can wreak havoc on filenames. In the digital era, it is very common for components to be shared on websites or in libraries. Spaces in filenames often confuse websites, and programming code commonly uses special characters. To ensure that errors do not occur, avoid both of these at all costs. A few of the better-known culprits are the inch symbol ["], the period [.], and the comma [,]. Databases use parentheses or the inch symbol to capture text, and in many cases become confused with the inch symbol if used in a name. Periods [.] are used to separate a filename from its extension and in some cases can confuse a database or website. Databases use commas as delimiters to separate fields. A comma added to a name can potentially trip up the database and create errors. Simply using *in* instead of ["] for inch will likely save you the headaches of having to go back and rename files that have tripped up a website or database.

PART II

BIM Content Basics

CHAPTER 6

Basic Modeling Considerations

Building information modeling objects are created by generating solid models that represent various components assemblies and products. When creating these models, we need to consider how detailed they should be and how they should be implemented into a project. BIM objects are best represented contextually. For many components, context is simple. It is little more than creating the object as a stand-alone item that can be implemented into a project based on the appropriate locations or the hosts it may be installed on. Developing the graphics becomes a difficult part. Some components are actually an assembly of several products and require multiple objects to be created, all of which work together.

Storage shelving is an example of a component made up of several components that develop the entire system. There may be wall-mounted standards or floor-mounted poles to which are attached some type of bracket, and a horizontal surface or shelf, all working together. Rather than expect the design team to place each one of these components individually, we should create the model based on how somebody will intuitively place the components, all at once. To create components like this, it is often effective to create individual objects for each component in the system and load them all into a BIM constellation object, which allows the user to select from the different bracket, pole, standard, and shelf options shown in Figure 6.1. The most important thing to remember when creating components that have multiple embedded options like brackets is that our insertion points must be identical among all components of a given category. Use the same insertion point for each bracket, the same insertion point for each pole, and the same insertion point for each shelf. Be careful with file size when dealing with components like this, as the graphic options can weigh down the file when they are not being used. Certain BIM software platforms allow components to be configured so that the options may be available even if the components are not loaded into the primary object. Provided the components are of the appropriate category, they may be loaded directly into the project, rather than into the object itself, and still allow for the options to be selected. These types of components in this loading method are discussed in greater depth in the chapter on BIM constellations.

In some cases, components are designed to be placed in multiples or arrays and have aspects of the individual object that is designed to be shared along the array. For instance, restroom partitions shown in Figure 6.2 may be designed such that two stalls are created with three walls and three pilasters, sharing a wall and pilaster between the two. To further complicate components like this, the stalls may be placed in a corner, with two panels and two pilasters, or in an

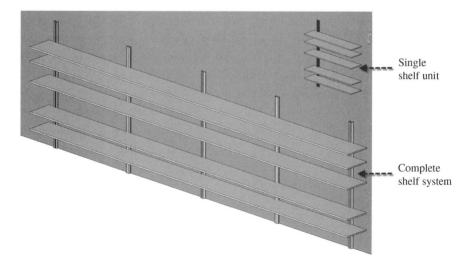

Single
shelf unit

Complete
shelf system

FIGURE 6.1   Shelf
systems

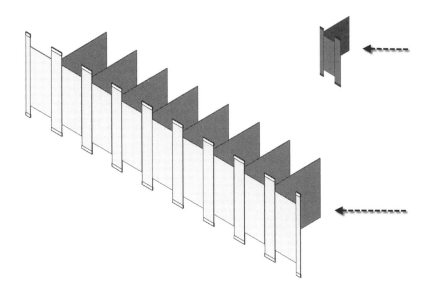

FIGURE 6.2 Restroom partition arrays

alcove with only one panel and one pilaster separating the stalls. The individual creating the BIM object that represents the partition will never know how many stalls will be used on a given project and how they will be configured in relationship to adjacent walls. Attempting to create an entire catalog of stalls that represent anywhere from 1 to 30 or more stalls in a battery, multiplied by the number of mounting options and multiplied again by their location, is impractical. It is far more effective to create only a few or even a single stall that has intelligent dimensions, graphics, and visibility controls. This will allow the architects to determine for themselves how many stalls are to be placed and in what configuration.

LEVELS OF DETAIL—AIA E202 AND THE LOD CONCEPT

The American Institute of Architects (AIA) released document E202, or the Building Information Modeling Protocol Exhibit. It is used to establish the protocols, expectations, and the unauthorized use of the models created for a given project. It also assigns responsibilities for specific elements of the model to specific individuals and, in Article 3, assigns a level of development (LOD) for each project phase. There are five levels of development, as noted by the AIA: LOD 100, LOD 200, LOD 300, LOD 400, and LOD 500. Each level of development corresponds to specific content requirements, authorized use of the model, and specific purposes of the model. Following are basic guidelines for accuracy at the various levels of detail.

LOD 100

LOD 100 is essentially a massing study of the overall project to determine the area, height, volume, location, and orientation. It generally does not take into consideration any "real" BIM content of the project, only masses. This level of detail is typically used for project preplanning, feasibility studies, and basic cost estimation. When working at LOD 100, there is not much information available other than the gross size of the building with some basic dimensions that represent the square area, included volume, and general shape. Figure 6.3 shows how a massing study performed at LOD 100 can transform into a completed project.

LOD 200

LOD 200 contains model elements as generalized systems or assemblies with approximate quantities, sizes, shapes, locations, and orientations. At this level, nongraphic attributes may be added into the components. LOD 200 takes into consideration what we described as primary components in Chapter 5, "Where to Begin." Our walls, floors, ceilings, roofs, and openings would be added in at this point but may not be specific to exact materials or components used in those assemblies. In some cases the actual dimensions may be known; in others they may not. Openings in walls or roofs at this point may not even be known as windows, doors, or skylights, but just as openings. Having an approximated thickness for the assemblies is acceptable at this time as well, as the point of LOD 200 is really more space determination and overall sizing of the project rather than detailed aspects of the individual assembly or component. BIM objects noted at LOD 200 in Figure 6.4 are really only representative and are more like placeholders or symbols than actual components.

At this point performance analysis of the various assemblies may be conducted to determine which components are to be used. Cost estimation is also possible using area, volume, and quantity of known elements.

LOD 300

LOD 300 elements become more accurate in terms of their quantity, size, shape, location, and orientation. They may not consider exact materials within assemblies or exactly specified components, but begin to add specific detail regarding the performance aspects of the component, dimensional preference or limitation, and specification information necessary to develop construction documents. Components such as Figure 6.5, listed at LOD 300 should contain

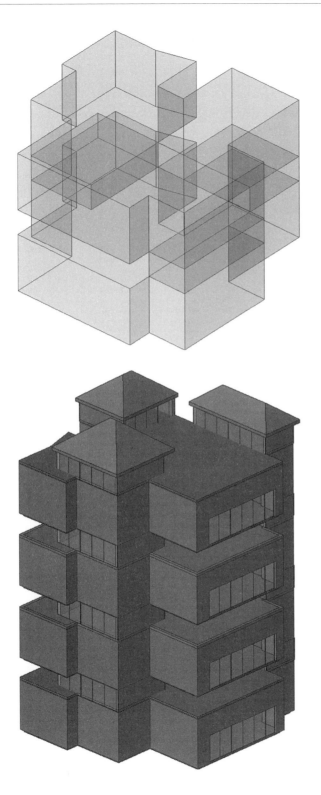

FIGURE 6.3 A BIM
project at LOD 100

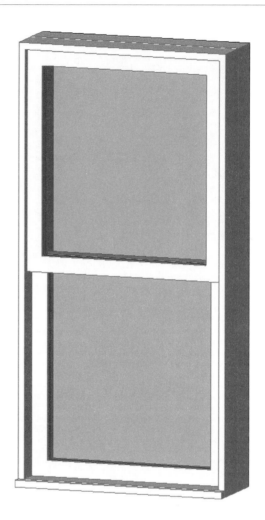

FIGURE 6.4 BIM component at LOD 200

the necessary performance criteria and have enough data to perform a detailed analysis of the systems within the project related to the component. Specific cost estimates may be generated based on components at LOD 300, as well as construction documents.

Most BIM development work is performed around LOD 300, so it becomes an excellent base point from which to develop content. It begins to show detail about individual components, but not precise detail related to their installation or maintenance.

LOD 400

Above and beyond the requirements of LOD 300, BIM objects that can be considered to be LOD 400 must either contain or have available related details associated with the two-dimensional roof aspect of its design, assembly, and

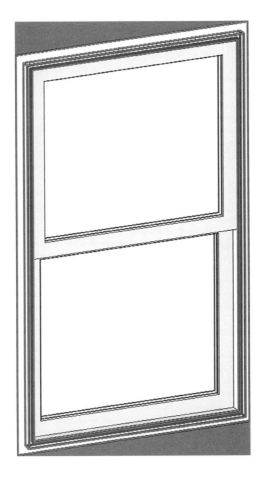

FIGURE 6.5 BIM
component at LOD 300

fabrication. Components must be accurate enough to create suitable construction documents, perform accurate model analysis, and be capable of containing accurate cost information.

The primary difference between LOD 300 and LOD 400 is the amount of information contained within the object, and the two-dimensional details that are either embedded or associated with the component itself. This is shown in Figure 6.6. To keep the file size manageable, it is more appropriate to create two-dimensional detail components, which may be added to the model at the appropriate time. This can greatly improve the performance of the software, as the various details that may be associated with a component can weigh it down considerably.

LOD 500

LOD 500 could be considered a fully accurate digital representation of a given manufacturer product. This level of detail is rarely necessary, except in the

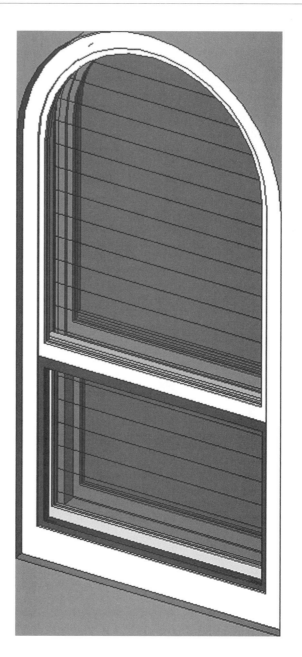

FIGURE 6.6 BIM component at LOD 400

case of highly detailed renderings, and is often not desired, as objects of this caliber generally lie heavy upon the project model. These types of objects should be reserved only for use in very high-resolution renderings that contain close-up views.

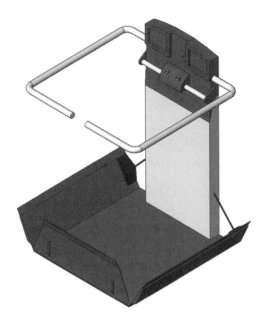

FIGURE 6.7 BIM component at LOD 500

While many manufacturers expect that their models will and should be created as shown in Figure 6.7, in most cases it is not practical. Because of the size and amount of detail associated with components at LOD 500, many architects will not use them. It is important to remember that product-specific BIM objects are designed to be used by the architect and provided by the manufacturer, so they should be created to fit the needs of the architect, not the manufacturer. Any time a component is created at this level of detail, a companion component should be created at a much lower level of development, 200 or 300, in order for the product to be useful during design.

The AIA LOD concept assigns a specific amount of development required for specific components, based on the needs of the design team in the project as a whole. It is not necessarily a one-to-one-to-one relationship between a type of component, the phase of the project, and the level of development. Only the design team determines how much detail is necessary at what points in the project for which components. This is a good thing for architects, because it gives them the ability to customize the amount of information and graphics necessary based on the needs and budget of the project, but for BIM content developers it can be quite confusing. Trying to make a determination of how to represent a specific manufacturer's component can be quite an undertaking when we consider all the possibilities, all of the project phases, and all of the preferences of the architects who may use that component.

Right in the middle of the road is LOD 300, which considers an appropriate amount of graphics and a considerable amount of product information, but keeps the individual components small enough to be manageable. LOD 300 does not always consider the exact details associated with the installation of the component or the associated views in which it may be found, but providing an additional set of construction details that augment the object can allow an LOD 300 object to be considered an LOD 400 with no additional work.

REPRESENTATIVE MODELING

Representative modeling is a concept that allows us to simplify graphics to represent multiple products using a single object. In many cases, the details of the graphics associated with a given component are less relevant than the amount of information contained within, so as to provide a good balance of form and functionality. Components selected based on their performance rather than their appearance are excellent candidates for representative modeling. Most recessed light fixtures are contained within a ceiling, so the graphics lose relevance altogether save the ceiling-mounted trim. It is the photometry, electrical, and performance aspects of the component that take precedence, so a single recessed light fixture with parametric controls for size will allow the graphics to be shown accurately enough for modeling and still detail the hundreds of lamp, ballast, and electrical options available.

Many components that are added to a project are not relevant within rendered views, or the graphic level of detail is just not important to the architect. This is why certain components come to be modeled in a representative fashion rather than in exact representations. Just as symbols are used in two-dimensional drawings to represent specific components, representative models can be looked at as three-dimensional symbols. As long as the model takes up the appropriate amount of volume, contains the correct and appropriate amount of information regarding the component, and follows the appropriate level of detail desired by the architect, representative modeling is an effective way to continue the growth of building information modeling without spending a considerable amount of money developing components.

In addition to the cost and time savings that representative modeling provides, representative models also minimize overall file size. When dealing with projects of considerable size, we need to look at components in terms of their scale and importance to the overall project. At this point, we can quickly see how graphically important a fire extinguisher cabinet or recessed light fixture actually is to the overall scope of the project. While all manufacturers want their BIM content to look exactly like the manufactured component, it is not practical to provide this level of detail until the software can manage it. Each time a component is placed into a project, it compounds the file size. Components such as electrical devices, light fixtures, fire signature cabinets, signage, and others that may be located hundreds or thousands of places within the project can cause a considerable lag during loading and regeneration of the file when the graphics are overly detailed.

Components that are highly ornate, but are relevant to the overall aesthetic of the project, are not likely candidates for representative modeling. These types of components are typically placed once or twice in a project, and their overall appearance is likely to be viewed in a rendered setting. Components such as chandeliers, elevators, escalators, and certain windows and doors are often showcased in rendered views, so their general appearance should be graphically modeled at a greater level of detail. Determining which components to model as representative versus realistic takes careful planning and discussion with the parties involved with modeling. For manufacturers, before having components developed, it is a good idea to discuss with architects and other designers what their needs and intentions are. This will ensure that the models provided to the architect will ultimately be used in projects rather than become overweight graphic models with little practical use other than for marketing brochures. For architects, spending a few moments planning with the BIM manager will set an expectation for the model, giving them a sense of what type of views will ultimately be presented to an owner and which aspects of the project will be showcased.

When beginning a project and working through the schematic design, representative components should be the only ones used. This will keep modeling speed up at the beginning and keep the file size small, allowing quick decision making and updating during the period of the project when the most critical decisions are made regarding sizes, shapes, and locations. Once these types of decisions have been made final, the representative models may be swapped out for more detailed versions where desired or necessary for rendered views. Think of it as a transition from LOD 200 to LOD 300 in a rolling fashion. As actual products are selected for use in the project, more detail may be necessary to convey them for final modeling and/or rendering purposes. This would be like a transition from LOD 300 to LOD 400. LOD 500 components might be added in certain locations when the design is finalized in order to create highly detailed rendered views for presentation to an owner but, in many cases, are omitted altogether to save valuable file space.

As we think about creating representative graphics, it is important to look at the component based on its installed position. Going back to my rule of thumb, if

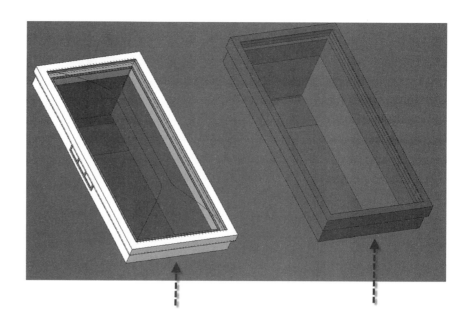

FIGURE 6.8

A representative object alongside a detailed object

it is not visible from 10 to 15 feet away in its installed position, carefully consider whether or not it needs to be modeled. Representative graphics, as shown in Figure 6.8, should take up the appropriate amount of area and volume necessary to perform interference checking, provide visual cues to the architect that the component exists, and contain the appropriate amount of information necessary to make decisions about which product will ultimately be used in its place. Graphically, representative models should be accurate to about ¼ to ⅛ inch. It need not carry exact details about specific options within the graphics, but might possibly have them available within the data so they may be updated later using more detailed models.

One method of creating scalable models that I prefer to use is to create a series of components that are embedded in the object and may be swapped out for more detailed versions as the level of development increases. For instance, a low-development window (LOD 200) may be created that has options in the data set for how the window operates and whether it has muntins, but no graphics associated with those embedded components. To change it from LOD 200 to LOD 300, the embedded components would be swapped out for graphically detailed components to show those components in more accurate detail. The same procedure can be done with any component, so rather than turning the visibility of certain graphics on and off to convey the level of detail, we will actually change the embedded components themselves. This allows not only the level of development to be consistent but the size of the components themselves to be smaller, which maintains modeling efficiency throughout the project, a critical aspect of the LOD concept.

USING SOLID MODELING TOOLS

Different BIM platforms have different methods of creating the solids that represent the objects we use in the project. The types of solids to be used depend greatly on how the component is implemented into a project. Some components are better implemented by simply drawing a line and allowing a solid or solids to follow that path, while others are a fixed unit that may have variable length width and depth dimensions. There are tools that will allow us to create spheres and rounded objects more easily than others, as well as those that can create ornate curvatures and twists. Understanding how each solid modeling tool works will allow us to create highly detailed components with fewer errors.

Solids may be created by either addition or subtraction. Addition is the act of creating a solid from nothing, and subtraction is the removal of volume from a solid by creating voids. Using void geometry to create facets within a solid is an effective method of creating ornate geometry that may not otherwise be possible. However, it can become confusing and somewhat overburdening to the model as voids are computationally larger than solids, and its volume can accidentally "hide" itself within the object if it is not actually cutting through a solid. Use great care in creating void geometry as the unexpected results that often occur in smaller file sizes often take more time to load and regenerate. Wherever possible, use solid geometry over void geometry to create the components that make up the object.

The most commonly used solids are extrusions, which are created by sketching an enclosed region without a two-dimensional plane and extruding upward a specific amount. Shown in Figure 6.9, extrusions take into consideration two aspects: the sketch and the distance. This type of geometry is used to create the core structure of most components, with additional geometry added to it or subtracted from it to detail its overall appearance. Extrusions provide us with the most flexibility in the overall shape, as each facet of the sketch can be made parametric so it may be controlled without having to resketch from scratch. To create an extrusion, a series of lines that enclose an area are drawn on a specific plane, which determines its point of origin. Multiple enclosed sketch loops will allow holes to be created within the extrusion, eliminating the need for void geometry. Once the sketch is completed, extrusions may be trained to project a certain distance either by attaching the

start and end points to a parameter, or affixing them to reference planes and dimensioning between them.

A revolution is a type of solid that spins a sketch around on axis rather than extruding it. A revolution is commonly used with components that are generally round in shape, but may have ornate detailing that is consistent along an edge. I think the best way to think about a revolution is as a long piece of wood on a lathe. If we spin the wood, chisels on the lathe will cut out volume from it. The profile in this case would be the space that is left over after the chisels do their work. Revolutions allow us to note specific start and end angles, so they do not have to spin 360° around. The most common BIM objects that use revolutions are architectural columns, balusters used on railings, door knobs, and drawer pulls.

Figure 6.10 shows the three primary aspects to a revolution: the sketch, the axis, and the angle. The sketch defines what the revolution would look like in a two-dimensional view looking straight upon it. The axis of the revolution is the center point from which the solid is created, or the centerline of the same two-dimensional view. It does not necessarily need to lie on the sketch or be one of the sketch lines. Where the axis is offset from the sketch, it will create an opening in the revolved solid, like the middle of a donut or the empty space left for structural support of an architectural column.

Shown in Figure 6.11, sweeps are very similar to extrusions in that they are developed using a sketch and a distance, but they also take direction into consideration. While extrusions can only go perpendicular to the sketch plane, a sweep runs along a line or path, which determines its shape. Sweeps are beneficial when creating graphics that have a set profile or sketch and need to follow a specific path, whether curved or angular. The frame of a window or door is an example of where a sweep may come in handy. When simplifying the

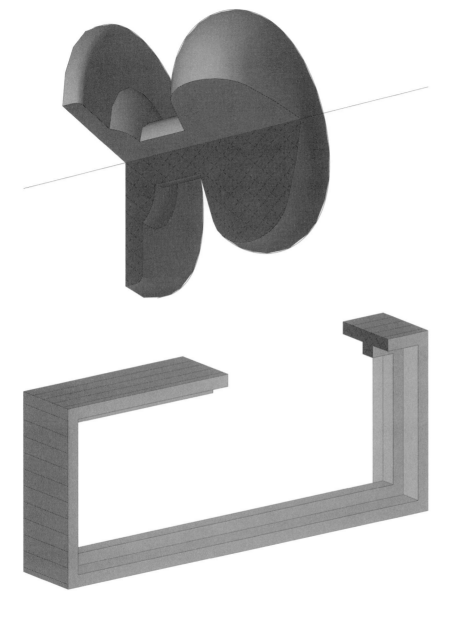

FIGURE 6.10 Typical revolution—sketch, axis, and angle

FIGURE 6.11 Typical sweep—sketch and direction

graphics of the frames, it is possible to represent the head, sill, and jambs using a single solid by creating that path that the sweep will follow, and the sketch that defines the profile that is to be extruded.

Sweeps give us additional control in that they are heavily driven by the profile. Rather than sketching the profile, a sweep can actually load specific profiles, allowing them to be swapped out at any point later on. This is especially helpful when dealing with components such as finish carpentry and casework.

Ornate trim is driven by its profile to determine how it appears, so by creating a series of profiles that represent each of the types of trim, a single sweep can represent every possible profile that may be used.

A word of caution regarding sweeps and profiles. If the profile is too large for the angle that is to be swept or a radius is too small for it to effectively turn, then errors may result. This is especially important when dealing with sweeps that have loaded profiles rather than sketched profiles, as there are likely several of them, all of which need to be tested to ensure that they work properly. When creating profile sketches, take care in the amount of detail, as highly ornate profiles with very minute detail can sometimes cause errors. In addition, it is essential to ensure that the profile sketch is a closed loop, else it will not be able to create the solid appropriately.

A blended solid is one that uses two sketches and a direction, as noted in Figure 6.12. Think of it as an extrusion with one sketch at the bottom and a different sketch at the top. It is not a widely used solid modeling method, but comes in very handy for unique situations when dealing with nonuniform geometry, such as toilets, tubs, and decorative light fixtures. There are also two types of blends: an extruded blend and one that follows a path. An extruded blend follows the same requirements of extrusion, only it has two sketches rather than one. A blend that follows a path has the same requirements as a sweep, with the exception that it has a sketch at the beginning and a sketch at the end. Another primary difference between an extrusion or a sweep and a blend is the ability to twist the solid as it moves along its direction or path.

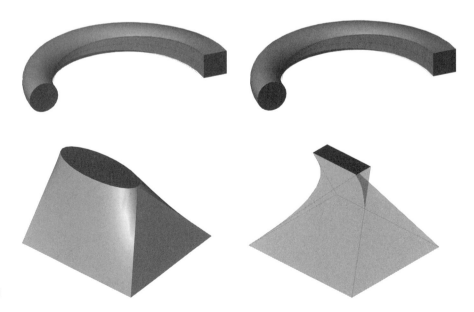

FIGURE 6.12 Blends—extrusions and path based

REFERENCE LINES AND PLANES

Three-dimensional graphics don't just use the X and Y directions from a Cartesian plane, but add the Z direction to create depth. To maintain control of not only our projects but our components, we use reference planes and reference lines to give us a sense of where we are located in space and which view we are looking from. Consider a cube, which has six sides all of equal size. It would be very difficult to know which side is supposed to be the top without some sort of notation or visual cue. Shown in Figure 6.13, reference planes provide us with not only a visual cue but a surface with from which we can work. They become the start and end points for all of our graphics solids, the references between which dimensions are placed, and, perhaps most importantly, the insertion points for our components.

The insertion or origin point of an object is arguably one of the most important aspects of its development. If an appropriate and consistent insertion point is not provided, it becomes difficult to quickly and easily place components into a project. If the insertion point of a window is not defined, or is defined as 20 feet off to the left and 6 feet below the window, it becomes difficult to insert the window into a wall. Appropriately naming and noting reference planes and defining which three planes make up the X, Y, and Z coordinates will ensure that components are always placed appropriately. When dealing with embedded components, maintaining consistency among reference planes is paramount. Suppose a door object is created with an embedded panel that may be swapped out through a user-defined option. Each one of the embedded panel objects must have an identical insertion point; otherwise, they will not locate appropriately and errors will occur when the object is updated. It is effective to come up with a strategy that works for your office, or, better yet, the industry as a whole, which defines insertion points for different types of components. For instance, all door panels would use the interior side of the door at its very top on the hinge side as the insertion point, or all door hardware would use the centerlines of the component as measured for placement height, with the face that is placed against the door as its third plane.

Reference lines are similar to reference planes, except they are more effective and useful in two-dimensional drawings. They assist in dimensioning the angle between two lines, which may need to be parametric, and are useful for dimensioning sketches in lieu of placing dimensions between two sketch lines themselves. When creating two-dimensional detail objects, reference lines are used in lieu of reference planes altogether, as there is no Z-axis in details.

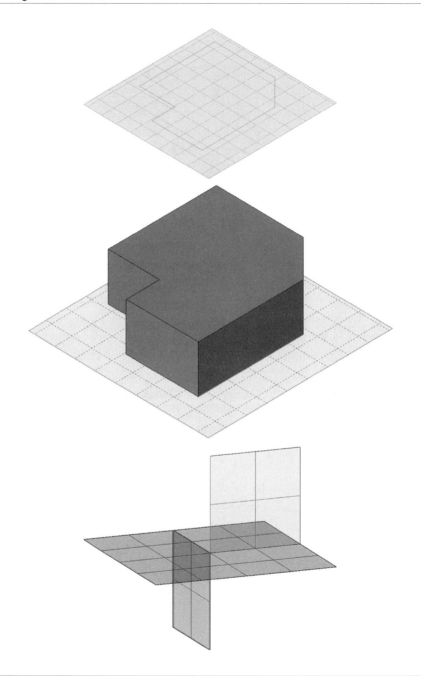

FIGURE 6.13
Three-dimensional
reference planes

DIMENSIONS AND TOLERANCES

As you begin to develop objects, take into consideration how accurate they must be to perform the task at hand. The purpose of a BIM object is to represent a specific component being used in a project. The active word here is *represent*.

Nobody is going to design a component or manufacture it using the graphics associated with a building information model. It is designed for the component to be implemented into a project, and as such should carry the dimensions and tolerances necessary to convey aspects of architectural design and construction, not of product engineering and manufacturing. This is not to say that a component could not be detailed enough for manufacturing, but the tools used for implementation are far less detailed and far less capable than those used for manufacturing. The typical construction tolerance is around $\frac{1}{16}$ of an inch, whereas in manufacturing, tolerances may be listed in microns. The solid modeling tools within BIM software may not be as accurate as they could be, but they are as accurate as they need to be. Architectural software looks at the macro view of components, whereas design and manufacturing software looks at the micro view. It comes down to intent and purpose. A single manufacturing software file may be as large as an entire architectural project due to the miniscule level of detail associated with specific components. Since nobody is going to see the innards of a furnace or air conditioning unit within a building information model, there is no sense in developing to that level of detail.

The dimensioning of objects may not be as simple as it seems. With CAD, a dimension was as simple as the distance between two points. With the addition of parameters, there must be a location in the data set for each parametric dimension. Creating a series of parameters to control dimensions allows us to put controls on them so they may be updated later with little effort. However, all of these dimensions ultimately end up in a data set, which may be viewed by an architect or other individual in the design team. When there are 20 dimension parameters, all but two of which are relevant to the design, it can become difficult to determine which ones should be modified and which should not. To differentiate between dimensions that are relevant to the design and those that were used strictly to develop the object, I place them in different locations within the data set. Dimension parameters that the designer may need to modify themselves are placed in one location in the data set; others that are relevant to the designer, but are a function of the actual type of component and should never be modified, are placed in another. When dimension parameters either are driven by calculations or are solely for the development of the object, I typically give them unreadable names, all in lowercase, and place them in an out-of-the-way place in the data set so it is understood that they are of no concern to the design team.

Developing solid geometry is a series of exercises in creating sketches that are dimensioned and in many cases controlled by parameters. When dimensioning sketches, it is often more effective to dimension between reference planes rather than the sketch lines themselves. This allows for more control and the ability to attach to solids together with the fewest number of errors. This does not, however, dictate that all dimensions should be based upon reference planes—only the most important ones. In the case of a sketch that contains 20 facets or lines and ultimately becomes a solid, the adjacent geometry will likely need to connect to it on one or more sides, as shown in Figure 6.14. Suppose we have geometry that will be connected on four of those faces; creating four reference planes to manage the four primary faces or sides will give us more control over how the solid behaves. In another case, where multiple disconnected lines are aligned with one another, it is more effective to align them both to a reference plane rather than to each other.

One main purpose in using reference planes to dimension sketches is so the reference plane may be used to align or lock the geometry to adjacent solids. For this to occur while maintaining the ability to effectively dimension the geometry, the reference planes must be created outside of sketch mode so that they may relate to geometry other than the sketch. In addition, when dimensioning between two reference planes, not only must the planes be outside of the sketch, but the dimensions must be as well. Certain BIM software is designed to be intuitive and make assumptions about what the designer intends to do when developing components. In some cases, sketch lines are automatically locked to reference planes that are nearby, which may cause unexpected results. In cases where this continually happens and is not desired, one solution is to develop the sketch prior to placing reference planes, and then to set the desired alignments manually.

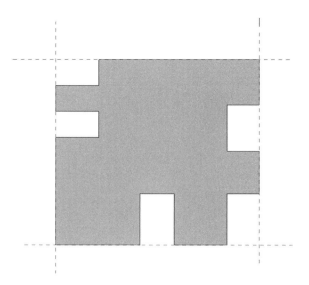

FIGURE 6.14 Sketch lines and reference planes

Dimensions that are created within BIM objects do not translate into the project visibly. They become a permanent fixture within the data set whose only function is to drive the appearance of the object. In most cases the dimensions for BIM objects become a function of the construction details, rather than the graphics that are placed within the model, so this is not a common dilemma. If dimensions for an object are necessary on a drawing sheet, they will need to be placed manually while within a project, or have an associated detail object created to complement the component.

Tip

In some cases, sketch lines are automatically locked to reference planes that are nearby, which may cause unexpected results. In cases where this continually happens and is not desired, one solution is to develop the sketch prior to placing reference planes and to set the desired alignments manually.

General construction tolerances are set at about $\frac{1}{16}$ of an inch. When we discuss tolerance within a BIM object, it may be more accurate to refer to it as clearance or offset. A window or door should be able to note the clearance necessary for its rough opening, the installation height of a hand dryer should note its clearance or distance from the floor, and a bathroom partition its clearance or distance from an adjoining wall. These types of dimensions added into components allow them to be more accurate for design without requiring them to be hyperaccurate in graphic accuracy. The distance from the floor to the bottom of a hand dryer is far more relevant to the designer than the rounded radius of its cover. Focusing on the information and dimensions that are necessary for the design team to do their job allows for models to be built with the needs of the architect in mind.

DEVELOPING CONTENT FOR CLASH DETECTION

Interference checking or "clash detection" is a function of BIM software that allows it to analyze two or more components to see whether they interfere with one another in the model. This is a widely used function of building information modeling and relies on the accuracy of components to do their job effectively. In most cases this function is reserved for the larger, first-order elements of a project, such as structural members, mechanical equipment, duct work, and piping; conflicts between these types of components can prove to be most problematic during design. If BIM content is developed with clash detection analysis taken into consideration, more detailed studies may be performed to determine whether or not a wall-mounted light switch or recessed fire extinguisher cabinet interferes with a pipe running up the wall.

Another method of developing components with clash detection in mind is actually to turn off any errors. For instance, creating a fireproofing object that both places sealant or a fireproofing collar around a pipe or HVAC duct and removes the volume from the wall will actually turn off the clash detection, as the volume where the pipe penetrates the wall has been removed. This allows the model to be studied in terms of its fireproofing, so anywhere a pipe penetrates a wall, annotation will be made to signal the design team that fireproofing has been missed in the location. This is a very low-level example of how this type of anti-clash detection analysis can benefit the design team provided that the components are created appropriately and made available, but creating content that can serve as a product representation as well as perform some type of building analysis opens the door for dual-purpose BIM content.

Because clash detection relies solely on graphics and category, it is important that components take up the appropriate amount of space and be within the correct category. A light switch, for instance, has a box behind it that is embedded in the wall. If the switch is designed for use in clash detection, it must carry with it graphics to represent the box, as simple as it may be. It does not need to be detailed, but only to take up the appropriate amount of space necessary to define necessary clearances from adjacent components. Categorizing objects should be done regardless of whether the components are designed for clash detection, but in a case such as this where the component will cause errors in the analysis if not formatted properly, it is even more critical to ensure that the categories are listed correctly.

CHAPTER 7

Creation and Management of Materials

WHAT ARE BIM MATERIALS?

BIM materials are the base unit used to create all other elements within a project. Each graphic solid used to create a component has a material assigned to it that details what it looks like in model view, its appearance in rendered views, and associated information about what it is and how it performs. Materials are built into components and assemblies to convey appearance in three-dimensional views and add information necessary to create attributes, or callouts, in section views. Just as with every other component within a project, materials can be counted. Whether we're looking at the area in square feet of paint applied to a surface or the volume in cubic yards of concrete in a foundation wall, adding exact materials to a model allows for the categorization of the different material types and estimation of the necessary amounts.

When working with materials in a project, it is often difficult to manage all of the information that surrounds them, both graphically and in terms of data. Putting together a protocol that will organize the appearance of different types of materials allows them to be quickly spotted and easily retrieved within a project. This is especially important when dealing with materials used in assemblies such as walls and roofs, as they are typically visible only in section views as described in Figure 7.1. During modeling, the project may be viewed in color, which allows the user to visually determine and delineate between different materials used in a wall assembly. This can prove as effective or, in some ways, more effective, than hatch patterns, which are commonly used today.

The data and information associated with the material can be used for more than informational purposes. Text added to a material may be used to mark the material or create an annotation for section views. This streamlines the detailing phase of a project and minimizes the opportunity for error by automatically placing the appropriate callout text that corresponds to the layer within a wall, floor, roof, or ceiling assembly. Creating a series of stock materials used throughout all projects allows an office to create a template file, or a BIM "warehouse," which carries all of the acceptable materials for use in projects. Attributes may be added to materials that will allow them to be categorized in a logical order. Adding manufacturers' names, specification section numbers, unique product categories, material classifications, and even performance values makes materials searchable within the file. If an installation is required to have in R-value of 19 and a Kraft paper facer, the attributes can be filtered such that only products that meet specific attributes are visible in the query.

Attributes that apply to materials, apply to all materials within a given project. Material subcategories cannot be created to limit the attributes that apply. For instance, insulation materials may have an attribute called "Facer Type." This attribute will show up within wood materials, concrete, steel, and any

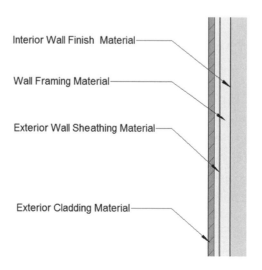

FIGURE 7.1 Materials within an assembly

Interior Wall Finish Material——

Wall Framing Material——

Exterior Wall Sheathing Material——

Exterior Cladding Material——

other materials created, even though the attribute does not apply. To keep the information easy to retrieve, creating a series of templates that apply to different product categories can be beneficial. An insulation material schedule would be limited only to the attributes that apply to it, such as R-value, facer type, density, and perm rating; a tile material schedule would be limited to slip resistance, abrasion resistance, frost resistance, and format (size).

Materials that are used in component objects are generally used only for graphic purposes. Where assemblies are made up of a series of materials placed independent of each other and specified for certain reasons, components are a single unit with multiple materials used in the construction of the unit. Because a component is generally specified as a single unit, not as a customizable sum of its manufactured parts, it is typically not necessary to contain information about the materials above and beyond their names and descriptions. There are some exceptions to this, glass being the most notable. Windows and doors typically provide the option to use more than one type of glass. Above and beyond the thickness of the material, it may be tempered, laminated, annealed, or wired, and could be one of a countless number of colors or tints. If we multiply out the options of the available glass types, in some cases we will find that there are more options than is practical to make family types of. This is where it is practical to add performance attributes of the glass at the material level and allow the glass type to be a user-selected option.

Whether a material is used on its own, within the component, or as a part of an assembly, a certain amount of information needs to be added to it for it to be qualified, quantified, and specified within a project accurately. Developing a naming convention, graphic representation method, and information storage and retrieval protocol will allow exact materials to be used on projects repeatedly.

WHY MATERIALS ARE IMPORTANT

The most notable and arguably the most important reason exact materials should be used within a project is to convey its visual appearance. Building information modeling allows us not only to work in three dimensions but to develop in full color and provide realistic rendered views. Different materials use different hatch patterns for section views and, in many cases, are assigned surface patterns for model views. These act as visual cues to the design team that a specific material has been assigned and is present at a given location. Without the use of different colors or different patterns, it would be difficult to differentiate between two types of wall or two layers within a wall without a lot of hunting and pecking through the model. A simple surface pattern is enough to graphically determine the difference between shingle siding and clapboard in a three-dimensional view, and alternating colors and cut patterns are enough to differentiate between layers of a wall in a section view.

Annotations and callouts are a function of the material that is created. Predefined annotations used within the BIM software are often mapped to an existing attribute of a material whose value is used as the text for a callout. This opens the door for some unique opportunities to create different types of annotations used within section views of projects. By creating a custom annotation that is mapped to a performance attribute, we can toggle all of the attributes at the same time to show different pieces of information. In one view, we may want to show the material names. In a different view we may want to show the R-value of each material, or the specification section number to which the material applies. By adding these types of attributes to the materials, global changes can be made to the drawings such that they apply to different individuals who may need to see them. The general contractor on the project may want to see the exact material name, including the manufacturer, in the annotation, whereas a specifier may only want to see the specification section number or a vendor-neutral material type.

Structural attributes allow materials to be used for more than just informational purposes and to show the appearance of a component or surface. Structural considerations allow third-party software to analyze the model to determine whether or not the design is sufficient to meet building codes and structural requirements. Since building information modeling is parametric, "what-if" scenarios can be staged to find the most effective component or material for a given situation based on trial and error. This is the baseline of digital prototyping, and with it the door is open to minimize over engineering of buildings in lieu of product research. Generally speaking, the three most common structural materials used on projects today are steel, wood, and concrete. The structural values of manufactured components such as steel beams, dimensional and engineered lumber, and cast-in-place concrete walls begin with the materials with which they are created.

Different types of steel have different maximum yield, compressive, and tensile strengths that correspond to stresses the beams experience based on applied loads. By creating specific materials for each type of steel, considering their different physical properties, exact calculations can be made regarding the type of steel that should be used and the source of the finished component. While minimum strengths of various types of steel are governed by ASTM standards as well as other test methods, the actual values will vary based on the foundry from which the steel was sourced. This allows us not only to design based on reference standards but to look at actual manufactured components to determine which steel is the most cost-effective solution while taking into consideration the ultimate goal of providing a perfectly engineered building.

Wood materials are categorized by their species and have specific tensile strengths, sheer strengths, and compressive strengths both parallel and perpendicular to the grain. The attributes associated with wood materials determine the amount of deflection it may experience based on the various loads applied to it. A floor joist or header is likely to experience a greater amount of deflection than the sill plate at the top of a wall. The amount of deflection that is acceptable in various locations is determined by building codes, and sometimes even requirements of the building product manufacturer, and is largely based on live loads, dead loads, and snow loads that are applied to the component in question. Leveraging the attributes within a wood material will allow the project to be modeled such that third-party software can perform a vector analysis of the building to determine how large of a parallel strand lumber (PSL) carrying beam is necessary for a large cathedral ceiling, the size of the laminated veneer lumber (LVL) header, or the maximum clear span for a 2 × 12 Douglas fir floor joist.

Concrete is mainly analyzed in terms of its compressive strength or its ability to handle a crushing force. Because concrete is monolithic, as a material, it is functionally nondirectional. It is only when it is formed into a specific shape, such as a precast twin-T concrete deck, that we begin to consider deflection. Yes, other attributes associated with concrete may be relevant, but in terms of how the model will leverage the information for structural analysis, the primary concern is its compressive strength. As with all materials, in cases where concrete is poured into slabs that are supported by structures beneath, its weight must be considered as well.

Structural performance is only one aspect of a material, and structural analysis is only one of many ways to leverage the information contained within a material. Many materials found throughout a project are located within several specification sections, so quantifying the amount of a specific material can become difficult. The United States Green Building Council (USGBC) developed a rating system that determines how efficiently a building has been designed and constructed, or how "green" the building is. The Leadership in Energy Efficient Design (LEED) rating system looks not at the individual component but at the building as a whole, and allows individual materials or components to contribute to various LEED credits based on how well the material or component performs, where it was sourced from, its recycled content, or one of many different criteria.

Paint is an excellent example of a material that is found throughout a project. It may be located in only one specification section, but it is located on wall and ceiling assemblies and sometimes even floors. The level of volatile organic compounds (VOC) found within the paint can determine whether or not it has the ability to contribute to a specific LEED credit. Further, VOC offsets can often be performed where a small amount of paint with a high VOC content is allowable when it is offset by a large amount of paint with a low VOC content. By adding VOC content as an attribute to materials where this type of offset may be performed, the model can derive percentages based on the sizes of the areas that have been painted.

Cost estimation is an essential aspect of designing a building. This is typically performed early on in the project design to determine an overall budget for the project. Typically, cost estimation is performed using square-foot calculations of the overall size of the building, but building information modeling provides the ability for models to be far more accurate in their estimation by looking at individual components. Creating actual cost data for an entire project is a double-edged sword, though, in that should any single component be without an associated cost, the accuracy of the estimate becomes questionable. This requires architects to evaluate each component and assign either a budgetary value or an assumed value based on weighted cost averages. When cost information is added into a model, it must assume not only the actual price, or manufacturer's suggested retail price, but also the labor cost for the installation of the component. On the one hand, architects can add this information in and determine a fairly rigid cost figure, but, on the other hand, prices of commodity products fluctuate rapidly, so leaving cost information in the hands of the contractors and subcontractors installing the components may be more effective. Information contained within a model allows the architect to provide accurate quantity takeoffs or unit counts of each component found in a project. This in and of itself is a very powerful tool, which can simplify the bidding process and decrease the amount of time necessary for a contractor to assemble and submit a bid.

An important differentiation between cost estimation and quantity takeoffs is how the information is displayed and organized. Cost estimation looks at areas and lengths, whereas quantity takeoffs look at sales units. A roof that has been created within a project has the ability to tell us how many square feet of roof material, insulation, fasteners, and adhesive are necessary on the project. What it does not tell us is the application rates of each component, and the units in which the component is sold. By adding attributes that allow an area to be transformed into a unit, we can use the model to perform unit calculations. Roof membrane adhesive may be applied at 60 ft^2 per gallon and sold in 5-gallon pails. By adding an attribute for theoretical application rate and unit size, we can calculate that a 3000-ft² roof would require 10 pails of adhesive.

Surface area / Theoretical application rate / Unit size = Number of units
3000 ft² / 60 ft² per gallon / 5 gallons / Pail = 10 pails

By adding a few simple attributes that apply to the coverage area and unit sizes of all materials used in assemblies, the architect has the ability to hand over a list of all components that may be necessary for project. Alternatively, if the architect were to give the contractor access to the model, the contractor could leverage the information himself and cross-check information for accuracy. The reality is that coverage rates are only theoretical, and those who install the products know best where waste factors will occur and where special calculations are necessary. For instance, if an architect determined the area of a roof that was mechanically attached with fasteners spaced one every 2 ft², the contractor would actually need to look at not only the area of the roof, but the perimeter of the roof as well to determine additional enhanced fastening patterns that may be necessary along the edge of the roof.

An important concept behind adding attributes into materials is to offer the ability for an architect or specifier to note not just what a component is, but why it was selected. One type of insulation might be used because of its high compressive strength, where another type might be used because of its thermal resistance or R-value. Vapor barriers have permeance ratings, tile has scratch resistance, gypsum wallboard has fire ratings and mold resistance, and roof shingles have wind resistance. No matter what type of building product we look at, there are performance and identification attributes associated with them that determine what they are and why they are used. Adding specific information into the model allows architects and specifiers the ability to search for components and assemblies that meet the criteria of the design. This is a far more effective method than having to hunt and peck through their libraries or websites on the Internet to find what they are looking for.

DATA—WHAT GOES INTO MATERIALS?

In terms of data located inside of materials, it is important not to overload them with unnecessary information. Much of the information surrounding any given building product is governed by ATSM, ANSI, ISO, UL, and other organizations involved with the standards and testing of products. While it is possible to put the results of each one of these values into the model, the question is its necessity. If the results of every test were added to every component used in a project, the amount of information would be so great that it would be difficult to search through and find what we're looking for. By adding only the salient points of a product that are used by architects and specifiers to determine which product should be used, a small data set may be generated that allows quick product comparison. First and foremost, an individual who is using the data from a model must be able to identify either the material or the product at hand. Beyond identification, basic performance information will allow the design team to analyze various materials and products and to make educated merit-based decisions on which will meet the design criteria of the project.

First and foremost, the material should have a name that allows it to be easily found within the project and a brief description of what it is. Developing a naming convention that works for your office is effective, as there are no accepted industry standards that govern this. The Uniform Drawing Standard and National CAD Standard do discuss naming conventions, but the naming of BIM materials has additional pitfalls that should be considered. Because information may be imported and exported to and from the model, the name of the material should not contain any characters that may cause confusion to a database. If any spreadsheet or database software is to be used in manipulating information, avoid the use of special characters and punctuation, especially the use of commas and inch symbols. These characters are used within spreadsheet and database software to delimit columns and to bracket text. When they are added into the actual values, they can trip up the data, potentially causing errors, especially when data are imported programmatically.

When thinking about how to name materials, consider how they are organized within the architecture and construction industries, and common methods of keynoting or calling out materials. Materials that are vendor neutral, or generic, should be named so that they contain the classification of the material, the type of the material, material descriptors such as finishes or colors, and an easy way to organize them. BIM software will generally organize materials alphanumerically, so as we see in Figure 7.2, an added prefix will keep materials of similar type grouped together. The most effective prefix I have found is the use of MasterFormat®, with a close second being OmniClass Table 23 – Products. I find MasterFormat® to provide a better prefix as it is an accepted standard within the architecture community and is limited to six digits or, in specific cases, eight digits. While OmniClass Table 23 is specifically designed to organize products, it is not widely used in architecture today, and uses far more numbers to describe various products. Since we are working with these materials on screen with specific pieces of software, text visibility can become an issue when names become too large.

FIGURE 7.2 Naming conventions of materials

[MasterFormat® Number]_[Category]-[Type]-[Descriptor 1]-[Descriptor 2]

Tip

Avoid using special characters in naming materials, as they can cause errors when importing and exporting information. Most importantly, avoid the use of commas and quotes as an inch symbol.

In many cases, the name of a material is used as a callout. In cases where this is the preference, the naming convention should consider readability not only on screen but on the drawing sheet as well. My preference is not to use the name of the material for its callout, but rather a specific description attribute for the material. This allows it to be more detailed in the drawings without making the material difficult to use within the model. Descriptions should be detailed enough to convey the information necessary for a contractor to determine which specific material or building products are to be used in a given location. Information contained in a description should be brief and informational, but avoid unnecessary descriptors like "High Performance" or "Extra Strength." Terms like these are used in marketing but have no technical merit with respect to the actual performance or strength of a material.

In the case of a vendor-specific building material, the model name is beneficial in that it allows the scheduling of the exact materials to be used on the project. In many cases a manufacturer may have a specific part number that can be added here, or a vendor's trade name or brand name. When specific model names or numbers are added into the project, they can be exported in various schedules such that a contractor or manufacturer could potentially import them into his sales system to generate a price quote. In addition, I have found that using the model name alongside other attributes added into the material can allow us to concatenate a product description. If we combine the manufacturer's name with the brand name and add other attributes as descriptors, we can programmatically create descriptions for different materials quickly and with little effort.

Materials typically will also let us add information about its source and links to additional information. If there is specification or test information that applies to a specific product or material, but is not relevant within the model, creating a series of links to various websites allows information to be managed and updated remotely. Test results for materials that change frequently are good candidates for hyperlinks. Rather than modifying the materials constantly based on the updated test results, if we place a static hyperlink within the material that points back to a website, the information can be maintained remotely. This will allow the user to always have the most current information regarding the material or product without having to download new versions of the BIM materials within a given project.

Above and beyond the basic information associated with a material, such as its manufacturer, model, description, and informational links, adding attributes that allow the materials to be organized into logical categories makes them easier to find within the project. With MasterFormat®, materials may be organized into logical categories that architects and specifiers understand. Materials used for rough carpentry would then all be categorized together in 06 11 00, and cast-in-place concrete materials would all be categorized together in 03 30 00. This method works well because building materials are used in context. While there may be a material in the world called "steel," it is not useful within a building information model or project infill that steel be put into context. Contextual materials allow the layers of an assembly to be very specific without the necessity of creating graphics that may not be required for a given project. For instance creating a material called "2 × 4 wood stud – 16-in spacing" allows a layer of a wall assembly to be created that takes into consideration not only the material, but the actual product and its installation criteria. This can eliminate the need to add each individual wall stud where it is impractical to do so, but still allows for a somewhat accurate quantity takeoff. It won't consider additional blocking in corners or additional studs required at openings, so it should not be used for exact piece counts, but it does take considerably less time and effort to develop than framing each wall in the model piece by piece.

The performance information associated with a material or building product should allow the user to locate, sort, and filter information based on industry-accepted criteria. Basic performance attributes for specific materials or products is typically what is used to make product decisions, so adding attributes that apply to each of these materials will allow them to be searchable based on practical information. The R-value of insulation, the compressive strength of concrete, and the visible light transmittance of glass are just a few examples of where attributes can be useful within the model and to create supporting documents for the project. Any attribute that is entered into the model may be extracted from the model, provided it is formatted appropriately. Construction specifications are widely based on attribute and value pairs, as the selection of components for use on a project is largely based on their performance.

Performance and structural data associated with materials will vary from category to category, and, generally, when attributes are added to one material, they are added to all materials. This can create a dilemma when attempting to access information. An effective solution is to create a series of template schedules that may be used to extract information from different material categories. For example, metal framing materials will all typically have the same attributes, so by creating a schedule unique to metal framing materials, the information can be viewed regardless of whether the components are found on the floor, ceiling, roof, wall, or as a part of a column.

It is not uncommon to see lifecycle and usage information added to materials and components. Most products have a specific warranty duration, are expected to last a certain amount of time, and need to be maintained periodically. Adding attributes of this nature into the materials will allow the information to be useful to facility managers and owners should the model be updated through construction and the owner is supplied with an as-built model upon completion. Knowing not only how much material is used on a project but how long it is intended to last will provide an owner with lifecycle assessment information regarding the ongoing maintenance of a facility. If an owner knows that the material cost of paint is half as much on a product that is designed to last half as long, he may see that there is no benefit in the less expensive material, as the labor costs to apply the material twice will eliminate the benefit. Conversely, if the owner spends twice as much on a product that lasts twice as long, the benefit becomes evident.

Product lifespan information may also be used by the design team in making decisions on appropriate products to use in an assembly. If a roof material is designed to last 50 years but has a substantial increase in cost, it would not be practical to use if the insulation beneath it was assumed to fail after 20 years. Regardless of how well and how long the roof performed, the owner would likely require replacement as the insulation beneath it failed. This would negate any cost benefit associated with a roof designed to last an extended amount of time. Being able to do cost-benefit analyses of specific products during the design of the project allows the architect to design a building with the expectation of product replacement at appropriate times. This type of analysis is sure to save a property owner a considerable amount of money over time.

APPEARANCE AND RENDERING

The outward appearance of the material is really the only graphics associated with it. A material has no geometry until it is applied to a surface or a solid, so this aspect of materials is fairly straightforward. Materials are handled in two ways: model view and renderings. Model view appearance determines what the material looks like as a design professional is working on the model. This is the day-to-day visual that architects and engineers see, so the model view should not use colors that are irritating to the eye or hatch patterns that add additional line work that may confuse the user. Renderings are the photorealistic outputs of the building information model that allow for far more accurate representation of the materials used in the project. Without accurately depicted materials, renderings are based on little more than the color of the material. BIM software has the ability to add transparency and translucency to materials, to add specific sheens and gloss levels and textures to surfaces, to control how the material reflects or refracts light, to create the appearance of indentations or perforations, and even to create a material that can illuminate itself. This type of material development differentiates a high-performance material from one that is just serviceable. In many cases it may not be absolutely necessary to get into this level of detail, as the BIM software generally comes preloaded with a series of standard materials that may be further customized to create an exact appearance.

In addition to manually configuring the rendered appearance of materials, the use of image files can be equally, and in some cases more, effective. Patterns for materials such as brick, pavers, or metals with unique finishes often are represented with high-resolution images. It is critical, however, to make sure that whenever a pattern is present the images represent the entire repeated pattern. In all cases, material images must have no white space at the perimeter, and have no shading or shadowing present on the image. Image files used for rendering are tiled along an entire surface, so a tiling effect becomes very noticeable when any shading or imperfections in the repeat pattern are present.

Bitmaps and bump maps are image files used to create recessed or raised sections of the surface. Figure 7.3 is a sample bump map used to add depth and texture to the appearance of grass. Bump maps allow for not only texture but a repeating pattern such as is seen with tile. Tiles are spaced a specific distance apart based on the format or size of the tile. Take, for instance, a 4 × 4 tile. The grout lines between each tile are slightly recessed. To take this into consideration, creating a map using positive and negative space will allow the software to make determinations of where areas must be raised or recessed. These are created using black and white images, where the black spaces are those to be raised or recessed, and the white areas are those at the standard surface level. These can be created using typical CAD drawings exported as an image file or simple drawing software. Exceptionally ornate patterns are possible when using these types of files, but, just as with rendering images, it is crucial that the entire repeating pattern be represented through the map, as it tiles itself throughout the entire material surface.

Hatch patterns are used to create simple line work that defines how a material appears in a model view. Specific hatch patterns may be used to represent clapboard siding, shingles, concrete, and any other material that may have a unique surface pattern of note. Hatch patterns are also used in section views

FIGURE 7.3 Sample bump map

to define the layers within an assembly. Some commonly used hatch patterns are shown in Figure 7.4. The UDS and NCS have definitions for types of hatch patterns to use for specific materials, but do not take into consideration every material possible. Hatch patterns are not designed to be highly detailed and don't take into consideration items such as the detail line work for a wood or metal stud, or the cavity locations of a concrete masonry unit. This level of detail is reserved for detail components rather than hatch patterns. When working in three dimensions, there are two types of hatch patterns—drafting patterns and model patterns. Drafting patterns are typically used in two-dimensional views, most commonly section views, and orient themselves to the view. Model patterns are more dynamic, in that they are a function of the surface in which they are placed not the angle at which they are seen. This allows the pattern to be placed onto a surface, such as a wall, and the three-dimensional view shifted without disturbing the appearance of the pattern. Highly detailed hatch patterns may be created to represent ornate and curved surfaces, but

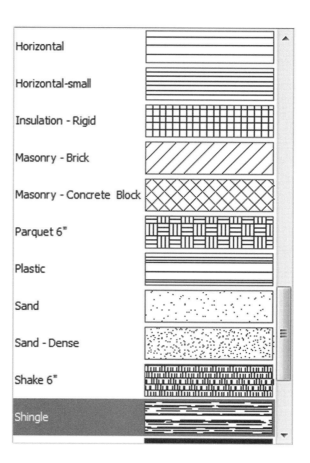

FIGURE 7.4 Detail and model hatch patterns

I advise against their becoming too detailed, as the line work becomes cluttered and curbs become a series of segmented lines.

The last and probably most noticeable aspect of a material is its color in model view. This is the appearance that a modeler will see on a day-to-day basis, and as such should be easy on the eye and in some cases follow a pattern with respect to the category of material. Surface materials such as siding and paint will always have exact colors, finishes, and appearances, so the color selected for model view should be relatively close to that of the actual product. For components that are embedded in an assembly, there is slightly more flexibility in the color used to represent the material. This makes it possible to create a set of standards used to represent various materials within an assembly. If each category of materials were assigned a base color from which to derive appearance, we could create shades of the color used to represent an attribute or type of that material. For instance, if all concrete materials were represented in shades of gray, we could use lighter gray for materials with a low compressive strength, and darker gray for materials with a higher compressive strength. This could provide a visual cue, and possibly even be used for model analysis. Suppose vapor and air barrier materials were all shades of green, with their permeance ratings used to determine how light or dark the shade was. The same could be done with insulation materials and their R-value, or adhesives and their VOC content. Whether shading is done with attributes in mind, material types in mind, or some other method, colorizing various materials based on attributes or performance can provide visual cues that are beneficial to the design team.

In a general sense, materials are the baseline and starting point for all building information modeling. Without appropriately created and managed materials, the information associated with projects is limited, in that a great deal of the project resides between the interior and exterior faces of assemblies. The aspects of those assemblies are often the most important in terms of specification and overall design of the project, so we mustn't sell their value short in the BIM arena. Taking the time to develop a high-quality set of materials early on will allow us to create thousands of projects for years to come with little or no effort required to maintain them.

CHAPTER 8

CAD Imports and Nonparametric Objects

At certain points within the development of a building information model, it may be necessary or effective to import files from other applications. If we are developing the topography for our project, it is far more effective to import a computer-aided design (CAD) file. Highly ornate components that are only being used once may also find their way into a project as an import, drawing sheets may contain image files, and, in some cases, raster images may be used to trace a layout from an idea. These file types should be used sparingly, as they are often large and can bloat a model quickly. Wherever possible, the addition of CAD and image imports should be done later in the design to keep file size low early. For image files used as tracers, they should be deleted immediately after use.

IMPORTING CAD FILES—PROS AND CONS

There are some positive and negative aspects associated with importing CAD files into a building information model. In terms of developing content, where three-dimensional CAD files have already been developed, it seems like a quick shortcut to create the geometry associated with the component. The primary issue with CAD files is that they are nonparametric. An imported CAD file is a block and cannot be modified in any way. The dimensions are fixed, so the graphics cannot stretch. In many cases this does not matter, as the component may be nothing more than a unique "one-off" component, but the nonparametric nature also applies to the materials. Even when dimensions cannot be changed in some ornate components, it is common for material options to be available. A geometrically complex toilet, bathtub, or light fixture might not change dimensionally, but it is usually available in several colors. For a CAD import to be useful to represent all of the product options, one would need to be created for each color.

On the upside, two-dimensional CAD files can be a tremendous benefit when creating detail objects, converting CAD-based plans into BIM-based models, or creating topography. When creating a detail object that pertains to a specific condition, such as a manufacturer's requirements for a roof edge termination, one can simplify the creation process by importing two-dimensional CAD details, as shown in Figure 8.1. By either exploding the existing file or tracing the line work, a BIM detail object can be created with very little effort. When importing CAD files, scale is critical. Everything drawn within a building information modeling platform is done at full scale. This is not always the case with computer-aided design. To ensure that the detail will become useful not only as a component on the drawing sheet but in overlay onto model graphics, keep a close eye on the import scale.

Many manufacturers have already created a robust series of construction details that apply to the conditions that their products may encounter during installation. These types of details are generally those that end up on drawing sheets, and often have little or no relevance to the three-dimensional model views. These types of "shop drawings" are usually placed for the benefit of the contractor more than the design team, as they are typically more specific than one would find in the model views. Manufacturers existing shop drawings may be imported directly into drawing sheets as CAD files in order to convey specific information about construction. This is not a preferred method for the development of details, but it is a shortcut that is commonly used. Several issues can arise from developing details in this fashion, from line weights to colors to scale. One major issue to consider when importing shop drawings is the quality of the CAD file. In many cases, title blocks have been drawn into CAD files in their model view. When attempting to import the file for use on a detail sheet, the title blocks should be removed prior to importing. The most effective way to create detail components is to redraw them from the CAD files and not to use the CAD files themselves.

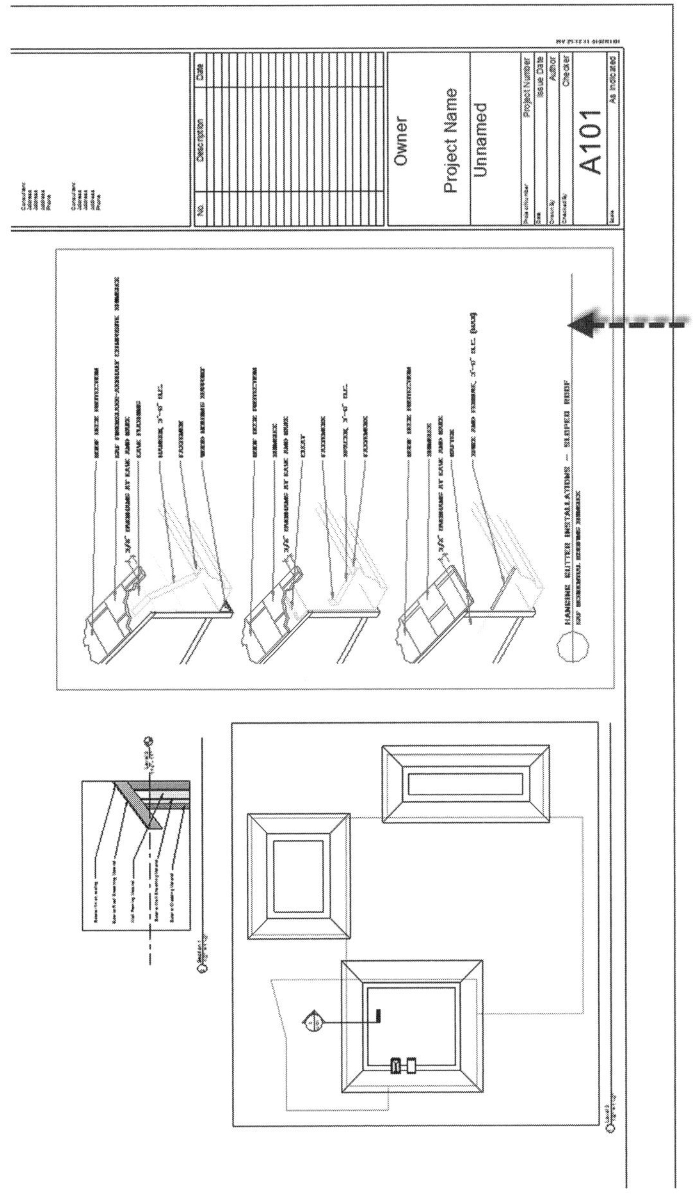

FIGURE 8.1 Importing CAD as a detail object

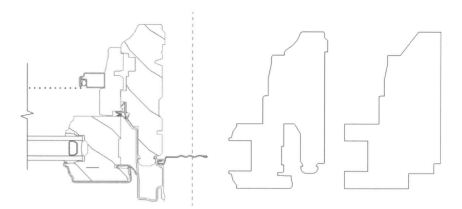

FIGURE 8.2 Simplified CAD as model sketch

Using CAD files to develop components can be a great benefit, especially when dealing with solids that need to be sketched. Creating profile and extrusion sketches from existing CAD files as we have done in Figure 8.2, can keep the process simple, especially when there is ornate geometry or extensive line work. When creating sketches from two-dimensional CAD files, it is important to remember to simplify the geometry. A CAD file may contain fillets and rounds that are too small to regenerate within a BIM file, so simplifying this type of geometry is essential.

In many cases it's not practical to create our own topography within a building information model. It is typically more of a reference component, supplied by a different contractor. Where it is necessary to create three-dimensional topography, an imported CAD file can act as a guideline to locate points, and in some cases may have the ability to generate elevations as well as locations within the project. By adding a site overlay to a building information model using a two-dimensional CAD file, we have the ability to locate site base components accurately, and use the contours of the land, benchmarks, and locations to place model components in their appropriate locations. If we're dealing with a project that contains site work created by multiple surveyors, we will probably end up with multiple CAD files. By bringing these files into the project, aligning them based on benchmarks, and adding the locations of important site base components, site components such as sewer lines, septic, gas mains, and buried electrical lines can be transitioned into the three-dimensional model, and the extraneous information can be deleted with the two-dimensional CAD file.

Do not expect to gain a considerable amount of benefit from the import of two-dimensional or three-dimensional CAD files. While they are quick solution to spending a considerable amount of time developing ornate objects, they have very limited functionality. Their use should be restricted to referential information for the creation of content, or as a symbol that represents where a component will be placed.

NONPARAMETRIC AND SEMI-PARAMETRIC OBJECTS

Static, nonparametric objects or "one-offs" are simple components that cannot be modified in any way. They take very little time to generate, and have very little functionality other than as the single object that they represent. Decorative components, such as furniture, light fixtures, and other elements that have a fixed shape are generally nonparametric. If a table is available in only one size and one color, there is no purpose or benefit to adding dimension or material parameters to its graphics. When geometry is created in this fashion, it can be turned out very quickly, but it is really little more than representative models or three-dimensional symbolic placeholders where real components may end up in the future.

Semi-parametric objects are those that may not have dimensional parameters but carry informational attributes with them alongside options for materials. The solid graphics remain fixed, but finishes may be modifiable. Light fixtures are typically modeled as semi-parametric, as they graphically do not change but may be modeled with different finishes for the fixture, the trim, or the diffuser.

Both semi-parametric and nonparametric objects are limited in what they are capable of doing and offering to a building information model. These types of objects are sort of a bridge between CAD and BIM, or BIM-lite. They are typically small and easy to create, but difficult to manage. To make a window or door as a nonparametric object, we would have to create thousands of single objects to represent all of the possible combinations of size and shape. Using these types of objects defeats the purpose of parameters within building information modeling and, in many ways, may as well put us back into a computer-aided design platform. The upside to semi-parametric objects is that they eliminate the ability for the design team to easily modify a manufacturer-specific component. If a manufacturer is concerned that an architect might want to change the size of the light fixture to suit his design, then he may choose to model these components without dimensional parameters. Modeling components that do not contain graphic parameters, but are specific to a manufacturer, should still contain dimensional attributes that note the size and shape of the unit. Even if they are not attached to any solid geometry, the dimensions will allow the design team to view the size and shape of the component within the data set. This hinders the design team from modifying the component, while providing the information about its dimensional requirements.

CONCLUSIONS

CAD imports and nonparametric objects have their place in design but are more of a point of entry for building information modeling. They assist us in making the move from CAD to BIM, provide us with resource documents to further our development, and act as something of a crutch during our transition. I have heard many architects say that they use BIM for schematic design and design development, but still detail the project by exporting it out to a CAD platform and creating the two-dimensional drawing sheets there. It is important to note that it is possible to go the other direction, where instead of exporting the BIM file, you import the CAD files that are necessary for detailing. CAD imports, especially three-dimensional ones, can be large and add a considerable amount of time to the regeneration of the model. By waiting to load CAD files until it is absolutely necessary to work with them or deleting them as soon as their usefulness has passed, we will keep our model optimized while still retaining the benefits of the elements added in.

Image files that are added into a project or created from renderings generated by the project can also weigh the file down considerably. While these may not cause issues with the regeneration of the model, they can make the model load slower. Export and eliminate image files from the project whenever they are no longer needed. In cases where image files are used to trace the geometry for a component, they should be eliminated immediately so their removal is not forgotten later on.

CHAPTER 9

BIM Data: The "I" in BIM

A primary difference between computer-aided design (CAD) and building information modeling (BIM) is the ability to add information, but what is the point of putting information into a project model? When information is added into a project, it may be used for model analysis, product selection, cost estimation, specification, facility management, and even has possibilities for fabrication and construction. A building information model is a relational database with a series of tables that contain the information that may be added, manipulated, viewed, extracted, and, if necessary, deleted after it is no longer useful. When properly formatted, nearly every piece of information placed into the model may be extracted for analysis using specialized software or imported into process management software, so the more information we add to the model, the more uses we will find for that information.

Development of the model usually begins with a series of assemblies that enclose the building, and a series of openings that allow access and visibility. These primary components are arguably the most important and probably the most used on any given project. While we may not have any information regarding specifics on these components at this time, ultimately, the actual product selected will be based on a series of criteria or attributes that determine what it is, what it looks like, how it performs, and why it is the best product for the specific situation. When attributes are added into a model, they do not necessarily need to have exact values immediately. If all exterior doors are chosen based on their thermal performance and forced entry ratings, then adding these attributes to the doors before they are placed in the model allows us to add values later on with little or no additional effort once they are known. Adding a series of component-specific attributes to each object placed in the model will give the architect the ability to "shake" the model, to extract information pertinent to every component in a neat and organized fashion.

If we think of adding attributes to BIM objects as documenting the project in a rolling fashion, it actually streamlines how product specification and project documentation occurs. Rather than specifying products all at once during the construction documents phase, products may be selected or specified as the information regarding them becomes known. When the attributed information for all components is completed, it can be handed to a specifier or spec writer to generate the construction documents based on the performance criteria within the model. There is already software on the market designed to automate this process further by creating keynotes and attaching or tagging specification sections based on the components in the model. Taking it a step further, where the actual values of the attributes within a model are passed into a specification is the real trick in creating specifications based on building data. Unfortunately, there is no one-to-one comparison between information in a model and the information in a specification. Much of the information contained within the model is not relevant to the specification, and an equal or greater amount of information in the specification has no bearing on the model. Rather than attempting to capture all of the specification information in a single component, or all of the data in the specification, an intermediary is a possible solution. Creating a centralized database that is housed remotely can allow information to be passed to both the specification and the model while using a Web-based interface that accesses that information. This interface will functionally create a bidirectional association between the information contained in the model and the information contained in the specification. This ensures consistency among all documentation, and lack of consistency is the root of all problems related to information exchange.

Whether we are working with vendor-neutral components or manufacturer-specific products within a project, adding performance information to the components allows them to be qualified, analyzed, and selected based on their merits. Since a BIM project is a database, it can be queried as such. When attributes are added, they can become functions of a query to select products based on whatever criterion is most relevant. If we work with vendor-neutral components early in design development, the attributes contained within those components may be used as a baseline or benchmark from which manufactured products are to be selected. Once the design has been completed and bidding begins, the model may be used as a "control" to select the most appropriate products and affirm that they meet the design criteria of the project, as we've done in Figure 9.1.

Developing a taxonomy for attributes is critical to ensure that this type of product analysis can be performed. A computer cannot differentiate between *U factor*, *U-factor,* and *U-value*, even though the attribute is actually the same. Using a consistent set of attributes will allow attributes from the model to line up in a neat and organized schedule so that multiple products may be looked at and their attributes assessed line by line, rather than by parsing through pages and pages of data sheets.

Tip

An attribute added to the model may be used as a "control" to select the most appropriate products and affirm that they meet the design criteria of the project.

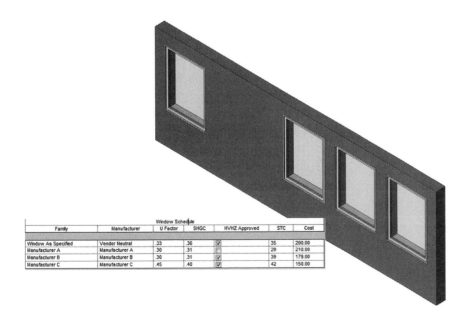

Window Schedule						
Family	Manufacturer	U Factor	SHGC	HVHZ Approved	STC	Cost
Window As Specified	Vendor Neutral	.33	.36	☑	35	200.00
Manufacturer A	Manufacturer A	.30	.31	☐	29	210.00
Manufacturer B	Manufacturer B	.30	.31	☑	39	179.00
Manufacturer C	Manufacturer C	.45	.40	☑	42	150.00

FIGURE 9.1 Using a BIM project for product comparison

Not only can this database allow us to organize the information, but we may sort and filter it as necessary to attain the information we are looking for. Sorting and filtering is done by telling the database what order to put information in or what information to show based on specific criteria. The decision criterion is based on the attributes that are built into the components and the model, so, again, the taxonomy and naming structure are critical. There is a series of built-in categories that define typical product classes. A component may be classified as a window, a door, a wall, a roof, or one of a few other classifications. Unfortunately, it is not practical to create a specific classification for every product category known to mankind. Rather than using intuitive categories, a series of industry standards and formats assists us in organizing our products into logical categories so we can quickly retrieve the information necessary. CSI MasterFormat® and CSI UniFormat™ are two of the most commonly used formats, and allow us to perform classification based on work result and elemental category, respectively. Since MasterFormat® is the architectural standard for project manuals, it seems only appropriate to use this as a high-level information attribute. More information about MasterFormat® is available in the chapter about standards and formats, or from masterformat.org and csinet.org.

When each component contains an attribute that notes its MasterFormat® category, the model data may be sorted such that every component aligns with its respective specification. When the model has been completed, the data can be exported and the specifier can develop the specifications with far less effort, as the salient information about the product's section of the specification is right at his fingertips in a tabular format. This is not without pitfalls, though. Many specification sections are listed in a project manual but are not modeled graphically. In cases such as this, it is possible to embed a graphically simple or nongraphic component in the model such that the information may be extracted alongside the graphic components. This is what I refer to as components that are placed in the *SpecAttic*.

The SpecAttic is made up of a series of BIM objects that are informational only. Figure 9.2 shows how we can create a project level that is far above or far below where any work is being performed, and place small, lightweight objects in an out-of-the-way location, while keeping their information available for analysis from within schedules and data exports. Product categories, such as caulks and sealants, fire-stopping, metal or concrete restoration work, finishes, or any other work that the architect deems unnecessary to model, may be placed in the SpecAttic with little effort but a considerable amount of benefit. Figure 9.3 shows us what the graphics for a typical spec attic volume might look like.

By adding attributes into the model, we create new potential opportunities to enhance or improve upon existing formats, as well as create new ways to

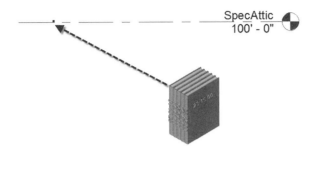

FIGURE 9.2   Placing the SpecAttic in a project

FIGURE 9.3   A typical SpecAttic volume

view architectural information. Creating a tabular specification based on information within the BIM project will allow the relevant points about specific work to be conveyed and will simplify the documentation process. The idea behind a tabular specification is something like a cross between a specification from the project manual and a submittal sheet from the manufacturer. It organizes information the same way a data sheet would, but the amount of information is limited to that which belongs in a specification. Often, manufacturers will place a considerable number of attributes on data sheets as supplementary information that architects, specifiers, and engineers might choose to leverage when making product decisions. This type of information may or may not be relevant within a BIM component and often is omitted from a specification for the sake of brevity.

As manufacturers become more and more involved with the architectural community and building information modeling as a whole, they may begin to see opportunities to organize their own internal information by leveraging building information modeling. By aligning their product information with a building information model that is used by an architect, they have the ability to streamline the procurement process by creating connections between information within the model and information within their internal sales structure. This is not to say that it is practical to add in internal sales tracking information such as SKU numbers for every component, but if we create a one-to-many relationship where one BIM object will apply to several SKU numbers in a sales database, there is a potential for automating sales and shipping based on information that is passed from the architect to the contractor and then to the manufacturer. Technical services, marketing, and research and development departments of building materials manufacturers can benefit from building information modeling because they can centrally locate all of the information that applies to construction details, architectural specifications, data sheets, installation instructions, and other related documents in a single database.

It is clear that the information contained within a model is useful not only to the architect but to all parties associated with the project. Adding information into models is advancing architecture, engineering, and construction disciplines by providing the ability to perform analysis during the design, create digital prototypes before construction, streamline documentation, simplify procurement, and offer a digital owner's manual for facilities management. There is a considerable amount of information that applies to projects and products. The most important things to remember about the addition and management of building information modeling data is to keep attributes consistent, accessible, and relevant. Building information models are technical documents and should be created and treated as such.

TYPES OF INFORMATION TO ADD

The usefulness of the building information model is dependent on the information that is added to it. There are several types of information that apply to products and projects; some are graphic, some are informational. Before adding information, it is important to determine the needs of the end user and the ultimate goal of the project. There's no point in spending a considerable amount of time up front creating data sets that are of no value to anybody.

Dimensional Information

Dimensional information makes up the sizes, shapes, and areas associated with the graphic elements created within a project. Highly detailed components may have dozens of dimensions associated with the construction of the object. When initially creating the object, consider carefully how to display the information about each of these dimensions, how to organize them within the software user interface, and whether or not they need to be parametric. When we're creating a solid that has a ⅛-inch-radius fillet around each corner, it is usually not necessary to make this type of dimension parametric; usually it can be left out of the data set altogether. When deciding on which dimensions to make parameteric and a part of the data set, think about which dimensions are likely to be changed, either by the user or by the manufacturer, during a potential product update later on.

Many objects can be made highly detailed if desired. The frame of a window, for instance, has several faces and angles, making for a highly detailed extrusion. Building information modeling is used to implement a product not manufacturer it, so these dimensions are irrelevant and in many ways their presence is a burden to the model. The relevant aspects of a window frame are its size in relation to the opening, its size in relation to the thickness of the wall, and, in a very general sense, how it interfaces with other components within the window object. Keeping the graphics and dimensions simplified will maximize the functionality and usability of the component.

When you think about which dimensions are necessary for a given component, think about how it is installed in a project, the types of clearances and tolerances that are necessary, and the types of information that may be extracted from the object itself. If we go back to the window as an example, the window is installed into a wall with an opening that is slightly larger than the window itself. This is what's known as the rough opening. Rough opening dimensions help the contractor determine how to prepare the opening to receive the window. Rough opening height and rough opening width are relevant dimensions. When a window is offered or sold by a specific manufacturer or fabricator, it is often available in certain specific sizes. These are the unit dimensions and they are relevant and necessary in determining how large the aforementioned rough opening is supposed to be, and the identification of the window. Many windows have optional jamb depths that correspond to common wall depths. The depths should be noted within a data set, in order to determine whether extension jambs are necessary. The last dimension of note with respect to a window applies to the analysis of the window itself. The clear opening dimensions of a window are used to determine suitability under building codes. Windows that are used in certain locations are required to be of a certain size to allow emergency egress. The clear opening area and clear opening width are dimensions that may be calculated based on the size of the frame or simply added in as informational attributes. I list them under dimensional attributes as it is often easier to calculate them than it is to add them into a catalog. Figure 9.4 is a common set of dimensions that apply to a window. Coupled with other secondary dimensions, we can calculate areas and sizing requirements that may be relevant to building codes or construction.

The window illustration is just one example of necessary dimensions within an object above and beyond their nominal unit sizes. Doors and cabinets require a certain amount of clearance in front of them to allow them to open, building codes may determine the minimum distance necessary between plumbing fixtures, and incandescent light fixtures may require a certain amount of space to be allotted around them for fire protection. Consider not only the design but the clearances, tolerances, installation, and analysis associated with any given object when making determinations of what dimensions are necessary.

Identification Information

Identification information is also necessary to determine what a product is. At bare minimum it should consists of a trade name or model number, a description that can be used for annotations, and a few attributes that will categorize the component so its information can be easily retrieved later. To enhance the functionality of a component, a series of hyperlinks may be added to reference related information in order to assist in the design, specification,

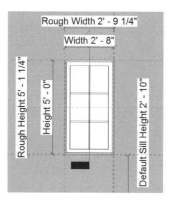

FIGURE 9.4 Relevant window dimensions

installation, purchase, or maintenance of the specific component. Adding links of this nature to the model is an excellent way to provide a considerable amount of information without overburdening the project file and to ensure that data are always up-to-date.

Information that is not necessary for analysis purposes is best linked back to a manufacturer's website or other hosted location. This allows the information to be updated in a single location and disseminated to each individual who is in possession of the BIM object. Revision control is essential when developing BIM objects, and, rather than revising every component as well as the information on related documents, referencing the document itself through a link is a far more effective approach. I always recommend against placing specific warranty information into an object. Warranty terms may change, and it will be unclear whether or not somebody has downloaded the most current version. So, rather than putting a specific warranty term into the model, linking directly to the warranty document will ensure that the information is always up-to-date, regardless of when the model was downloaded.

Adding an attribute into objects for comments can be helpful, but should be done sparingly. If every component carries a comment related to it, then it should likely have its own specific attribute. Comments should be reserved for very specific information about a component. If the same comment is used for more than three or four objects within the same category, then it is likely time to add an additional attribute to address the comments. An example of an acceptable comment might be "Model 24406 not available in green." An example of a comment to avoid might be "Available at better supply houses everywhere." Not only is the second comment marketing fluff, but it likely applies to every other component sold by the manufacturer. This type of information is unnecessary. Rather than placing a comment of this nature in the model, creating a link to the manufacturer's sales or distribution page would be more appropriate.

Performance Information

Performance information is far and away the most important nongraphic data to add into a model. It qualifies a product based on industry standards and assists the design and specification team in determining why a product was selected. Most products have a considerable amount of performance information that could be added. Determining which aspects of a component are relevant within a building information model and which should be linked as related information is essential to keeping the information within the model organized and avoiding information overload.

Test standards, such as ASTM, ANSI, ISO, Underwriters Laboratories, and FM Global, are commonly used to test aspects of a product under certain circumstances. ASTM has created test standards that apply to nearly every situation imaginable in the world of building materials, and most products must undergo several of these tests to be considered suitable for use in many building codes. Often it is unnecessary to add the results of every one of these tests. The only ones that are necessary are those that are ultimately used to determine suitability for the project or why the product was selected. Code bodies such as the International Code Council (ICC) and the Florida Building Code (FBC) have adopted specific standards for products, so in some cases simply to note that they comply with the ICC or the FBC is enough information for the object.

When multiple performance attributes are to be added to a model, they should be organized in such a manner that they may be easily viewed or retrieved, and be uniformly located within the user interface, as shown in Figure 9.5. This will allow the information to be used from within the model as well as outside the model. For instance, if an architect is researching the forced entry rating of a door, he would be able to click on the door itself and quickly and easily find the value he is looking for, rather than having to search through multiple locations. Certain pieces of performance information are not only informational, but analytical. Many BIM software platforms have applications built in that will analyze energy and structural performance of the project, and third-party plug-ins are available that perform the same types of tasks. The information associated with these plug-ins and applications needs to come from somewhere, so to analyze thermal performance of the building, we must know the R-values of the walls and roofs, the U-factors of the windows, and the amount of space that is taken up by windows or skylights within the walls and roofs.

Building codes are often determined based on the performance of a project as a whole, and the suitability of certain products is dependent on their performance. Certain structural members must be used to span specific distances and carry a maximum amount of weight; doors may be required to attain specific thermal properties, and specific types of glass may be necessary in certain locations in the project or based on where the project is located. Adding information about performance opens the door for automation of code compliance documentation. The performance criteria associated with building codes changes frequently, so, in some cases, it is better to note the attributes that are firm code compliance rather than simply noting that a component is compliant with a specific building code. This will allow the determination of code compliance to be extrapolated and eliminate the possibility of incorrect information being passed on should a building code change in the future.

Parameter	Value	
Construction		
Graphics		
Text		
Materials and Finishes		
Glass Type	Glass - Laminated - Clear	=
Frame Material	Vinyl - PVC - 0.070" - Tan	=
Dimensions		
Rough Width	3' 1 1/4"	= V
Rough Height	6' 8 5/8"	= H
Height	6' 8"	=
Glass Thickness	0' 0 7/8"	=
Sill Height (default)	2' 0"	=
Width	3' 0"	=
Thickness		=
Identity Data		
Phasing		
Warranty Duration (Years)	0	=
Maintenance Schedule (Months)	0	=
Installation Phase	Exterior Enclosure	=
Expected Lifespan (Years)	0	=
Energy Analysis		
U_Factor (default)	0.330000	=
SHGC (default)	0.300000	=
R_Value (default)	12.000000	=
IFC Parameters		
Operation	LH	=
Analytical Model		
F588_Forced-Entry	As Specified in 08 53 13	=
E547_Water-Resistance	As Specified in 08 53 13	=
E330_Structural-Test-Pressure	As Specified in 08 53 13	=
E283_Air-Infiltration	As Specified in 08 53 13	=
AAMA Conformance	As Specified in 08 53 13	=
Other		

FIGURE 9.5 Grouping performance attributes

Installation/Application Information

In situations where a general contractor either develops the model or will ultimately receive the model after design, the addition of installation, fabrication, or application information will provide contractors and subcontractors criteria that they must follow to complete the work that has been specified. In many cases the most effective way to add installation information is to link back to a manufacturer's website where it is hosted. It's not practical or necessary to add a set of step-by-step instructions regarding the installation of components, as it is assumed that the contractor responsible for the installation of the component is already knowledgeable.

Projects may be organized in terms of phases of construction, where specific elements of the project are installed at specific times. This allows us to create time schedules for work, which can help us become more efficient with resources and allow fast-track construction to succeed by figuring out where trades may overlap each other and work concurrently. Adding attributes that apply to whichever trade is responsible for the installation of a component can allow us to sort them by phases, locate them within the project, and make determinations of what work should be done and at what time to minimize foot traffic over completed work and minimize delays due to trade overruns.

Depending on how accurate the model and its components are, there is a potential for direct-to-fabrication exports. Claims have been made that HVAC (heating, ventilating, and air conditioning) contractors have been able to export model information right to a plasma cutter in order to have their ductwork created with little oversight. Whether or not this is practical or even possible in mainstream use remains to be seen, but the ideas are out there, so we should, at the very least, attempt to streamline these processes in order to further the industry as a whole.

Sustainability/Usage Information

Everybody wants to build the most efficient building possible. Whether it's because we are attempting to gain accolades from achieving the highest Leadership in Energy Efficient Design (LEED) rating possible, are looking to save money over the lifespan of the building through energy savings, or are just very environmentally conscious individuals, building efficiency and sustainability has been placed at the forefront of design and construction today. The United States Green Building Council (USGBC) LEED rating system is based on a project as a whole, not on individual components. A product cannot be LEED certified or LEED compliant; it can only contribute toward the certification or compliance of a project. This is an important item to note when considering what sustainability information to add into a model. LEED credits are a valuable attribute within a project that is to be analyzed for certification, but it is not as simple as adding up the credits associated with given products to attain a total.

As LEED attributes and values are added to the project through specific components, the information would need to be extracted and analyzed by a professional who understands how the rating system works and can make determinations of where certain components can have an effect on the rating. Adding credits gives us a starting point to work from, rather than requiring us to hunt through manufacturers information to make determinations of what products contribute to which credits. Adding LEED credits to the components may simplify the research process of certification, but will not automate the analysis of the building as a whole.

Above and beyond its use in rating systems such as LEED, the addition of sustainability information can address the frequency in which a component should be replaced, how the product may affect the quality of life for occupants of the building, and even the cost to maintain the component over the lifespan of the building. Selecting products based on the amount of energy they use or how efficient they are speaks to sustainability information, but implementing and using those products begins to speak to the management and operations of the building. A considerable amount of information within the model may be leveraged for lifecycle assessment, facility maintenance, and budgeting.

Management and Maintenance Information

A building information model is a gold mine of data for facility managers and property owners. When the model is finalized as a true as-built representation of the project and made available to the owner, the owner can then leverage the information for facility management, maintenance, forecasting, and budgeting. Possibilities exist for integrating a building information model into control systems for HVAC, security, and fire protection in order to create a three-dimensional user interface, which would allow a facility engineer or manager to control an entire buildings' systems remotely.

Every component used in a project will eventually require maintenance and replacement. Attributes that speak to the expected lifespan and maintenance frequency will allow facility managers to schedule routine maintenance and forecast for replacement of components well in advance. Having this type of information available for every component will ensure that the building is cared for appropriately and maintenance items are not inadvertently overlooked. The roof of a building is often overlooked in terms of maintenance, as it is out of sight and, so, out of mind. Adding a notation that shows the frequency at which a component or assembly should be inspected will allow the information to be either passed to or used as a facility management database to schedule when a member of the facility staff or contractor is required to perform routine maintenance.

Many aspects of the building have an anticipated replacement point, which can become an unforeseen expense if it has not been budgeted for. If the roof is expected to last 20 years and costs $250,000 to install, by the time it is necessary to replace it, this expense is likely long forgotten and probably has not been budgeted. An owner or facility manager can add an expected replacement cost to the model, divide it by the expected lifespan, and calculate an annual budget figure for replacement. It is a good practice to create this type of budget analysis for all large expenditures that may be necessary on the building later in its lifecycle. A fully completed building model contains all of the components used on the project, so it is in many ways the most effective location to begin performing building lifecycle analysis.

Perhaps one day a building information model will allow us to set and change the temperature in different rooms accordingly, or automatically activate a camera when a security sensor has been tripped. There are a considerable number of automation possibilities when we add the important information into the model. The key to successfully implementing them is to have the necessary information about each component available for access and retrieval.

Specification Information

Specification information can be defined as the data or attributes used to determine not just what product was used, but why it was selected. It is something of a combination between informational properties, material properties, performance properties, and sustainability properties. A door may be specified because it has a high R-value for better thermal performance or because is made of oak for better sound attenuation. Bamboo flooring may be specified because it is a rapidly renewable product or because it is inexpensive. Specification information is specific to the work result, and, in many cases, every specifier is looking for something a little bit different. There are initiatives happening today to unify specification information by creating a consistent property set. The specifiers property information exchange or (SPie) is one such initiative that sets specific attributes and specific values to each specification section.

METHODS OF DATA ENTRY

After thinking about all of this information that can be contained within a model, a big question arises: how and when do we put all of this information in? If we make the conscious decision to add information into the models, then the next step is determining when to put it in. This, in many ways, will drive how the information is placed in the model and how it is managed. Information may be managed within the individual components or within the project itself, depending on whether or not components are reused on multiple projects. Manufacturer-specific BIM content lends itself to adding information to the component itself, as it is to sign to carry exact attributes and values that pertain to a specific product. This type of BIM content is also designed to be disseminated to the design and construction communities. Architects, contractors, specifiers, and facility managers will likely find information that is not relevant to their focus within the project, but should understand that other individuals involved with the project may deem it important.

A building information model is a central database that houses information about all of the components and assemblies used on a project, as well as the project as a whole. The project model may contain information that speaks to the overall design criteria, the location of the project, building codes, the responsible individuals on the project, and a whole host of general information that applies to all work to be performed. Within this project model is a series of assemblies and components that have been used, each with its own specific attributes and values. Within components and assemblies, there are specific materials to be used that also contain attributes that apply to the material itself, not the element in which it is placed. This creates a top-down hierarchy from project to object or assembly, and object or assembly to material, each layer having a series of attributes that apply to their respective level. End users may look at this as a top-down hierarchy, but during BIM content development, it should be looked as a bottom-up process to maintain accuracy within the information. Materials that are used in specific objects and assemblies have certain attributes. These material attributes should be sovereign and standardized so that the material may be reused in any object or assembly deemed necessary in the future. Objects and assemblies contain a series of attributes that apply to what the component is and how it behaves as an independent element of the project. It takes from materials, and puts itself into projects, making itself an intermediate component. Be careful when selecting attributes that apply to this level, especially with assemblies, as adding information that is redundant with materials can cause inconsistencies within the data sets. Project-level information is user defined and specific to the exact project, so, in many cases, it requires the user to start from scratch. Templates may be created without that contain information about specific projects types. Hospitals may carry specific attributes that apply to the project as a whole, schools may have a different set of attributes, residences another, and commercial office buildings yet another. This allows the user to select a standardized project that carries specific attributes, and in some cases even has specific BIM objects preloaded to speed up the model development and shorten the design timeline.

There are often attributes that apply to every component within a category, regardless of whether the values available with a component have been tested. For instance, all insulation has an R-value, all windows have a U-factor and solar heat gain coefficient, and all doors have an hourly fire rating. Rather than adding these attributes to every component of that category, it is practical to create templates that carry the important information right from the onset. This speeds up the development process by minimizing the amount of time and effort required to create the data set for a given component. The forthcoming chapters in the book that apply to different product categories will go into more depth about specific attributes that should be added to the different objects. Adding these attributes to the individual objects prior to developing them is a proactive approach, but in many cases the objects have already been built but do not contain the attributes necessary.

An alternative method for managing information about the components used is to build attributes into the project itself. Adding attributes to the project that apply to different product categories will allow the information about the components to be maintained without adding the attributes to the objects themselves. The attributes and values seem to "pass through" to the objects in schedules and data sets. Because the attributes are project-based, they do not actually attach themselves to the BIM objects, so once the project is completed, the information regarding a specific component cannot be reused in a different project. Attributes at the project level also pertain to every component in a given category, so while windows and doors may have a fairly standardized set of attributes, many components used in a project do not have their own specific category, and are not so cut and dry. Adding an attribute that applies to all components in a category opens the door for potential errors in data management when values are added to attributes that do not apply to a given component. Project-level attributes are effective for a short-term solution to "Oops, I forgot that. . . ." on a Friday afternoon deadline, but there is no substitute for a well thought out plan for BIM content management.

DATA USAGE

Once we have this information in the model, it needs to be used to maintain its relevance. Information that is unused is useless information. I look at information users in terms of two categories—upstream and downstream. The upstream users are all the individuals associated with the design of the project, from the architects, to the specifiers, to the engineers, to the consultants, and in some cases the contractors. Each of these individuals contributes to the information as well as leverages it for his own purposes. This allows it to grow with each discipline that becomes involved. Architects may add design attributes to a component, specifiers may add product selection information to a component, engineers may add performance and usage information to the component, and specialized consultants may add specific attributes that apply to their expertise. Contractors are the pivot point between upstream and downstream data management and usage. With the growth of design-build firms in the architecture and construction industries, many contractors are becoming more and more involved with building information models. This allows them not only to leverage the information within the model, but to contribute to and sometimes even to be in control of the model during the design phase.

Once the data set is fully grown and is finalized, it may be handed off to other individuals who will use the information and are associated with the implementation, maintenance, and usage of the project. These are the downstream users.

Upstream—The Design Team

During the design of the project, architects use BIM data to perform building analysis. For everything from energy analysis, to spatial relationships, to what-if scenarios regarding design considerations of various components, the data within the model are used to streamline the design process. Architects may choose to swap out elements based on their size, shape, or appearance to confirm that they achieve the desired aesthetic qualities. This visual analysis is an opportunity for an owner to view progress drawings to confirm design intent. As hundreds of elements are added into a project, there is a real opportunity for components to interfere with one another. Architects can perform interference-checking studies that determine whether a component of one category interferes with a component of another category anywhere in the project. This analysis will return a list of any "clashes" that may have occurred, allowing the design professional the opportunity to rectify the situation before construction.

Specifiers can be either developers or users of BIM data, depending on how involved they want to become. A specifier has the ability to take an active role in data development and management earlier in the development of the project rather than performing only the responsibilities related to creating construction documents. The concept of the specifier as knowledge manager takes the expertise in the selection of products and assemblies, and leverages it to streamline the design process by allowing certain design decisions that relate to specific elements of the project to be documented in a rolling fashion, rather than all at once. The management of building information modeling data is heavily reliant on expertise in standards and formats that are commonly accepted in the industry. Specifiers have the greatest amount of knowledge in this area, making them the most appropriate individuals to maintain responsibility for project model information. Where model information is maintained by individuals other than specifiers, it may be leveraged for the creation of construction documents. The data associated with the model may be organized and exported so the specifier may quickly see which elements are used in the project, and to which specification section they belong. This can drastically reduce the amount of time necessary to create a project manual by organizing specification information up front.

Engineers leverage BIM data to perform load and usage calculations necessary to ensure that a building is safe, sustainable, and as efficient as possible. Analysis is based on usage attributes being built into the model appropriately, and their values set and adjusted to suit the needs of the project. An electrical engineer who is designing a wiring system for project needs to have basic electrical power attributes built into each component. In addition, a series of more detailed attributes specific to the type of electrical device is added in to determine placement and usage. Occupancy sensors, for instance, have specific spread patterns that determine at what point a switch will activate. Building this information into the model will allow it to be analyzed both in terms of information and graphically. Mechanical and structural engineers will have specific attributes that apply to their disciplines and allow them to perform analysis during the design and to streamline their workflow.

General contractors and subcontractors have an opportunity to input their opinions and requirements during the design, should the design team give them an occasion to do so. They may offer relevant information regarding how specific trades should be phased in order to shorten the timeline for project execution. Their vast field experience may offer insight to specific products that may perform better or worse under certain circumstances, as well as offer design assistance associated with their respective trades. Design-build firms are, by their nature, building this type of information and expertise into the model, as it is a single entity that is responsible for both the design and the execution of a project. Whether it is a design-build firm on a project or a close collaboration between the design team and the general contractor, building information modeling is showing us that the general contractors and their subcontractors have a great deal of expertise to offer to the design of the project.

Downstream—The Implementation and Usage Team

BIM data can be used by contractors to simplify estimation by automating quantity takeoffs and to perform clash detection studies to confirm that the design is buildable, ultimately minimizing errors and change orders. When architects export information from the model and make it available to the general contractors, it is usually possible for the contractors to import it directly into their construction management software. This allows them to estimate, analyze, schedule, and phase the project accordingly, using explicit information about components, products, and assemblies that the design team has specified.

When model data contains a list of every component to be used on the project, and the dimensions and areas of each assembly, preliminary cost estimation may be performed almost automatically, and more detailed estimation for bidding purposes is streamlined considerably by eliminating the need to measure and calculate based on field conditions or existing two-dimensional plans. Specific installed costs may be assigned to different elements from the project and sorted based on the trade responsible for it. This will allow general contractors to separate out information relevant to different trades so their subcontractors will have the same ability to estimate.

General contractors who have access to both the graphics and the data can visually analyze how projects may be phased so they are completed in the least amount of time. Rather than waiting for one trade to finish before another begins, overlaps may be created whereby one trade has finished working in a specific area, allowing another trade to begin even though the scope of work of the first trade is not fully completed. Contractors can also schedule just-in-time deliveries of building materials and place them at appropriate locations so they will not need to be moved throughout the project multiple times. When contractors leverage the building information model for execution purposes, there is a potential for cost savings to be passed along to the owner when labor resources are minimized and operating expenses are decreased based on fewer days required on a specific project.

At final completion, facilities managers and owners may be provided with a "digital owner's manual" of a facility, giving them the ability to schedule maintenance, forecast and budget for replacement, and track usage throughout the lifecycle of the facility. This affords them the opportunity to integrate these activities into their current facility management process and to streamline or automate routine maintenance scheduling. The information from the model may be used for budgeting, systems controls, maintenance, resource usage calculations, or a whole host of other potential analyses. Allowing owners to maintain the building information model will further the automation of facility management.

CHAPTER 10

Quality Control

Quality control is probably the most important aspect of BIM content development. It should be understood that the models we develop may ultimately become a part of a construction contract, whether it is in the form of construction drawings or the data exported from the model to create specifications. When dealing with manufacturer-specific content, this carries an even greater importance, as the content is not just a graphic representation of a model, but is also the product data embedded in the model. It is the manufacturer's first line of marketing and advertising to a design professional.

If an architect downloads a window manufacturer's BIM of a specific component, there are certain expectations that come with it. First and foremost, it should be a reasonable facsimile of the product that is to be installed. Reasonable is a subjective term, so consider the usage of the component when developing it. This is discussed in depth in the specific content types. It is usually not necessary to make every indentation or chamfer in the graphics, but dimensional attributes and requirement sizes like rough openings and necessary clearances need to be accurate to typical construction tolerances. This ensures that the unit will fit in the location it is designed for and also work appropriately.

The data in a model are expected to be clear, concise, complete, correct, and consistent with other documentation, such as corresponding guide specifications or associated data sheets. Incorrect data can translate into incorrect specifying and potentially specifying the wrong product. While not all BIM content carries data, when data are added, they should be added with care and updated constantly to ensure that they are always correct at the time they are implemented into the model. Data tables and reference spreadsheets often allow easier model updating and also provide a conduit between the manufacturer or supplier and the designer or content manager.

Where practical, assigning a single accountable party for maintenance of BIM data and graphics is good practice. This individual can keep a constant watch on the information and, through good information organization practices, be able to update and refresh models very quickly. In addition, a single responsible party can generally work more effectively by developing an understanding of the subtle nuances of how specific components were created. Just as a doctor needs to understand how a certain patient behaves and lives to provide appropriate healthcare, a BIM developer knows how his models were assembled, which allows him to assess where and how changes should be implemented when updates are made.

Graphics play a vital role in the success or failure of a BIM component. It is not necessarily how accurate the graphics are that makes this determination, rather the correctness of the development. Various solid modeling techniques are available, all of them appropriate for specific conditions.

Tip

Where possible, assign a single individual to be responsible for quality control of all content in a library. This ensures a uniform level of detail and quality.

QUALITY CONTROL PROCEDURES

Putting together a procedure for quality control allows us to streamline the content development process and minimize redundant work. If we take a modular approach to quality control, we'll likely find that it takes less time than testing and retesting everything over and again. First and foremost the content needs to work. There should be no errors when implemented into a project, all solids should be driven by a material parameter, and it should look appropriate.

Above and beyond graphics, the information contained within the model should be assumed to be correct. Therefore, all information should be put under a strict quality control procedure, which involves individuals who have the ability to check the information for accuracy. In the case of manufacturer-specific content, typically an individual from research and development, technical services, or marketing will handle this task.

Once the graphics and data are developed, an assembly procedure needs to be performed to align the information in the model with the graphics. This takes one piece of graphic and prepares it to be used for multiple versions, or types. Information that is not graphics may be considered, but it is not data either. Options such as materials or finishes may be user-selected items, so it is essential to make sure that all materials are developed appropriately and limited to the models to which they apply. After a final assembly is performed and all graphics, information, and options are added, the models need to be tested in a real-world scenario, or a project. This is basically a BIM beta test. Without this type of affirmation it is difficult to be completely sure that the models are working correctly.

After much trial and error, I have found that it is effective to break down the quality control process for content development into four basic modules: graphics, data, final assembly, and implementation. Graphics consider all of the solids in the object working together to create a reasonable facsimile of the product. Data organizes and controls the information associated with a given component or product and organizes it based on the different types of associated objects. Final assembly takes the data and implements them into the object and the options and prepares them for final testing in a project. The implementation of the model is what determines whether there will be errors on each type of component that is developed. It's not uncommon for errors to occur when a dimension goes out of a given range or a reference plane is not locked appropriately with the depth of a host component, such as a wall, floor, roof, or ceiling.

Quality Control of Graphics

Performing quality control on graphics is probably the hardest part, and is often the most overlooked. There are so many facets of the graphics that the individual performing the quality control (QC) task must have a clear understanding of what goes wrong inside of models, common mistakes, and solutions. The QC manager should also be something of an educator, allowing the developers to learn from their mistakes and saving themselves time down the road.

The graphics within a given component are generally made up of several solids working together to create the whole object. Depending on how detailed the component is there can be upward of 20 or 30 dimensions, all of which need to be tested for accuracy and assurance that they work appropriately. The more quality control that's done during development, through "flexing" the object, the less work is necessary down the road. In many cases the locations of certain solids may be reliant on the locations of others, so the use of reference planes and reference lines allows points in space to be used for dimensioning. In most cases, before I develop any solids in object, I create the reference planes necessary to develop the dimensions associated with the object. This does two things: it dimensions the model up front before solids are entered, and it minimizes the bad habit of dimensioning solids themselves. It is always preferable to dimension the reference planes rather than the solids themselves as it minimizes the chances for errors in the model.

Once the reference planes are all in place and dimensioned, I typically start by modeling the larger components and work my way in to the smaller, less important components in the model. In some cases I may work from the outside to the inside, or the inside out, depending on the type of component that's being developed. For example, the frame is the outermost component of a door and is typically fixed to the wall in which it is placed. This makes it the most effective location to start from. Conversely, an item such as an architectural column may start from the center shaft and work outward toward its base, capital, and surface appearance.

For each geometric solid that is created, a material needs to be assigned. Every component is made up of something in the real world and as such should never be left as a generic material or, even worse, unassigned altogether. A good practice is to create a set of test materials that can be used during the development process to check whether materials have been attached to each solid. Using bright primary colors gives a strong visual cue that material parameters exist and have been assigned to the graphics solids. Changing the material parameters periodically ensures that the graphics are being created appropriately and the material parameters are not being forgotten.

When we run into components that may have multiple options, it is usually more effective to develop them as their own objects and embed or "nest" them into the object that is being created, as we show in Figure 10.1. In terms of a window, this may be the glass sash, the dividers, or both. In terms of an architectural column, this may be the different base or capital types available. The most important thing to consider when adding components to other components is the reference points used to determine where they are to be inserted. Consistent naming and locating will save a lot of headaches and time in development, and over time will become second nature. BIM software platforms usually

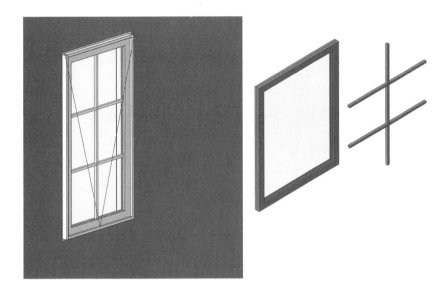

FIGURE 10.1   Nested components

allow us to name reference planes and assign categories or types to them. Using named reference planes that are listed as having a purpose, such as top, bottom, or center, allows us to create multiple components with the same point of origin. Once these nested components are brought into the object, the reference planes that define the origin can be locked in place such that every component that is swapped out will always be in the same location.

After the nested components are completed, one aspect that is often overlooked is the creation of dimension and material controls. In many cases, these nested objects rely on the parameters of the host object for their dimensions or materials. A series of links are created that allow parameters to pass from the higher level object into the nested object. While a door handle is nested in a door, it may be desirable to add a parameter in the door that will control the finish of that door handle. Creating this link makes it easy for the user to control information without having to dig into the object to find it. When there is more than one option for a nested component, it is effective to add a label to the component for it to be controlled within the data set. This simple parameter can create a drop-down list that includes all of the available options for the component. When there are multiple components that may be switched out, such as bases and capitals in an architectural column, it is a good idea to create categories for each type of component. The bases should be one category and capitals should be another. This minimizes confusion and limits the potential for capital to be selected as a base and vice versa.

Unless specially designed to do so, nested components will not show up in a schedule. In cases where it is necessary for them to show up individually within a schedule, there are two options. The first is to create those components as their own individual objects, and the second is to create what is known as a shared component. Not all BIM software allows for the latter, but where possible, it is a very effective approach to creating modular components and minimizing file size of the individual object. The principle is to allow each option to be its own file, which is loaded into the project. All components of a given category become available as options within a project. Because the number of categories that may be used is finite, and there are likely additional unrelated objects within that category in a project, this approach should be used sparingly and only when the components are required within a schedule or make an object's file size inordinately large.

Quality Control and Review of Data

Data are the "I" in BIM. This is what differentiates building information modeling from standard 2D or even 3D vector graphics. BIM can effectively store and manage information about individual components, products, materials, assemblies, and the project as a whole. All of this information may be used by different individuals at different points in the project, so it is critical for it to be accurate from the onset. When a manufacturer-specific component is created and added to a project, there is an expectation that all of the information contained within will be correct. For this reason, quality control of the information slated to be contained in the model is paramount.

First and foremost, never create the data set inside the BIM software. Most of the time, the individuals responsible for reviewing the information are not proficient with the use of BIM software, and the individuals who are developing the graphics are not capable of reviewing the data. It saves a lot of time and effort to create the information in a spreadsheet or database as shown in Figure 10.2 and translate it into the objects once it has been approved. Parameters are expressed in terms of attribute and value pairs, with each attribute being of a certain category or unit, such as text, length, number, integer, or Boolean (yes/no). When organizing information for review, place each attribute in its own column of a spreadsheet and note each unit of measure in its header. The rows of the spreadsheet are for each type of object, so if we're creating a data set for windows, each size would be its own row.

Much of the information contained in each type of object is repetitive. To streamline and simplify the review process, it is helpful for the reviewer to have all redundant information listed only once in its own row just below the header. If the opportunity arises where this repetitive information can be reviewed and approved prior to development of the component, often a template file or files may be created that preloads all this information before

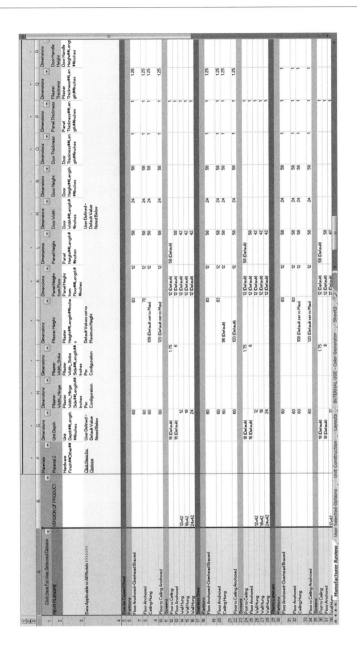

FIGURE 10.2 Typical review data set layout

creating the graphics. This allows a content developer the ability to clone this file over and over to create the individual components, without having to add attributes and values to each one. This is especially beneficial when dealing with manufacturer-specific components and when dealing with a large number of similar components. If 600 cabinets are all made by the same manufacturer and all have the same values for most of their attributes, it saves a considerable amount of time and effort if we create a template file with these attributes and values preloaded and create each cabinet based on that.

There are two ways an attribute can be assigned to a component: a type attribute applies to a type or version of the component, and an instance attribute applies to a specific unit that has been placed in the project. Each of these has specific purposes and it is critical to ensure that attributes are assigned properly or undesirable results may occur. Colors and finishes are the most common instance parameters, as many components in a project have hundreds of different material, color, and finish options available to them. Generally speaking, early in project design, colors and finishes are not selected, so if they are left as an instance attribute, they can be quickly found, selected, and updated in later phases of project design. Dimensions are often used as instance attributes as well. Dimensions that cannot be defined by the component itself but are critical to the appearance of the component are best left as instance attributes. The height from floor to ceiling in a building is a good example of this. A component such as a floor-to-ceiling mounted toilet partition relies on the distance between the floor and ceiling to create its graphics appropriately, yet this value is unknown until it is placed in a project. By creating an instance attribute in the component called ceiling height that controls the pilaster height, the design professional has the ability to stretch that height to fit the ceiling space, or enter it manually. Figure 10.3 shows the different type and instance attributes that might apply to a component.

Highly customizable components also use a considerable number of instance attributes, as they leave the decisions in the hands of the design

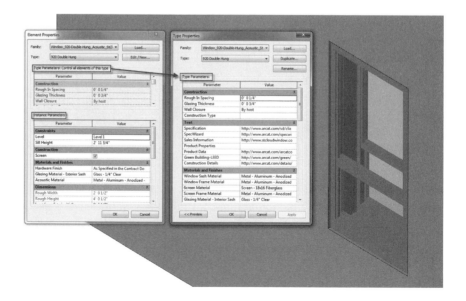

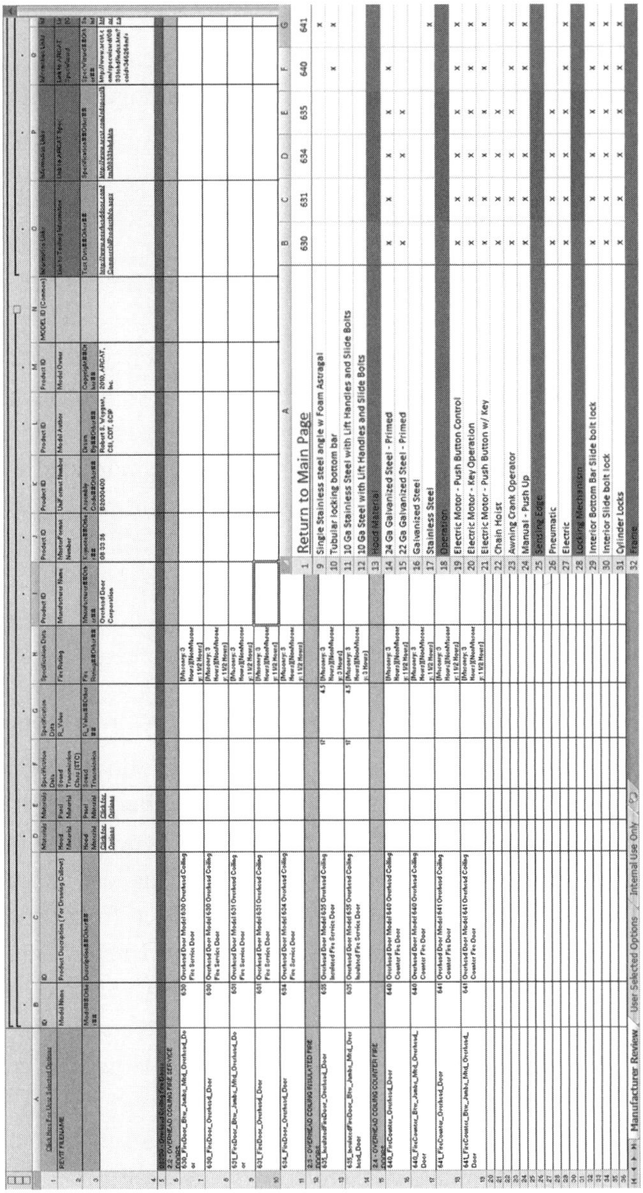

FIGURE 10.3 Instance attributes and type attributes

professional while they are making decisions. Windows that may be fabricated to any size may have instance attributes for height and width, an elevator that moves anywhere from 2 to 200 floors may have an instance attribute for the number of stops, or a door that could be one of 20 different styles may have an instance attribute for the door slab.

Final Assembly

Once all the graphics and data have been completed, checked, and approved, the data must be merged into the graphics to create a singular unit of information, or the completed BIM object. This can be done in several ways. The data can be entered manually, which is very time-consuming and labor-intensive; it can be done programmatically by developing an application that can manage the information within the components; or, where the software allows, the most effective method is to create a catalog file that houses the data for the individual types.

Most components have several options, versions, or types of the product. For instance, a double-hung window is a single component that can represent every size available. This can lead to hundreds and even thousands of potential combinations. It is important to keep in mind that the more versions or types of the component that are placed in the model, the slower it becomes, as it takes a considerable amount of time to load and regenerate. Generally speaking, it is not wise to add more than three or four types to an object, as is likely that only a few of them will be used within a project. Where more than a few types of a component exist, it is far more effective to create a catalog that can load the information.

Not all software platforms allow for the creation of a catalog that will load multiple versions of the object. For the ones that do have this ability, it is typically a text-based file with some type of delimiter, either a comma or a tab. These types of catalogs are very helpful when developing components that may have hundreds of possible combinations. This text file carries all of the information associated with a specific type of object, from the dimensions and materials to the performance and informational attributes. This essentially allows the user to begin developing with the component that carries attributes but no values, and as decisions are made during project development, the components can be selected and further updated without a considerable amount of effort. If the information about the components has been created in a spreadsheet or database, transferring it into a catalog is actually a very simple operation requiring little additional effort.

Most spreadsheet software will allow us to save the file as a comma-separated value or CSV file. This is basically a text file that uses commas as delimiters, so changing the file extension from .csv to .txt will allow the file to be read by the BIM software. BIM software will typically have a specific syntax that needs to be followed to ensure that the values associated with each attribute are entered correctly. Length is a good example. A length attribute does not define what the unit of measure is, so entering a number as the value may not be correct unless the catalog defines the prescribed unit of measure. If the value for length in the catalog is listed as three, but no unit of measure is defined, the catalog will generally use the default value set in the project into which it is being loaded. This leaves a lot of room for error, as some individuals work in metric units and others in SI units. If the unit is not predefined, what is supposed to be 3 mm may end up being 3 feet!

There are other pitfalls to consider when creating catalogs of this nature. Even though you are working in a spreadsheet when developing the data set, always remember that the values in the catalog end up being separated by commas. I think the biggest culprit among catalog errors that I have come across occurs when adding addresses as an attribute into a component. An address usually has a comma separating the street address, city, and state when written in a single line or single field in a data set. To combat this, you can either avoid using commas altogether and substitute a different character, such as a semicolon or comma, or identify the field as a whole by putting quotation marks around the entire text string that contains the comma.

Tip

Saving a spreadsheet file as comma-separated values and changing the file extension from .csv to .txt will create a text-based catalog file.

Implementation

Once the components have been created, the data have been approved, the models have been assembled, the catalogs have been created, and everything seems to work correctly, the model must be tested in a project. This is especially important when dealing with components that rely on a host component such as a wall or a roof, as changes to that host may cause unexpected and undesirable results if not tested properly.

First and foremost, no component should ever raise an error. If errors occur, something is fundamentally wrong with the object and must be corrected within the component or the catalog itself. Components should be loaded into projects and tested to see whether they have the correct appearance, appropriate controls and limitations, and the ability to be placed in the model from the view in which they are typically located. In most cases components are located from a plan view, but in some cases one may choose to locate the component from an elevation or in a three-dimensional view.

After components are placed in a model and the graphics are correct, the instance attributes should be tested to find where errors may occur. This is especially important when dealing with attributes that control materials or turn graphics on and off. By changing materials to a contrasting color, it is easy to find any solid geometry that may not have been attached to a material attribute, and by turning graphic control attributes on and off, appearance attributes may be found as well.

EDUCATING STAFF ON QUALITY CONTROL

While it is always best to have a single individual responsible for the quality control of the models within a library, each individual associated with the creation of the components should have a clear understanding of how the model should be developed, the standard of care and level of detail associated with the library, and the intent of the models that are being created. As content developers become more educated in quality control, less effort is necessary from the individual responsible for oversight of the content and the faster the content is completed. As with any aspect of business, time is money, so as a quality control ritual is developed, more money can be made on either the components or the project itself, depending on what business we're in.

Even though time is money, there is no substitute for quality. Poorly and quickly made models are far less effective than well-made models that took a little more effort to create, but have far more functionality and far fewer errors. Each time a poorly created component is used and creates an error, time is taken from each individual using the component in a project, compounding the amount of time associated with the development of an individual object. Building an object right the first time and developing a structure by which the information can be updated easily and quickly will cut down the amount of time associated with the component, and in the long term will save countless hours and dollars in development and redevelopment.

CHAPTER 11

Knowledge Management

WHAT IS KNOWLEDGE MANAGEMENT?

Knowledge management is the supply, maintenance, and delivery of graphical and topical information related to a project. With the advent of building information modeling (BIM), there has been a considerable increase in the amount of information and collaboration during the design of the project. Because so much information is being passed between so many different parties, a single responsible party or team should be assigned to manage this information to ensure consistency between the plans, specifications, model, and other supporting documents.

In previous iterations of the design team, an architect would design a building and sometimes collaborate with engineers and advisors, such as interior designers, roof consultants, or other specialists highly knowledgeable in areas of the project. Once the design was completed, a specifier would come in to document the project and provide a project manual for use during the bidding phase. While this method was, and still remains, a highly effective approach for design, when working on a BIM-based project, there is an opportunity for

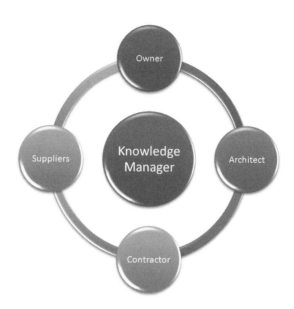

FIGURE 11.1 Knowledge manager—the project hub

the design team to leverage the expertise that the specifier, contractors, subcontractors, and product representatives have regarding their specialties.

Through the years the role of the specifier has diminished to that of an editor of form documents. The expertise and knowledge that a specifier has regarding specific products and assemblies within a project seems to have been forgotten. A well-trained specifier can provide documentation for not only how products and assemblies are used in a project, but why those specific components and assemblies were selected. There are reasons for using a solid wood door in certain areas of the project and reasons for not using copper flashings for roofs in certain areas. Specifiers also see the success or failure of not only specific components within a project, but actual manufactured products. This gives them the ability not only to determine a type of component to be used on a project, but perhaps to provide product selection assistance based on their knowledge of product quality under a specific set of conditions in the environment in which the project is located. Having an individual on the project design team who can assist in component selection can allow for better decision making earlier in the design process.

It is not uncommon for general contractors to become involved in the design process today. With the growth of the design-build firm, it is almost a requirement, as the general contractor has a substantial amount of expertise and experience in how the project is executed and constructed. A great deal of information regarding the assembly of the project is often overlooked or otherwise not considered, as architects are not expected to have this type of experience in their practice. Integrated project delivery, or IPD, is a project delivery method that focuses on the collaboration between architect and contractor to deliver a project that meets an owner's requirements and streamline the design and construction processes to create the greatest cost benefit for all parties involved. There have been several successful case studies where an IPD project has saved the owner a substantial amount of money, the contractor a considerable amount of time, and the architect from numerous change orders and potential design flaws or errors.

General contractors often have a series of subcontractors who they use based on their previous successes and failures. Understanding that one drywall contractor is good on a single-floor project, where a different contractor is good on high-rise buildings, allows the contractor the ability to select the right individual for the project based on merit. Having the contractor involved with the design early allows the architect to receive input about design aspects related to staging and scheduling the specific subcontractors. This can help minimize the amount of time necessary to bring materials onto a project, move them around, and protect finished work by staging a project accordingly. If we look at this as a larger-scale project and think about the heavy machinery and cranes that may be necessary at different points in the project, the cost savings becomes greater. Imagine a new stadium being built without taking into consideration the locations of cranes used to erect heavy steel. In a worst-case scenario, imagine a crane being stuck at the 50 yard line because its deconstruction and removal were not considered.

Project documentation really begins at the onset of a project when *feasibility studies* are done and *preliminary cost estimates* are created. In many cases this information disappears or gets lost in the shuffle during schematic design and design development, as they in many cases do not apply to the design team. If this information were kept as a baseline, it could be used for development of preliminary project descriptions, short-form specifications, long-form specifications, construction implementation documents, and, ultimately, facilities management documents. Rather than looking at a series of modular documents, look at documentation as a whole. Just like writing a textbook, we start with an outline and as information is added it fleshes out the text for the chapters, which ultimately become the book. If we think of project documentation the same way, we organize a series of notes in terms of project requirements, budgetary concerns, owner preferences, and pre-projects studies to create a preliminary project document, or outline, which discusses the basics of a project to be created. This type of document can be used to discuss the project with the owner, for the owner to discuss the project with financiers, and for the architect to discuss the project with potential future members of the project team.

Schematic design takes this preliminary project document and fleshes it out further, adding more specifics about size, shape, and specific elements of the building. The preliminary project document becomes larger, evolving into a short-form specification. This point in the project is a good place for additional parties to become involved, such as contractors, subcontractors, specialty consultants, and advisors. These individuals can provide input that can streamline the design development process by minimizing the amount of research necessary to make appropriate decisions. The contractor responsible for interior finishes and partitions can discuss locations for necessary structural components, such as king studs, as well as review potential locations to stage his work. Mechanical contractors can review the information and provide feedback regarding appropriately sized components and types of mechanical systems that could be used.

During *design development*, the project as a whole is fleshed out in design, wall, floor, ceiling, and roof assemblies are located, and the most important components are located. Openings such as windows and doors are often the first to be added, as they are the most critical in terms of baseline location. This is not to say that the locations of openings will not change, only to note that a room requires a door in order for it to be accessed. As each of these wall, floor, ceiling, roof, and opening components are added to the project, there is an ability for each one of them to carry the salient information that determines what it is and, in some ways, why it was selected. In a hotel, walls between rooms and common areas may note the required sound attenuation performance attributes or Sound Transmission Classification (STC) rating, as well as the required fire ratings. The windows and doors may carry the desired U-factor, solar heat gain coefficient (SHGC), and glass type attributes. Prior to bid, these attributes act as baseline requirements from which suppliers and contractors determine the actual products to use on the project. Adding the information to the model with the components allows the attributes to be extracted from the model during the construction documentation phase, thereby creating a series of schedules, or tabular specifications, if you will.

The *construction documents* phase as we know it today takes all of the information obtained during schematic design and design development and organizes it into a document that is used during the bidding phase of a project to complement the information found in the drawings and to set forth minimum requirements for the components to be used on the project. Building information modeling affords the design team a new opportunity to rethink how construction documents are created. Not only is there a possibility of automating the process of construction documents, there is a potential for creating new ways of viewing the information. In many cases construction specifications can be difficult to read and interpret mainly because they are usually written in paragraph form. Much of the information within a specification is actually attribute and value pairs, which lend themselves to being viewed in a tabular form. Data export templates allow attributes of the project to be organized and viewed by the individuals or teams that the information applies to. General contractors may need to see all of the information within the specification, as all of it applies to them and their contract with the owner. Subcontractors, however, only need to see a limited amount of information, that which pertains to their scope of work. The electrical contractor does not need to see information about wall finishes, and the concrete foundation contractor does not need to see information about the roof finishes. Organizing information in a tabular form allows it to be cross-referenced easily, so that if the roof contractor needs to see information regarding the scope of work on an adjacent wall, he can find it quickly and easily.

The *bidding phase* of a project has traditionally been a demarcation point, or the delimiter between design and construction. Contractors offer their services, manufacturers offer their components, and the owner and design team make decisions on which products to use and who is to install them. The bid review process requires that the design team review a series of informational packages sent by contractors offering their services, which can be a very time-consuming undertaking when we consider the potential number of contractors bidding on a single project. When baseline information regarding the requirements of a project is embedded in the model itself, the model can become a reference standard used to qualify products. If a manufacturer submits its components for consideration in the project carrying the salient attributes necessary to determine whether or not each component meets the project requirements, the information may be viewed in a tabular form, and apples-to-apples comparisons can be made with less effort and less paperwork. This concept is especially beneficial when dealing with substitution requests. When a substitution request is submitted, a manufacturer or contractor is attempting to submit his product for consideration in the project. To be considered as an approved alternate, the product must have the same performance capabilities as the reference standard, so if a manufacturer is asked to submit a BIM component for review in addition to or instead of data sheets and supporting documentation, the architect can quickly and almost programmatically determine whether or not the component meets the requirements of the project.

Once the contract is awarded and the construction phase begins, rare is the project that has no changes to the original design. While building information modeling does offer clash detection and the ability for collaboration, there is always something that requires a change. Whether it's a discontinued product that was specified, a design flaw that was not caught, or the owner of the building changing his mind, there is an expectation that a certain degree of field engineering will be performed during construction. The construction documents used for bidding don't take this into consideration, as the documentation of the building typically leaves off with addenda issued by the architect. Field changes are often overlooked and do not become officially documented. The future of BIM seems to be headed toward intelligent access to information regarding a project by owners and facility managers. For owners to get the most of their documentation, it should be accurate at completion, not at the bidding phase, as actual installed products often change during construction.

Once the construction of a project has been completed, the information contained within a model can be of considerable value to the owner and facility manager as long as the information is correct. To provide a true as-built project model, documentation should continue through the construction cycle, through the punch list, and into substantial and final completion and owner acquisition. This provides the owner with documentation of the entire project from start to finish, which can act as a digital owner's manual of an entire facility. Figure 11.2 considers a project not just in terms of the design and construction of a project but from the concept of the project through the re-tasking of the facility years down the road. Facilities managers can use a document of this nature to forecast maintenance and replacement of components, and owners can use it to analyze and budget for future development. In the event that something goes wrong on the project, it is important to have information about who the installer and the manufacturer were, as well as

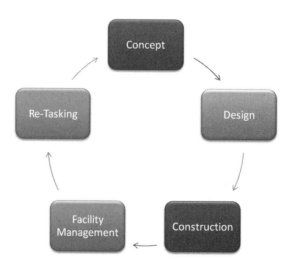

FIGURE 11.2
The project cycle

supporting documentation regarding what the product was, and the type of remedial action necessary.

It's plain to see that managing all of this information is no small task. Having an individual associated with the project whose sole responsibility is to maintain project information can minimize or eliminate reinventing the informational wheel at each project phase. Project information is larger than any single individual in the project and extends from before design to after construction, so the question is not so much when and how to manage the information, but which individual or team should perform the task and who should supervise the knowledge manager. If the design team is responsible for knowledge management, there is a possibility that information will not be exchanged prior to design or after the bidding. If the construction team is responsible for knowledge management, information regarding the design would need to be added into the model after design in order to create a fully accurate model. If the responsibility of knowledge management becomes a function of the owner or facility manager, there is a greater likelihood that all of the information associated with a project will be accurate after design and construction, provided the facility manager exists and becomes involved with the project prior to design.

Knowledge management is a scalable task that can apply only to design, only to construction, only to facility management, or all of the above, depending on the needs of the project and the owner. Larger facilities and larger projects will see the most benefit, mainly from the management perspective, but projects of any size will benefit from consistent information among all components of the construction documents, as well as having an individual or team whose expertise is in the administration of product, project, and construction information. It is rare to find a single individual with expertise in design, specification, and construction, along with the ability to work within specific BIM software platforms. At the onset, the role may be delegated to a team while individuals become educated to take on the role for future tasks and projects.

THE KNOWLEDGE MANAGER

What is a knowledge manager? To fully understand what a knowledge manager is, we must first understand what he is responsible for and the tasks he is to perform. The core information that makes up a BIM-based project lies in the components used to develop the project. The materials, components, and assemblies used in any given project carry all of the pertinent information necessary for the design, specification, construction, and management of not only the product, but the project as a whole. At an absolute minimum, a knowledge manager should be able to administrate this information within the software platform the used by the design team. Whether an application is developed that can translate information from a database to the BIM software, or the knowledge manager is working within the BIM software, project information must be accessible through the model.

The knowledge manager is something of a hybrid of specifier, CAD manager, and BIM content developer. Having a strong understanding of standards and formats used in design and construction allows him to work in an environment that all members of the design team are familiar with. Information is passed to the knowledge manager from the design team, construction team, and management team, whereupon he sorts, filters, arranges, manipulates, and exports the information as necessary during various points in the design and construction phases. As decisions are made regarding the performance of specific components, the knowledge manager updates model information accordingly. As manufactured products are selected to replace specific components based on bids awarded, the knowledge manager updates that information as well. The knowledge manager notes changes made to selected products during construction and, upon completion, finalizes and checks the information in the model against the actual project and prepares it for the owner.

With the amount of time a knowledge manager may spend dealing with BIM content, it seems only natural that he become responsible for providing content used during the design phase. A knowledge manager's involvement during schematic design will allow him to format and provide wall, floor, ceiling, roof, and opening components as necessary to develop the basis of design. Then the components can be entered carrying the attributes necessary for product selection. These components may not necessarily carry values at this time as decisions have not been made this early on in the project, but when components carry attributes necessary for product selection, updating the model later in the design phase requires considerably less effort.

During schematic design, a knowledge manager may provide a series of walls based on basic usage characteristics. There may be a foundation wall, an exterior wall, an interior partition wall, and firewalls. At this point in design that may be the only information in each of the wall types, but the interior partition walls may have an attribute for STC rating with no value, the firewalls may have an attribute for fire rating with no value, and the exterior walls may have an attribute for R-value with no value. As determinations are made for each of the requirements, the values can easily be added within the scheduling environment.

As openings are added in walls, the type of opening may not be clear. A knowledge manager may provide one window and one door at this point, each with the attributes necessary to determine and differentiate between the various types of windows and doors. As decisions about the type of window or door used at various locations in the project are made, the knowledge manager can create additional types of windows and doors to suit the needs of the project at a given time. An opening may be a window, a window may become an aluminum window, and an aluminum window may become a blast-resistant aluminum casement window with a U-factor of 0.30 and a solar heat gain coefficient of 0.30. After the bidding phase, this specified window will ultimately become an aluminum casement window meeting specific performance criteria as manufactured by a specific company. If the information and components are managed appropriately, the components themselves can be easily updated without disturbing surrounding design elements or causing modeling errors.

As construction documents are created and the project manual is assembled, the knowledge manager can organize information based on its specification section and export the information from the model for use by the specifier. In many cases, the specifier is the individual who makes decisions regarding the performance attributes of certain components. Cases such as this lead me to believe that a seasoned specifier may be the most appropriate individual to take on the role of knowledge management. A seasoned specifier is not an individual who simply understands how to edit a form document, but one who understands the differences between products based on their performance values, when to use certain components, and the appropriate methods for documenting them. Regardless of whether or not the specifier is involved with knowledge management, the information associated with the specific components and assemblies may be exported from the model to the specifier to assist in creation of the project manual. Where attributes are determined by the specifier, that information is passed back to the knowledge manager, who can insert it into the project.

During the bidding phase, a snapshot of the model can be taken and used for bid review. As contractors and manufacturers submit products for consideration, the knowledge manager can insert them into the "control" model and provide exportable schedules showing line-by-line comparisons of various manufacturers and how they stack up against one another in terms of their performance attributes as outlined by the "control." This will allow architects to review bids much more quickly, as the information about all prospective manufactured products can be viewed together, rather than on separate pages in separate bid packages. As decisions are made by the design team regarding which products are to be used, the knowledge manager updates the design model with the information determined by bid review from the control model.

Once the contracts are awarded and construction begins, changes are inevitable. As changes occur, the contractor passes information to the knowledge manager, who updates and maintains the model postdesign. If alternate products are used on a project due to availability concerns or contractor preference, the knowledge manager updates the model accordingly. Where conflicts between design and implementation occur, the knowledge manager notes them and, in cases where design changes must be made to reflect actual construction, notifies the design team, which can update the model as necessary. Upon completion of the project, the finalized model and data set are prepared for the owner to become a new deliverable as an additional closeout submittal. Providing a finalized digital owner's manual gives the owner complete documentation of the entire project from preplanning through construction. Where practical or applicable, even actual cost information could be added for use in future budgeting.

Facility managers have the ability to take a finalized as built BIM project and implement it into their facilities management documents, or, taking it a step further, create a facilities management database that may be used for maintenance scheduling, systems integration, budgeting, and even space planning for rented areas of the facility. This begs the question, though, of who owns the model upon completion. Traditionally, the architect has held ownership of the digital files associated with a project in order to maintain his intellectual property. With building information modeling, it becomes a bit more unclear as to who owns what at the end of a project. It is entirely possible for an architect to provide a protected version of the final model that allows access to the graphics and information without giving up the model used to create the design. Negotiations between owner and architect will ultimately determine who owns the model, but to further the growth of building information modeling, it is far more practical for the property owner to retain, at bare minimum, perpetual licensure of the model for internal purposes. Perhaps limiting the owner to usage of the current model without allowing for creation of derivative works may be a solution to model ownership and control. Someday we may have a clear understanding of this, but for now it is all in the hands of property owners, architects, and their respective legal teams.

The role of knowledge manager provides a bright future for the specifier, as it provides an opportunity for individuals with a vast knowledge of component, assembly, and building product selection to become more involved in overall project delivery. Today, the role of the specifier has been limited to that of a documents manager, whereas evolving that role into the knowledge manager can bring this expertise to the forefront while providing a valuable service to the building owner, architect, and contractor. In addition to providing the typical construction documents seen today, the knowledge manager has the ability to leverage the information within the model to provide a series of new information components that apply to specific members of the project team, from the smallest subcontractor all the way to the property owner.

NEW DOCUMENTS AND DELIVERABLES

While there is nothing wrong with the methods used today to document projects, technology is providing new opportunities to become more accurate and more detailed in our information structures. The project manual, containing the construction specifications, is the most widely used and largest piece of documentation found on a project. The problem with the project manual is that it is only used during the two-week period of the design phase during which bids are collected and reviewed. After the bidding phase, the project manual seems to end up on a shelf somewhere collecting dust, while the information associated with that project manual lives on in the building being built. A building information model is essentially a relational database that houses all of the information about the project from the littlest component to the primary assemblies used to create the building.

During the design phase this type of information can be used to examine the project for code compliance, energy modeling, structural design, and a whole host of other design analyses. There is a potential for new forms and formats to be created that will allow this type of information to be viewed quickly and easily, the same way a construction specification is organized to allow information to be retrieved. Since the model is a database, it is not intuitive enough to understand that a human will see U-factor and U-value as the same thing, so a standardized language must be created that a machine can understand. By creating a standardized set of terms to define specific attributes used within a project, we create a taxonomy that will allow apples-to-apples comparisons of information regarding specific component categories. This taxonomy becomes the root of all future documents and deliverables, which may be made available to members of the project team.

Because much of the information that surrounds components, assemblies, and products can be organized in attribute and value pairs, the most logical type of new document would be a tabular specification like the one seen in Figure 11.3. Organizing the information within a model by its designated specifications section, and listing the individual components and their attributes within that section as a set of attribute and value pairs will provide a document that details not only what component was used, but the information that was

CASEMENT WINDOW - 30x46

Identification Properties

Element	Window
MasterFormat Section	08 52 13
UniFormat Code	B2020130
Omniclass Product Code	23.30.20.17.21.14
Manufacturer	As Specified in 08 52 13
Model	30x46 LH Casement
Description	30" x 46" LH Outswing Casement Window

Dimensions

Unit Width	30 5/8"
Unit Height	46 3/4"
Rough Opening Width	31 3/8"
Rough Opening Height	47 1/2"
Window Depth	3 5/8"
Glass Thickness	11/16"
Operation	LH Outswing

Materials

Frame Material	Northern White Pine
Cladding	Aluminum AAMA 2605 Finish
Glass Type	Fully Tempered Sealed IG - Low E, Argon Filled
Muntin Material	PVC, Extruded - White
Frame Finish	White
Hardware Finish	Oil Rubbed Bronze
Screen Material	8x16 Fiberglass - Charcoal

Performance Properties

U-Factor	0.55
SHGC	0.41
Water Penetration	No infiltration at 15 psf
Structural Test Pressure	No deformation @ 90 psf
Air Infiltration	0.06 cfm @ 6.24 psf
Condensation Resistance Factor (CRF)	
Forced Entry Rating	Type A; Grade 40
Sound Transmission Class (STC)	44
OITC	30

Lifecycle Properties

Warranty Duration	15 Years on Glass / 20 Years on All Other Components
Maintenance Schedule	Inspect and Oil Actualtion Hardware Annually
Installation Phase	Exterior Enclosure
Expected Lifespan	25 Years

FIGURE 11.3 Tabular specifications

leveraged to determine its suitability. Attribute and value pairs lend themselves to analysis, as the information is easily sorted, filtered, and organized. When an entire project is documented in this fashion, it becomes easy to analyze the information for code compliance or energy modeling.

In many ways, a tabular specification is very similar to a submittal sheet or manufacturer's data sheet, except that it follows a standard format accepted by the industry. There is nothing to say that the tabular specification could not be used to create a standardized submittal sheet, as many submittal sheets already contain product performance information listed in a table somewhere on the page. If we were to adopt a standardized submittal sheet that carries all of the information relevant to a specific component that is necessary to select one product over another, individuals attempting to parse through submittal packages manually would always know where to look for the information regarding specific attributes. A standardized submittal document, as we see in Figure 11.4,

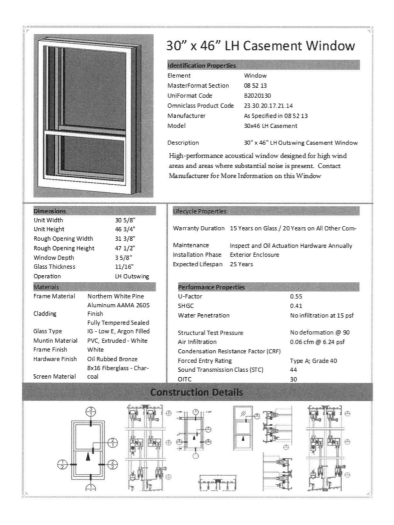

FIGURE 11.4
Standardized submittal document

would always have an image of the product in the same location on the page, product performance in the same location on the page, as well as other relevant aspects of the product that the design team deems necessary to determine which product they are selecting. Taking it a step further, in addition to standardizing the individual submittal sheet, an entire bid package could be standardized such that the whole series of submittals requested are in a specific order and a specific format.

The digital owner's manual is about as robust a deliverable as one could hope for. The idea of the digital owner's manual is to provide a true as-built model of the entire facility, which has been documented from the first day of design through the last day of construction. It allows the owner to see where every component is in a project, regardless of whether it is visible or buried in the ceiling. A fully dimensioned and fully attributed owner's manual can prove to be extremely helpful, especially when things go wrong. If a problem arises with the electrical system in a building and a finished wall must be opened up to fix the issue, a digital owner's manual can locate exactly where the problem lies and minimize the amount of demolition necessary to correct the problem. The digital owner's manual may also become a living database where information about maintenance is stored for analysis. A model such as this carries the ability to document dates and locations of maintenance procedures and to provide reports that dictate when maintenance and replacement should occur. This is the type of information that could turn a digital owner's manual into a working facilities management database.

Plenty of commercially available facility management databases can consider the operation and maintenance of the facility. None of them has the ability to provide a graphic interface that is as accurate as the actual model used to create the facility. The model carries not only the attributes that reside in a facility management database, but the graphics that dictate where each component is. This can open the door for the creation of a very powerful tool: using the BIM as a graphic user interface for building systems control, as well as security, access, and detection. If cameras throughout a facility were integrated into a BIM alongside security systems, in the event of unauthorized access, a facility manager or member of the security team could automatically see notification of a threat as well as visual confirmation through the integrated camera system. This could also work in reverse—detention facilities could monitor an entire prison facility using a three-dimensional user interface that can track locations of individuals throughout the facility as well as the status of each electronically controlled passageway.

Building information modeling and the growth of knowledge management certainly offers a considerable number of opportunities for advancement of construction documentation. Don't be surprised to see new standards and formats that apply to model analysis during design, specific information about subcontractor trades, enhanced schedules and more of them, new documentation formats that apply to project execution, and more emphasis on facility management.

CHAPTER 12

BIM Data and Specifications

CHANGING SPECIFICATION PRACTICE

Throughout time, specification has played an integral role in construction. It documents the products, processes, and procedures necessary to create an element found in the built environment, be it a building, a tower, or a bridge. The role of the specifier entails not only the creation of construction documents, but also the act of selecting the appropriate products and systems for a given set of circumstances. The sheer number of product and system possibilities makes the concept of specification a critical element within the design and construction process. This intuition makes replacing the specifier with building information modeling (BIM) impossible for the foreseeable future.

A specifier is responsible for determining which products and systems to implement in a project, and should be able to convey not only which components are used, but why they were chosen. In most cases, there are several options available for any given product or system. Some solutions are better than others, based on the location of the project, environmental conditions, local building codes, available options, and performance. Determining which product to use is largely achieved by weighing the performance and cost benefit of each product and determining the most effective option for the owner.

Building information modeling opens a new door that can allow a specifier to qualify products side by side and determine which meet the criteria necessary to select it. The ability for BIM to allow this to happen is contingent on not only the data actually being in the model, but the attributes having a consistent naming convention and a standardized set of formats that can be used to organize the information. Currently, CSI MasterFormat® and UniFormat™ are the two most common methods for organizing construction information, but they do not organize information at a level deep enough to consider the attributes necessary for product selection and qualification. The OmniClass tables can potentially fill this void. Specifically, the *Properties, Materials,* and *Products* tables can have the most benefit to the specifier, as they can effectively categorize the products, materials, and attributes associated with the work that is being performed on a project.

STANDARDS AND FORMATS FOR BIM

A BIM project is a database of information about not just spaces and dimensions, but attributed information about actual elements and systems. Unlike traditional CAD-designed projects, BIM projects have a unique ability to carry information about the products and systems implemented in the project. Provided the data are available, the model can know everything from the composition of each type of wall to the exact type and performance of windows to be installed, down to specific physical properties of paints and coatings. The database can be as small or as large as the modeler sees fit for the project at hand, or for a specific workflow process. When information that categorizes actual products based on performance and physical characteristics is added, it allows for powerful model analysis and exporting of information to streamline final documentation. Having information available in the model is a benefit to all parties involved.

Standards and formats are what drive the ability of the data to be useful outside of the BIM project file. If the data are not organized in such a way that they can later be retrieved, then they have little use to the specification, construction, or project management teams. Using standards and formats that already exist will allow information to be used at the project level, but do not allow for qualification of products and systems at their basic product and material levels. Leveraging new and different formats is necessary to accomplish this.

MasterFormat® for BIM

MasterFormat® is the most common method of organizing building information. It is the most widely used format and is built into most BIM software. MasterFormat® allows the design team to keep track of the work results of the project and organize them in such a fashion that the specifier can automatically know which sections are necessary for the project manual. After all elements are placed within a BIM, a report can be run that organizes the data based on its MasterFormat® number. This can simplify the creation of the project manual considerably by providing the specifier with a single report carrying all of the products that require documentation for each given section.

Because MasterFormat® organizes information based on work results, certain elements are more difficult to consider and organize within a BIM project. Building systems such as walls, floor/ceiling construction, and roof systems are excellent examples of this. Within a BIM, these types of components are placed as a whole, not as their individual parts, so an 8-inch metal framed wall with interior and exterior wall sheathing, air barrier, interior paint, and EIFS will have information in several MasterFormat® sections. It is important to be able to view these components both as a whole and as their individual components.

UniFormat™ for BIM

UniFormat™ groups information in terms of element classification, be it a wall, a window, a chair, or a heating, ventilating, and air conditioning system. Components are grouped together as they are installed. UniFormat™ is most widely used as a cost-estimation tool, and allows quick square-foot costing as well as specific information applicable to different options of materials and components. Tagging BIM components with UniFormat™ codes allows the information to be leveraged by the contractor and owner after the model is completed, and the data are made available.

OmniClass for BIM

OmniClass is a series of tables used for classifying information. UniFormat™ and MasterFormat® are two of the tables found in the series, but the information drills into a much deeper level to not just classify, but quantify and qualify specific elements, systems, and processes involved with construction. The tables apply to different aspects of the BIM based on the level of information in the model. Because of this grouping, it is a very effective method of categorizing complex components that contain multiple products and materials, such as walls, roofs, floors, and ceilings in a BIM project. The following are the

OmniClass tables existing at the time of publication. Those tables in bold type are currently being used within Building Information Modeling today.

- Table 11 – Construction Entities by Function
- Table 12 – Construction Entities by Form
- Table 13 – Spaces by Function
- Table 14 – Spaces by Form
- **Table 21 – Elements (UniFormat™)**
- **Table 22 – Work Results (MasterFormat®)**
- **Table 23 – Products**
- Table 31 – Phases
- Table 32 – Services
- Table 33 – Disciplines
- Table 34 – Organizational Roles
- Table 35 – Tools
- Table 36 – Information
- **Table 41 – Materials**
- **Table 49 – Properties**

OmniClass Table 23 – Products, is the most commonly used table, and effectively organizes not by work result or element, but by the actual product being installed. In terms of BIM, it is a tremendously effective way to find and organize products to make the model very searchable. It organizes products into logical categories and, as with similar formats, is hierarchical, making it easy to navigate.

ORGANIZING BIM DATA

The specifier has the opportunity to become the keeper of information within a project. He can act as not only the individual who inserts the information into the model, but the one who leverages it for model analysis, updates it as actual products are determined, and organizes it into tabular outputs, such as schedules and tables and, ultimately, a text specification. While the information contained in all three parts of a specification is not contained in the BIM component, it is appropriate for it to contain the information relevant to the products within the model. Thus, the component serves two purposes: it allows active product selection and analysis, and it contains the information necessary to create the part 2 "Products" section of a construction specification.

BIM data are found at all levels of the project, from raw materials to the geographic location of the project. The information is organized using a series of standard tables, and is hierarchical and thus scalable to suit the project requirements. While usually not necessary, the hierarchy can start with the organization of materials into solids, liquids, or gases. Typically, the information is categorized beginning with basic furnished materials, such as "cherry wood," "⅝" type X gypsum wallboard," or "type III roofing asphalt."

Element and work results are used together to classify information and are not mutually exclusive or inclusive. Element B2010.05 41 00 – *Exterior Metal Framed Wall Construction* considers the framing and sheathing, but not the insulation or finishes. Work Result 05 41 00 – *Structural Metal Stud Framing* considers only the framing members. This can make classifying a wall within a BIM a bit confusing. Because every component involved with the wall, from the interior finish to the exterior finish, is placed as a single unit, multiple methods of organization must be implemented to categorize each material. Organizing information beginning at the material level, followed by the furnished material, element/work result, and project levels allows data to be found quickly and easily. Depending on the scope and size of a project, additional levels of detail can be added to organize the information.

- Project (Result)
- Element (Component)
- Work Result (Finished Product or System)
  - Furnished Material (Building Material)
    - Material (Raw Material)

With this type of hierarchy, a material can be tied to a component that is used for a specific work result or within a specific element. Gypsum board may be used on either a ceiling or a wall: one product, two work results, and two elements. For costing purposes if we are trying to find the amount of wallboard on a project, we can query the square-foot area based on the material rather than the element. For specification purposes, we can sort the information based on work result to find in which sections wallboard is found.

At each level, projects, elements, work results, and materials carry applicable information. Just as a specifier understands where to look in a specification for the information, a clear understanding of where to look for information within a model is essential. When looking for thermal performance information about the insulation within a wall cavity, the insulation material carries the data, not the wall. If you are looking for the thermal value of the entire wall system, the wall carries it. When looking for the location of the wall in relation to other walls and spaces, the project carries it.

Here are some examples of a hierarchy at various levels of detail using one or more OmniClass tables.

Material Organization
Material: Cherry Wood, S4S, Polyurethane Finish
- Material class: Wood – OmniClass 41-30 30 14
  - Type: Cherry – OmniClass 41-30 30 14 11 14 21
    - Surfacing – S4S – OmniClass Table 49 – *Properties*
    - Finish: Polyurethane – OmniClass Table 49 – *Properties*
    - Certification: FSC certified – OmniClass Table 49 – *Properties*

Material: Roofing Asphalt, Type III
- Material class: Bituminous Minerals – OmniClass 41-30 10 21
  - Type: Asphalt – OmniClass 41-30 10 21 11 11
    - Usage: Roofing asphalt – OmniClass 23-20 10 11 17
    - Classification: Type III – OmniClass Table 49 – *Properties*

Material: Interior Latex Paint, Eggshell Finish, White
- Material class: Applied coatings – OmniClass 23-35 90 00
  - Type: Latex paint – OmniClass 23-35 90 11 11 14
    - Finish: Eggshell – OmniClass 23-20 10 11 17
    - Color: White – OmniClass Table 49 – *Properties*

Element Organization
Element: B2020.08 51 13 – Aluminum Windows
- Component 1: 36 × 48 Aluminum Casement Window, White – MasterFormat 08 51 13
  - Usage: Window – OmniClass 23-30 20 00
  - Type: Casement – OmniClass 23-30 20 17 21 14
  - Width: 36" – OmniClass Table 49 – *Properties*
  - Height: 48" – OmniClass Table 49 – *Properties*
  - Finish: White – OmniClass Table 49 – *Properties*

- Operation: Outswing – OmniClass Table 49 – *Properties*
  - Handing: LH – OmniClass Table 49 – *Properties*
  - Glazing: Insulated, tempered – OmniClass Table 49 – *Properties*
  - SHGC: .30 – OmniClass Table 49 – *Properties*
  - U-value: .30 – OmniClass Table 49 – *Properties*
- Component 2: 24 × 36 Aluminum double-hung window, white – MasterFormat® 08 51 13
  - Usage: Window – OmniClass 23-30 20 00
  - Type: Double-hung – OmniClass 23-30 20 17 17 14
  - Width: 24" – OmniClass Table 49 – *Properties*
  - Height: 36" – OmniClass Table 49 – *Properties*
  - Finish: White – OmniClass Table 49 – *Properties*
  - Operation: Outswing – OmniClass Table 49 – *Properties*
  - Glazing: Insulated, laminated – OmniClass Table 49 – *Properties*
  - SHGC: .33 – OmniClass Table 49 – *Properties*
  - U-value: .33 – OmniClass Table 49 – *Properties*
- Component 3: 6" Butyl window flashing – MasterFormat® 07 25 00
  - Usage: Window installation accessory – OmniClass 23-35 05 17
  - Type: Flexible flashing – OmniClass 23-35 05 17 21
  - Width: 6" – OmniClass Table 49 – *Properties*
  - Attachment: Self-adhering – OmniClass Table 49 – *Properties*

Element: B3010.07 54 00 – **Thermoplastic Membrane Roofing**

- Component 1: .045" TPO Roofing Membrane, White – MasterFormat® 07 54 00
  - Usage: Roof covering – OmniClass 23-35 20 21 11 14
  - Type: TPO – OmniClass 23-35 20 21 11 14 17
  - Thickness: 0.045" – OmniClass Table 49 – *Properties*
  - Width: 120" – OmniClass Table 49 – *Properties*
  - Finish: White
- Component 2: Synthetic, Water-based, Low VOC TPO Adhesive – MasterFormat® 07 54 00
  - Usage: Adhesive – OmniClass 23-20 40 17
  - Type: Water-based – OmniClass 23-20 40 17 14
  - VOC: <250 g/L – OmniClass Table 49 – *Properties*

- Component 3: Insulation Fasteners and Plates – MasterFormat® 07 22 16
  - Usage: Mechanical fasteners – OmniClass 23-20 40 11
  - Type: Insulation screws – OmniClass 23-20 40 11 14 24
- Component 4: 3" Rigid polyisocyanurate roof insulation – Master-Format 07 22 16
  - Usage: Thermal insulation – OmniClass 23-20 50 24
  - Type: Polyisocyanurate – OmniClass 23-20 50 24 24
  - Thickness: 3" – OmniClass Table 49 – *Properties*
  - Thermal resistance: R-8.1 – OmniClass Table 49 – *Properties*
  - Compressive strength: 25 psi – OmniClass Table 49 – *Properties*

Element: C3010.06 46 00 – Wall Trim and Decoration

- Component 1: 1" × 4" Colonial Window Moldings – Cherry Wood, S4S, Polyurethane Finish – MasterFormat® 06 46 13
  - Usage: Window molding – OmniClass 23-35 10 34 17
  - Type: Cherry – OmniClass 41-30 30 14 11 14 21
  - Breadth: 1" – OmniClass Table 49 – *Properties*
  - Depth: 4" – OmniClass Table 49 – *Properties*
  - Pattern: Colonial – OmniClass Table 49 – *Properties*
  - Surfacing: S4S – OmniClass Table 49 – *Properties*
  - Finish: Polyurethane – OmniClass Table 49 – *Properties*
- Component 2: 1" × 2" Fluted chair rail – Cherry Wood, S4S, Polyurethane Finish – MasterFormat® 06 46 13
  - Usage: Chair rail – OmniClass 23-35 10 34 17
  - Type: Cherry – OmniClass 41-30 30 14 11 14 21
  - Depth: 1" – OmniClass Table 49 – *Properties*
  - Height: 2" – OmniClass Table 49 – *Properties*
  - Pattern: Fluted – OmniClass Table 49 – *Properties*
  - Surfacing: S4S – OmniClass Table 49 – *Properties*
  - Finish: Polyurethane – OmniClass Table 49 – *Properties*
- Component 3: ¾" × 6" Base moldings – pine wood, S4S, prime painted – MasterFormat® 06 46 19
  - Usage: Base molding – OmniClass 23-35 10 34 17
  - Type: Pine – OmniClass 41-30 30 14 11 11 11
  - Depth: 1¼" – OmniClass Table 49 – *Properties*
  - Height: 6" – OmniClass Table 49 – *Properties*

- Pattern: Shaker – OmniClass Table 49 – *Properties*
- Surfacing: S4S – OmniClass Table 49 – *Properties*
- Finish: Prime painted – OmniClass Table 49 – *Properties*

Work Result Organization
Work Result: 06 46 13 – Wood Window Casings

- Component 1: 1" × 4" Colonial Window Moldings – Cherry Wood, S4S, Polyurethane Finish
  - Usage: Window molding – OmniClass 23-35 10 34 17
  - Type: Cherry – OmniClass 41-30 30 14 11 14 21
  - Breadth: 1" – OmniClass Table 49 – *Properties*
  - Depth: 4" – OmniClass Table 49 – *Properties*
  - Pattern: Colonial – OmniClass Table 49 – *Properties*
  - Surfacing: S4S – OmniClass Table 49 – *Properties*
  - Finish: Polyurethane – OmniClass Table 49 – *Properties*

Work Result: 06 46 19 – Wood Base Moldings

- Component 3: ¾" × 6" Base moldings – pine wood, S4S, prime painted
  - Usage: Base molding – OmniClass 23-35 10 34 17
  - Type: Pine – OmniClass 41-30 30 14 11 11 11
  - Depth: 1¼" – OmniClass Table 49 – *Properties*
  - Height: 6" – OmniClass Table 49 – *Properties*
  - Pattern: Shaker – OmniClass Table 49 – *Properties*
  - Surfacing: S4S – OmniClass Table 49 – *Properties*
  - Finish: Prime painted – OmniClass Table 49 – *Properties*

Work Result: 06 46 23 – Wood Chair Rails

- Component 2: 1" × 2" Fluted Chair Rail – Cherry Wood, S4S, Polyurethane Finish – MasterFormat® 06 46 13
  - Usage: Chair rail – OmniClass 23-35 10 34 17
  - Type: Cherry – OmniClass 41-30 30 14 11 14 21
  - Depth: 1" – OmniClass Table 49 – *Properties*
  - Height: 2" – OmniClass Table 49 – *Properties*
  - Pattern: Fluted – OmniClass Table 49 – *Properties*
  - Surfacing: S4S – OmniClass Table 49 – *Properties*
  - Finish: Polyurethane – OmniClass Table 49 – *Properties*

Work Result: 07 22 16 – Roof Board Insulation

- Component 1: 3" Rigid Polyisocyanurate Roof Insulation
  - Usage: Roof insulation – OmniClass 23-20 50 24
  - Type: Polyisocyanurate – OmniClass 23-20 50 24 24
  - Thickness: 3" – OmniClass Table 49 – *Properties*
  - Thermal resistance: R-8.1 – OmniClass Table 49 – *Properties*
  - Compressive strength: 25psi – OmniClass Table 49 – *Properties*
- Component 2: Insulation Fasteners and Plates
  - Usage: Mechanical fasteners – OmniClass 23-20 40 11
  - Type: Roof insulation screws – OmniClass 23-20 40 11 14 24

Work Result: 07 25 00 – Weather Barriers

- Component 1: 6" Butyl Window Flashing
  - Usage: Window installation accessory – OmniClass 23-35 05 17
  - Type: Flexible flashing – OmniClass 23-35 05 17 21
  - Width: 6" – OmniClass Table 49 – *Properties*
  - Attachment: Self-adhering – OmniClass Table 49 – *Properties*

Work Result: 07 54 00 – Thermoplastic Membrane Roofing

- Component 1: .045" TPO Roofing Membrane, White
  - Usage: Roof covering – OmniClass 23-35 20 21 11 14
  - Type: TPO – OmniClass 23-35 20 21 11 14 17
  - Thickness: 0.045" – OmniClass Table 49 – *Properties*
  - Width: 120" – OmniClass Table 49 – *Properties*
  - Finish: White
- Component 2: Synthetic, Water Based, Low VOC TPO Adhesive
  - Usage: Adhesive – OmniClass 23-20 40 17
  - Type: Water-based – OmniClass 23-20 40 17 14
  - VOC: <250 g/L – OmniClass Table 49 – *Properties*

Work Result: 08 51 13 – Aluminum Windows

- Component 1: 36 × 48 Aluminum Casement Window, White
  - Usage: Window – OmniClass 23-30 20 00
  - Type: Casement – OmniClass 23-30 20 17 21 14
  - Width: 36" – OmniClass Table 49 – *Properties*
  - Height: 48" – OmniClass Table 49 – *Properties*

- Finish: White – OmniClass Table 49 – *Properties*
- Operation: Outswing – OmniClass Table 49 – *Properties*
- Handing: LH – OmniClass Table 49 – *Properties*
- Glazing: Insulated, tempered – OmniClass Table 49 – *Properties*
- SHGC: .30 – OmniClass Table 49 – *Properties*
- U-Value: .30 – OmniClass Table 49 – *Properties*
- Component 2: 24 × 36 Aluminum Double-hung Window, White
  - Usage: Window – OmniClass 23-30 20 00
  - Type: Double-hung – OmniClass 23-30 20 17 17 14
  - Width: 24" – OmniClass Table 49 – *Properties*
  - Height: 36" – OmniClass Table 49 – *Properties*
  - Finish: White – OmniClass Table 49 – *Properties*
  - Operation: Outswing – OmniClass Table 49 – *Properties*
  - Glazing: Insulated, laminated – OmniClass Table 49 – *Properties*
  - SHGC: .33 – OmniClass Table 49 – *Properties*
  - U-Value: .33 – OmniClass Table 49 – *Properties*

Now that the information has been classified and categorized, what does it all mean? The information can be organized and exported from a BIM based on UniFormat™, MasterFormat®, or OmniClass code, depending on who needs the information. The cost estimator may want a list of everything in the model categorized by UniFormat™ code. The final information for the project manual can be leveraged by organizing the information by MasterFormat® code, and a series of model queries can be performed based on OmniClass codes.

For LEED certification, if someone wanted to find how much FSC-certified wood was on the project, he could query the model based on OmniClass 41-30 30 14 – Wood and filter it by Property – Certification so only the FSC materials are counted.

For volatile organic compound (VOC) levels for paints and coatings when performing indoor air-quality studies, the information can found under OmniClass 23-35 90 00 – Applied Coatings, filtered by location, and sorted by VOC levels and covered areas.

PROCESS AUTOMATION

Construction specifications are integral to the construction practice. As long as there are projects that need to be built, specifications will exist in some form.

The role of the specification is to provide written documentation and affirmation of the exact processes required to complete a project. They provide the general information, product data, and installation requirements for various tasks that are performed during a project. While it is possible for all of this information to be embedded into BIM components, it is not practical. Elements of a specification that have no bearing on the graphical or analytical aspect of the components are better linked or associated with the model, rather than being a part of the model itself. Most of the information found in the individual elements of a BIM are found within Part 2 – *Products* in any given specification section.

Specifications are structured in a commonly accepted three-part format, which defines the General Requirements, Product Requirements, and Execution Requirements. The information is detailed but concise and ultimately is used as a contract document between a project owner and the contractor or contractors responsible for completing the project. Since the specification outlines the scope of work to be performed, it is an essential element in affirming that the work performed was in fact what was requested. This system of checks and balances minimizes the risk for conflicts or discrepancies and clarifies any information that would be too cumbersome or detailed to be added to drawing sheets.

Drawing sheets carry enough information to convey what an element of a building is, its size, and its relationship to adjacent elements. It typically does not go into detail about why an element was selected, the performance aspects of the element, or where the element came from. For instance, a detail showing the connection between a roof and a wall carries the general information about the type of wall, the different layers of the roof structure, and the dimensions associated with the connection. It will likely omit information on who manufactures the roof, specifics on the roof's performance, how long the roof is warranted, how to store the roofing materials prior to installation, installation procedures, and other information too detailed to add to drawing sheets.

All information that complements the information on drawing sheets needs to be stored in some form for easy access and retrieval. Regardless of whether the information is stored in a database or in a document, it needs to be easily understood in a consistent format, thus making the construction specification document an important and relevant document, regardless of whether the project is designed using a BIM platform, a CAD platform, or a drawing board.

THE EVOLVING ROLE OF THE SPECIFIER

Specifiers have an opportunity to increase their role and add responsibilities to their current charges within a project. On the surface, it seems as though the only task that a specifier performs is that of the spec writer, where, in actuality, he has the responsibility of ensuring that the correct type of component is used in certain circumstances. In the current process, the primary responsibility of the specifier is to provide a project manual to the architect. On a BIM project, the specifier has an opportunity to assist in product selection and implementation early in the project, allowing the architect and engineer more resources and time to develop a project from an aesthetic perspective.

Allowing the specifier direct access to a project during conception allows him to view and modify components that have already been placed in a model as well as proactively select the correct products before they are brought into a project. Product selection can be a tricky undertaking, as the selection of a component can affect the adjacent and surrounding components. Selecting and analyzing a product before placing it in a model can save a considerable amount of trial-and-error product selection scenarios. For instance, while the selection of a fire extinguisher cabinet may seem trivial and simplistic, the choice of a recessed, semi-recessed, or flush model based on location and wall depth are crucial. The type of window used in a project is based on many factors that must be considered. Location within a building can affect the type of glass used; the codes that govern a building's performance can affect the structural ratings and energy performance; operation method (awning, casement, double hung, etc.) can be affected by life safety considerations and owner preference.

Having a single individual who can maintain responsibility for this type of product selection on demand can streamline the architect's workflow. Morphing the specifier into a project information and product knowledge consultant creates a single point of responsibility for the information for which they are already responsible in the form of the project manual. Having this individual managing the information inside of a building information model ensures homogeneous information that is correct, consistent, and congruent. There is an assumption that drawings and specifications are supposed to complement one another. Since BIM connects construction drawings and project specifications to create a single project entity, that line becomes blurred to some degree. When information is placed in a BIM model, it becomes a data set that can be leveraged during the construction documentation phase. Ensuring that these data are correct early on simplifies creation of the project manual and minimizes inconsistencies and errors.

THE EVER-EVOLVING SPECIFICATION

BIM has two main parts: graphics and information. It is the responsibility of the architect to ensure that the graphics are correct and appropriate for construction, and the role of the specifier to ensure that the project information is correct on the behalf of the architect. It seems only natural then to place the responsibility of BIM information management in the hands of the specifier. Over the years, the tools of the specifier have improved—beginning with the pen and moving to the typewriter, followed by the word processor. Once again, the specifier is experiencing a process improvement, which inevitably leads him to the *database*.

Databases house the salient parts of a specification for easy and repetitive retrieval while maintaining the consistency of the final delivered specification. The *office master* is the most common example of this. Most specifiers and architects offices have guide specifications that are used over and over; to simplify the task of specification writing, this is a rudimentary but effective method of making a database of project information for reuse. The shortcoming of the office master is that it needs constant maintenance as products, building codes, and design requirements change over the years.

ARCAT SpecWizard, BSD SpecLink, and other similar online "guide specification" libraries allow for the simplified creation of project manuals on an individual basis by providing ready-to-use formatted specifications that can be easily implemented into projects based on required performance values, industry standards, or actual products. The most appropriate type to use is dependent on the project delivery method used on a given project. These online libraries are giving way to the concept of integrating the information from a BIM model with the project manual by providing a single database where product information is stored for multiple products. Where a specification and BIM object are sourced from the same location and driven by the same database, there is a level of consistency not easily attainable by other means.

The possibility exists to create a short-form or outline specification, a long-form specification, and a BIM component all using the same series of drop-downs. Rather than a printed document being the only deliverable of a specifier, consider just how critical the responsibility of selecting the most appropriate component for a given project is. If the ability to review and select products and systems for a project extended to formatting a BIM component based on the required performance and appearance characteristics, the final project documentation and specification would be simplified considerably.

The concept of a specification is to provide documentation of specific elements of a project. It expands upon *what* is selected to explain *why* it is used. If we think of a specification in terms of what it is designed to do, much of it is broken into pairs of *attribute* and *value*, where the attribute is the "what" and the *value* is the "why." This is the baseline concept for creating a specification from a database. Some examples of attribute and value pairs are

- Color: Green
- Length: 12 inches
- R-value: 19
- Tensile strength: 1000 ksi
- Warranty: Ten (10) Years

While not all aspects of a specification can be broken into these pairs, they can encompass most if not all of the critical aspects of product selection and implementation. The balance of the specification can be formatted through development of a preformatted guide specification—a form used for filling in the data.

CHANGING THE SPECIFIER'S WORKFLOW

With wholesale changes to the design and construction process come changes to the specifier's workflow. Changes should be looked at in terms of short-term pain for long-term gain. If someone takes the plunge into learning a new technology, he can position himself as unique in his ability to provide a service that few specifiers can offer: the ability to provide BIM integrated specification services. Historically, a specifier has held responsibility only during the construction documentation phase of a project. An enhanced role of information and documentation consultant throughout the project lifecycle can translate into additional responsibilities and increased revenue.

Certain tasks need to be performed, whether by the specifier or by a different party, to get the BIM from concept to facilities management while providing a model useful to the architect, contractor, facility manager, and owner. We can break down the project into two categories in which the specifier might add substantial value to the overall success of the project: prior to bid solicitation and post bid solicitation.

Prior to Bid Solicitation

Having the information necessary to determine which specific products will meet the design criteria is essential for model analysis to be performed during the design phase. Just as the aerospace industry creates digital prototypes of aircraft prior to construction, the building industry is beginning to develop the same capabilities. To analyze a project as a whole, whether for cost estimation, performance analysis, code compliance, or structural integrity, the information about every component needs to be correct and available. On a large scale, this can be a considerable amount of information to maintain, so the individual or individuals with the most knowledge and expertise on products and systems should be responsible for providing and maintaining the information. In addition to product knowledge, the ability to organize and categorize information effectively is essential. The specifier is basic to both of these areas, thus making him the ideal person for this undertaking.

During the design phase, the specifier can enhance his role to that of a consultant to the design team or knowledge manager responsible for the BIM data. To streamline the overall design process, the specifier can assist in specific areas, based on the timeline. When the specifier interviews an architect to determine the preliminary project description, he gets a sense of what the project scope and requirements are. During this interview, the specifier can determine the types of elements that need to be implemented in a project, the requirements that the owner may have, and the performance qualifications necessary for the products that are to be used. The information gathered should be enough to begin creating an outline specification and formatting BIM elements that can be implemented into a project. Whether by creating them first hand or using generic or manufacturer-supplied BIM components, the specifier can enter the attributes and values that are critical for the success of the elements in a given project prior to or during their being modeled into the project.

Based on the information gathered from the interview with the architect, the specifier may choose to create an outline specification, which is functionally a working document from which a final long-form specification section may be derived. As a project becomes more developed, the outline specification becomes more specific, allowing the outline to morph into the final specification by the time all project information has been attained and implemented. As the information about elements is received, decisions are made about specific components, and actual products are selected, the specifier may update the BIM components on his end and provide an updated set for the architect to use to amend the project.

Prior to bid, especially, the graphics and information in a BIM project are constantly changing as more design choices are made. Thus, the attributed information surrounding the changes must change as well. A qualified specifier can update the model throughout the project to maintain the most current information and allow accurate analysis of the BIM. Model analysis is only as accurate as the data provided. For an accurate portrayal of how much energy a building will consume, actual components need to be considered, since devices, fixtures, and fittings used in the project all have varying performance characteristics.

Long-form specifications are created based on the information that has been provided throughout the entire design process and exported from the BIM. Leveraging the accumulated information saves a considerable amount of time in research and organization. Another method that can be an even more efficient is to develop outline specifications that can be scaled and amended as the project progresses—a working document with rolling changes. The final document would eventually carry all of the information and, with a few small revisions, can be organized into a final project manual.

While the specifier is probably not proficient in the use of a BIM platform, there is an opportunity for him to add value to the project prior to bid. Whether he chooses to become proficient or to hire a proficient individual in his firm to act as a BIM data modeler, value is added to the overall project. The concept is not for the specifier to actually create the graphics associated with the product or system in question, but to be capable enough to manipulate an existing BIM object to suit the needs of the project.

Post-Bid Solicitation
Active Specification and Product Analysis
The information included in the BIM can streamline bid review by allowing active specification and product analysis. During bid review, a copy of the model can be used as a "control" from which the proposals of competitive bidders can be analyzed for suitability. The data from the bidder's models can be compared with the control data line by line to quickly weed out inferior or otherwise unsuitable products. In addition to the architect's ability to select products based on the model data, a contractor can use the same process to select subcontractors based on the products he is proposing, costs for the work, and amount of time allotted for the project.

The ability to analyze bids this way can minimize both the time and effort required to process bids. In addition, there is a potential to allow bidding to happen in a rolling fashion, rather than all at once on "fast-track" projects where portions of the work are bid and performed at different times. The specifier can become involved during bid review by preparing the information about actual products from competitive manufacturers' products and prepare apples-to-apples product comparisons.

From this table, we see that the important aspects of the windows for the project are appropriate U-value and solar heat gain coefficient (SHGC),

Table 12.1   Product comparison—windows

Manufacturer	Element	U-value	SHGC	HVHZ approved	Cost
Basis of design	30 × 46 Casement window	.30	.30	Yes	$400.00
Manufacturer A	30 × 46 Casement window	.27	.30	No	$355.00
Manufacturer B	30 × 46 Casement window	.35	.46	No	$265.00
Manufacturer C	30 × 46 Casement window	.27	.29	Yes	$410.00
Manufacturer D	30 × 46 Casement window	.30	.30	Yes	$380.00

high-velocity hurricane zone (HVHZ) approval, and a maximum cost of $400.00. The values that meet the design requirements are noted in bold type.

The *basis of design* carries the specified values, and manufacturers provide their information either in the form of data that the design team enters themselves or by providing BIM components representing not just the graphics of their products, but the associated data necessary to make accurate product comparisons—in this case U-value, SHGC, and HVHZ. Cost is typically a value added independent of the component, as prices change constantly and vary by location due to shipping and other factors. Cost information is best attained at the time of bidding and entered during specific comparisons after all design criteria have been considered. For example,

- Manufacturer A has an acceptable U-value and SHGC, but is not HVHZ approved.
- Manufacturer B has inferior U-value and SHGC, and is not HVHZ approved.
- Manufacturer C has acceptable U-value and SHGC, and is approved for HVHZ.
- Manufacturer D has acceptable U-value and SHGC, and is approved for HVHZ.

Based on design criteria, manufacturers C and D should be considered for supplying products, since they meet all design criteria. Adding cost information to the products and closer analysis of the data reveals that manufacturer C is slightly more expensive than the requirement, but also has a better performance record. Manufacturer D has acceptable values in all categories. Choosing between manufacturers C and D can be further analyzed by looking at the model as a whole, and calculating the potential energy savings of the more efficient windows against the price differential between products.

The use of a BIM to analyze this type of specification information can save a considerable amount of time and make it possible to look at performance aspects of the building as a whole to study the impact that a single product may have on the entire project.

Element Updating

Once all of the bids have been awarded and products have been selected, an optional service of updating the model has the potential for further involvement. Even after the design is completed, all bids are awarded, and construction is underway, the project will likely receive change orders and alternate products. As changes are made and products are substituted, the specifier can analyze these product changes, affirm their conformance with design criteria and intent, and, again, prepare models the design team can use to amend the model.

While this level of post design detail may provide no benefit to the specifier or design team, the owner may be willing to pay a premium to receive an *as-built* model of the project for future analysis. An as-built model can allow a facility manager to schedule maintenance and replacement based on product lifecycle and recommendations from the product manufacturers. It can also allow for budgeting of the same considerations. A BIM that carries all of the actual information about an entire building from the dimensions and locations to the performance and usage characteristics to the lifespan and cost information of every component is tantamount to a digital owner's manual of the entire project.

CONCLUSIONS

Since BIM is very much in its infancy, most architects are only scratching its surface. It is primarily being used as a 3D modeling tool to speed up the design process, but the data that can be captured and manipulated are not being used. Much of this is due to a disconnect between the BIM and the specifier. Currently, the specifier holds no role in the development of a BIM model, and is left out of any integrated project coordination that may occur. By bringing the specifier into the BIM model and allowing him to specify systems and products for the project, the data that are missed within the project can be provided and maintained by the specifier for the design team, contractors, facility managers, and owners. Essentially, the specifier has the opportunity to take on an additional role, which will benefit not just the design professionals, but anyone who may set foot in the finished building.

Currently, during the design process, most BIM projects are developed with generic products and systems rather than manufacturer-specific components that carry data about an individual product's performance, lifecycle, impact, and efficiency. It is too cost and time prohibitive to require a design professional to update an entire project with manufacturer-specific components after the design has been completed. If the specifier has the opportunity to specify through the BIM model in real time, products and systems can be specified earlier in the design phase and potentially streamline the bidding process by setting available and visible performance standards in real time.

First and foremost, the specifier needs to understand what BIM means to the built environment and the benefits BIM brings to his business and current workflow. Once the concepts of what it is designed for and, more importantly, what it is capable of doing are understood, there is no reason not to make this change and take the leap into the brave new world of building information modeling.

PART III

BIM Content Types

CHAPTER 13

Walls

ANATOMY

Walls are assemblies comprising multiple products or materials that work together to act as partitions within an interior space or enclosures of the building. Countless combinations of wall types can be created and used within projects. There are, however, basic categories of walls that can be used to organize the information based on the specific components used in a wall. Framed walls are those that have some type of structural member, typically a wood or metal stud, that is wrapped with interior and exterior sheathing and contains interior and exterior finishes. Cavity walls, just as the name implies, have an airspace or cavity between the exterior cladding and exterior sheathing. This is typically used in masonry construction to allow any accumulated moisture to flow down a wall and out of the building before it penetrates the interior wall. I use the term monolithic wall to describe a wall whose structure is solid throughout. This may be something of a misnomer, as it does include concrete masonry units that have a cavity, which may or may not be filled.

Nevertheless, the term monolithic is used to describe the overall structural aspect of the wall, not the individual material or component.

Within a well-developed wall, each component should be called out to its exactly specified product or type. Each component in a wall carries its own set of information and often is used for specific reason. If we think about the openings that go into a wall and how they must be handled in terms of framing and flashings, we see that certain products can only be used with certain wall types, and that many manufacturers of products have required substrates or surfaces on which their products may be applied.

Walls must have some type of structural component that allows them to stand up. Whether it is cast-in-place concrete, 2 × 4 wood studs, or dry stacked stone, the structural component is the core element within a wall. Because this component is structural in nature, it has physical properties that should be taken into consideration within the model to allow structural analysis to be performed in order for appropriate documentation to be created. For cast-in-place concrete we must consider, among other things, its compressive strength and reinforcement type and location, as well as wall height, length, and thickness. Wood- and steel-framed walls are designed based on the spacing of the framing member and wall height, thickness, and length. These aspects take into consideration the structural aspects of a wall as a whole with no openings. Headers must be placed in locations where openings occur in walls to support the load from above, but this is considered using not typical wall tools but structural components that we discuss later in this book.

Sheathing, whether used for interior or exterior purposes, is designed to act as a covering over structural components and provide a surface on which to apply final finishes. The most widely used interior finish is gypsum wallboard.

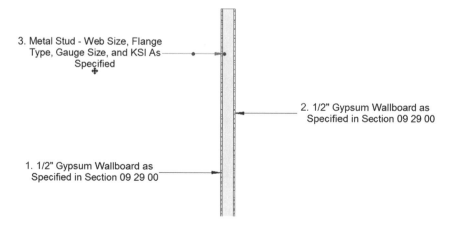

FIGURE 13.1 Typical framed wall construction: 1- exterior wall sheathing; 2- interior wall sheathing; 3- structural framing.

3. Metal Stud - Web Size, Flange Type, Gauge Size, and KSI As Specified

2. 1/2" Gypsum Wallboard as Specified in Section 09 29 00

1. 1/2" Gypsum Wallboard as Specified in Section 09 29 00

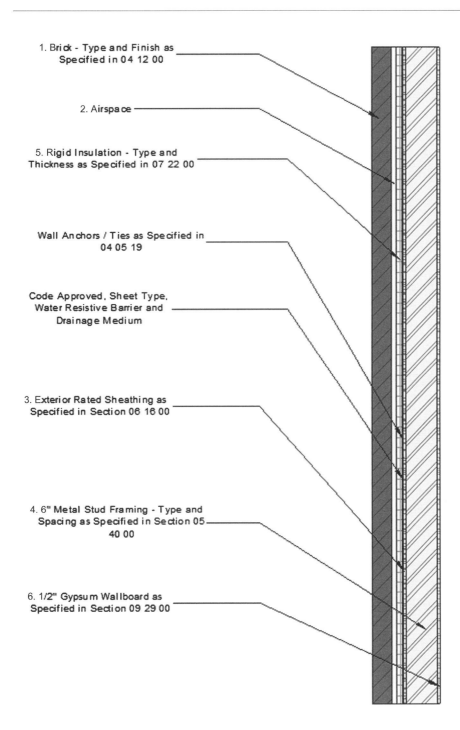

1. Brick - Type and Finish as Specified in 04 12 00

2. Airspace

5. Rigid Insulation - Type and Thickness as Specified in 07 22 00

Wall Anchors / Ties as Specified in 04 05 19

Code Approved, Sheet Type, Water Resistive Barrier and Drainage Medium

3. Exterior Rated Sheathing as Specified in Section 06 16 00

4. 6" Metal Stud Framing - Type and Spacing as Specified in Section 05 40 00

6. 1/2" Gypsum Wallboard as Specified in Section 09 29 00

FIGURE 13.2 Typical cavity wall construction: 1- exterior wall finish; 2- airspace; 3- exterior wall sheathing; 4- structural component; 5- insulation; 6- interior wall sheathing

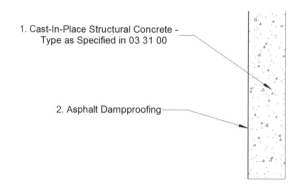

1. Cast-In-Place Structural Concrete -
Type as Specified in 03 31 00

2. Asphalt Dampproofing

FIGURE 13.3

Typical monolithic
wall construction:
1- exterior wall finish;
2- waterproofing/
dampproofing

Because of its somewhat noncombustible nature, it is an easy to install, fire-resistant finish that can accept nearly any final finish product, from paint to wallpaper to tile. In many cases it is also used to provide enhanced fire ratings or moisture protection, in the case of fire-resistant or moisture-resistant gypsum wallboard. Plywood or oriented strand board are two of the most commonly used exterior sheathing types. Gypsum and fiberglass-based sheathing products are also available, but all of these materials really serve the same purpose—to cover the exterior of the building before its final finish is installed.

CONSIDERATIONS

Because walls are material-driven, creating the callouts within the materials is an important aspect of the walls. While the wall will have its own callout, the relevance is diminished by the callouts for the individual components. Wall sections are used in contract and construction drawings, so the assemblies should be able to contain each component and note its nominal thickness, and be able to be implemented into drawing sheets in the form of section views of the assembly, transitions, and terminations. Not every last detail is found in the overall assembly, as the assembly pertains only to the wall, not the conditions that may arise in the openings in the wall or where the wall meets and adjacent surface.

If we think about tile being placed onto a wall, we see that there is more to it than a surface and a piece of tile. Tile manufacturers may recommend or require the use of a water-resistant wallboard or cementitious backer board. Above the substrate, an adhesive is used to attach the tile, and grout is used between the tiles. Each of the materials used in the assembly should be clearly visible and, in many cases, in alternating colors so the user can visually distinguish between the layers. This is especially important when several thin layers are next to each other. With a wall assembly of this nature, only the face layers on either side of the wall are actually visible, so those are the only ones that need to have an exact rendering appearance.

Gypsum wallboard is a generic term describing a type of interior sheathing. In terms of design and specification, a ⅝-inch type X gypsum wallboard may be used in areas that need fire containment. A ½-inch water-resistant wallboard may be used in areas such as bathrooms that have a considerable amount of moisture, and ½-inch wallboard may be used in common areas throughout a building. Components in an assembly should be called out to their specifics, as in the real world. Gypsum wallboard is not a product, but ⅝-inch type X gypsum is.

Walls should be created based on logical configurations and how they are designed. They may need to achieve specific thermal or fire ratings or to have specific acoustical properties. This type of information should always be added to the assembly itself, and to the individual materials that make up the assembly as necessary. Using thermal resistance, or R-value, as an example, each component within the wall assembly has an R-value, as minimal as it may be. The insulation used in the wall assembly is what carries most of the R-value, but if we add the thermal resistance properties from all other components, we can aggregate the overall thermal resistance of the wall.

A critical aspect of assemblies such as walls is the ability to create section views and quickly annotate each component. Even if a component such as an air barrier is too thin to represent at its actual thickness, it should be noted at the minimum thickness that the software is capable of showing. The same holds true for components that may not cover the entire surface, but nevertheless are integral to the wall. Insulation fasteners on the outside of a wall and masonry wall ties are perfect examples of this. Rather than modeling each fastener that may be found on a wall, creating a wall layer that represents the fasteners or wall ties will allow the component to be annotated and the placement density to be listed. If fasteners are supposed to be spaced at the rate of one every 2 square feet and this is noted within the component material in the wall assembly, the approximate number of fasteners may be extrapolated by dividing the area of the wall by the fastener density.

When it comes to creating walls, the bottom line is that the assembly needs to be thought of as both a whole and a sum of its parts. Each material within the assembly should carry the pertinent information about the product, and the assembly as a whole should carry the pertinent information relevant to the performance of that assembly. Informational aspects of the wall that pertain to performance and building codes should always be accurate and never assumed. Assuming a fire rating on a wall that has not been tested leads to unreliable data and inaccurate information that could end up being used for code compliance. If somebody looking at the model finds one piece of incorrect information, he may find himself in a situation where all information must be considered incorrect.

GRAPHICS

Graphics for walls are mainly at the detailing level, providing appropriate surface and cut patterns to allow for good visual representation. Wall graphics are a function of the materials used to create the wall, so it is more important to create the graphics at the material level and use them to drive the appearance of the walls. The materials on the surface of a wall assembly are graphically the most important as they carry a rendering appearance as well as hatch patterns used on the surface and in section views. Because wall surfaces take up a considerable amount of area within a model, the image files used to create the rendering appearances should be as accurate and as large as possible. This minimizes the amount of tiling necessary to create the surface, and provides a visualization that appears more seamless and realistic.

Hatch patterns for cut and surface appearances are often dictated by the uniform drawings standard (UDS) and/or national CAD standard (NCS). Using appropriate patterns for the different types of materials allows each material to be reused over and over and cloned to create similar materials with little or no effort. Two types of hatch patterns may be used on a project: model patterns and detail patterns. Both are shown in Figure 13.4. The primary difference between these two is how they are used. A model pattern orients itself to the surface on which it is placed, so regardless of the angle at which it is viewed, it appears accurate in terms of its appearance in the real world. This is commonly used for surface patterns. Detail patterns orient themselves to the view in which they are placed, so as the view angle changes, the pattern orients itself differently. This is typically used for cut patterns in section views, as the angle of the view never changes.

For surface materials we need to consider the overall appearance of the product, including its color or color pattern, transparency, translucency or opacity, glossiness, reflectivity, and any surface texture it may contain. This is a considerable amount of information, and the accuracy of it should be based on the needs of the project or the intent of the model. If little or no rendering is necessary, then the materials themselves can be simplified so that no rendering appearance is developed. When a considerable amount of rendering is done in an office, developing a library of materials with high-quality rendering attributes

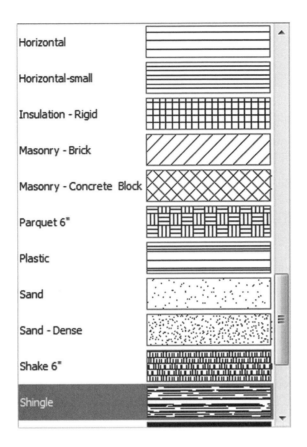

FIGURE 13.4 Model hatch patterns and detail hatch patterns

allows for more professional-looking renderings during project development. In many cases image files are a very practical way and sometimes the only way to develop the surface pattern necessary to convey materials. Figure 13.5 is an example of an image file used to convey the rendering appearance of brick, by tiling it over a surface. Instead of attempting to model every brick in a wall, adding a surface hatch pattern that somewhat resembles the appearance is acceptable for model view, followed by an image file with the brick size and shape, grout, and actual color for use in rendered views.

Walls behave differently within a model depending on how they are formatted. Above and beyond materials, they are layers within the assembly. In the real world, as two walls join, certain layers may wrap around corners, while others do not. If we take this into consideration when developing the wall assembly, little effort will be required when modeling a project to ensure that walls join appropriately. In the case of the typically framed wall with gypsum wallboard on either side, the wallboard is designed to wrap around corners, while the framing itself is not. In the case of a cast-in-place concrete wall with

FIGURE 13.5 Typical rendering image file

furring strips and gypsum wallboard on one side and asphalt waterproofing on the other, the asphalt waterproofing, concrete, and gypsum wallboard should be designed to wrap, whereas the furring strips do not wrap.

BIM software allows us to assign a purpose to each layer of an assembly, as well as note it as being a part of the core or outside of the core. Think of the core as the structural aspect of a wall. In terms of a common framed wall, it would consist of the framing members. In a cast-in-place concrete wall, it would be the concrete. This helps the software determine not only what the material is, but how it behaves in relation to adjacent components in the project as a whole.

Wall studs are placed a specific distance apart, insulation is placed between the studs, and fasteners are affixed to the assembly at a designated spacing or density. It is impractical to expect anyone to place every insulation fastener within a project in order to count the number necessary. Alternatively, we can add a material to the assembly called "fasteners," assign a specific fastening rate to it, and calculate the number of fasteners based on the areas in which the material is found.

MATERIALS

Just as with other assemblies, materials drive the appearance and behavior of the wall assembly. The two most graphically relevant layers of a wall are the interior and exterior face layers. As noted before, this is because they carry graphic relevance in rendered and three-dimensional views. Above and beyond the attributed data, attention should be given to the rendering aspect of these materials. Materials found in layers beneath the face layers are visible only in section views, so the most important aspect is the hatch pattern used to visually note what the material is and the color with which it is noted in the model.

More detailed assemblies may have upward of 20 layers within them, so using contrasting colors for each of the wall components assists in creating annotations in detail in section views. It is good practice to create a series of categories into which the wall layers fall. For instance, creating categories for structural components, thermal components, interior finish components, exterior finish components, and air and vapor barrier components allows organization and easy retrieval of materials that may need to be used later in the project. If a color is assigned to each category, or even a color range, the design team has a visual cue as to the type of components that are found in the wall. Making all insulation materials in shades of red, structural components in shades of gray, and air barriers in shades of green, is an example of this. The hatch pattern used on the individual material further details which material within a given category is being viewed. There is no prescribed standard that I am aware of for colorization of product categories. Developing one which works for your office is an acceptable solution, provided that everyone that is involved with the projects is aware of and proficient with using the color standard.

Tip

More detailed assemblies may have upward of 20 layers within them, so using contrasting colors for each of the wall components assists when creating annotations in detail in section views.

Each material within an assembly will carry the pertinent information about why it was selected for use in the assembly. Insulation will carry thermal resistance properties, interior finishes will carry appearance properties, and perhaps properties related to indoor air quality, air barriers have permeability properties associated with them, and structural components will carry strength properties. Even if there is no intention of the design team to perform any type of analysis, the presence of these properties allows the information to be extracted later on for documentation and facilities management purposes. Building information modeling is larger than any single project participant, so the information contained within it should apply to the project as a whole, rather than the professional who is involved with developing the model. Specifiers may want certain information in the model, while architects require

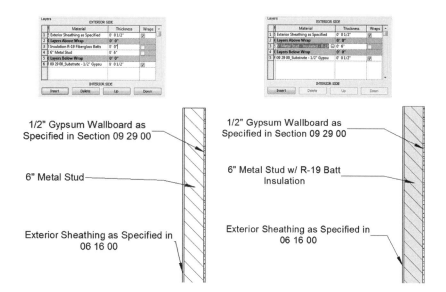

FIGURE 13.6 Two ways of representing materials within a wall assembly

1/2" Gypsum Wallboard as Specified in Section 09 29 00

6" Metal Stud

Exterior Sheathing as Specified in 06 16 00

1/2" Gypsum Wallboard as Specified in Section 09 29 00

6" Metal Stud w/ R-19 Batt Insulation

Exterior Sheathing as Specified in 06 16 00

other unrelated information. Engineers and contractors also involved in the project may have requirements for model information as well. Thinking about who the model is for, and what its purpose is, aids in understanding what type of information should be contained.

In certain instances two materials may align with each other within a single layer. Batt insulation often falls into the same layer as the framing members. A vertical cut view of a wall will show this. Figure 13.6 shows how one of two methods could be used to represent both of these layers within the project.

(1) By creating a layer that has no thickness, one of the two conflicting materials can be represented within the information of the assembly. While it will show up in schedules as being a part of the assembly, in section views, it is invisible, and as such cannot carry an automatically generated annotation.

(2) By merging two materials into one, both graphic and nongraphic information regarding two materials can be carried together. If we merge wall framing materials and thermal insulation materials into a single material, for example, we could create *4" metal studs – 16" O.C. w/ R-13 fiberglass batt insulation.*

DATA—ATTRIBUTES AND EQUATIONS

Below are a series of commonly used wall assembly attributes and wall material attributes. Obviously, this is not an all-inclusive list, but it contains some of the most important aspects that should be considered for any type of wall being created on a BIM project. It is important to carefully consider whether an attribute belongs within the wall, or within the material, as flooding a wall with information may cause more harm than good when trying to extract information back out from it. If we think in terms of an automobile, in which thousands of different components make up the vehicle, the information associated with each one is rightfully located with its respective components. If every performance aspect of each component within the vehicle were located in the owner's manual, it likely would not fit in the glove compartment, so the owner's manual carries information relevant to the vehicle and its performance as a whole, with supporting documentation available in various shop manuals regarding the individual components. This creates an information hierarchy that lets an individual drill in to the level of detail he is attempting to attain.

Wall Assembly Attributes

- *Fire rating*: A rating expressed in terms of class A, B, or C, which classifies how resistant to fire and flame spread a wall assembly is
- *Assembly R-value*: The thermal resistance of the entire wall assembly expressed in sq ft * F * H/BTU
- *Sound transmission classification (STC)*: A rating of how well a partition attenuates sound
- *Dew point*: The point within a wall where water vapor will condense into water
- *Wall usage*: Categorization of the wall into its purpose. (i.e., interior partiton, load bearing, sheer, foundation, retaining)

Wall Material Attributes

- *Compressive strength*: The maximum (or rated) strength that a material (typically concrete and masonry) can withstand when compressive force is applied
- *R-value*: The thermal resistance of a specific material expressed in sq ft * F * H/BTU
- *Permeability (perm) rating*: The amount of moisture (expressed in perms) that is allowed to pass through a building material
- *Grade*: The industry-accepted quality classification rating for a building material
- *Thickness*: The depth of the material or its required application
- *Color/finish*: The surface texture and appearance of a material

- *Application rate*: The rate at which a material is applied based on its commonly distributed unit (i.e., gallon, square foot, lineal foot)
- *Face value*: The area of each modular component used in a wall assembly (i.e., CMU, brick)

A few basic equations that may be used for quantity takeoff and estimation purposes are also noted below. With all estimation procedures, everybody has a different method, so equations act as guidelines from which to start, not hard and fast rules for calculation. Calculations for wall assemblies are typically created within a wall schedule and performed by operating on two or more number or dimensional values.

- Equations

  - *Fastener count/adhesive amount*: wall area/application rate
  - *Rebar/reinforcement length*: (wall length/rebar spacing) * wall height
  - *Common wall stud count*: (wall length/stud spacing) + 2 (I add 2 to the stud count of each wall to consider for blocking in corners)
  - *Unit count*: wall area/face value

Especially at the material level, some specific performance values apply to individual materials that may be used on a wall assembly. Paints and coatings may note the amount of volatile organic compounds (VOC) and solids

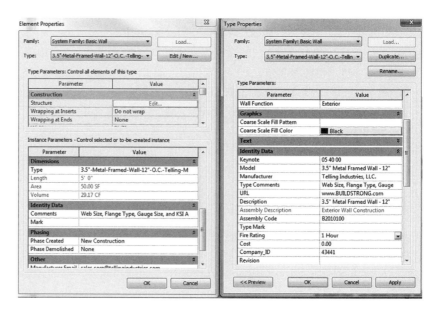

FIGURE 13.7 Typical wall assembly data set

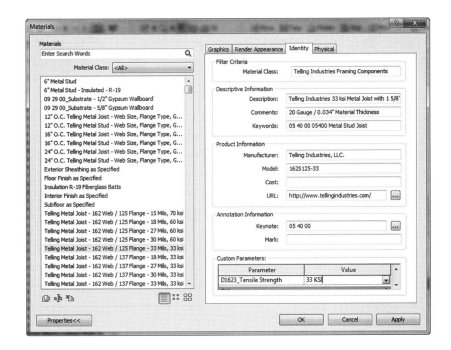

FIGURE 13.8   Typical wall material data set

content. The scratch resistance and frost resistance of a ceramic tile and the facer material of gypsum wallboard may be important attributes as well. In determining whether or not to put these types of attributes within the model, we should carefully think about why the attribute is relevant. If data are strictly for informational purposes, and not leveraged for model analysis, it is often far more practical to link back to a manufacturer's product information page on a website rather than embedding the information within a model. When adding an attribute to a material, it is important to note that the attribute will apply to all materials, so without filtering information in schedules, there is the ability to inadvertently add values to attributes that may not apply to specific materials.

When adding attributes that apply to specific materials, it is good practice to create a schedule for each material type in order to view the data; otherwise, the schedule itself may end up becoming very wide, with dozens of columns, many of which are empty in most rows.

USAGE—LEVERAGING THE INFORMATION

In today's BIM, probably the most common use for the information within a wall assembly is for quantity takeoff. Noted above are equations that can calculate quantities based on attributes built into individual components used in the assembly. Third-party software vendors are developing applications that can analyze many of these data for code compliance, energy modeling, structural performance, and a whole host of other potential analytics. If we look strictly at the abilities for quantity takeoff, simple equations based on the attributes added into the materials and assemblies can cut down the amount of time necessary to bid on a project, as baseline unit figures are available through the model, rather than requiring us to scan through hundreds of pages of drawing sheets.

Unique opportunities for contractors and subcontractors to become involved with the development of a BIM-based project are becoming evident. The growth of design-build firms today makes this obvious. If contractors and subcontractors are willing to become advisers to the architect or design team during schematic design or design development, they have the potential to provide the actual assemblies necessary for the design such that they can be located appropriately based on exact figures rather than assumed values. The more trades that work on a project, the more important this becomes, as structural components, HVAC ductwork, piping, and electrical requirements can all be considered when determining where and how to place partition walls, how deep the walls should be, and what fire ratings they should attain.

BIM has a very bright future in that the information housed within a model could be used by everyone from future designers to facility managers to city planners and even to first responders. Consider the possibility of firefighters having a device that can tell them what the critical path of egress might be in the event of a fire. The data from a building information model carries the fire rating of each wall, floor, and ceiling within a building. If that type of information were housed in a citywide first-responders database, firefighters, paramedics, and law enforcement could have a clear understanding of how to handle a situation based on their environment. I know this sounds like something out of a Hollywood blockbuster action movie, but, to me, this possibility is not as far off as it may seem.

On a slightly smaller scale, building information modeling already offers the ability to integrate building systems and control them through a single point of reference. If a fire alarm goes off, a building information model can locate and activate cameras and countermeasures. Electrical sensors and devices allow for control of temperature and lighting. Integrating this with a project model can add a three-dimensional user interface to the equation, where a facility manager or building engineer can potentially click on a room and change its temperature or lighting settings, or click on a camera to view activity within a space.

EXAMPLE WALL ASSEMBLIES AND THEIR ATTRIBUTE SETS

FIGURE 13.9

Typical interior wall assembly

- Fire rating: 90 minute
- Assembly R-value: 15
- Sound transmission classification (STC): 29
- Wall usage: interior partition
- Structure:
  - Side 1 finish: $5/8''$ type X gypsum wallboard
  - Structural element: $4''$ metal stud – $16''$ O.C.
  - Side 2 finish: $5/8''$ type X gypsum wallboard

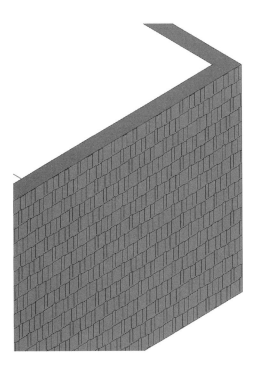

FIGURE 13.10

Typical exterior wall assembly

- Fire rating: 90 minute
- Assembly R-value: 22.5
- Sound transmission classification (STC): 35
- Dew point: $1.6''$ from exterior face
- Wall usage: exterior bearing wall
- Structure:
  - Interior finish: $1/2''$ gypsum wallboard
  - Structural element: $2 \times 6''$ SPF wood stud – $16''$ O.C. – insulated w/R-19 fiberglass batt
  - Exterior substrate: $1/2''$ CDX plywood
  - Air barrier: asphalt-saturated building paper – ASTM D226 type I
  - Exterior wall covering: wood shingle – $6''$ exposure #1 cedar perfections
  - Exterior finish: paint – latex flat – olive green

FIGURE 13.11

Typical foundation wall assembly

- Fire rating: 3 hour
- Assembly R-value: 14
- Sound transmission classification (STC): 42
- Dew point: 1″ from exterior face
- Wall usage: structural foundation
- Compressive strength: 4000 psi
- Structure:
  - Structural element: 8″ cast-in-place concrete – reinforced w/#5 rebar 48″ O.C.
  - Dampproofing: asphalt coating meeting ASTM D 449

CHAPTER 14

Roofs

ANATOMY

The roof of a building is an assembly of multiple components that work together to create a waterproofing or water-shedding system. The purpose of a roof is to deter or prohibit moisture from passing into the building at horizontal or near horizontal surfaces. In addition to the field covering of the roof, a roof system also contains components that consider how to inhibit moisture at penetrations through the roof and where terminations occur. There are two basic types of roof assemblies—low-slope roofs and steep-slope roofs—and the design and purpose of each are significantly different.

Rarely will we see a roof that is perfectly flat. Low-slope roofs typically carry a slope between ⅛ inch per foot and 3 inches per foot and are generally designed to be little more than a waterproofing element. They are not typically thought of as an aesthetic design element, so the overall appearance of the surface is diminished in terms of building information modeling. To create an effective low-slope roof assembly, we must consider all of the elements contained within in order to portray them in section views, which are commonly used to create flashing details. With low-slope roofing, the devil is in the details, as they say. This is why it is essential to create not just the roof surface, but the details at penetrations, terminations, and transitions between roofs and walls. These details are by-products of the section views that are cut through a roof and wall, or roof and penetration, and carry the annotations or callouts that note each component of the assembly in its proper location. Many of the components within an assembly are too thin to accurately portray as more than a line, but it is effective to note them at $1/16$ of an inch rather than omit them altogether.

BIM has the ability to accurately portray structural members, so the most effective way to create a low-slope roof is to create each layer of the assembly from the substrate, or roof deck, all the way to the surfacing or coating that covers the roof. Depending on the type of roof framing, the structural members may or may not be shown. Wood framing, for instance, is often included in the assembly to simplify the design process. Trusses and other heavy-gauge metal framing elements are often created beneath the roof so they can be used for structural analysis of the building. Figure 14-1 shows the basic anatomy of the different components found in a low-slope roof, and the order in which they are typically found from bottom to top.

When thinking about the anatomy a roof in terms of BIM, we must decide which components should be included and which should be omitted. Above and beyond the roof assembly itself there is series of penetrations, terminations, and transitions between roof and wall. Graphically, it may not be practical to represent each of these components in all cases. The level of accuracy in representing roof components may vary drastically based on the scope of the project and type of work being performed.

Hundreds of pipes may penetrate a roof, each of which will actually need to be waterproofed, but it is not practical to provide a flashing component for each and every one. Rather than flashing the individual pipe, the

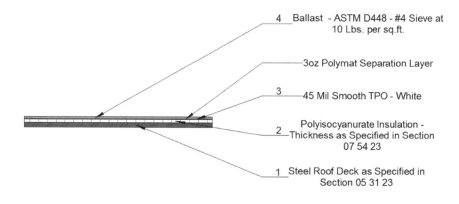

FIGURE 14.1 Anatomy of a low-slope roof: 1- deck/substrate; 2- insulation; 3- roof covering; 4- overburden/ballast/paver

4   Ballast - ASTM D448 - #4 Sieve at 10 Lbs. per sq.ft.

3oz Polymat Separation Layer

3   45 Mil Smooth TPO - White

2   Polyisocyanurate Insulation - Thickness as Specified in Section 07 54 23

1   Steel Roof Deck as Specified in Section 05 31 23

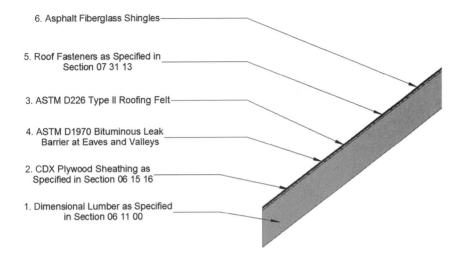

6. Asphalt Fiberglass Shingles

5. Roof Fasteners as Specified in
Section 07 31 13

3. ASTM D226 Type II Roofing Felt

4. ASTM D1970 Bituminous Leak
Barrier at Eaves and Valleys

2. CDX Plywood Sheathing as
Specified in Section 06 15 16

1. Dimensional Lumber as Specified
in Section 06 11 00

FIGURE 14.2 Anatomy of a steep slope roof: 1- structural members; 2- deck/substrate; 3- leak barrier; 4- underlayment; 5- fasteners; 6- roof covering

roof assembly itself could carry an attribute that points the user to a series of flashing details available from the manufacturer or the appropriate trade association. While the number of flashings around roof penetrations cannot be counted, the number of pipes penetrating the roof can be.

Roof-to-wall transitions, or base flashings, are often represented in models, as they are generally their own assembly specified by the manufacturer, and carry a large amount of material that should be considered during the estimation process. A base flashing may be made of the same materials as the roof membrane, or a set of specialized materials. Roof edge terminations, gravel stops, and gutters are also commonly represented. In many cases their visibility is why they are chosen to be modeled graphically, but their presence allows them to be counted. Both transitions and terminations are counted or expressed in terms of lineal footage, so they may easily be represented by a "line-driven" object that automatically counts the running length of the component.

CONSIDERATIONS

Roof assemblies are made up of multiple products that work together to provide a waterproof or water-shedding system for a building or other structure. Roofs can be broken into two primary categories, low slope and steep slope. Low slope is used to describe roofs with a slope that is less than 2 inches of rise for every 12 inches of run. Steep slope applies to roof slopes above 2 inches. Low-slope roofs have more to do with the thermal and waterproofing aspects of their design, while steep-slope roofs have more to do with aesthetics and appearance.

Low-Slope Roofs

A low-slope roof is primarily a waterproofing system made up of one or more waterproofing membranes attached to a substrate (roof deck). In many cases insulation is added to the system to provide thermal resistance, hindering warm air from escaping. In addition to the roof assembly, additional components or "flashings" are placed anywhere another component, such as a plumbing pipe or skylight, penetrates the roof.

Whether done graphically in the model, added to the 2D drawing sheets, or embedded as BIM data, properly conveying all aspects of a low-slope roof can ensure that it follows the design intent of the roof and minimize improper placement of roof penetrations. A low-slope roof is more than a sheet of rubber or plastic affixed to the top of the building. There are structural components (the deck), thermal components, (the insulation), and waterproofing components (the membrane), all working together to provide a thermal and waterproofing system. Just as a hat keeps our body heat from escaping in the winter, the insulation in a roof system stops heat from escaping through the top of the building.

One of the most important aspects of low-slope roofing is how it is attached. Attaching a low-slope roof to its substrate is performed by one of three common methods: mechanical, adhered, or ballasted. Mechanically attached roofs use a series of screws, nails, or other anchors; adhered roofs use an adhesive specific to the type of roof used; and ballasted roofs use specialized gravel or paving stones. Regardless of the method of attachment, its inclusion in a BIM should be done such that it can be called out on drawing sheets and quantified. Fasteners are installed at a certain rate, in some cases by the number of fasteners per square foot and other times in terms of fasteners per lineal foot. Either way, we're dealing with a number, which should have an attribute assigned to it for calculation purposes. Not only does this afford the contractor an ability to determine how much adhesive or how many fasteners are required, it also conveys the appropriate installation procedure to meet manufacturer and building codes.

Steep-Slope Roofs

When dealing with a steep-slope roof, quality renderings are crucial in creating functional models. Typically, renderings are a function of an image file that represents a specific roof type, so the higher the resolution image, the better the rendering.

There are several different types of roof coverings, from asphalt shingles to metal panels to high-performance thermoplastic membranes such PVC and TPO membranes. Each type of roof covering has its own design, performance, installation, and maintenance attributes that need to be considered.

Roof design is based on a series of industry standards and principles, such as Factory Mutual (FM Global), Underwriters Laboratories (UL), Single Ply Roofing Institute (SPRI), Roof Consultant's Institute (RCI), and the National Roofing Contractors Association (NRCA). These standards determine what should and should not be designed under certain circumstances. Considering industry standards when developing roof models is essential to providing consistent and appropriate roof configurations.

Building codes determine where certain roof configurations can be used and when enhanced measures need to be implemented to combat forces of nature. It is not necessarily an aspect to be built into the intelligence of a roof component, but the component should carry enough intelligence to qualify if and where the roof system would meet an applicable building code.

A roof is a system made up of two primary assemblies that work together to provide a water-shedding or waterproof covering on the top surfaces of a structure.

- *Roof covering*: The roof covering is a series of components layered on top of each other to create the primary waterproofing of a building.
- *Roof flashing*: No roof is without some sort of penetration or termination passing through or around it. Whether it is the perimeter edge where the roof stops, the junction where the roof meets a wall, or the penetration where a pipe passes through the roof, the type of flashing used is a consideration of every roof system.

GRAPHICS

Roof coverings are developed graphically by drawing an area and selecting a roof type. The user predefines the roof type and instantiates it into his project. The roof type is created by combining a series of layers that compose the roof system. Each layer is its own material carrying material properties and a thickness. When dealing with assemblies like a roof, the thickness must often be made larger than it is in real life. For instance, a roofing ply sheet is less than $1/16$ of an inch, which becomes difficult to detail in a project. For this reason thin layers should be noted at $1/16$ of an inch or greater. Because BIM software allows for structural calculations, in many cases the structural members are not a part of the roof system, but are their own entity, which we will address in a different chapter. For this chapter let's discuss everything from the substrate up.

The substrate or sheathing of a roof is generally the base layer and composed of one of six typical types found on projects. Steel, wood, lightweight insulating concrete, structural concrete, cementitious wood fiber, and gypsum make up most of the roof substrates seen in general construction today.

Insulation is not always used in roof systems but when it is it should be considered carefully as it is important to the energy modeling of the building. Insulation should be implemented in a system such that the thickness can be easily modified by the user to suit the project needs. Where possible, having the R-value calculated based on the insulation thickness allows for less user modification and more computer analysis of the project. Other than the cut pattern associated with the insulation and perhaps the color to differentiate types, there is very little graphic information necessary to develop roof insulation within an assembly.

Ply sheets are what make up the waterproofing aspect of a low-slope roof. They are typically not found in steep-slope roofing except in the form of underlayment or leak barrier membranes. These, however, are not considered a waterproofing aspect of the roof system. In a low-slope roof there are one or more ply sheets in any given roof system and they are attached either using an adhesive or by a mechanical method, or are laid down and ballasted with some type of surface weight. Ply sheets are often too thin to accurately represent their thickness, so it is effective to represent them as $1/16$ of an inch so that they can be called out on the drawings. In addition to each sheet, it is good practice to show each layer of adhesive or fastener independently. This will allow the software to calculate how much adhesive or how many fasteners are necessary on the entire project. When content is developed appropriately, accurate quantity takeoffs become a by-product of the model.

Roof coverings such as shingles, shakes, tiles, membranes, or cap sheets are interchangeable terms to some degree. For the purposes of this book, we can look at them the same way because, for the most part, they are the top layer of the roof. From a conceptualization standpoint this is the most important aspect of the roof assembly, as it shows the outward appearance of the roof. When dealing with steep-slope roofs, such as shakes, shingles, tiles, slate, or other roof types selected by their appearance, it must be conveyed accurately to show what the project will truly look like. There are two sides to the graphics of a roof covering: the surface pattern and the rendered appearance. The surface pattern only shows in a model view and is more of a visual cue to the draftsman of what he is looking at. The rendering appearance determines what the roof will look like when the project is rendered for conceptualization and appearance study. Both are equally important, but in many cases it's not practical or possible to have a rendered image for every type of available roof covering, so a basic color may be the only driver for a rendered view of a roof.

MATERIALS DRIVE THE ROOF

Materials determine the actual products used in a project. The ability to count, qualify, and quantify them is one of the primary benefits of using BIM rather than traditional CAD methods. For this reason, specific materials should be called out such that they are different from similar materials that have slightly different attributes. This not only allows comparison of different materials from different manufacturers, but makes it possible to count how much of each material is being used. When dealing with components such as fasteners or adhesives, it's not practical to model them one by one as there are literally thousands on any given project. A more effective way to determine how many fasteners or how much adhesive is used on a given project is to list these items as layers of the assembly and assign an installation rate. The software will automatically determine the overall area of the roof, and when this is divided by the application rate the number of fasteners or amount of adhesive can be extrapolated.

In addition to material takeoffs, general appearance within the model becomes important since BIM uses color along with hatch patterns and vector graphics to display differences in layers. When dealing with very thin layers sandwiched together it is important to represent them in contrasting colors for visibility rather than a color that is a closer representation of the actual product. This is more for the benefit of the design team in creating visual cues for differences in products, as the drawings typically will still end up in black-and-white or grayscale on paper.

The materials themselves carry a series of performance attributes, which should be embedded at the material level, not the roof assembly level. While it is not always necessary to build this level of information into the model, it is the base level of information found within a project and, as technology grows, will allow model analysis to be performed and help the specifier determine which components to use on a project. If we think of it in terms of a peanut butter and jelly sandwich, this would be like looking at the calorie count of the peanut butter when trying to decide which brand to use. Adding attributes into materials can also assist in performing quantity takeoffs. An adhesive used in a roof assembly may be applied at a specific coverage rate. Adding an attribute to consider this will allow an equation to be developed that will translate the coverage rate into a unit quantity that can be used by cost estimators during procurement.

DATA—ATTRIBUTES AND EQUATIONS

Roof assemblies carry information that pertains to the roof as a whole. The materials themselves carry information that pertains to the performance of the individual materials. For instance, the fire rating of a roof is determined not by its covering but by the assembly from the roof deck to the finish surface, so a fire rating attribute should be located within the roof system rather than within a material. Figures 14.3 and 14.4 show a set of commonly used roof attributes. While this list is not all inclusive, it contains the attributes that should be contained in roof objects as a minimum.

Roof Assembly Attributes
- *Fire rating*: a rating expressed in terms of class A, B, or C, which classifies how resistant to fire and flame spread a roof assembly is
- *Wind uplift rating/design pressure*: a rating that qualifies how susceptible the roof is to blowing off due to internal pressure
- *Fastener density*: the rate at which mechanical anchors are applied to the roof
- *Adhesive application rate*: the rate at which adhesive is applied to the roof
- *Substrate type*: the material used in the construction of the roof deck. (i.e., plywood, concrete, 22-Ga steel)
- *Insulation type*: the specific insulation used in the assembly. (i.e., polyisocyanurate, extruded polystyrene, perlite)

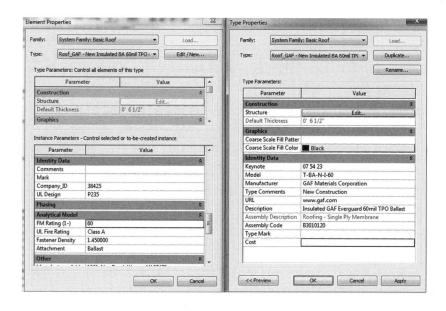

FIGURE 14.3 Typical roof assembly data set

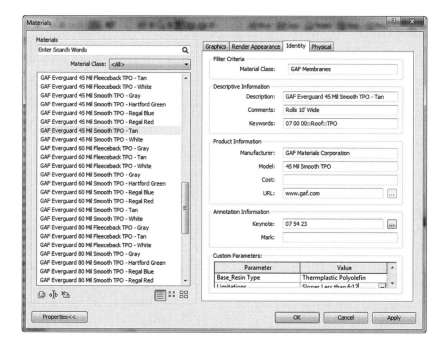

FIGURE 14.4 Typical roof material data set

- *Ply sheet/underlayment type*: the specific roofing sheets used beneath the surface membrane.
- *Membrane/roof covering type*: the specific surface material used in the roof assembly

Roof Material Attributes

- *Coverage rate*: the rate at which a material is applied
- *Insulation R value*: the thermal resistance value of the insulation used in the roof assembly
- *Insulation density*: the compressive strength or amount of weight and insulation a board can hold without being crushed
- *Roll width*: the unit width of roll goods used in roof assemblies
- *Roll length*: the unit length of roll goods used in roof assemblies
- *Membrane tensile strength*: the resistance to breakage of the roof membrane by tensive (pulling) forces
- *Membrane tear strength*: the resistance to breakage of the roof membrane by tearing forces:
- *Membrane UV resistance*: the resistance of a membrane to degradation from exposure to ultraviolet light.

Equations

- *Fastener count/adhesive amount*: roof area/coverage rate
- *Membrane rolls*: roof area/(membrane roll width * membrane roll length)

USAGE—LEVERAGING THE INFORMATION

Now that all of the information associated with the roof system is listed in the project, what do we do with it? Several types of analysis can be performed by the BIM itself as well as by outside facility management software or even through a series of exported schedules.

Code compliance is important aspect of roof assemblies. The roof may need to achieve specific fire ratings, have the ability to withstand certain wind speeds or design pressures, or be able to survive the impact of hurricane-borne debris. This speaks to design in a roof system such that it takes into consideration not just what it is but why it was selected. The data we embed in the model allow this type of analysis to be performed either by computer or, at the very least, as a simplified process done manually.

Contractors have a lot to gain by leveraging the data within a BIM. Roof systems contain much of the information necessary to simplify the estimator's job and to help make determinations of how to schedule workflow to minimize roof traffic, and allows for speculating for "just in time" material deliveries. When contractors work alongside the design team they have the potential to offer input regarding design elements that may not be practical in real-world scenarios. Above and beyond clash detection, which points out when two elements are in conflict with each other, a contractor often finds conflicts that are nongraphical in nature.

Specifiers and roof consultants can use the data within a model for quickly writing specifications, creating layouts, tapering insulation takeoffs, locating drains, visually noticing potential failures prior to construction, and suggesting changes during the design. Both the specifier and roof consultant have the potential to work alongside the architect as a member of the project team during design in order to assist in product selection and assembly design.

Manufacturers and manufacturers' representatives are becoming more and more involved with BIM as it evolves into a tool that they may be able to leverage internally. When a manufacturer's representative becomes involved with the design of the project, he has the ability to assist in the design process, as well as potentially receive preliminary information regarding the size and scope of the project in order to accurately determine how much material is necessary.

Owners and facility managers can use the information contained in a BIM for maintenance and replacement purposes. Not only is the size known but the type of roof, when it was installed, who installed it, how long the warranty is valid for, and the basis of design that was initially specified are known as well. When forecasting how much it will cost to replace the roof, an owner can take the size of the roof and perhaps the installed cost, attach a percentage for inflation, and determine how much should be budgeted over a specific number of years based on either the roof warranty or its expected lifespan.

TYPICAL ROOF ASSEMBLIES AND THEIR ATTRIBUTE SETS

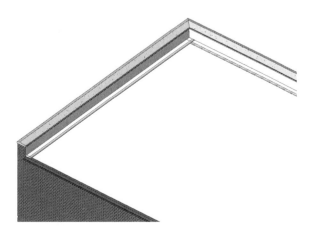

FIGURE 14.5

Typical low-slope roof assembly

- Fire rating
- Wind uplift rating/ design pressure
- Fastener density
- Adhesive application rate
- Insulation R-value
- Substrate type
- Insulation type
- Ply sheet/underlayment type
- Membrane type

FIGURE 14.6

Typical steep-slope roof assembly

- Roof materials
  - Coverage rate
  - Insulation R-value
  - Membrane roll width
  - Membrane roll length
  - Membrane tensile strength
  - Membrane tear strength
  - Membrane UV resistance

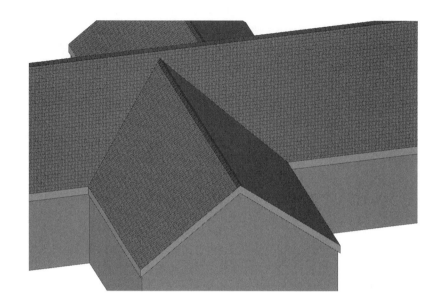

CHAPTER 15

Floors and Ceilings

Floors and ceilings can be looked at in a very similar sense and in some cases are one and the same. They are both created by drawing a series of lines that enclose an area. This area is assigned a specific assembly and is located based on a user-defined elevation. In terms of their presence within the project, they are both internal horizontal elements that divide and enclose spaces based on their elevations. In terms of fire ratings, there are floor-to-ceiling constructions that take into consideration every component, from the carpet or finish on the floor to the paints or finishes on the ceiling, and everything in between. Because many building information modeling platforms have both floor-based and ceiling-based host components, it can get difficult to create these types of elements properly.

Related elements that may be placed into or against a ceiling, such as recessed lighting or a ceiling fan, require that a ceiling be present for them to be instantiated. This raises the question of whether to create a floor-to-ceiling assembly as a floor or as a ceiling. Because there are more components and products that are installed into a ceiling than a floor, it seems more practical to create entire assemblies as ceilings rather than as floors. Alternatively, if we think about not how the assemblies will manage the components, but how the components relate to the assemblies, there may be a more effective solution. Rather than generating ceiling-mounted or floor-mounted components as reliant on a ceiling or floor host, creating them as hosted by a face will allow them to be placed and located regardless of whether the ceiling is a function of a floor assembly above, or the floor is a function of the ceiling assembly below.

ANATOMY

Floors

Floors are made up of several materials in an assembly, which provide a structural surface that can withstand traffic. While there are thousands of ways to construct a floor assembly based on various types of materials, categorizing them into compound floors and slabs as noted in Figure 15.1 and Figure 15.2 may simplify how floors are organized. In terms of graphics, the important aspect of a floor is its finish surface and, in the case of a floor-to-ceiling assembly, both top and bottom surfaces.

FIGURE 15.1 Typical compound floor construction: 1- floor finish; 2- underlayment; 3- subfloor; 4- floor framing/structure

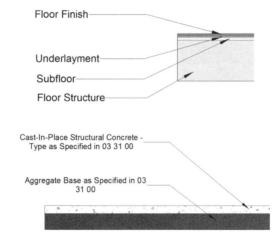

FIGURE 15.2 Typical slab floor construction: 1- floor finish; 2- underlayment; 3- slab; 4- vapor retarder; 5- aggregate base

Ceilings

Ceilings can be developed in one of two ways as we see in Figures 15.3 and 15.4: as a single material designed to cover the underside of the structure above, or as a compound ceiling, which contains the structural, thermal, and other components related to the ceiling construction. A drop ceiling, for instance, is a simple ceiling that uses one material to drive the appearance of the surface. Gypsum board ceilings are created the same way and can be placed against the underside

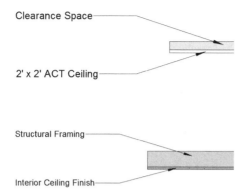

FIGURE 15.3 Typical simple ceiling construction: 1- ceiling tile; 2- ceiling grid; 3- gypsum board

FIGURE 15.4 Typical compound ceiling construction: 1- ceiling finish; 2- structural framing

of the floor structure above. A ceiling that encloses an attic or other uninhabited space above will often contain the structural members that support it.

CONSIDERATIONS

It is generally accepted that the floors take precedence over ceilings in a project, as they are required to accept live loads. As such, it is critical that structural elements that are associated with the construction of the assembly be located appropriately. There are several different types of floors to consider. A slab is a type of poured-in-place monolithic floor, but also may contain other aspects that should be considered. For a suspended slab, which may make up the upper floor construction of a high-rise, we may also want to consider the pan on which it was poured. For a slab on grade or below grade, we should consider the vapor barrier and coarse aggregate that is placed beneath it. A compound floor is a series of materials placed in an assembly to represent each of the products associated with the floor. In some cases we take into consideration the structural members, but in other cases the structural members are modeled independently. A third type of floor is a subassembly, which is used to overlay a finish onto any structural floor.

Where multiple floor finishes exist on a project, the design team may choose to create a structural floor that considers everything from the structural members up to the subfloor, and then add secondary floors above it that consider only the finish as described in Figure 15.5. Using this type of floor is beneficial when dealing with a specific set of materials. Bathroom floors on the project may have a cementitious underlayment, adhesive, tile, and grout, where the common areas are carpeted with an underlayment pad beneath it. These floor finishes are placed atop the structural floor but are substantially different in their construction. Developing and instantiating floor finish

FIGURE 15.5
Floor subassembly

subassemblies as independent floor types can make it considerably easier to calculate the amount of each type of material used on the project.

> ## Tip
>
> By developing and instantiating floor finish subassemblies, we can make it considerably easier to calculate the amount of each material used on the project.

Ceilings, on the other hand, are not really structural unless they are designed as a function of the structural floor above. BIM software platforms allow us to create ceilings based on a single material, such as gypsum board, or multiple materials, which include the framing and insulation elements in the case of a ceiling that encloses an uninhabited crawlspace or attic. Component ceilings, such as an acoustical tile suspended ceiling, are not as easy to represent properly. In all cases, their appearance is driven by the surface material, and its space is generated by drawing a series of lines to enclose an area. Wherever possible, it is effective to create floor-to-ceiling assemblies that take into consideration all materials from top to bottom. The major benefit of this is the simplification of many structural aspects; the downside is that many light fixtures and ceiling-based components require that a ceiling be present for them to be placed in the model.

Just like walls, floors and ceilings rely heavily on their materials. While the floor will have its own callout, which can give an overall description of the assembly, the relevance is diminished by the callouts for the individual components. The assembly as a whole may be referenced by a UniFormat code or simple annotation for large-format views, but the section views used in construction drawings will often annotate each specific material used in the assembly.

Span and slope should be considered when developing the models. If a specific material within the floor's structure is what drives its slope, it should be adjustable independent of the rest of the floor. This allows the user to quickly and easily update the slope while maintaining the integrity and accuracy of the rest of the floor's structure. This is a common function of slab floors. In many cases slabs will contain a slight slope to promote proper drainage. If the floor being developed is a concrete slab with vinyl flooring, the floor should be configured such that the thickness of the concrete is variable, but the thickness of the vinyl flooring is fixed.

Floor framing can be either a part of the floor's structure or placed independently. There are situations where either or both of these methods will work. When the structure of the building is to be analyzed for integrity and structural merit, framing members should always be placed on their own. In the case of a tenant fit-out or a commercial interiors project where the structure of the building carries little relevance other than dimensional, it is a substantial savings in time to bundle framing members with the balance of the floor components.

GRAPHICS

When considering the graphics associated with floors and ceilings, the most important aspect is to create them so they accurately represent the assemblies being used in the project. If we start by creating floors and ceilings that will work for every situation, we can quickly duplicate and modify them for use in other situations. The first step is to create a series of floors that consider all of the structural component options, such as dimensional lumber, metal, engineered joists of various sizes, and poured-in-place lightweight concrete. Add the necessary vapor barrier, subfloor, pan, and underlayment requirements for each of the constructions, and we can create a small library from which to build customized assemblies quickly. Once we have developed a warehouse of assemblies that consider all of the configurations that we're likely to find on the projects that we take on, we can modify them as needed to add additional components, change thicknesses and materials, and customize them to the situation at hand. These floors and ceilings can become our structural floor options, which can develop large areas of the project.

Creating floor finish assemblies can make it easy to not only divide the floor areas and place the appropriate finishes but simplify material takeoffs. Because there is more to installing carpet than just the carpet itself, the sub-assembly can carry with it not just the finish material, but the underlayment pad, adhesive, and, because it's its own assembly, the perimeter dimension. Being able to parse out this type of information from the assembly will assist estimators when dealing with flooring takeoffs, as many materials related to the installation of the floor are based not just on square foot area but on perimeter and shape of the area.

Building a library of floor and ceiling assemblies is an ongoing process, as different floor finishes are always being used. Rather than developing an assembly for every tile that is being used, it's better to develop an assembly that takes into consideration the use of tile, and a series of materials that represent the appearance of each of the tiles. This will allow the assembly to be used over and over on different projects, and not be specific to a certain tile. Industry organizations such as the Tile Council of North America (TCNA) have a series of standard constructions that are used with floor tile. Building each of these constructions as a floor type, and leaving the tile in the assembly "As Specified," will allow the necessary related materials to be brought into the project and the tile itself to be chosen later.

MATERIALS

Materials drive the appearance and behavior of floors and ceilings the same way they do with walls and roofs. Visually, the most important aspect of a ceiling or floor is the exposed surface layer, as it carries graphic relevance in rendered and three-dimensional views. Above and beyond the attributed data, attention should be given to the rendering aspect of these materials. Materials found in layers beneath the face layers are visible only in section views, so the most important aspect is the hatch pattern used to visually note what the material is and the color with which it is noted in the model. One of the most common types of ceiling is a suspended acoustical ceiling tile, more commonly known as a drop ceiling.

The ceiling tools in most building information modeling systems do not allow for the control of different types of grids and panels using traditional ceiling tools. Rather than modeling them graphically, each type of panel has its own material assigned to it, and the material uses an image file to generate the rendered appearance. While this diminishes our ability to perform accurate piece counts of the different components associated with the ceiling, it is a quick method of developing the graphic aspect of these types of ceilings.

The same method is used to control the appearance and behavior of the surface material of floors. It is highly unlikely that the design team will place each individual tile in a pattern or each paver in a patio. Rather than using graphic modeling to represent these types of finishes, developing a material that corresponds to the appearance allows the visual appearance of a large area to be swapped out quickly. The difficulty comes when we are dealing with many different finish types. It can require a considerable amount of effort to maintain them when we consider the various materials, colors, sizes, and grout colors associated with a tile floor, or the countless stain colors associated with a wood floor. In cases where there are far too many options to create materials for them, an effective approach is to create a material such as "Hardwood flooring – Stain as specified" and let the user determine which stain applies based on either an RGB-value or an image file associated with the flooring.

While ceilings typically are made of only one or two materials, detailed floor assemblies may have upward of 10 layers within them when we take into consideration all of the underlayments, membranes, adhesives, and mortars associated with the installation of tile. Using contrasting colors for each of the components assists when creating annotations in section views. It is good practice to create a series of categories for the layers. Just as with walls, creating categories for structural components, thermal components, interior finish components, exterior finish components, and air and vapor barrier components allows organization and easy retrieval of materials that may need to be used later in the project. If a color is assigned to each category, or even a color range, the design team has a visual cue as to the type of components that are found in the wall. Making all insulation materials in shades of red, structural components in shades of gray, and air barriers in shades of green is an example of this. The hatch pattern used on the individual material further details which material within a given category is being viewed.

Each material within an assembly will carry the pertinent information about why it was selected for use in the assembly. Insulation will carry thermal resistance properties, floor finishes will carry appearance properties, and perhaps properties related to durability, adhesives have adhesion performance associated with them, and structural components will carry strength properties. Even if there is no intention of the design team to perform any type of analysis, the presence of these properties allows the information to be extracted later on for documentation and facilities management purposes. Building information modeling is larger than any single project participant, so the information contained within it should apply to the project as a whole, rather than the professional who is developing the model.

There are certain instances where two materials may align with each other within a single layer. Batt insulation is a material that often falls into the same layer as the framing members. In a section view of a floor or ceiling, we will see that both insulation and framing are in the same layer. To represent both of these layers within the project, one of two methods could be used:

1. By creating a layer that has no thickness, one of the two conflicting materials can be represented within the information of the assembly. While it will show up in schedules as being a part of the assembly, in section views, it is invisible and as such cannot carry an automatically generated annotation.

2. By merging two materials into one, we can allow both graphic and nongraphic information regarding the two materials to be carried together. If we merge floor framing materials and thermal insulation materials into a single material, we could create, as an example, 2 × 12 wood joists – 16″ O.C. w/ R-19 fiberglass batt insulation.

DATA—ATTRIBUTES, CONSTRAINTS, AND EQUATIONS

Below are a series of commonly used floor and ceiling assembly attributes and some sample material attributes. It is important to carefully consider whether an attribute belongs within the assembly or within the material. Adding too much information may cause more harm than good when trying to extract information from the model. When adding attributes to an assembly, realize that the attributes that apply to one assembly will apply to all assemblies of the component category. If we create a subassembly that pertains to tile installation, added attributes that pertain to tile will ultimately end up in the subassemblies that pertain to wood flooring, vinyl tile, and carpet, because they are a part of the object category for floors. By adding more information to the materials, or linking information back to websites or other data storage locations, the data remain available, but are located externally rather than as a part of the model itself.

Floor and Ceiling Assembly Attributes
- *Fire rating*: a rating expressed in terms of class A, B, or C, which classifies how resistant to fire and flame spread a floor or ceiling assembly is

- *Assembly R-value*: the thermal resistance of the entire wall assembly expressed in sq ft * F * H/BTU
- *Sound transmission classification (STC)*: a rating of how well a floor or ceiling attenuates sound
- *Area*: the total area of a floor or ceiling assembly
- *Perimeter*: the total length of all floor or ceiling edges
- *Live load*: the total allowable static load that the assembly must be able to carry; this may also be added as a material attribute
- *Dead load*: the total allowable dynamic load (snow, traffic) that the assembly must be able to carry; this may also be added as a material attribute
- *Clear span*: the maximum clear distance that a structural member can span unsupported; this may also be added as a material attribute

Material Attributes

- *Compressive strength*: the maximum (or rated) strength that a material (typically concrete and masonry) can withstand when compressive force is applied
- *R-value*: the thermal resistance of a specific material expressed in sq ft * F * H/BTU
- *Permeability (perm) rating*: the amount of moisture (expressed in perms) that is allowed to pass through a building material
- *Grade*: the industry-accepted quality classification rating for a building material.
- *Thickness*: the depth of the material or its required application
- *Color/finish*: the surface texture and appearance of a material
- *Application rate*: the rate at which a material is applied based on its commonly distributed unit (i.e., gallon, square foot, lineal foot)
- *Format*: the size, shape of a modular component used in an assembly (i.e., tile, pavers)
- *Unit area*: the area per unit of a modular component used in an assembly (i.e., tile, pavers)

There are equations that may be used for quantity takeoff and estimation purposes. As with all estimation procedures, everybody has a different method, so equations act as guidelines from which to start, not hard and fast rules for calculation. Calculations for floor and ceiling assemblies are typically created within a floor or ceiling schedule and performed by operating on two or more number or dimensional values.

Equations

- *Adhesive amount*: floor area/application rate
- *Unit count*: wall area/unit area
- *Tack strip or baseboard unit count*: perimeter/unit length

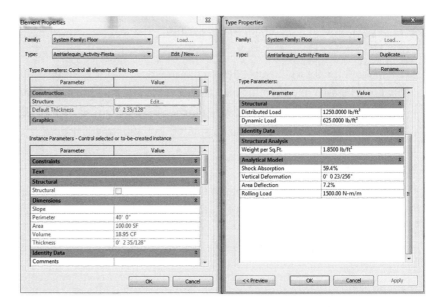

FIGURE 15.6 Typical assembly data set

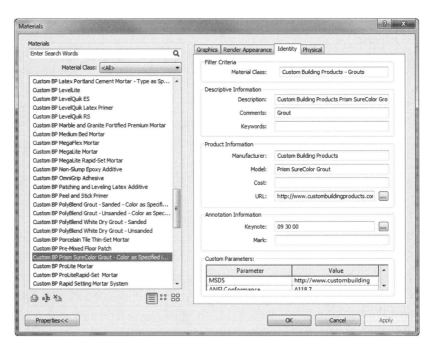

FIGURE 15.7 Typical material data set

Especially at the material level, there are specific performance values that may be used in a floor or ceiling assembly. Paints and coatings may note the amount of volatile organic compounds (VOC) and solids content. The scratch resistance and frost resistance of a ceramic tile and the facer material of gypsum wallboard may be important attributes as well. Determining whether or not to put these types of attributes within the model should be weighed carefully against why the attribute is relevant. If data are strictly for informational purposes and not leveraged for model analysis, it is often far more practical to link back to a manufacturer's product information page on a website rather than embedding them within a model. Just as with assemblies, when adding an attribute to a material, it is important to note that the attribute will apply to all materials, so without filtering information in schedules, there is the ability to inadvertently add values to attributes that may not apply to specific materials.

When adding attributes that apply to specific materials, it is good practice to create a schedule for each material type in order to view the data; otherwise, the schedule itself may end up becoming very wide, with dozens of columns, many of which are empty in most rows.

USAGE—LEVERAGING THE INFORMATION

The most common use for the information contained within floor and ceiling assemblies is for the structural analysis and quantity of takeoffs that may be performed. Not only is the area automatically generated by the software, but perimeter is as well. Because many components associated with the project are reliant on not just area but lengths that are attributed to perimeters, the information contained within will provide more accurate cost and quantity estimation. To attain unit counts, unit sizes must be attached to each material associated with a project. Even though a tack strip used with carpet applies only to the perimeter, if it is added to the assembly as a material and is noted with a unit length, the number of tack strip units necessary (Pieces or Boxes) can be calculated.

Many materials require a repeating pattern to be achieved when they are estimated. This creates some difficulty when attempting to perform quantity takeoffs. Carpet, for instance, may have a pattern associated with it, so the amount of material necessary may be far greater than the area that is being estimated. To determine the estimated amount of carpet necessary for an area, creating a simple detail object that is a rectangle that has alignment points will act as an overlay. The rectangle shown in Figure 15.8 may be shaped to

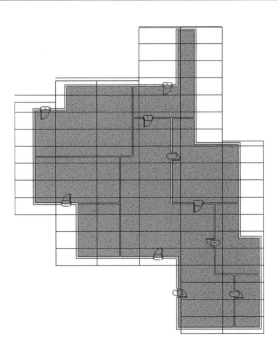

FIGURE 15.8 Potential
carpet takeoff

the width of a carpet roll, placed over the area in question, and repeated using alignment marks. This will allow estimators to do trial-and-error work and also minimize the amount of leftover scrap material by finding other places that it may be used.

The sound transmission classifications associated with floor and ceiling assemblies can be used to make determinations of how to plan space effectively within a building, such as where to place specific areas, such as rooms that may require a quieter environment. Components that need to be isolated because of the amount of sound they produce may need to be located within spaces that are enclosed by partitions with high STC ratings. By creating an annotation that tags the sound transmission classification rating of an assembly, a view can be created that notes the corresponding values for each wall, floor, ceiling, and roof assembly.

The information that is put into a model can also be driven by what somebody may want out of it. Building information modeling is very dynamic in this respect. Rather than thinking about what we can get from the information contained within the model, we should think about what we want from the model, and build the appropriate information into the components in order to extract it later on.

TYPICAL FLOOR AND CEILING ASSEMBLIES AND THEIR ATTRIBUTES

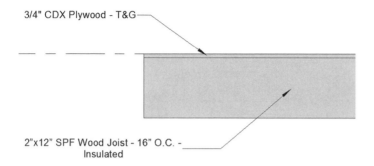

3/4" CDX Plywood - T&G

2"x12" SPF Wood Joist - 16" O.C. - Insulated

FIGURE 15.9

Typical structural floor assembly

- Fire rating: 90 minute
- Assembly R-value: 20
- Sound transmission classification (STC): 6
- Structure:
  - Structural element: 12" joist – 16" O.C. – insulated w/R-19 fiberglass batt
  - Substrate: ¾" CDX plywood – T&G

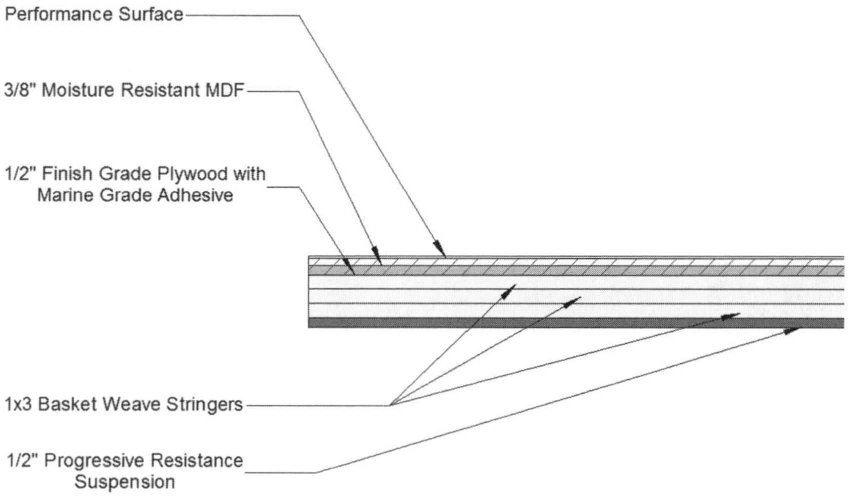

FIGURE 15.10

Typical finish floor subassembly

- Assembly R-value: 2.5
- Sound transmission classification (STC): 36
- Usage: performance flooring
- Structure:
  - Finish: performance flooring as specified
  - Underlayment: ⅜" MDF – moisture resistant
  - Subfloor: ½" AC plywood adhered w/marine-grade adhesive
  - Shock dampening: 3 rows 1 × 3 spruce stringers – basket woven
  - Base: progressive resistance suspension

Performance Surface

3/8" Moisture Resistant MDF

1/2" Finish Grade Plywood with Marine Grade Adhesive

1x3 Basket Weave Stringers

1/2" Progressive Resistance Suspension

FIGURE 15.11

Typical compound ceiling assembly

- Fire rating: 90 minute
- Assembly R-value: 49.5
- Sound transmission classification (STC): 19
- Structure:
  - Interior finish: ½" gypsum wallboard
  - Structural element: 2 × 6" SPF wood joist – 16" O.C. – insulated w/ R-19 fiberglass batt
  - Thermal insulation: R 30 fiberglass blanket

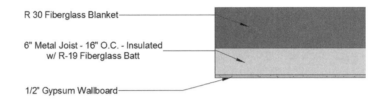

R 30 Fiberglass Blanket

6" Metal Joist - 16" O.C. - Insulated w/ R-19 Fiberglass Batt

1/2" Gypsum Wallboard

FIGURE 15.12

Typical ACT ceiling assembly

- Assembly R-value: 1.5
- Sound transmission classification (STC): 23
- Structure:
  - Clearance space: 4"
  - Finish: 2' × 2' ACT – white w/white grids

CHAPTER 16

Windows and Skylights

ANATOMY

A typical window is made up of two basic components and a series of optional and secondary ones. The most important aspects of the window are the frame and the sash. The frame is the outside component that mounts to a wall, and the sash is the fixed or operable unit that contains the glass or glazing. Secondary aspects of the window are its operation and locking mechanisms, hardware, muntins or glass dividers, mullions, which join windows together, and the glass itself. Figure 16.1 depicts the most commonly used window types based on the method of operation. It is proper for all window objects to carry the frame and sash at bare minimum, with the secondary components that describe their operation and appearance added when necessary.

CONSIDERATIONS

The purpose of windows and skylights is to allow transmission of light while limiting the passage of moisture and air and, in some cases, to allow egress in

FIGURE 16.1 Typical window types

case of emergencies. When designing the window or skylight, it is important to consider not only what is graphically necessary, but also what data are relevant to the selection and analysis of the unit.

Windows and skylights have multiple components, which often come from multiple manufacturers. To qualify and quantify the individual components accurately, they need to be created and implemented into a window or skylight model, rather than called out in a simple text notation that identifies what the product or component is. The type of glass used in a window or skylight is often driven by the building codes for a given locale and can dramatically affect energy performance. The type of flashing may change based on the type of roof. Including specifics about the components that make up the unit provides an understanding of why the individual components that make up a window or skylight were selected. This in turn allows appropriate products to be selected based on specific environmental and conditions.

In many cases, windows may be ganged or "mulled" together where they share common framework between the units. When window objects are being developed, they should be built such that graphics may be turned off in the case of mulled units, or specific units are developed that consider two or more windows within the same opening. Developing these types of units can often become difficult and confusing, especially with casement units, where the handing of each window in the group must be adjustable independently. If the graphics are simplified, single window units can butted against or overlap each other to simulate an array of windows. This works graphically but is limited in the amount of actual information associated with the rough opening and required dimensions for installation. Figure 16.2 shows us some common configuration options of multiple (mulled) units and grids (muntins) that divide the glass panes.

Components such as hardware, flashing, and weather stripping are maintenance items. Creating them as components within a window or skylight model allows them to be date stamped or otherwise noted independent from other aspects of the complete window or skylight unit. This allows for the

ability to consider maintenance of the unit throughout the lifecycle of the building.

Light transmission is probably the most noticeable aspect of a window or skylight and is generally the purpose for installing the unit. While the relevance of this value to the unit itself is of little importance, appropriate light transmission values allow daylighting studies to be performed to determine if, where, and how much artificial light must be placed in a given space.

Window and skylight dimensions can be confusing. In real-world scenarios, they are often nominal dimensions. A window that is noted as 30" wide by 46" tall may in fact be 29½" by 47¼". Accuracy of the real dimensions is critical to ensure that a specified window fits in an actual opening. In addition, the rough opening dimensions should be considered to ensure that the openings created in the field are designed for the unit. The depth of the jam is also a relevant dimension, as jambs are not always designed to be as thick as a wall. Having a jamb depth dimension notifies the modeler both graphically and through the data that an extension jamb or other finish condition must be considered in connection with a given window or skylight unit.

Performance aspects of windows and skylights are of utmost importance. They have little or no graphic relevance but allow good analysis of the models for energy and daylighting studies. Energy codes require specific thermal values, locations may merit specific acoustical properties, and wind or seismic considerations may require specific structural performance criteria. Without the addition of these performance attributes, the window is primarily a graphic representation, rather than the fully functional analysis tool that it should be.

Most BIM authoring tools let us switch the orientation of a component with a single click. We can switch a window from left-handed to right-handed or from awning to hopper using a control. While this simplifies the creation of the object, I recommend against this, as it limits the accuracy of door

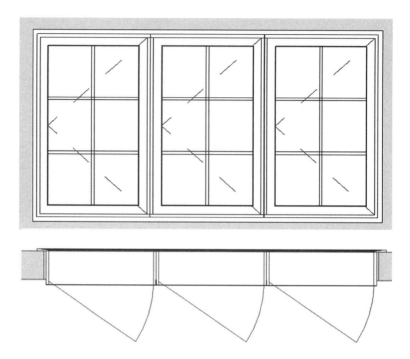

FIGURE 16.3   Window handing

schedules by requiring the user to insert the handing of the unit manually. If the operation of a window is considered individually and is created as a unique type of the object, the operation can be taken into account automatically.

GRAPHICS

Frame and Sash

Head and jamb components are essentially the basic framework for a given window or skylight and typically become the host or primary object. All other components, including the sash, glass, and hardware and grilles, can vary in type, color, appearance, and performance. While the frame can also have different characteristics or even be of differing types, shapes, or materials, it is the one component that is fixed to its host component, making it the most logical component to use as the primary.

Where present, the sash is the most visibly noticeable part, and thus a graphically important part of a window or skylight. The sash encapsulates the glass and provides the most visible facets of the window. Where any substantial graphic detail is to be added to a window, the sash is the most appropriate location to provide the most visual benefit. A sash can be a fairly standard component in that it may be reused regardless of how the window operates. If the sash is created as its own component and embedded it into the window, the size and configuration may be modified so that it is able to represent a fixed, casement, awning, hopper, double-hung, or any other type of window. By creating an appropriate insertion point, two sashes may be placed in the object for hung or rolling windows, and a single sash for all others. Developing a window as a series of modules allows the subcomponents to be reused on other objects or swapped out for other types.

Tip

If the window sash is created as its own component and embedded it into the window, the size and configuration may be modified so that it is able to represent a fixed, casement, awning, hopper, double-hung, or any other type of window.

The cross-section view of a window or skylight frame is usually quite detailed. It is not necessary to note every facet of a frame. The goal is to convey design intent and provide information on how to design and install a window, not how to manufacture it. It is better that the unit be graphically minimized to show an approximate representation of the unit rather than the exacting appearance, as shown in Figure 16.4. A good rule of thumb for determining the level of detail is to consider the component in its installed condition and model what is visible from 5 to 10 feet. If it is not visible at that point but still carries relevance to the model, it can then be created as a two-dimensional detail component.

Figure 16.5 shows us how the graphics of the frame can be created in any one of several ways, depending on its complexity and the desired level of detail. Where more detail is desired, the head, sill, and jambs can be created as individual components; where that level of detail is not necessary, a sweep or single extrusion is a quick and easy way to represent the graphics. Another benefit to using a sweep is the ability to control its appearance by use of a profile. If it is unclear as to what the profile of the frame will look like, it may be simplified early in the design phase. Once more information is obtained, the profile may be swapped out for one that is more detailed and contains the exact appearance of the window that is to be used. Alternatively, the frame can be treated the same way the sash—as its own embedded object.

Glazing

Glazing, glass, vision lites, and panes all refer to the same component—the portion of a window or skylight through which light is transmitted—and graphically, light transmission is the primary consideration. Creating glass

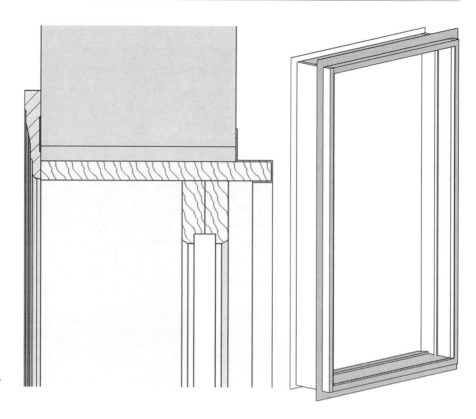

FIGURE 16.4 Window
and skylight frame

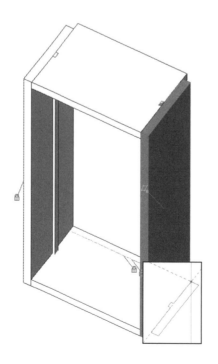
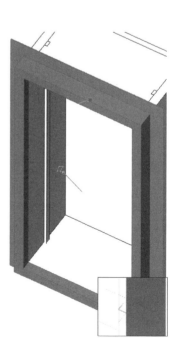

FIGURE 16.5 Frame
creation methods

with appropriate light transmission allows accurate light rendering inside of the BIM model. Glass can be considered as either a solid component or a material, depending on the unit in which it is being installed and how accurate the model needs to be. Creating glass as a material is the simplest method, and can carry the necessary characteristics, such as U-factor and solar heat gain coefficient (SHGC) data, which are essential in making the determinations necessary for energy code compliance. Impact performance of glass can be largely attributed to the thickness and type of interlayer used with a laminated glass pane. The color of the glass is often a function of one of the panes or a tinted interlayer. Deciding on whether to create glass as a material or as a solid is dependent on how frequently back glass is to be used.

Little effort is required to create the glass as a material, but it can be limited in its ability to accurately convey all of the information about the unit. If we plan on using the same glass configurations in many different objects, it may make sense to create the glass as its own object that can be inserted into a window, skylight, door, or curtain wall panel. When glass is its own component as shown in Figure 16.6, the configurations can be more exact and the model will take into consideration that an insulating glass unit has multiple components. Typical components in an insulating glass unit are panes of differing types, a spacer, muntins, low emissivity coatings, and, often, an inert gas between the panes. Generally, it is not necessary to provide this level of detail, but there are specific instances where it can be beneficial or even necessary. When a glass pane is created as its own object, it makes it easier to extract information about the glass, even if it is embedded into another object. If formatted properly as a subcomponent, it can show up in schedules, allowing all of the performance data to be reviewed by the architect or specifier. Another benefit of adding

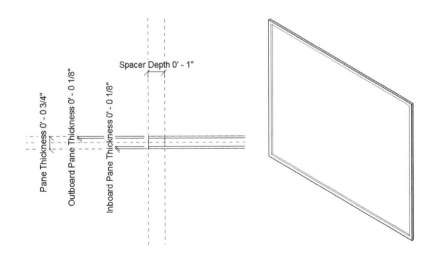

FIGURE 16.6 Typical glazing configuration

glass as its own object is the ability to modify performance values based on the thickness and type of glass. U-factors and solar heat gain coefficients can vary considerably based on the type of glass that is used in the window. Since most manufacturers offer several glass types, making the glass type a user-defined option within the object minimizes the amount of manual data entry and potential user error. The glass carries its own attributes, which change subject to its thickness or size, so to allow the information to pass into the model without multiplying size options by glass options, embedding the glass into the window as its own object seems to be the most effective approach.

Hardware and Accessories

Muntins (or grilles) are partitions that divide, or simulate the division of, window glass. They can be surface mounted or located between glass panes and are available in various shapes and configurations. They are generally options determined by the user, so it is important to allow the presence of muntins to be controlled, either by providing a parameter to turn them on or off or as a selectable option that is a function of the type of glass. Muntins can affect the energy performance values of a window, so if they are created with the glass, they can take these values into consideration, allowing a more accurate representation and minimizing the amount of user data entry. By creating muntins as solid geometry that is a function of the glass, glass types can be created with and without them. In instances where the performance data are not relevant or affected by muntins, it can be more practical to create them as a component of the window rather than the glass. The graphics have equal functionality with respect to visibility and appearance, but have less control over the data.

Hardware consists of multiple components, such as crank operators, hinges, pivots, weather stripping, and flashings, that can be created either as a part of the window or skylight, separately, or not at all. If and how they are created and managed is determined largely by how the unit is sold. If the hardware is an integral component of the unit with no available options other than color, then the only real purpose of adding these components is for graphical accuracy.

The data associated with components provided by a single manufacturer are best contained in ancillary documentation rather than directly in the BIM model. This type of information is typically used for reference purposes rather than actual product decision making.

MATERIALS

Materials collectively determine what the product is and, in the case of the glass, how it performs. It is important to recognize that the materials used in the models carry much of the information necessary to do analysis and provide notations on drawing sheets. Callouts and annotations in section views are a function of the materials used, so providing accurate material descriptions will automate the detailing and annotation process and eliminate the need to enter text manually.

Even when using image files of specific finishes, we should recognize that there is no substitute for seeing the actual product. Attempting to create a perfect copy of a material or finish is impractical, and in some cases impossible. The rendering capabilities of BIM software are not in the same category as the high-performance rendering software designed solely to mimic exact appearance. Adding links to color palettes or available finish types from a website can allow the designer to represent the finish in a model as well as provide more information for more accurate appearances.

The frame and sash materials are essential in determining what a window will look like in two-dimensional and three-dimensional views. Use appropriate cut patterns to further automate the two-dimensional detailing process and improve the accuracy of construction details on drawing sheets. For three-dimensional rendering purposes, the use of image files to represent finishes instead of default finishes installed with the software provides the ability to be more accurate. This is especially noticeable when dealing with unpainted wood or metal components where wood grain and metal texture are what make the finish unique.

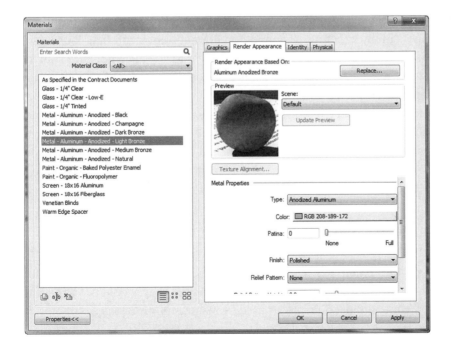

FIGURE 16.7   Materials for windows

The glass drives the ability to perform energy and daylight studies. Regardless of whether the glass is created as a material or a component, it should carry the appropriate light transmission values. The tinting and opacity of the glass should be as accurate as possible to allow high-quality daylighting and glare studies. Glass materials should be created so that they are specific to the thickness, type, color, and any other attributes that will directly affect the performance of the glass within a window or skylight. Simply creating the material as "glass" is not acceptable, as specific types of glass are required for use in specific locations. As such, the model should be able to parse out the types of glass used in these locations for analysis purposes.

Hardware and accessory materials have the same importance as the frame and sash components for rendering purposes. Often, hardware is selected by finish and form, rather than its functionality, so providing reasonable representations of color and finish provides a benefit to the designer.

DATA—ATTRIBUTES, CONSTRAINTS, AND EQUATIONS

Energy codes are performed by leveraging all of the data in the model, from the R-values of the walls, floors, and roofs to the U-values and solar heat gain coefficients of the windows, doors, and other openings. Having this information available within each window or skylight minimizes the need for manual data entry.

Egress code calculations can be easily accomplished inside the window component by creating a simple conditional statement that looks at the opening width, clear open area, and sill height to affirm compliance with local code. For instance in Figure 16.8, let's suppose that the building code requires a clear open area of 5 sq ft and a clear open width of 30 inches, the data contained in the model can affirm conformance to these values. If the code sets a maximum height for a finished floor, the sill height can consider this. Egress requirements can differ based on the height from grade or the floor in which the window is located, so it should be made as adjustable as possible, so the user can easily modify the code requirement to suit his project.

Commonly Used Window and Skylight Attributes
Dimensions

- *Unit dimensions*: Unit dimensions are generally expressed in terms of width and height, and are exact to the size. They should not be confused with nominal dimensions used by manufacturer for sales purposes.

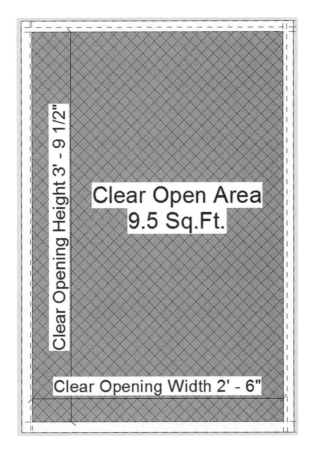

FIGURE 16.8 Typical egress code sizing requirements

- *Jamb depth*: The depth of the frame from its outer mounting surface to the inside edge of the frame. For windows that are mounted flush to the exterior wall using a nailing fin, it is often necessary to add extension jambs when dealing with nonstandard wall depths.

- *Rough opening dimensions*: Dimensions given to notify architects and contractors of the clear opening that is necessary to install a window properly. Generally, a rough opening provides ¼" or more spacing on either side of the window to allow for discrepancies in framing.

- *Clear opening width*: A dimension used to determine whether or not the window meets egress code. It measures the clear lateral distance that a human can pass through. Often this dimension is added as data rather than as a calculated value or modeled dimension.

- *Open egress area*: Also used to determine whether or not a window meets egress code. Measures the total area that is available to pass through in the event of an emergency. Because building codes differ from location to location, and the requirement is based on where in the project the window is located, it is more effective to note the open egress area than whether or not it meets egress code.

- *Sill/head height*: Used to place the window vertically in a wall. In some cases the head height is relevant, as it may need to align with the tops of doors, where in other cases the sill height is more relevant, as the distance from the floor is the basis of design.

- *Aperture (effective daylighting area)*: Helps determine how much natural light will pass into the room. A very wide sash minimizes the aperture of the window, so a nominal 36 × 36" window with a 1-inch frame and a 2-inch-wide sash would have only a 30 × 30" aperture.

Performance

- *Solar heat gain coefficient (SHGC)*: A performance value associated with glazed openings that refers to the increase in temperature resulting from sunlight passing through the glass. It is expressed as a percentage of solar heat that is absorbed versus reflected when it comes in contact with the window. The lower the solar heat gain coefficient, the more effective the window is at blocking heat from sunlight.

- *U-value/U-factor*: A measure of heat conductivity through the glass. Where R-value relates to thermal resistance, U-factor relates to thermal transmission. In colder climates, it is used to measure how much heat is lost through a window and to help determine whether or not windows meet energy codes. The lower the U-factor, the less heat is lost through the window.

- *Sound transmission class (STC)*: Measures how well a window attenuates airborne sound. Acoustical windows are measured based on their STC rating. It is expressed in terms of decibels reduced, where the larger the value, the better the window is at reducing sound.

- *Air infiltration*: Based on an ASTM standard that measures how much air is allowed to pass through a window at specific atmospheric pressures. Since most windows are operable, they have a tendency to allow a certain amount of air to pass through. The less air that passes through, the more efficient the window is. Air infiltration is typically expressed in terms of cubic feet per square foot (cfm/sf) at a given air pressure.

- *Water penetration*: Based on an ASTM standard that measures the amount of air pressure required to force water through the void around a window in its installed position. It is generally expressed in terms of its air pressure at the point of failure.

- *Structural test pressure/design pressure*: Measures how much internal or external pressure is required to break a window during weather events, such as hurricanes, in which extreme internal and external pressures are common.

- *Forced entry rating*: Determines how effective a window is at preventing a forced entry.

EXAMPLE WINDOW AND SKYLIGHT COMPONENTS AND THEIR ATTRIBUTE SETS

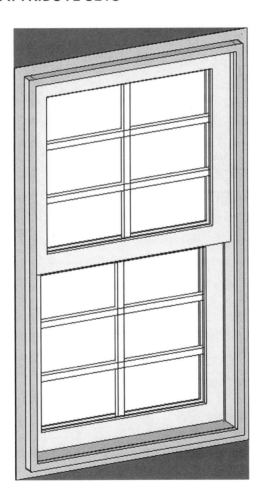

FIGURE 16.9

Typical window object
- Width: 36½"
- Height: 48¾"
- Rough width: 37"
- Rough height: 49¼"
- Jamb depth: 4⁹⁄₁₆"
- Glass type: low E argon-filled clear tempered glass
- Operation: double hung
- Air infiltration: maximum 0.08 cfm/sq ft at 1.57 psf (25 mph) in accordance with ASTM E 283
- Water penetration: no leakage when tested at 6.0 psf in accordance with ASTM E 547
- Structural test pressure: 52.5 psf positive and negative in accordance with ASTM E 330.
- U-factor: 0.30
- SHGC: 0.25
- STC: 29
- Forced entry: type D, grade 20 in accordance with ASTM F 588

FIGURE 16.10

Typical skylight object

- Width: 24″
- Height: 48″
- Rough width: 25¼″
- Rough height: 48″
- Frame depth/ projection: 3″
- Glass type: low E argon-filled clear laminated glass
- Operation: fixed
- Air infiltration: maximum 0.08 cfm/sq ft at 1.57 psf (25 mph) in accordance with ASTM E 283
- Water penetration: no leakage when tested at 6.0 psf in accordance with ASTM E 547
- Structural test pressure: 52.5 psf positive and negative in accordance with ASTM E 330
- U-factor: 0.30
- SHGC: 0.25

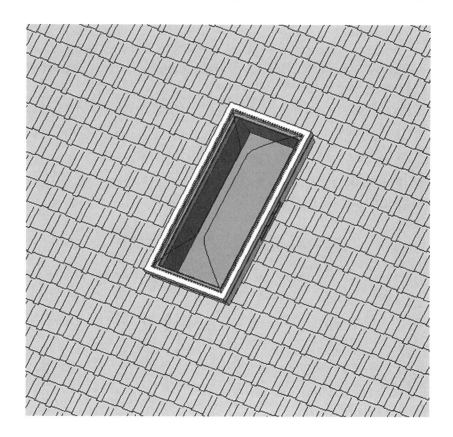

CHAPTER 17

Doors

ANATOMY

What is a door? In a general sense, a door is an opening designed to allow access between two spaces within a building. In many cases it is also designed to allow the transmission of light while limiting the passage of moisture and air. When designing a door we must consider what is graphically important and what data are relevant to the selection of the door. Different types of doors can be categorized either by what they're made of or how they operate. There are steel doors and wood doors, and swing doors and overhead doors. When thinking about a door, consider not just what it looks like, but what it is, how it is installed, and how it operates. Figures 17.1, 17.2, and 17.3 show how doors are categorized in terms of how they operate.

CONSIDERATIONS

Doors have multiple components, which often come from multiple manufac-turers. For the individual components to be qualified and quantified accurately,

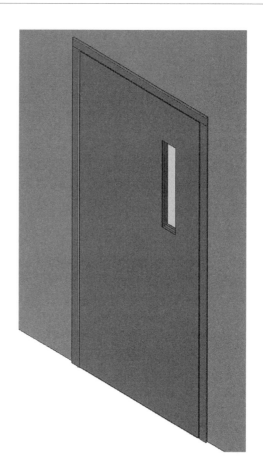

FIGURE 17.1 Typical swing door

FIGURE 17.2 Typical sliding door

they need to be actually created and implemented into the model by creating graphics for the larger more visible components, and either simplified graphics or simple data notations to call out secondary components, such as hinges, weather stripping, access hardware, and accessories. It is important to keep in mind that hardware sourced from the original manufacturer of the door does not always have to be shown in terms of graphics or data. Items such as hinges and weather stripping that are standard equipment and have no alternatives for selection can be omitted.

The most common identifier of a door is its width and height and the appearance of the slab or leaf. When measuring or calling out a door, it is proper to note the width first followed by the height. There are several different types of slabs, such as flush, two panel, four panel, and six panel, and countless specialties styles. The door may have a solid core, it may have a hollow core, or it may be constructed of solid material. While graphically the core may not be visible, for information and specification the type of core should be noted, as it determines performance aspects, such as sound transmission, thermal resistance, and fire rating.

In many cases doors contain glazing or vision lites, which allow light to pass through. Using appropriate sizes and materials will allow the software to consider the amount of natural light that comes into a project through an opening such as a door, render it, and analyze the model to determine how much artificial light should be placed in the building. The level of detail surrounding the creation of glass within a door can be tricky. Creating a lot of detailed graphics to represent the muntins (grids) can make the model slow, so simplifying the graphics will allow them to be shown without overburdening the project.

Most doors are available in both single and double configurations, so when developing the door object, we should take this into consideration, as shown

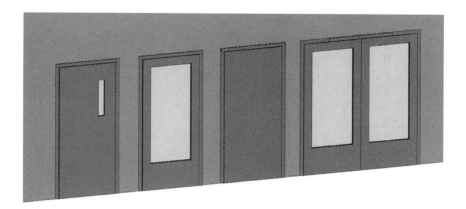

FIGURE 17.4 Typical door configurations

in Figure 17.4. Rather than developing the slab as a geometric solid within the object, it is more effective to create the slab as its own object and insert it into a larger door object. This can be said for all components associated with the door. If we create the hinge, handle, exit device, closer, frame, or other accessory as its own component, we can use them as building blocks and quickly swap them out as necessary on a given project.

Where modeled, components such as hardware and weather stripping are maintenance items and as such perhaps should be considered independent of other components. Many of the decisions about whether to create and how to create secondary or accessory components such as this are driven by the intent of the model. If nobody outside the design team will use the information, then taking the time to develop it may be impractical. Creating the accessories as separate components that can be date stamped or otherwise noting them from other aspects of the opening allows for the ability to consider maintenance throughout the lifecycle of the building.

SIZE/DIMENSIONS

The typical formatting for the size is feet and inches with an "×" between the two sizes. Common examples are 2-6 × 6-8 or 3-0 × 7-0. When developing objects, all available sizes from a given manufacturer should be created to minimize the possibility for user error or the creation of an object that does not exist in the real world. Another aspect of size is the jamb depth of a door. In many cases, especially with wood doors, there are specific sizes of the jamb. Because BIM software often resizes items like jambs to suit the door, often it will not consider a properly sized jamb with the necessary extension jamb. There are multiple solutions to this, depending on the needs of the component developed. Graphically, once an extension jamb is installed to a door, it becomes invisible, so simply noting the jamb depth within the object can assist those on the receiving end of a door schedule.

The actual size of a door is larger than the noted size, as the noted size considers the size of the door opening, not the overall size including the frame and the space necessary to properly shim and install it. This size is referred to as the rough opening and should be taken into consideration through either a calculation or a parameter value within the object.

Most BIM authoring tools allow us to switch the orientation of a component with a single click. A door can be switched from left-handed to right-handed or a window from awning to hopper using a control. While this simplifies the creation of the object, I recommend against this, as it limits the accuracy of door schedules by requiring the user to insert the handing of the unit manually. If the operation of a window or door is considered individually, and is created as unique types of the object, the operation can be taken into account automatically.

Tip

Adding a checkbox that notes the handing of a door will allow for accurate door schedules to be created.

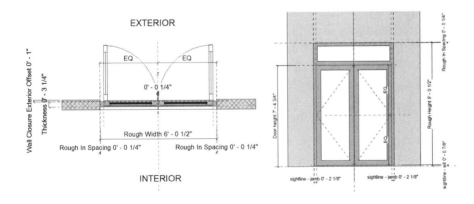

FIGURE 17.5 Door dimensions

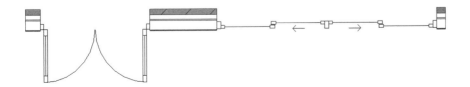

FIGURE 17.6 Door handing/operation

PERFORMANCE

There are countless performance criteria associated with doors, but in most instances it comes down to just a few that are the determining factors as to why a specific type of door is used on a project. Below are some of the most common performance aspects seen in a door, which should be built into every door object that is used on a project requiring data management.

Egress/ADA: Specific dimensions are necessary in determining egress and accessibility compliance. Those dimensions should be developed so they may be visible in schedules and accessible by model analysis software. Generally speaking, egress/ADA compliance is determined by the clear opening sizes of the door, including the clear opening width, and the floor on which the door is installed. It is important to note that egress and ADA requirements vary based on the project location, so adding calculations to determine this is not recommended. Instead of noting whether it meets code requirements, note the values that the code uses to determine compliance. Always check with local code bodies to get the most current information.

Energy efficiency: One of the most important aspects of an exterior door is how energy-efficient it is. In this time of sustainable design and green building, saving energy everywhere we can becomes a paramount design consideration. Just as a wall is insulated and carries a specific R-value, the openings, such as doors, carry R-values as well. These values are taken into consideration when calculations are done to determine the energy efficiency of the building as a whole. BIM affords us the ability to analyze a building as a whole rather than as the sum of its parts, looking at the sizes of openings and the variation in R-value. The U-factor and solar heat gain coefficient are also used when doors contain glass or other glazing. Building these values into the model allows for more robust calculation through third-party software to streamline and simplify energy modeling.

Physical performance: Many code bodies in different parts of the country, especially those in hurricane-prone regions, require that exterior doors be tested to withstand specific air infiltration, water penetration, structural design, and impact resistance criteria. In a hurricane doors can be subject to extreme wind, water, and pressure, and to ensure human safety, must be designed appropriately. Adding the attributes that qualify these performance criteria will allow the architect and specifier to quickly and easily determine whether or not the door meets the design criteria set forth by either local code or the owner/architect.

Sound transmission: Both interior and exterior doors may be rated with a sound transmission classification (STC) rating, which determines how much sound passes through the door. This is an important aspect in design consideration of many types of buildings, be it a hotel, hospital, residence, or sound studio. Having an STC attribute within the model allows the architect or specifier to quickly determine whether or not the door meets the necessary design standards.

GRAPHICS

Frame

The frame of a door is composed of head and jamb components and typically becomes the host, or primary object. All other components, including the leaf, sash, glass, and hardware, can vary in type, color, appearance, or performance. While even the frame can have different characteristics or be of differing types, it is the one component that is fixed to its host component, the wall, making it the most logical component to use as the primary. The level of detail in the frame can be subjective and can vary based on the necessity of the project. The head may look different than the jambs in real life, but in the model it may not be necessary to convey to that detail. It is more important to showcase where the door slab sits in the frame and where integral casing may be located as well, as these have the potential to affect adjacent components and the actual swing of the door.

Glazing

Glazing, glass, and vision lites all refer to the same component—the portion of the unit that light can transmit through. Graphically, the primary consideration is light transmission. Creating glass with appropriate light transmission allows accurate light rendering inside of the BIM. Glass can be considered as a solid component or as a material, depending on the unit in which it is being installed and how accurate the model needs to be. As a material is the most effective method, as it has the ability to carry the necessary characteristics, such as U-factor and solar heat gain, that are necessary to make determinations for code compliance.

In the real world an insulated glass panel is made up of two or more panes of glass, a spacer, and air or some noble gas trapped in the middle. This level of detail is not usually necessary, as visually it is rarely if ever seen. If there is a need to convey what each pane of glass comprises, it is better done as a material listed in the data set of the object.

Door Slab/Leaf/Curtain

The slab, leaf, or curtain is the most visibly noticeable part and in many cases the most graphically important part of a door. There are thousands of different door types in terms of the appearance of the operable component. How detailed should we get when creating a BIM component to represent each of these doors? Much of that is determined based on the needs of the individual firm and the intent of the model after design. If the model will never be rendered and the actual appearance is not relevant within the model, then a simplified flat slab will suffice for every project, with identifiers in place to quickly determine which door is which. On the other hand, if aspects are the primary driver of the model and substantial rendering will be done, it may be necessary to model a door slab down to its last detail.

A good middle-of-the-road solution is to provide a basic appearance of the slab, which outlines details that may be visible from 15 feet away. This allows rendering to occur that will provide the approximate appearance of the door, without increasing the file size to an unmanageable level. Since doors tend to be very ornate objects, with recessed or raised panels or delicate scribe work, it's important to keep our eye on the file size. Try not to model anything less than ⅛ inch in size, and simplify panel profiles to a manageable level.

Door Hardware

Door hardware consists of several components that can be created either as a part of the door or each as its own component. Any time there is an option for multiple types of door hardware, it is recommended to create it as a stand-alone component that can be built into the door.

Levers and knobs are probably the most commonly used forms of access hardware. While several components are embedded within the door, graphically they are of little relevance. It's not likely that somebody will take a section view of the door within a model, and these components are never visible when installed, so their graphic relevance is diminished to almost none. The important aspects of levers and knobs are those that can be seen from the inside and outside of the door. It is important to keep in mind, though, that items of this nature might be placed in hundreds or thousands of locations within a project, so graphics such as keyholes and thumb-turns should not be modeled. In many cases the graphics of door hardware are irrelevant. If there is no intention of rendering the door hardware, it is possible to simplify the graphics altogether. This will allow it to act as a simple placeholder, to be found in finish schedules, and to provide a graphic notation that a piece of door hardware is present. In extreme cases it may be acceptable to simply model a knob as a cylinder.

Exit devices and closers are commercially used devices to permit, limit, and automate door access. Many of these components can become very detailed graphically and can slow the model down if they are overmodeled. Generally, their presence is all that is necessary within a BIM, so it is perfectly acceptable to simplify their graphics considerably. In many cases a simple rectangle will suffice.

Accessories

Hinges are often original equipment from the manufacturer of the door. In some cases, though, specific hinges may be called out. Correctional facilities, hospitals, and schools may have specific requirements for types of hinges to be used. In cases where hinges are added, it should be done such that they show up in hardware schedules and may be swapped out for alternate types.

Thresholds and weather stripping may or may not be added into a door model, based on need, on their presence, or just on simplifying the model. As with hinges, often this is original equipment from the manufacturer of the door. Components like this can easily be omitted, as they are referenced in the manufacturer's product information. Where items like this are added, they should be placed such that they may be swapped out for alternate types without sacrificing the performance of the object.

Kickplates and push plates are often added solely for graphical purposes. Just as with other accessories and other hardware, if they are present, they should be able to show up in hardware schedules and be swapped out for alternate types.

MATERIALS

Materials collectively determine what the product is and, ultimately, how it performs. The frame material is essential in determining whether a door will achieve a specific fire rating. The leaf material will give us some insight into the weight of the door, how much force is required to open it, and what type of sound characteristics the door is capable of achieving. The glass determines how much daylight comes into the building and its color.

Basic door components: Because a door can be painted just about any color, it is important to note the material appropriately and leave the finish "as specified" so the architect can insert whatever color he chooses after selection has been made. What is important, though, is the material from which the door is constructed. A steel door has different characteristics than a wood door, which has different characteristics than a hollow core door. Door types are often selected based on what the material is, so it is important to clearly define the materials within the door such that they can be called out in a door schedule. In some cases the manufacturer will have specific finish options available for the door. These should be called out and created to minimize user error and the creation of a finish that is not available by the manufacturer.

Glass: Glass is more than a clear solid used to let light through an opening. There are several different types of glass, each with different properties, and certain types of glass need to be used in certain locations. It's not uncommon to see the requirement for a tempered glass in bathroom doors, or laminated glass in hurricane-prone regions. Taking into consideration a specific type of glass is essential in determining whether or not the door meets certain code restrictions. The most commonly seen types of glass are tempered, laminated, annealed, and heat strengthened. In certain scenarios we may see other types of glass, such as wired, but for the purposes of this book, the aforementioned types will suffice. In addition to the different types of glass, colors or tints may be applied to the glass to change the color or amount of light that enters the building. Creating the available colors for the different types of glass is equally important to allow daylight studies of the model without requiring the user to develop tint colors, which may not be available.

Hardware and accessories: Materials associated with door hardware have actually become fairly standardized by organizations such as the American National Standards Institute (ANSI) and the Builders Hardware Manufacturers Association (BHMA). These organizations have created standardized finishes and categories for material type, color, and texture of different metals. The hardware and accessory components used in a project in many cases are specified not only by their performance and usage but by their appearance, so it is essential that they be built in such that they can be extracted through a door hardware schedule.

DATA—ATTRIBUTES, CONSTRAINTS, AND EQUATIONS

Dimensions

- *Unit dimensions*: Unit dimensions are generally expressed in terms of width and height, and are exact to the size. They should not be confused with nominal dimensions used by manufacturers for sales purposes.
- *Jamb depth*: The depth of the frame from its outer mounting surface to the inside edge of the frame. For doors that are mounted flush to the

exterior wall using a nailing fin or casing, it is often necessary to add extension jambs when dealing with nonstandard wall depths.

- *Rough opening dimensions*: Dimensions given to notify architects and contractors of the clear opening that is necessary to install a door properly. Generally, a rough opening provides ¼″ or more spacing on either side of the door to allow for discrepancies in framing.

Performance

- *Solar heat gain coefficient (SHGC)*: A performance value associated with glazed doors that refers to the increase in temperature resulting from sunlight passing through the glass. It is expressed as a percentage of solar heat that is absorbed versus reflected when it comes in contact with the door. The lower the solar heat gain coefficient, the more effective the door is at blocking heat from sunlight.

- *U-value/U-factor*: A measure of heat conductivity through the glass. Where R-value relates to thermal resistance, U-factor relates to thermal transmission. In colder climates, it is used to measure how much heat is lost through a door and to assist in determinations of whether or not doors meet energy codes. The lower the U-factor, the less heat is lost through the door.

- *Sound transmission class (STC)*: Measures how well a door attenuates airborne sound. It is expressed in terms of decibels reduced, where the larger the value, the better the door is at reducing sound.

- *Air infiltration*: Based on an ASTM standard that measures how much air is allowed to pass through a door at specific atmospheric pressures. Since most doors are operable, they have a tendency to allow a certain amount of air to pass through. The less air that passes through, the more efficient the door is. Air infiltration is typically expressed in terms of cubic feet per square foot (cfm/sf) at a given air pressure.

- *Water penetration*: Based on an ASTM standard that measures the amount of air pressure required to force water through the void around a door in its installed position. It is generally expressed in terms of its air pressure at the point of failure.

- *Structural test pressure/design pressure*: Design pressure measures how much internal or external pressure is required to break a door during weather events, such as hurricanes, in which extreme internal and external pressures are common.

- *Forced entry rating*: A grading system that determines how effective a door is at preventing a forced entry.

USAGE—LEVERAGING THE INFORMATION

Door Schedules

Schedules are standardized documents that show every door and door hardware components used in a project. Doors are often categorized by their function or usage. Each door in a category may have specific pieces of hardware, specific fire ratings, sound transmission classifications, and other aspects that determine why a door is being used for its specific purpose. Door schedules can be as simplified or as detailed as necessary for the individual receiving the schedule. A specifier may need a door schedule with a considerable amount of information, as these data may be used to assist in developing the project specification. The contractor, on the other hand, may only need the names, sizes, and identifying properties of each door and door hardware component. It is not uncommon for multiple door schedules to be created tailored to different parties.

As schedules are created within the software, design professionals now have the ability to analyze the information in a tabular form. Previously, there was no simplified way to look at two products of a given category and make determinations about their acceptability or performance. If the building code requires a door to meet a specific fire rating, or to be able to withstand impact from a hurricane, the information contained within the model will allow design professionals to view multiple manufacturers of a door during bid review in order to determine which products should be selected based on the design requirements.

Figures 17.7 and 17.8 show two examples of door schedules, one detailed and one simplified. The architect and specifier may use the detailed version for

FIGURE 17.7 Typical door schedule—detailed

Identity				
Count	Type	Manufacturer	Model	Description
Assembly_Door_SDI				
1	As Specif	Steel Door Institute	As Specified in 08 11 13	SDI Steel Door as Specified in 08 11 13
As Specified in 08 11 13: 1				
Assembly_DoubleDoor_SDI				
1	As Specif	Steel Door Institute	As Specified in 08 11 13	SDI Steel Door as Specified in 08 11 13
As Specified in 08 11 13: 1				
DblDoor-2-Panel				
1	(2)-3-0 x	Generic	Generic	6-0 x 8-0 Raised 2-Panel Steel Double Door
1	(2)-3-0 x	Generic	Generic	6-0 x 8-0 Raised 2-Panel Steel Double Door
(2)-3-0 x 8-0 Steel: 2				
Door_Astragals_Amweld				
1	Door_Ast	Amweld International,	Astragals	Double Door Astragals
Door_Astragals_Amweld: 1				
Door_FullLight_BulletResistant_BulletGuard				
1	As Specif	Bulletguard	Full Light	Bullet Resistant Door as specified in 13 20 00
As Specified in 13 20 00: 1				
Door_Sidelite_CGI_Transom				
1	As Specif	CGI Windows and Do	As Specified in 08 57 00	Hurricane Resistant Door as Specified in 08 57 00
As Specified in the Contract Documents: 1				
Door_SolidCore_w_Lite_BulletResistant_BulletGuard				
1	As Specif	Bulletguard	Solid Core w/ Lite	Bullet Resistant Door as specified in 13 20 00
1	As Specif	Bulletguard	Solid Core w/ Lite	Bullet Resistant Door as specified in 13 20 00
1	As Specif	Bulletguard	Solid Core w/ Lite	Bullet Resistant Door as specified in 13 20 00
1	As Specif	Bulletguard	Solid Core w/ Lite	Bullet Resistant Door as specified in 13 20 00
As Specified in 13 20 00: 4				
Door_Transom_CGI				
1	As Specif	CGI Windows and Do	As Specified in 08 57 00	Hurricane Resistant Door as Specified in 08 57 00
As Specified in the Contract Documents: 1				
DoorSlab_Stamped_SDI				
1	Door as Spe	Steel Door Institute	As Specified in 08 11 13	SDI Steel Door as Specified in 08 11 13
1	Door as Spe	Steel Door Institute	As Specified in 08 11 13	SDI Steel Door as Specified in 08 11 13
Door as Specified in 08 11 13: 2				
None				
1	None	None	No Panel Specified	Door Constellation Needs Panel
1	None	None	No Panel Specified	Door Constellation Needs Panel
1	None	None	No Panel Specified	Door Constellation Needs Panel
1	None	None	No Panel Specified	Door Constellation Needs Panel
1	None	None	No Panel Specified	Door Constellation Needs Panel
1	None	None	No Panel Specified	Door Constellation Needs Panel
1	None	None	No Panel Specified	Door Constellation Needs Panel
1	None	None	No Panel Specified	Door Constellation Needs Panel
1	None	None	No Panel Specified	Door Constellation Needs Panel
1	None	None	No Panel Specified	Door Constellation Needs Panel
1	None	None	No Panel Specified	Door Constellation Needs Panel
1	None	None	No Panel Specified	Door Constellation Needs Panel
1	None	None	No Panel Specified	Door Constellation Needs Panel

FIGURE 17.8 Typical door schedule—simplified

product analysis and construction documents, and the simplified version may be used when soliciting bids, compiling cost data, and during procurement.

Model Analysis

BIM has the ability to perform egress and accessibility analysis based on the information contained within the door objects. A model can look at a space, determine what the space is, and analyze it in terms of its usage, function, and components necessary to achieve the design intent and building codes required of the project. In some cases human interaction is still necessary to perform a full analysis of the building, but specific aspects may be automated or simplified by the addition of attributes into objects. For accessibility requirements, a door may need to be of a certain width. Provided this door accurately depicts this dimension, the software needs to consider only the size of the door and the function of the space in which the door is located.

Energy modeling software must be able to consider not only the walls of the building but the openings that are contained within the exterior walls. Exterior doors may make up a considerable amount of surface area and drastically change the energy performance of the building. Glazed doors are an excellent example of this. Where U-factor, solar heat gain coefficient, and R-value are present in a given door, the information can be extracted and analyzed to determine actual energy performance of the building.

Facilities managers have the ability to leverage the information within door objects for maintenance and forecasting purposes. For instance, fire doors must be tested periodically, so tagging each fire door allows facility managers to quickly and easily determine how many doors must be tested, when they were tested last, and where they are located. Maintenance equipment within the door, such as batteries for electromechanical hardware or weather stripping, can be tagged with installation dates. This allows components to be maintained efficiently and minimizes the risk of downtime due to broken equipment.

EXAMPLE DOOR OBJECTS AND THEIR ATTRIBUTE SETS

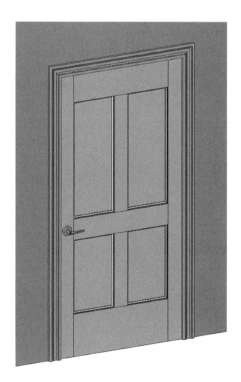

FIGURE 17.9

Typical interior swing door object

- Width: 30"
- Height: 80"
- Rough width: 33 1/4"
- Rough height: 80 3/4"
- Jamb depth: 4 9/16"
- Panel material/finish: solid core composite
- Panel style: 6 panel
- Frame material/finish: FJ pine – primed
- Operation/handing: LH
- Function: interior passage
- Fire rating: 30 minute
- STC: 29

FIGURE 17.10
Typical exterior swing door object

- Width: 36"
- Height: 80"
- Rough width: 39¼"
- Rough height: 80¾"
- Jamb depth: 4⁹⁄₁₆"
- Panel material/finish: honeycomb core steel
- Panel style: 6 panel
- Frame material/finish: FJ pine – primed
- Operation/handing: LH
- Function: exterior fire door
- Fire rating: 90 minute
- R-value: 8.0
- Air infiltration: maximum 0.08 cfm/sq ft at 1.57 psf (25 mph) in accordance with ASTM E 283
- Water penetration: no leakage when tested at 6.0 psf in accordance with ASTM E 547
- Structural test pressure: 52.5 psf positive and negative in accordance with ASTM E 330.
- STC: 29
- Forced entry rating: type D, grade 30 in accordance with ASTM F 588

FIGURE 17.11

Typical exterior glazed swing door object

- Width: 36"
- Height: 80"
- Rough width: 39¼"
- Rough height: 80¾"
- Jamb depth: 4⁹⁄₁₆
- Panel material/finish: pine – northern white
- Panel style: single lite glazed
- Frame material/finish: clear pine
- Operation/handing: LH
- Function: exterior fire door
- Fire rating: 30 minute
- R-value: 8.0
- Glass type: ⅝" IG – clear tempered
- U-factor: 0.30
- SHGC: 0.25
- Air infiltration: maximum 0.06 cfm/sq ft at 1.57 psf (25 mph) in accordance with ASTM E 283
- Water penetration: no leakage when tested at 6.0 psf in accordance with ASTM E 547
- Structural test pressure: 52.5 psf positive and negative in accordance with ASTM E 330.
- STC: 35
- Forced entry rating: grade 10 in accordance with ASTM F 588

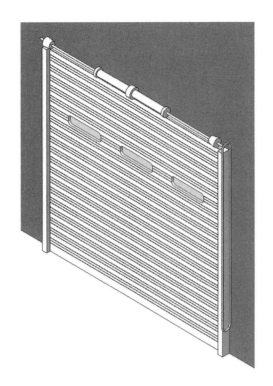

FIGURE 17.12

Typical Overhead Door Object

- Width: 96″
- Height: 120″
- Rough width: 94″
- Rough height: 116″
- Panel material/finish: solid core composite
- Panel style: 6 panel
- Frame material/finish: FJ pine – primed
- Operation/handing: LH
- Function: exterior fire door
- Fire rating: 2 hour
- R-value: 4.0
- STC: 21

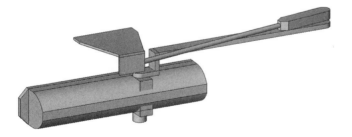

FIGURE 17.13

Typical exit device object
- Color/finish: 605 bright brass
- Mounting: surface
- Spring size: 3
- ANSI rating: A156.3 grade 1
- Fire rating: panic only
- Function: delayed egress

CHAPTER 18

Stairs and Railings

ANATOMY

Stairs

A typical stair is made up of three basic components: stringers, treads, and risers. Stringers are the structural supports that hold up the surfaces that are stepped upon, the treads are the surfaces that are stepped upon, and the risers are the vertical components that cover the area between two treads. Creating objects that allow all of these components to work together has been simplified by BIM software. Most BIM software has a series of stair tools that automatically assembles these components and makes calculations as to how deep the tread should be and how tall the riser should be based on the vertical and horizontal distances traveled, or the rise and run. Building code and good design practice both dictate that treads should be a specific minimum depth, riser height should fall between a specific minimum and maximum, and the height between steps should be equal throughout the entire stair set.

In situations where the stair may turn a corner or the vertical distance between two floors is too great, a landing is placed in the middle of the stair run to accommodate this. In most cases the landings are structural components and must be supported either by the surrounding walls or supports from above or below. Typical BIM stair tools do have the ability to add landings, but do not accurately detail construction dimensions or support locations; these must be placed manually.

Other types of stairs include curved stairs, spiral stairs, and basic monolithic stairs, which may be constructed of solid concrete. These stairs carry the same requirements for their basic anatomy and procedure for design, but the differences in their anatomy are noticeable and should be considered carefully when developing BIM objects. Spiral stairs, for instance, have treads and risers, but don't use a stringer as their structural support member. They use a center column and have treads and risers cantilevered out and supported by the shaft with the gusset. Monolithic stairs, as their name says, are a single component typically made of cast-in-place or precast concrete.

FIGURE 18.1 Typical stair construction:
1- tread; 2- riser;
3- stringer; 4- nosing;
5- handrail

FIGURE 18.2 Typical spiral stair construction: 1- tread; 2- center column; 3- handrail; 4- baluster

The treads, the risers, and the structural support are all part of one single monolithic unit.

Railings

Three primary components make up a railing: horizontal rails, vertical support posts, and infill. Several different types of infill may be used, from vertical pickets to horizontal cables to solid panels, and everything in between. When developing railing objects, we should consider carefully the spacing of posts, heights of handrails and grab rails, and spacing of the infill. Building codes and structural considerations often dictate the specifications and should be modeled such that they are close to actual dimensions, if not exact. The reality of BIM is that it is ultimately a static image once created. That means that regardless of the actual spacing of the infill, nobody is really going to attempt to pass a 4-inch-diameter sphere to determine whether or not the railing meets building code. The concept is more to show an approximate appearance of the railing and to focus more on the unit length and structural considerations rather than the exact placement of the individual components.

Just as with stairs, building information modeling software typically has a series of tools that will generate an entire railing based on which rails, posts, and infill are selected. This simplifies object creation considerably, but is also limited, as the software is not intuitive enough to understand how corners may happen or angles may join. For this reason it is often not practical to attempt to model a railing to its exact location or exact size as the joins will likely never match up exactly unless a considerable amount of manual effort is added. In many cases, railings do play an integral part in the rendering of a BIM project. Creating pickets or other infill types that look appropriate can be important, but I would caution you that attempting to make exact

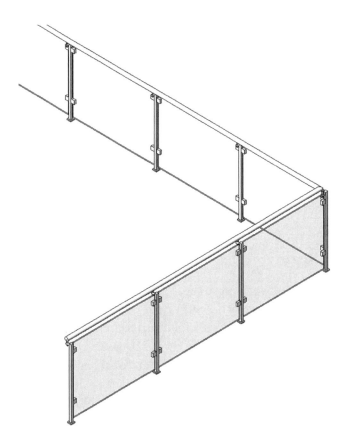

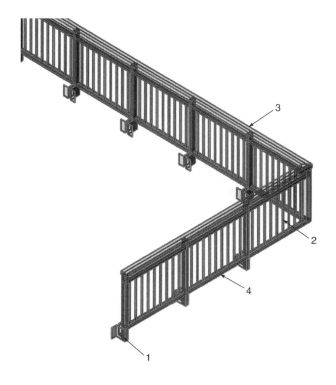

FIGURE 18.3 Typical railing construction: 1- post; 2- baluster/infill; 3- handrail; 4- base rail

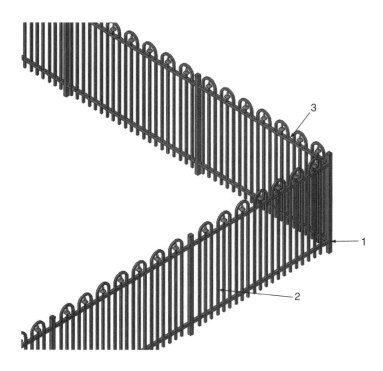

FIGURE 18.4 Typical fence construction: 1- post; 2- fencing infill; 3- rail

appearances, especially at junctions and terminations, may require additional effort prior to rendering.

Another component similar to railings that we will cover in a general sense is fences. They are typically created in the same manner, using horizontal rails, vertical posts, and some type of infill or fence fabric. Using the railing tools within BIM software provides an excellent opportunity to quickly create good-looking fences. I will caution you again, though, that when dealing with meshes and fence fabrics, it is often easier and more effective to create them as solids rather than trying to mimic the appearance of a chain-link fence. Surface patterns and rendering images are ultimately the most effective way to provide the overall appearance within the rendering but still keep the modeling speed up.

CONSIDERATIONS

As I noted, stairs are made up of multiple components, typically treads, risers, and stringers. The stair construction itself dictates whether the stringers may be located underneath or beside the treads. Taking this into consideration is important, as it will determine the actual width of the stair. In close dimension situations, being off by 1½ inches may be the difference between meeting building code requirements or a very expensive change order. Some BIM software packages handle stairs and railings better than others, so the graphic element of the stair will be dictated by the quality of the software. Where possible, it's a good idea to note the profile of the stringer, whether it is a C-channel, a wood 2 × 12, or flat plate steel. The profile of the stringer can potentially affect where and how the stairs are structurally supported.

Treads are mainly affected by their appearance and the material from which they were created. The leading edge of a stair tread, or "nosing," may be curved, beveled, or contain an ornate profile to match the surrounding trim. Where possible, adding these details in provides for a more accurate rendering and allows us to call out a specific stair tread. This will assist not only the architect's design, but the specifier's documents, the estimator's cost figures, and the accuracy of the schedules exported for the benefit of the contractor. When adding surface materials and patterns to a stair, adding it to the tread is typically done by adding it to the stair as a whole. This allows the material and surface pattern to be added to every tread, regardless of the final count. If we add a surface material or pattern to each individual tread, then if the number of treads increases, the pattern may not carry to the additional treads.

Risers are fairly straightforward and simple components, and in many cases either exist or don't exist. It is possible to have them sloped or vertical and add material and surface patterns to them, but outside of manually adding customized appearances to the risers there is little more that can be done to modify them.

Spiral stairs are tricky components, and this BIM developer has spent countless hours trying to perfect the best way to represent a set. While traditional stair tools will handle a spiral, they don't handle the center shaft, so additional components are necessary to accurately portray the entire unit. Treads get to be a tricky aspect as well, as spiral stairs typically have treads that taper in toward the center shaft. Modeling spiral stairs requires a considerable amount of patience and a lot of thinking outside of the box. Later in this chapter we will discuss in a little more depth some good practices for creating spiral stairs.

There are several types of railings to consider: wall-mounted handrails, basic handrails that mount to the stair or floor, and guardrails, which may or may not contain a handrail and are typically found around balconies. With each of these types, the posts may be mounted either to the floor or against a vertical face. Creating components that can take into consideration the multiple types of mounting is important, as structural considerations take precedence when dealing with railings. The easiest way I've found to achieve this without creating a whole series of objects is to create a vertical and horizontal offset, which allows the railing to move without changing the reference line used to determine its location. Generally, the easiest reference line is the edge of the floor, stair, or other face on which the railing is to be mounted. Creating a simple offset from that edge lets the railing move as necessary without having to redraw every time.

Horizontal rails are probably the easiest component within a railing to create. A horizontal rail is generally based on its profile, or cross-section appearance, and is created using simple line drawings and loaded into a project. Making the cross sections parametric will keep file size down and minimize the need to load additional objects into the project. This works for rectangular and round profiles, but with more ornate shapes it may become more of a headache than it's worth. Either way, profile sketches allow us to change the appearance of a railing with little more than a single mouse click. Where the rails start and end in relation to the support posts is typically handled by using offsets. The railing that is mounted atop a post may begin on one side of the post, where a railing that is mounted between posts may begin on the other side. Setting offsets will allow the model to create an appropriate appearance.

There are limitations and pitfalls surrounding stair and railing tools that require a considerable amount of manual effort to achieve the desired appearance. For instance, ornate wall returns in stairs at the beginning and end of a railing can be exceptionally difficult to model effectively. In many cases it is better to infer that graphics of this nature are present, rather than spending an inordinate amount of time trying to model them. Because even the slightest change in the angle of the stair will modify how the railing joins, most software is not capable of considering graphics at this aggregate level accurately. Proceed with caution when trying to model a set of stairs, as you may find yourself spending too much time on finite details that may or may not be relevant in the big picture of the project.

Above and beyond the basic components that are associated with a set of stairs and railings, there is a set of informational attributes that are relevant to the design, specification, and installation of a set of stairs. Most of this information is determined by building codes and design considerations. One must consider tread depths and riser heights at a bare minimum. The clear distance is that from nosing edge to nosing edge between treads. Risers should be no greater than 7¾ inch high with no greater than ⅜ of an inch difference among all the risers. Building code also dictates that there be a minimum headroom between the tread and any obstruction above. As a general rule it should be 6 feet 8 inches high.

Handrails and railings must be placed at specific heights and be continuous for the full length of a flight. They also have minimum and maximum dimensions to allow a hand to grasp them appropriately. For safety purposes, the distance between balusters is governed by building code as well. As a general rule, balusters should be spaced such that they do not allow the passage of a 4⅜-inch sphere between them on stairs or 4-inch sphere between them on guardrails.

Even though they are very much an aesthetic aspect of the building, stairs should represent the dimensions and sizes just as much as the appearance of the actual component. The limitations of the BIM software tools today give us little ability to control specific aspects of the aesthetic qualities and graphic representations of the structural design of stairs and railings. Unless we intend to add a considerable amount of manual effort to improve the overall appearance of the stairs and railings, keeping the appearance simplified to that of the treads and risers will often suit the needs of the project when rendering is performed. Even though the structural aspects are not accurately represented graphically, creating options for the various components in terms of data will allow the information to be pulled back out and used for specification and construction.

GRAPHICS

The graphical limitations to the development of stairs within some BIM software tools minimize the accuracy of the stairs' appearance. It can be difficult, and in some cases impossible, to modify the profile of the stringers or use a specific ornamental tread without a considerable amount of manual effort. Much of a graphic aspect of stairs is driven by the materials used. As I noted, stairs are very much an aesthetic item and often find themselves in rendered views, so when creating materials to represent treads and risers, take into consideration what they will look like when rendered, as well as the model view. Nosing profiles are another driver of the graphics within a set of stairs. Different manufacturers have different nosing profiles, so if we're developing a set of stairs for specific manufacturer, we create the profiles that match their offering and develop a specific set of stairs for each profile to make it easier for the design professional to select a specific stair without having to make considerable modifications on his own.

Railings offer slightly more control of the graphic aspect and appearance of the component. Ornate balusters, posts, and railings can be created to match any exact profile or appearance that is desired. A repeating pattern may be created that dictates the spacing of the balusters and the spacing of the posts along the length of the railing. This is where the intelligence of the BIM software begins to drop off. The behavior of railings at vertical angles and horizontal angles may change based on how they are joined—they may be welded, fastened, or joined with a fitting. In addition, the software often trips up where the railing does not finish its pattern. Often the user must manually resize components or reconfigure the railing to correct its appearance.

We must look at spiral stairs more as individual components than as an entire set of stairs, as shown in Figure 18.5. This is mainly geared to the

FIGURE 18.5 Laying out spiral stair components

limitations of the stair tools within the software. Because they cannot consider the shaft and the appearance of the treads in a set of spiral stairs, each tread really needs to be its own component. The stair tool can create an outline of where the components should be placed, but ultimately the best solution I've found is to trick the railing into creating each tread by making a tread type that is a baluster and setting the railing tool to assign one baluster per tread. While not scheduled appropriately, they will provide the desired appearance, and ultimately give the design professional a replica of the stair set to be used within the model.

DATA—ATTRIBUTES AND EQUATIONS

Most of the attributes and equations associated with a set of stairs and railings are actually built into the BIM software platform. It is more a matter of creating schedules that will export the information effectively, then entering the information. There are a few additional attributes to the structural aspects of railings, such as uniform load and concentrated load, so, for the most part, stairs and railings need little additional information above and beyond their appearance in order to be useful to the architect, specifier, or estimator. The software will also calculate the number and nominal dimensions of each component, so little is necessary in terms of equations as well. Below is a set of typical attributes that may be used within a set of stairs and a set of railings.

- Typical Stair Attribute Set
  - *Tread width*: the distance between walls, stringers, or railings on a given tread; this is the effective width that can be stepped upon
  - *Tread depth*: the horizontal distance between the nosing of one tread and the nosing of the next
  - *Riser height*: the vertical distance between the top of one tread and the top of the next
  - *Tread material*: the material and finish of the horizontal stepping surface
  - *Riser material*: the material and finish of the vertical stair closure surface
  - *Stringer material*: the material and finish of the structural support members of the stair
  - *Tread nosing type*: the appearance of the leading edge of the treads

- Typical Railing Attribute Set
  - *Handrail type*: the appearance of the top, bottom, and middle rails as applicable to the railing design
  - *Handrail height*: the height to the top of the uppermost railing
  - *Handrail material*: the material and finish of the top, bottom, and middle rails as applicable to the railing design
  - *Baluster/infill type*: the appearance of the balusters or other infill used in the railing.
  - *Baluster/infill spacing*: the spacing of the balusters or other infill used in a railing
  - *Baluster/infill material*: the material and finish of the balusters or other infill used in a railing
  - *Post type*: the appearance of the vertical support members used in the railing
  - *Post spacing*: the center-to-center spacing between the vertical support members used in the railing
  - *Post material*: the material and finish of the vertical support members used in the railing
  - *Concentrated load*: the minimum load that the railing must carry at any given point in any given direction
  - *Uniform load*: the minimum load that the railing must carry over its entire length

Usage—Leveraging the information

It's probably not practical to expect stair fabricators to be able to use the dimensions from a BIM software platform to actually engineer and build their stairs, as each manufacturer uses different tolerances, different design considerations, and different structural members. The data contained within a set of stairs are more likely useful to the specifier when creating construction documentation, and the building code official who needs to determine whether or not the stairs meet the local building code. A fabricator can, however, extract the information regarding the materials used to fabricate a set of stairs, as-specified finishes, and components that speak to the aesthetic of the stair. Stairs and railings are fabricated components, which means that they are engineered to fit specific design considerations. When a fabricator designs a set of stairs and a series of railings, the important elements are the gross dimensions and the space limitations that are allotted for the stair set. Making sure this information can pass through the model is what is most appropriate in terms of information leverage.

EXAMPLE STAIR AND RAILING COMPONENTS AND THEIR ATTRIBUTE SETS

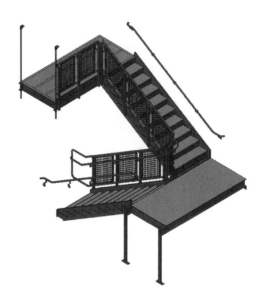

FIGURE 18.6
Typical stair object

- Stair width
- Tread depth
- Riser height
- Tread material
- Riser material
- Stringer material
- Tread nosing profile

FIGURE 18.7
Typical spiral stair object

- Stair width
- Tread depth
- Riser height
- Tread material
- Riser material
- Stringer material
- Tread nosing profile

FIGURE 18.8

Typical railing object

- Handrail type
- Handrail height
- Handrail material
- Baluster type
- Baluster spacing
- Baluster material
- Concentrated load
- Uniform load

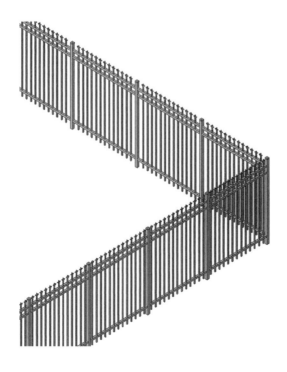

FIGURE 18.9

Typical fence object

- Handrail type
- Handrail height
- Handrail material
- Baluster type
- Baluster spacing
- Baluster material
- Concentrated load
- Uniform load

CHAPTER 19

Curtain Walls and Storefronts

A curtain wall can be looked at as a thin wall that is framed with mullions around the outer edges and filled in with panels. In many cases there are intermediate framing members with specialty hardware that secures the panels laterally. In terms of graphics, it is basically a grid where the lines represent the locations of mullions or framing members, and the panels are some sort of infill. Typically, curtain walls are nonstructural in nature and do not carry floor or roof loads the same way bearing walls do. Curtain walls are typically used to enclose the outside of a building, but can often be found as interior partitions as well. Storefronts are similar to curtain walls in their construction, but behave more like windows or doors. They are designed to be embedded within a structural wall with a header or lintel spanning the length of the opening.

In terms of building information modeling software, the curtain wall tools can provide far more possibilities for content than your typical wall enclosure or storefront. They can be used to develop operable partitions, caged enclosures, or any other type of construction that may rely on the vertical and horizontal components and some type of infill. One unique opportunity that I have found is to use curtain tools to develop structural framing components.

If we think of the frame lines as studs, and the panels as insulation, we can actually draw an entire wall framing system with a single line.

ANATOMY

To develop a curtain wall, storefront, or any other elements adapted from the curtain tools within building information modeling software, there are three primary components: the panels, or infill; the lines, or mullions; and the profile, which drives the appearance of the mullions found on the project. Curtain tools let us effectively control the appearance of an assembly by customizing it with different mullions on the top, bottom, left, right, and internal horizontal and vertical lines. They can be trained to place mullions a specific distance apart or have a fixed number of mullions, set minimum or maximum distances between mullions, and use different mullions at corners. The panels themselves may be customized to suit anything from a simple rectangular glass panel to a highly ornate decorative geometric structure. It is also important to note that mullions and panels can both be omitted altogether, allowing a repeated pattern to be generated without the need to place each component over and over.

Curtain tools are not limited to walls or vertical faces. They can be used to create a grid pattern on any uniform surface provided a mass is available to superimpose it on. A simple way to create a glazed dome is to generate a mass of the appropriate size and instantiate a specific curtain system on it. The software is intuitive enough to understand that the curved surface terminates at a point, which is different from a wall that terminates at a height. This will

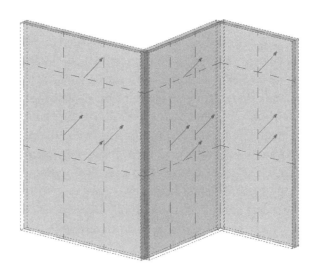

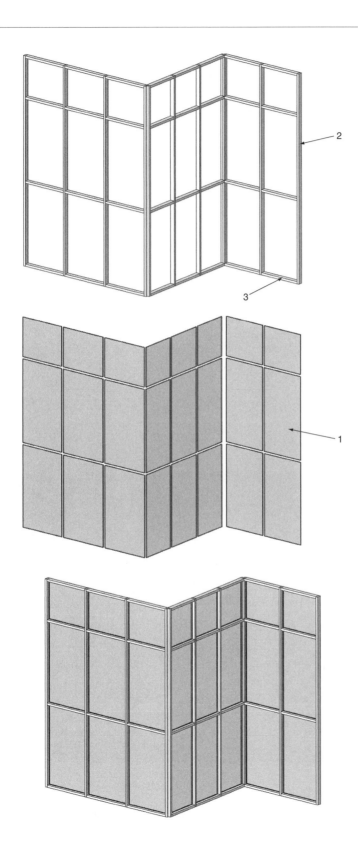

FIGURE 19.1 Anatomy of a curtain system: 1- panel/infill; 2- vertical mullion; 3- horizontal mullion

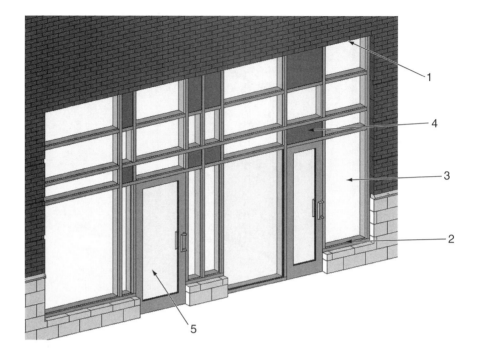

FIGURE 19.2   Anatomy of curtain wall or storefront: 1- top mullion; 2- bottom mullion; 3- glazed panel; 4- solid panel; 5- door

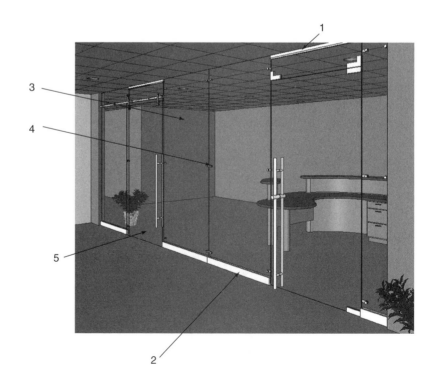

FIGURE 19.3   Anatomy of a glazed partition: 1- top mullion; 2- bottom mullion; 3- glazed panel; 4- connecting hardware; 5- door

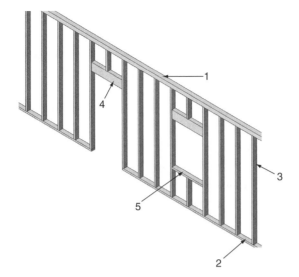

FIGURE 19.4 Anatomy of a framed wall: 1- sill plate; 2- sole plate; 3- common stud; 4- header; 5- stool

begin the mullions at a specific distance apart, and bring them in toward a center point.

Curtain walls, just like any other wall type, must allow for openings. Doors and windows may be generated as specialized curtain panels that can be substituted for any panel and the opening resized to the desired dimensions. Doors are generally not created to be embedded in curtain panels; they must be generated for this specific purpose. If a door may be used with both curtain wall construction and traditional wall construction, it may be a good idea to develop it as based on a face rather than on a wall. This will allow the same object to serve two purposes.

Tip

Curtain tools can be used to create a grid pattern on any uniform surface provided a mass is available to superimpose it upon.

CONSIDERATIONS

There is no limit to the possibilities available when using curtain tools, only limitations to the software. It is important to keep in mind that the panels are based on a rectangle, so if we're dealing with ornate shapes we can expect to encounter errors along the way. While the software is capable of designing curtain systems around complex curves, in many cases it trips up when attempting to align mullions. For representation purposes, this typically is not a big issue, as ornate geometry of this nature is generally fully engineered, and, as such, model graphics are not used for anything other than representation. When attempting to render, however, we may end up with some unsightly appearances.

The key to developing good curtain systems is to minimize the amount of manual effort necessary to use the tools. This is especially important when dealing with corner mullions and repeating patterns throughout the walls. By developing end mullions that can double as corner mullions, less effort is required to update the model to an exact appearance. In terms of mullion appearance, we should hold back our desire to become highly detailed. While some of the critical differences between various curtain walls and storefronts lie in the construction of the mullion, the primary differences are invisible to the naked eye. Where a thermal break is located, the internal construction, gaskets, glazing beads, and similar aspects of a mullion are better represented through data than graphics. Curtain tools use a considerable amount of resources to generate the graphics. By overburdening the graphics, we can slow down the performance and regeneration of the model considerably.

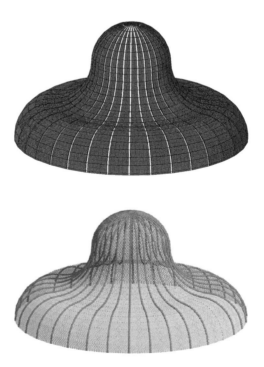

FIGURE 19.5 Creating an aviary along complex curves by using curtain systems

Developing a radial curtain system or one located along complex curves may require a great deal of trial and error to make it look appropriate. When curtain systems are developed with a fixed number of vertical or horizontal mullions, they can join appropriately with the least amount of effort. Because features such as domes have a termination point in the center, panels are not rectangular. When the rectangular panel does not fit, the software defaults to a standard infill that suits the shape, so in cases where we're trying to attain a specific appearance, creating that appearance through materials rather than graphics solids will simplify the process and allow us to attain the desired results. In the case illustrated in Figure 19.5, let's suppose we're developing an aviary that has a mesh netting attached to framework in a highly ornate complex shape. We can develop the framework using standard curtain systems and represent the infill by creating a mesh material that perforates each of the panels to represent a netted appearance.

GRAPHICS

Frame/Mullions

The framework of a curtain wall is made up of the mullions that are created using a one or more profiles drawn along the lines that mark the outer boundaries and separation between panels. The level of detail associated with these mullions should be commensurate with the desired accuracy in rendering. If rendering is not a concern, the mullion profiles could functionally be circles or rectangles. The more graphic detail that is put into the mullions, the more the software will have to work to generate the curtain wall, so if there are a considerable number of curtain walls on the project, try to keep the detail level to a minimum. The profile appearance should consider only the exterior appearance, not the exact extrusion in terms of its internal construction. In a finished model setting and in rendered views, nobody can see the innards of a mullion. This level of accuracy should be represented using detail objects rather than the profile mullions.

In some cases, mullions may be omitted altogether based on the construction of the wall. Panel walls, rainscreens, and glazing that are joined using specialty hardware are examples of this. Rather than mullions being used as frame components, the hardware becomes a subcomponent of the panel. When simple visibility parameters are created for each corner, the hardware may be turned on and off depending on its location within the wall. If a door is placed adjacent to a panel or the panel is at a corner, the hardware may need to be turned off or swapped out for a different type. In other cases, the framing is put at the

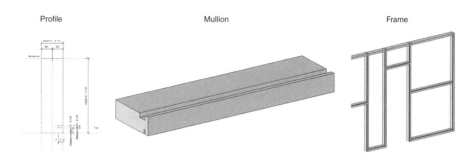

Profile   Mullion   Frame

FIGURE 19.6   Profile to
mullion to frame

forefront and the panels are omitted. In a case such as structural wall framing, the mullions may be developed so that they represent wall studs, sole and sill plates, headers, and specific framing components for wall openings.

To create curtain mullions, we start with a profile. The profile is a specific object formatted for use in curtain systems and contains a single closed line that determines the shape of the extrusion. We may make a single parametric profile that is called "dimensional lumber," which may consider everything from a 2 × 4 up to a 2 × 12 with a single object. The profile is embedded into a mullion object formatted for a specific purpose and assigned a material and a series of attributes that pertain to what it is and how it performs. Because every curtain system is slightly different, creating a series of mullions for all of the possible combinations will allow somebody to quickly customize the system to exactly what he is looking for, or for manufacturers to represent not only the graphics of each of the extrusions they offer, but the data associated with them as well.

Mullions may be assigned to the left hand, right hand, top, bottom, and infill gridlines associated with a curtain system. Each one may be different, and some or all of them may be omitted.

Glazing

Glazing, glass, and vision lites all refer to the same component; the portion of the unit through which light can be transmitted. Graphically, the primary consideration is light transmission. Creating glass with appropriate light transmission makes accurate light rendering possible inside the project model. Glass can be created as either a solid panel or as a material, depending on the shape of unit in which it is being installed. A material is the most effective method, as it can work in both complex and simple shapes, and has the ability to carry the necessary performance characteristics, such as U-factor, solar heat gain, and visible light transmittance.

Building information modeling software starts with default solid and glazed panels for use with curtain systems. If we create a series of materials that represent the various types of glass that may be used, then no additional panel objects would be required. Simply assigning a material to the panel is sufficient to represent the glazing. These materials can manage not only the identification information, energy, and structural performance, but the color, transparency, reflectivity, and surface texture. Regardless of whether custom panels are created, accurate materials must be created for each type of glass to mimic real-world glazing situations.

There are few situations where actual panel objects are necessary for curtain glazing. The primary reason for creating them is to accurately represent a specific manufacturer's product line in a nice neat package. Materials must be easily transferable from one project to another, so as graphically simple as they may be, a manufacturer-specific curtain panel likely carries a considerable amount of information regarding exact glass types, performance values, and available options. Once the object is transferred into a project, the panels or the materials themselves may be transferred into curtain systems. How the operation is performed is very much dependent on the preference of the user.

Panels

Curtain panels represent the infill between the gridlines within a curtain wall system. Whether it is glass, aluminum, or wall insulation, the idea is to create some type of infill using a grid structure rather than a single surface. This is a very effective method of representing panel-based assemblies without having to do a whole lot of work. Whether we are trying to represent the panels of a metal building, interior acoustical wall panels, the insulation between wall studs, or even office cubicles, the ability to draw a single line and represent height and depth and specific configuration at the same time seems to me to be a real timesaver. Depending on how we develop the panel, it can be placed either between mullions or on the face of a mullion. In the case of panel walls, it is likely that the panels will run vertically over a series of purlins that are configured as horizontal mullions. In the case of glass or wall cavity insulation, the insulation panel may be designed to fit between each mullion. Whether the element being created dictates that only panels, only mullions, or both be used, the tools are dynamic enough to reasonably represent nearly all of the situations we may run across.

Panel wall systems and rainscreens are good examples of curtain walls that do not leverage mullions. The panels overlap each other, creating a water-shedding exterior cladding, and are often mitered at the corners, or specialty corner panels are fabricated. Curtain system tools are not capable of creating corner conditions such as a specialty panel with any great ease, so by overlapping or mitering the corners, we can graphically depict the panels. This may not be the best solution for those who are trying to count every panel on a project and perform an exact takeoff, but walls of this type are better estimated in a square foot fashion rather than a specific panel count.

Panels that do not use mullions need to be attached to something using some type of device. Specific hardware components are designed to attach either to the back or to the corners of these types of panels to affix them to a wall behind or the panel adjacent to it. These types of hardware should be a function of the panel and have the ability to control their presence at all locations. A panel that has hardware at the top left, top right, bottom left, and bottom right corners should have a control for each location that allows the hardware type to be selected, as well as having a control for no hardware at all. Where a panel may join to an opening in the wall, the hardware types may be different or not present, and therefore should be easy to modify.

To represent structural wall framing, such as light-gauge metal or wood, click curtain assemblies can be created using only a couple different profile objects formatted into a few different mullions, which can represent the core components of the framing assembly. While it is possible to represent nearly every component from king studs to cripple studs, from the sole plate to the sill, in many cases it may not be practical. Some software applications are already available that can generate this type of design effectively, and most BIM software platforms are already developing additional functionality to take into consideration lightweight framing types.

The graphics associated with panels can tend to get ornate, especially when dealing with corrugated or ribbed panels. These types of panels will typically have a fixed profile, where the ribs or corrugations are a specific distance apart. Because a panel can stretch from side to side and top to bottom, it can be difficult to represent these without overburdening the software. If we attempt to create an array that calculates the number of records based on the width of the panel, the curtain system will slow down the model considerably. To represent each rib of a panel effectively, the best method that I have found is to create a panel that is larger than would ever be necessary and use void geometry to cut it off at the sides of the panel. This allows very detailed geometry to be created without worrying about computationally large objects.

Tip

When creating ribbed panels, create a panel that is larger than would ever be necessary and use void geometry to cut it off at the sides.

FIGURE 19.7 Creating corrugated panels

If we think of a curtain panel as just a rectangle that can be anything, the possibilities for development are limitless. If we look around, we see that there are countless different products that may find their way into a project that can leverage curtain systems. Any type of component that is designed on a grid is a candidate for this type of assembly. From an acoustical tile ceiling to a panel access floor to structural wall framing, curtain tools allow us to quickly place multiple components that may otherwise have taken a considerable amount of time to instantiate.

Doors

Doors that are used in curtain assemblies are different from those used in typical walls. In many cases this can cause a problem, especially when wall types are being adapted for use as curtain walls. A traditional door may be used in a metal building, but the wall that is used may be a curtain panel. Deciding how best to develop associated components depends on how we choose to work. If we create doors a stand-alone objects, they can then be nested into either a wall-based object or a panel-based object. This allows for maximum flexibility among all types of wall assemblies. In terms of panel-based doors, a door width is typically fixed, whereas a panel must be dynamic.

There are two ways to go about creating a curtain panel door: (1) a door can be created as a panel that may be dropped in where a fixed panel was, or (2) a specific door may be nested within a panel that has sidelights on one or

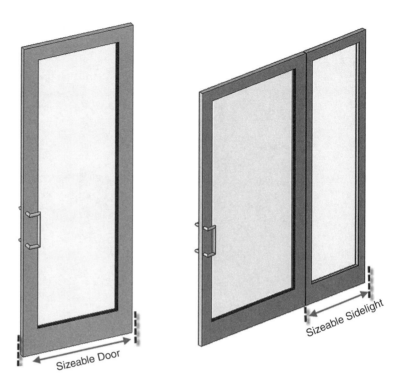

FIGURE 19.8   Curtain door types

both sides. The first method will allow the door to stretch to any size, whereas the second will limit the door to specific sizes and allow the sidelights to take up the remaining space. Each method has its benefits and drawbacks, but both are perfectly acceptable, depending on the given situation.

Where a door is an entire panel, it will adapt to the size of the opening, right, wrong, or indifferent. This is a difficult proposition for manufacturers as they seem to find themselves concerned with design team modeling products that do not exist. While we cannot limit the size of the door, it is typically the best method for creating doors for use in curtain systems. They are easy to drop in and have the least chance for errors. Further, in most cases, panels above and alongside the doors typically line up with the edge of the door, so if sidelights or additional panels are placed alongside the door, it can cause issues with adjacent panel alignment. When we develop a door that is a partial panel with one or more adjacent sidelights, it is important to clearly note what the minimum size of the panel must be for the opening to accommodate it. If the opening is too small, the software will return an error and the panel will not be placed. When creating sidelight panels, it is also a good idea to create a transom panel above. This will help make sure that all of the panels line up after the door has been placed.

Hardware/Accessories

Panel clamps, door hardware, and specialty accessories associated with a wall system are generally developed in the same fashion as any other fixture. Door hardware should be a function of the door and be selectable so it may be swapped out for additional types as necessary. Where door hardware is a function of the manufacturer of the door, it is often easier to either simplify its representation within the model or offer each hardware type as a selectable option. When hardware is a function of a different manufacturer than the door, it is best to format the hardware so that it may be selected from other types that may be loaded into the project. Doing this offers more possibilities for representing the hardware and also allows the hardware itself to show up in schedules.

MATERIALS

The mullion is often the most noticeable aspect of a curtain assembly, so accurately representing its overall appearance will allow for better renderings. Because curtain walls are typically nonstructural, it is usually not necessary to add very much in the way of performance attributes to the materials themselves. The most important aspect of materials in curtain assemblies is its outward appearance. In many cases, the material is available in almost any color or finish, so listing it by the finish type and noting "as specified" will give a cue to the design team that a color must be selected. In cases where manufacturers have a standard color offering, developing each color will limit the design team to only choices that are available.

Glass materials are handled the same way as they are in windows or doors, by developing materials that can carry the attributes associated with their appearance, performance, and how they are affected by light. With curtain assemblies, it is critical to accurately represent how glass changes the behavior of light, as they are typically found in large areas that tend to be considered for their ability to bring in natural light. Developing a specific material for each glass type, thickness, and color may seem like overkill, but when we can accurately represent how light behaves with each of these types of glass, we can perform very accurate daylighting studies, ultimately resulting in more efficient buildings.

While panel materials are handled pretty much the same way as mullions, large format areas may be anodized or finished and are often available in virtually any color. When developing colors, we should use manufacturers RGB values wherever possible to provide the most accurate renderings. When dealing with anodized finishes, it is typically more effective to use the tools within the software to create the finishes rather than to attempt to photograph metal without shading.

DATA—ATTRIBUTES, CONSTRAINTS, AND EQUATIONS

Commonly Used Curtain Wall and Storefront Attributes
Performance

- *Solar heat gain coefficient (SHGC)*: A performance value associated with glazing, which refers to the increase in temperature resulting from sunlight passing through the glass. It is expressed as a percentage of solar heat that is absorbed versus reflected when comes in contact with the window. The lower the solar heat gain coefficient, the more effective the window is at blocking heat from sunlight.

- *U-value/U-factor*: A measure of heat conductivity through the glass. Where an R-value relates to thermal resistance, the U-factor relates to thermal transmission. In colder climates, it is used to measure how much heat is lost through a window and to assist in determinations of whether or not windows meet energy codes. The lower the U-factor, the less heat is lost through the window.

- *Sound transmission class (STC)*: Measures how well glazing attenuates airborne sound. Acoustical windows are measured based on their STC rating. STC is expressed in terms of decibels reduced, where the larger the value, the better the window is at reducing sound.

- *Air infiltration*: Is based on an ASTM standard that measures how much air is allowed to pass through a glazed opening at specific atmospheric pressures. Since most windows are operable, they have a tendency to allow a certain amount of air to pass through. The less air that passes through, the more efficient the window is. Air infiltration is typically expressed in terms of cubic feet per square foot (cfm/sf) at a given air pressure.

- *Water penetration*: Is based on an ASTM standard that measures the amount of air pressure required to force water through the void around a glazed opening in its installed position. It is generally expressed in terms of its air pressure at the point of failure.

- *Structural test pressure/design pressure*: Measures how much internal or external pressure is required to break the glazing during weather events such as hurricanes, where extreme internal and external pressures are common.

- *Forced entry rating*: A grading system that determines how effective a glazed opening or door is at preventing a forced entry.

EXAMPLE CURTAIN WALLS AND THEIR ATTRIBUTE SETS

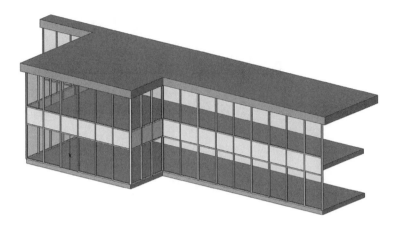

FIGURE 19.9
Typical curtain wall assembly

- Max panel width: 48″
- Max panel height: 96″
- Mullion: thermally broken 3 × 4″
- Frame material: aluminum – T6 anodized – clear
- Glass type: 1″ sealed IG panel – low-E argon-filled
- Panel material: aluminum – AAMA 2604 finish – beige
- U-factor: .30
- SHGC: .30

FIGURE 19.10
Typical storefront assembly

- Max panel width: 48″
- Max panel height: 96″
- Mullion: thermally broken 2 × 6″
- Frame material: aluminum – T6 anodized – clear
- Glass type: $^{11}/_{16}$″ sealed IG panel – low-E
- U-factor: .35
- SHGC: .40

FIGURE 19.11

Typical panel wall
assembly

- Max panel width: 48"
- Max panel height: 24"
- Vertical frame material:
  aluminum 6063-T6
- Attachment clips:
  aluminum 6063-T6
- Panel material:
  aluminum – .060"
  insulated
- Panel finish: AAMA
  2605 fluoropolymer –
  burgundy
- Fastening: concealed
- R-value: 7.2

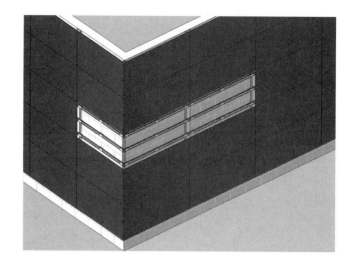

FIGURE 19.12

Typical wall framing
assembly

- Lumber species: SPF
- Sill plate: (2) 2 × 6
- Sole plate: (2 × 6)
- Stud: 2 × 6
- Spacing: 16" O.C.
- Corners: double-
  blocked
- Maximum unrein-
  forced height: 120"

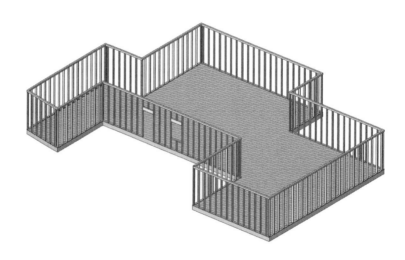

CHAPTER 20

Fixtures and Fittings

ANATOMY

For obvious reasons, the anatomy of various fixtures and fittings will vary based on what we are creating. Casework and cabinetry will differ considerably from sinks and tubs, which can make it difficult to think through how to create each of these components. If we break them into categories based on their level of importance within the project, we can get a better sense of how to graphically represent these types of components as BIM objects.

A fixture can be classified as a component that is relevant to the overall design and dimensional aspects of the project. Without knowledge of their locations and sizes, design considerations cannot be fully understood. If we were creating a commercial bathroom within a project, the toilet partitions would be considered a fixture, as they require certain amount of space to meet building codes. While toilet partitions may be built around the locations of walls, locating them in views and on drawing sheets is essential to determine whether enough space has been allotted for the required amount of stalls necessary for that bathroom. In terms of a residential project, kitchen cabinetry would be considered a fixture, as the design of the kitchen and the amount of space available cannot be determined without their presence. In both cases, the exact style, design, and detail may not be relevant to the overall project, but where components may be created that consider both their space and their appearance, they should be. The level of detail within the model, the analysis abilities that the components afford, and their ability to conceptualize the project in context provide tremendous benefits over simply locating them in two dimensions within a project.

Another way to look at a fixture is based on its reliance on other components, or another component's dependence on it. If it is relatively easy to move a component, it is likely a fitting, whereas a fixture, as its name suggests, is fixed to a given location. The location of a toilet may be dependent on where a wet wall is placed within a building, making the toilet more of a fixture than a fitting. The same can be said with showers and baths. Much of this type of determination is based on whether project is initially designed around function or form. A functionally designed building may first have its systems, plumbing, electrical, and HVAC located, whereas a project designed around form may locate specific fixtures based on their aesthetic qualities and design the building systems around them. To consider either case, developing these types of components with the consideration of them being fixtures is appropriate.

Fixture and fitting components may or may not end up in a building information model, and are generally not shown on high-level drawing sheets, such as plan views. It is unlikely that the soap dispenser or hand dryer mounted on a wall in a bathroom will find its way into plan view, based on the sheer number of these types of components that are likely to be found in a project. They create clutter in these types of views, so often they are omitted altogether in favor of a faster design process that requires less manipulation of the views to achieve the desired appearance of drawing sheets. Building information modeling software allows us to control which elements are shown in a view and which are hidden. Thus, the benefits of adding every component to a model and filtering them out far outweighs the amount of time necessary to create template views that automatically omit certain features within the drawing sheet. Two important aspects of building information modeling are the abilities to visualize a project and to provide quantity takeoffs. Adding fittings such as faucets, hand dryers, door hardware, furnishings, and equipment allows us to put the project into context, making it feel more realistic as we scroll through various views. While seeing how an empty space will look in a rendered view once the building is complete is a tremendous benefit, it does not put the space into context. Adding people and fittings into the project brings the model to life and allows an owner not just to see but to feel the space he is looking at.

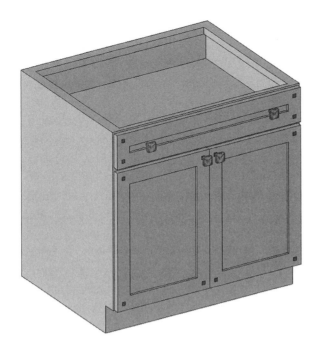

FIGURE 20.1 Anatomy of a typical fitting

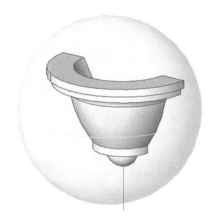 

FIGURE 20.2 Anatomy of a typical fixture

CONSIDERATIONS

Fixtures and fittings are the interior and exterior components used to complete the conceptualization of the project. In typical architectural design, many of these components are not commonly added. With building information modeling, however, the ability to accurately visualize an entire space makes the addition of these components more relevant. Previously, the addition of fixtures and fittings was limited to large components that were essential to the overall design, such as kitchen and bath fixtures, cabinetry, lockers, and partitions. When we visualize a space with BIM, we have the ability to view every last detail, so in many cases the addition of more detailed components, such as faucets, door hardware, and accessories, becomes important to affirming that the project has achieved its goals for the overall aesthetic.

By adding these components, not only can we visualize them, but we can count them as well. Larger projects, which may have thousands of fixture and fitting components, such as fire extinguisher cabinets, see a true benefit from simplifying the estimation process through the model. Each time a component is added, it is noted in the database, and all of the salient information about it is included. The relevant information regarding fixtures and fittings differs, depending on which category they are in. Furnishings such as desks, chairs, and tables may only carry information regarding the materials from which they are created and possibly maximum allowable weights or storage capacity. Bath fittings like showers, tubs, sinks, and toilets may carry slightly more information, as they are also plumbing components, which we will discuss later in this book.

Components that are added to the model can be categorized as primary, secondary, and tertiary. If you think of these three categories of components as elements of design, elements of space planning, and elements of conceptualization, it may help you in determining which category the different components belong in. Primary components are made up of the core elements used to enclose and access spaces—floors, walls, ceilings, roofs, and openings. Fixtures will fall into the secondary category, containing elements that outline the building systems of the project and help us plan our space effectively. Tertiary components make up the fine detail of the project as well as the detail elements of the design that are not relevant to the structure or the overall space, but are critical to the aesthetic and the feel of the space.

As different as many of the fixtures may be, there are similarities among all of them. Most fixtures are made up of multiple components that work together to create a single product. A cabinet has a body, a door, and shelves; a toilet partition has pilasters, panels, hardware, and a door; a toilet has a bowl, a tank, a seat, and hardware. Regardless of the type of component, some of the graphic aspects of the product should be modeled, while some can be optional. Fixtures are a hybrid of form and function, and as such are selected that way. Cabinets have many door and drawer styles and are selected based on their appearance as well as their ability to store goods. More effort should be spent on graphically representing the doors and drawers in this case than the number of shelves contained within the cabinet, which are not visible from any practical view. Before we attempt to model every curve and angle of a bathtub, we should think about the angles from which the tub will be visible and focus on the visible graphic aspects rather than those that are more relevant to the manufacturing of the unit.

A building information model is not designed to and never will replace the ability to see actual products in real life. Just as a paint manufacturer would not want us to select colors based on what we see on screen, those who manufacture cabinetry and plumbing fixtures would rather we stop into a showroom to select products rather than assuming that what we see on screen is exactly what the component looks like. The primary purpose of the building information model is to create and visualize the overall project, not the individual component, so the amount of detail with fixtures and fittings should be commensurate with the views in which they will be found. If a component is not likely to be rendered at any time, the graphics may be simplified considerably. If the element is being showcased in rendered views, it is more likely that additional detail should be added.

Furnishings can be considered fittings in a way, in that they serve the same purpose and are equally likely to be placed within a project. The only real difference in terms of design is that most furnishings are usually omitted from the specifications and construction drawings. With building information

FIGURE 20.3
Photo-realistic tree in rendered view

modeling, the fact that something is in the model does not mean that it needs to be on the drawing sheets. Adding furnishings during design allows various areas of the building to be planned effectively and the overall spaces to be viewed contextually. Moveable furnishings need not be exact in appearance, as there are far too many options to consider during the design phase. It is more important to accurately depict the overall shape and size of the furnishing to determine how much space it will take up. Once the space has been planned and renderings are being performed, it may be necessary to create more accurate depictions of the furnishings, taking into consideration exact styles and materials used in the furnishings. In some cases, specialized photographically represented rendering objects are available through companies such as ArchVision (at archvision.com) that create certain furnishings the same way that planting components and people are represented in rendered views.

It is difficult to expand upon every type of fixture and fitting that may be found in a project or from the building materials industry. Rather than discussing each component individually, some basic considerations apply to all types of fixture, fitting, and furnishing components. First and foremost, think of the component in context. Where is it being placed? How is it being implemented into the project? What is its relevance to the overall design? How is the product selected? These three aspects are the core of deciding how to appropriately model a fixture or fitting, or nearly any BIM object, for that matter.

If we first think about where the component is placed, we can assess the level of detail necessary. If the component or a part of the component is never visible because it is embedded in a wall, then the simpler the geometry the better. Items such as recessed lights, the electrical box that houses a light fixture or wall switch, or the container that holds the soap in a surface-mounted soap dispenser are perfect examples of this. While it may be necessary to represent these aspects of the component for interference-checking purposes, all they need to do is take up space. Adding ornate graphics in these cases is a waste of time and resources.

How is the component being implemented in the project? To understand this question, we must understand the procedures by which architects work as well as how the product is actually used. Much of this type of information is used to determine what type of template to build the component from. Should it be wall based or based on a surface or should placement be allowed anywhere throughout the project? Avoid using wall, floor, and ceiling templates as much as possible when dealing with electrical, plumbing, and HVAC components. Most engineers do not add walls, floors, ceilings, or roofs to the project. They work based on a series of surfaces and allow the architect to implement his design into the project, or vice versa. It is important to give the design team enough freedom to use components any way they choose, right, wrong, or indifferent. While the soap dispenser may be designed to be mounted against the wall, it may end up against a specially created backsplash that is a part of the countertop. If the soap dispenser was created using a wall-based template, instantiating it in the model may prove to be difficult or impossible.

After we understand how a component should be implemented in the project and have decided which template to use, determining its level of detail is largely based on its relevance to the overall design and how the product or component is selected. In terms of relevance, components relate to the design and are selected with two primary considerations: form and function. Fixtures and fittings that are selected by their form require considerably more detail for them to be represented appropriately. Generally speaking, selecting a component based on its form adds more to the overall aesthetic of the space or building, and as such it is more likely to be showcased in rendered views. Components that are selected based on their function carry less weight graphically. Hand dryers and fire extinguisher cabinets are good examples of components that are selected primarily based on their function. While finishes may end up a consideration when selecting these types of components, the overall aesthetic is not one that is generally showcased in the model. While it may end up in the background of a rendering, the chances of an architect demanding a close-up rendering of a fire extinguisher cabinet is very unlikely.

Tip

Think of the component in context. Where is it being placed? How is it being implemented into the project? What is its relevance to the overall design? How is the product selected?

GRAPHICS

The graphics associated with fixtures and fittings can be very complex in nature, and in many cases creating embedded objects will allow for more control using less components. If we take a cabinet as an example, we'll see that all base cabinets use basically the same construction, all wall cabinets use basically the same construction, and all pantry or full height cabinets use basically the same construction. With the exception of corners and specialty cabinets, this allows a single object to be created for each category, and one or more door styles to be embedded in each so that they may be easily managed. Controls can be set so that a door style changed on one will change on all of them, or they may be set so changes can be independent of one other. These types of components can work as constellations, or objects that can source their graphics from other objects within the project to complete their appearance. By training the objects correctly, we can create small, lightweight cabinets, and small, lightweight cabinet doors, which are loaded into the project independently of each other and work together to create the overall appearance of the component.

Some types of fixtures are seen as single components, and others are never seen on their own, but in a battery or array of objects that are placed together. Lockers and partitions are rarely placed as single units, but as a series of items that fit together. When developing these types of components, it's important to consider that they may share geometry. If a toilet partition or locker is created with both left-hand and right-hand panels, placing them in an array doubles up the number of panels in the middle stalls. If the geometry aligns exactly in rendered views it's not a real consideration, but it's not good practice to develop components this way. Creating visibility controls that allow panels to be turned on and off based on their configuration will give the architect the ability to create accurate graphics for the design at hand without becoming confused by how he is supposed to design using the given component.

For example, the primary components of a partition are a pilaster, panel, and door as shown in Figure 20.4. While a single partition that stands in the middle of a room may have two panels, two pilasters, and one door, as they are ganged together, the middle stalls really only have one panel, one pilaster, and a door. By adding visibility controls to the panel and pilaster on each side, it is

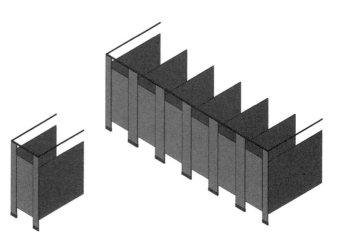

FIGURE 20.4 Typical partition object—single and ganged

possible to create a single BIM object that will work for any situation, whether it is a single freestanding stall, or an array of stalls within a corner or alcove.

By creating options for graphics that can be swapped out and a series of visibility controls to turn geometry on and off, fewer objects can represent many. In some cases, this type of object construction may generate considerably larger file sizes than desired. Much of this is due to the embedded objects on which the component relies. One solution to this is to create multiple light-weight components, which are loaded into the project independent of each other but work together. Another solution is to clarify that the object itself should be manipulated by the design team outside of the project before it is loaded into the project. This gives the design team the ability to select options and to clear out the unnecessary embedded components before it goes into the project. This minimizes general file size and speeds up the efficiency of the model.

Because of their aesthetic nature, most fixtures may be graphically complex. While the geometry may be slightly more difficult to generate, the objects as a whole are far simpler, as few or no parametric controls are necessary within the object. Hand dryers are typically a single size and shape, but most decorative light fixtures are all so different that each will require its own object, and it is rare to find two faucets with graphics that can be shared. This increases the overall number of objects that are necessary for fixtures but decreases the amount of time necessary to create each one. Less graphic parametrics means less flexing of the objects. This translates into far less time spent maintaining quality control and more time spent generating the objects themselves.

MATERIALS AND FINISHES

It is often beneficial to create to parameters to manage the graphic appearance of fixtures and fittings. In some cases, creating one parameter that speaks to the material of the component and another that speaks to the finish of the component will allow the information to be passed to the design team effectively with the least amount of effort. If we multiply the number of materials by the number of finishes available for a given product, it is often possible to end up in the thousands, when in many cases all of the materials are available in all of the finishes. A series of lockers or partitions that are available in either phenolic or fiberglass-reinforced plastic may have the same 60 color options for both. In a case such as this, offering 2 materials as options under one attribute and 60 colors under another attribute will require the creation of 62 materials rather than 120 materials. Not only does this method simplify the creation of the BIM object, it minimizes the amount of searching that the design team will need to do to find what they are looking for. In addition, the material is likely selected well before the color is, so allowing the architect to select the material at one point and the color at a different point gives him slightly more control of the data set during the design of the building. Unfortunately, this doesn't always work. Wood is an example where a finish will change considerably based on its material.

Many cabinets are commonly available in cherry, pine, oak, or maple. A given cabinet manufacturer may have 25 standard finishes available on all four species of wood. Because of the differences in the grain pattern, basic wood color, and how they absorb the stain, the differences in color between a stain placed on oak and a stain placed on maple can often be night and day. To accurately represent the finish of something as relevant as a cabinet, it is a good practice to create a material and finish combination. This will provide the architect and the owner with a far closer representation of what the finished, installed space will look like in a rendered view.

Metal components can often be difficult to represent using image files, as lighting generally reflects off of these materials and creates inconsistencies within the pattern. Most building information modeling software has built-in metal finishes that can be augmented by adding patterns and textures to create closer representations of the finish. Checker plate or diamond plate is a good example of a texture that is added to a material. Creating a bump map for each of the textures will allow them to be placed within any given material.

Materials and finishes are a critical aspect of fixtures and fittings, as they are often selected based on their aesthetic. Most manufacturers have custom colors and finishes for each of their components, so, in many cases, the use of image files to represent the finishes is more accurate. Simply adding color numbers to materials is fine for modeling views, but in rendered views, the color does not take into consideration the sheen, reflectivity, and how light behaves as it hits the surface at different angles. Without a considerable amount of expertise in creating materials and finishes, I would suggest starting with image files to represent specific colors and sheens that are available from manufacturers.

DATA—ATTRIBUTES AND EQUATIONS

As mentioned earlier, the attributes and equations that may apply to fixtures and fittings are directly related to the type of object is being created. General fixtures and fittings carry dimensional information as well as materials and finishes used in the product. In cases where product options are available, such as different hardware types, door and drawer options, or diffusers and shades, these options are usually not related to the overall design of the project and should be organized so that the design team can easily select from the options at any given time. In addition to basic dimension and material information, data may be necessary that assist in space planning. If a certain amount of surrounding space is necessary to the component, creating linework that shows up in plan view will allow this type of information to be noted. Where a cabinet or partition door may be present, noting the direction in space necessary to allow it to swing clearly will give a sense of minimum space requirements for the component.

Plumbing and electrical fixtures carry relevant information about how they apply to the building systems to which they are attached. Plumbing components generally have specific piping requirements and connection sizes, so noting these accordingly will ensure that the plumbing design is accurate from the beginning of the supply line to the fixture at its terminus. Electrical components have similar necessities and require the addition of connections that allow them to be used in circuits. These fixtures may have set requirements for voltage as well as maximum rated amperage. The presence of these attributes allows electrical systems to be created as well as analysis of potential electrical usage within the building. If we think of an electrical receptacle not as the terminus of the circuit, but as a stop along the way to the device plugged into it, the devices could potentially be added as electrical components along the circuit. If too many devices are placed within the circuit, the software is capable of alerting the engineer that a change to the design may be necessary.

Lighting components should carry both photometry and electrical information for them to be used as fully functional components. Light fixtures not only cast light, but use power. Having electrical attributes alongside the photometry attributes will allow the architect or a lighting designer to consider a lighting criteria when planning the space and allow the engineer to plan electrical circuits necessary for the design of the building's electrical system.

Certain fixtures, such as cabinetry and storage components, are designed into the building to provide locations to place goods or equipment. Their usefulness within the project is directly related to the amount of equipment that they are capable of storing, so attributes related to storage capacities of the components will allow facility planners to analyze how much storage space is available within the building. While it is possible to calculate the amount of storage space that is available within a component such as a cabinet or locker, in most cases manufacturers publicize these values, so rather than attempting to train the BIM object to calculate the size of the interior volume of the component and then subtract solid spaces, such as the frame of a drawer, shelving, and related components that subtract from the overall storage volume, using defined values provides a more accurate depiction of the available storage volume.

EXAMPLE FIXTURE AND FITTING COMPONENTS AND THEIR ATTRIBUTE SETS

FIGURE 20.5

Typical cabinet fixture

- Width: 18"
- Height: 35"
- Depth: 22"
- Style: flush
- Configuration: 1 door/ 8 drawers
- Material: American cherry – honey spice finish
- Hardware type: rectangular pulls
- Hardware finish: stainless steel
- Shelves: 2
- Storage volume: 11.6 cu ft

FIGURE 20.6

Typical toilet partition fixture

- Unit width: 36"
- Unit depth: 60"
- Partition height: 72"
- Door width: 24"
- Panel height from floor: 12"
- Mounting: floor mount w/headrail
- Material: painted steel
- Finish: olive green
- Hardware type: standard saddle type
- Hardware finish: stainless steel

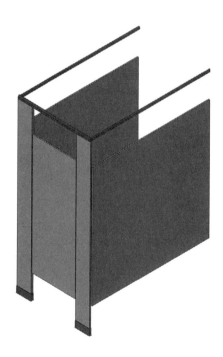

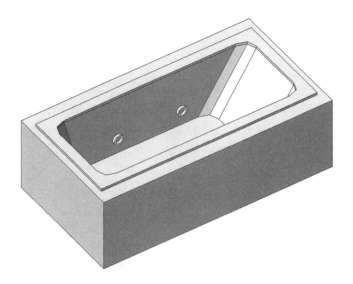

FIGURE 20.7

Typical tub fixture

- Unit width: 36"
- Unit depth: 72"
- Unit depth: 20"
- Mounting: alcove
- Operation: 6 jet whirlpool
- Motor: ½ hp
- Voltage: 240 VAC
- Amperage: 20 A
- Material: encapsulated fiberglass
- Finish: bone

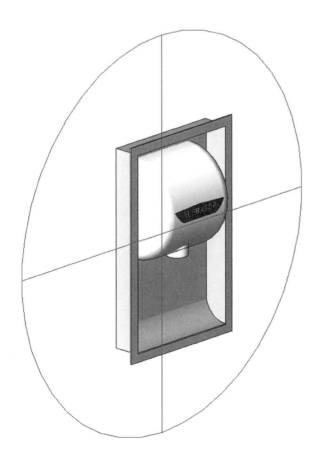

FIGURE 20.8

Typical hand dryer fitting

- Unit width: 15"
- Unit height: 12"
- Projection: 7½"
- Mounting: recessed
- Mounting height: 48"
- Recessed depth: 3"
- Material: cast iron
- Finish: white
- Hardware finish: stainless steel
- Air output: 1500 lfm
- Motor: ½ hp
- Voltage: 120 VAC
- Amperage: 11 A
- Wattage: 1320 W

FIGURE 20.9

Typical faucet fitting

- Material: steel
- Finish: oil-rubbed bronze
- Operation: dual control
- Flow rate: low flow – 1.2 gpm
- Supply fittings: ½" brass

CHAPTER 21

Lighting

Based on their usage, light fixtures are some of the most in-depth BIM objects. They must be capable of carrying information relevant to their appearance, their energy usage, and the actual photometry that determines how the light will render in a given environment. A great deal of thought must be put into the development of lighting components to ensure that they meet the needs of both the architect, engineer, lighting consultant, and manufacturer. Each of these parties is likely looking for different information, all of which is relevant and important to the overall project. Lighting is unique in that it is more than a fixed component; it also adds action and description to a space. Light, both natural and artificial, is a series of waves that reflect and refract based on adjacent materials. Photometry conveys how a very specific type of light is cast into an area and is dependent on the time of day, colors, and sheens of adjacent materials to represent a scene. It is a powerful tool that helps us make determinations of where we may save energy and money by harnessing natural light while ensuring that are affected areas have the appropriate visibility. Light fixtures are also electrical devices, which use power and can be connected to a circuit within the building information model. The value of the fixture may be analyzed by performing what-if scenarios between the quality and amount of light versus the amount of energy consumed versus the replacement costs of maintenance items in a whole building lifecycle assessment. Building this level of information into lighting fixtures allows architects and lighting designers to provide proven solutions for building lighting without needing to perform a considerable amount of extra work.

ANATOMY

The anatomy of a light fixture is dependent on its type or category. Fluorescent and incandescent are the most common types, followed by several other types of high-powered and high-efficiency specialty lights. LED lighting is experiencing tremendous growth and acceptance based on its energy efficiency and expected lifespan.

Incandescent bulbs produce light when an electric current is passed through a filament. When the filament is heated to extreme temperatures, it becomes hot enough to produce light. Incandescent bulbs were the industry standard for home lighting, but due to their lack of efficiency compared to

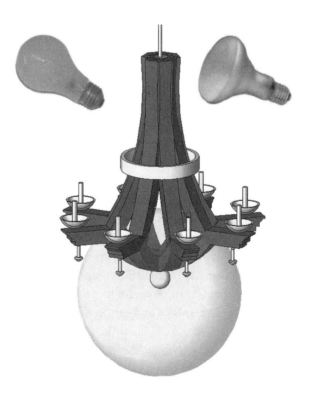

FIGURE 21.1 Typical appearance-based incandescent light fixture

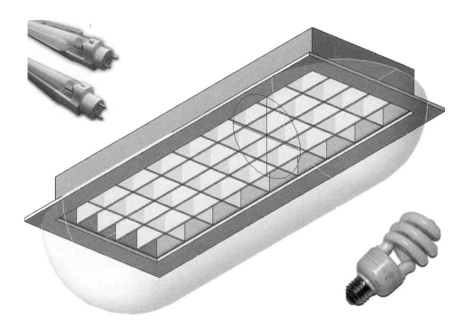

FIGURE 21.2 Typical task-based fluorescent light fixture

other sources, they are slowly being phased out of existence. Incandescent bulbs are available in a wide array of wattages and color temperatures and do not require any additional components, such as ballasts, to make them work. In comparison to other lighting types, they are very inexpensive, but do not last as long and are not as efficient.

Fluorescent bulbs use electricity to excite mercury vapor within a vacuum tube to create light. They are far more efficient than incandescent bulbs, and are designed to last considerably longer. The initial cost of a fluorescent bulb is significantly higher than that of a typical incandescent bulb, but because of their increased lifespan and decreased energy consumption, they are a far more cost-effective lighting solution in the long run. Historically, fluorescent fixtures have had a bad reputation for emitting light with an unpleasant feel and having a flicker and sound, which many found unappealing. Over the past decade florescent technology has improved considerably, providing faster ballasts and an increased range of color temperatures, which equate to a more inviting light.

CONSIDERATIONS

While the primary purpose of lighting components within a BIM project is to render light, many light fixtures are also aesthetic in nature. For wall-mounted fixtures that are selected solely based on their appearance, the model should be able to accurately represent not just a light, but the aesthetic qualities that the fixture brings during daylight hours. These types of fixtures are stylized to complement the decor of the space they are in. They require a considerable amount of detail and often can end up larger than anticipated or desired. Chandeliers can be one of the larger lighting files because they are usually very ornate and highly detailed. Deciding how much detail to build into the component should be done carefully, and considering multiple objects to represent the fixture is appropriate. The rendering of projects is limited only to specific views at specific times during project development. For highly ornate components, such as chandeliers and sconces, it is often effective to create a development model, which is more of a placeholder, and a second, more detailed model that may be swapped out later if highly detailed appearance renderings are necessary. In either case the light is cast same way using the same photometry files, so the only difference between the two is the accuracy of the model graphics.

Light fixtures are used in architecture, lighting design and study, and building systems engineering. Architects want to see the aesthetic qualities of the light fixture, lighting designers want to know how the light will be cast within a space, and building systems engineers need the energy usage information necessary to develop circuits within the building. Adding all of this information to a single component while trying to maintain a reasonable file size and optimum performance is no small undertaking. By developing lighting components such that they are modular and so graphics not visible to the eye or the rendering are minimized, we can maximize the overall appearance without overburdening the size of the project. Recessed lights are a simple example of this. A considerable amount of detail surrounds the component as it is installed in the ceiling, but the only visible part of the fixture is the trim ring, bulb, and diffuser or baffle. The rest of the fixture is embedded in the ceiling and invisible to the naked eye. Rather than taking a considerable amount of time and effort to detail the embedded portion of the fixture, looking at it in terms of gross space required to install will allow us to represent that portion of the component for interference checking and keep the file size at a bare minimum.

Depending on the type of project or the needs of the architect, not all aspects of the light fixture need be represented. As components are being created strictly for lighting analysis, graphically the models can be very simplistic so long as they carry the appropriate photometry information. If lighting studies are never to be performed, the photometry loses its relevance, giving way to the aesthetic qualities and perhaps the electrical usage information. Having a clear and open discussion about the intent and purpose of the light fixtures prior to development will help outline the needs of the end user and provide him with the best model for his purposes. Where graphic accuracy is not a paramount concern, it is possible for only a few, or even a single light fixture to represent hundreds or even thousands of lighting combinations. The parameters built into the fixture can allow it to change its clearance dimensions within a wall or ceiling, control the photometry, change the materials and sizes of the visible components, and even provide options for specific bulbs or ballasts. Simplifying the graphics to maximize the number of combinations that may be portrayed is known as *representative modeling.*

Representative modeling allows several light fixtures of similar appearance to be modeled together. Ultimately, the goal of a light fixture is to provide light. The appearance of the fixture can often be sacrificed in the name of budget to convey the photometry and usage aspects using fewer models. With as few as three or four objects, it is possible to represent every light fixture necessary on a project so long as the appearance is not critical. Creating a recessed lighting fixture, a surface-mounted lighting fixture, a free-standing lighting fixture, and a linear lighting fixture can cover nearly all of the lighting needs of most projects. The information that corresponds to the exact photometry and usage information can be contained within a catalog for easy retrieval as a component becomes necessary.

Another aspect of lighting fixtures that makes them unique is their importance to facility management and building lifecycle. Light fixtures use a considerable amount of energy and require maintenance more often than most components found in a building. Walls are designed to last a specific amount of time, ballasts need periodic replacement, and there are several options for both, depending on the type of light and type of lighting controls necessary on the project. Components such as bulbs and ballasts are actually embedded components within a light fixture and should be treated as such. It is not uncommon to have several ballast options and several bulb options. It may not be necessary to model these items graphically, but if they are created as informational objects that are embedded in the light fixture itself, they can carry a considerable amount of information that may be necessary for facility management. If modeled individually as data families, they can be shown in schedules and, with the appropriate attributed data, leveraged by facilities managers for speculated replacement times and costs.

GRAPHICS

When developing the graphics for a light fixture, the first consideration is who will use it. For a manufacturer-specific component, the model should be developed so as to consider not only the needs of the architect but also those of the engineer and the lighting designer. In some cases this may mean either larger file sizes or multiple models to represent a fixture, or, as an alternative, a less decorative graphic appearance. Lighting components that contain ornate features may sometimes require multiple representations, but in most cases may be modeled using a single fixture when done appropriately.

First and foremost, picking the correct template to begin with is essential. Lighting components are used within multiple software platforms, some of which do not rely on hosts such as walls or ceilings to be placed. For this reason, I strongly recommend using templates that are face based or free-standing to allow for maximum functionality and usability. A face-based object may be used on a ceiling, but a ceiling-based object cannot be used unless a ceiling is present. Electrical engineers often omit walls, floors, and ceilings from their designs to allow their components to be more visible.

Graphically model only what is visible and necessary, keeping embedded aspects of the fixture as simple as possible. The best case scenario would be to use a cube or cylinder shape to represent the clearance space necessary within the ceiling or wall. These models are not being used to manufacture a light fixture but to represent them in a project, so the closer to a symbol the object can be, the more effective it actually is in many cases. Architectural lighting is required to be slightly more detailed, but it is not necessary to model every last detail unless it is the focal point of a rendering. This level of detail should be reserved for very large and highly ornate light fixtures, such as chandeliers, which are used in spaces primarily for their decorative value.

When creating the behavior of light itself, the light source must be defined and the shape must be assigned. In many cases this is determined automatically by the photometry files provided by the manufacturer, but even those files are based on the light source coming from a specific point in space. The location of the light source must be located outside of a solid. This is a common mistake when developing lighting. The software imitates light based on a specific point in space. If that space is embedded in a solid, then light cannot be emitted through it. When developing components for specific manufacturers, confirm the location of light sources' origins against their photometry files so that light will always be rendered appropriately.

Specific types of lighting have specific clearances that must be met for building code, fire protection, and general installation requirements. These clearances may be represented as transparent solids, which will allow interference checking to be performed, while providing a visual notation that the space is representative and not real. Making these dimensions parametric will allow the space to be modified based on the exact fixture that is to be used, ultimately allowing the fixture to be reused for multiple product types; for example, a 4-inch, 5-inch, 6-inch, or 7½-inch recessed light fixture can be created using the same component.

Information about the components of a light fixture does not always need to be modeled graphically. Bulbs and ballasts are very important aspects of light fixtures, but they do not always need to be shown in the model. BIM objects can be created that carry the information about a bulb or ballast and are then embedded into the light fixture. These objects may be assigned a parameter, and when formatted properly will allow all of the information regarding the specific component to be viewed in data exports and schedules. There are typically multiple options for bulbs and ballasts, and when created as embedded components they can be selected from a drop-down menu as a user-defined option.

FIGURE 21.3   Recessed light fixture

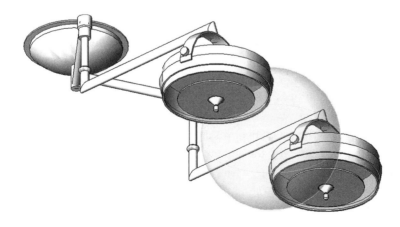

FIGURE 21.4
Surface-mounted light fixture

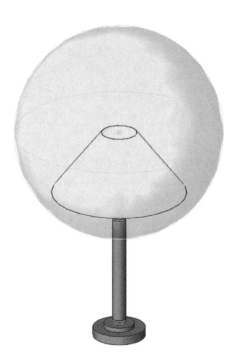

FIGURE 21.5
Free-standing light fixture

MATERIALS

The materials used within light fixtures are generally not as relevant as many other components. Only the diffusers, shades, and other decorative elements should be as accurate as possible, as they are designed to control and redirect light as it is emitted from the fixture. Materials that relate to the housing do not need to be render ready and may remain simplified, as they will never be seen in a rendered view. Pay careful attention to the reflectivity associated with different metals and finishes used in the objects. Metals cause light to bounce, often with undesired results. In addition, shades and diffusers are often made of semi-transparent or semi-opaque materials and are designed to illuminate when light shines from behind them. Much of the management of materials within light fixtures is trial and error, but there are some basic principles that we can follow.

BIM software affords the user a considerable amount of flexibility when manipulating materials. We can control not only the surface color and sheen of a material but also the way it behaves around light sources. The reflectivity of a material allows us to control the amount of light that bounces off the surface and creates reflections. The transparency of a material defines the amount of light that passes through a solid rather than creating reflections or being absorbed. Adjusting the translucency of a material controls the amount of light that is absorbed by a solid, and the index of refraction gives us control of how much light bends as it passes through a solid. By manipulating these controls, we can create a series of materials to represent various types of shades, diffusers, lenses, and ornamental glass elements, which can affect how light is perceived in space with respect to its source.

DATA—ATTRIBUTES AND EQUATIONS

General

- *Housing/fixture type*: graphics/materials used to represent the housing or decorative fixture
- *Shade/diffuser type*: graphics/materials used to represent the shrouds, shades, or other light augmenting facets of the fixture
- *Reflector/baffle type*: graphics/materials used to represent the aspects of the fixture that reflect or refract light
- *Lamp/bulb type*: graphic or nongraphic representations of the type or style of lamp
- *Ballast type*: graphic or nongraphic representations of the type of ballast
- *Bulb life*: the expected lifespan or replacement frequency of the lamp or bulb
- *Ballast life*: the expected lifespan or replacement frequency of the ballast

Photometry—Light Output

- *Light intensity*: the amount of light the fixture emits; can be expressed in terms of its efficacy (lumens/watt), luminous flux (lumens), luminous intensity (candela), or illuminance (lux)
- *Color temperature*: measured in kelvins, indicates the color and "feel" of the light—warmer, more yellow lights, such as incandescent bulbs, have a lower temperature, whereas whiter, cooler lights have a higher temperature
- *Light color*: the actual color of the light that is cast; can be controlled directly through the light source or based on a colored transparent lens or diffuser
- *Light loss factor*: an index used to determine the amount of light lost over time from dust, degradation lamp aging, lamp tilt, and outside environmental factors
- *Photometry file*: the source file used to recreate the actual rendered light

Electrical

- *Voltage*: also known as electrical potential, it is the amount of energy necessary to move an electric charge along a path; common residential applications are 120 and 240 volts, whereas commercial applications are 240 and 440 volts and greater
- *Wattage*: also known as power,it is the amount of electricity used by a device; may be simply calculated by multiplying voltage by the amperage
- *Amperage*: also known as electric current, it is the rate at which an electric charge flows, or simply, how quickly a device will use power

Calculations

Joules law: $P = VI$, where

P is the power consumption, or wattage

V is the electrical potential, or voltage

I is the current, or amperage

Luminous flux: lm = (lm/W)W, where

lm is the total lumen output

lm/W is the luminous efficacy of the lamp

W is the amount of power the lamp uses

Footcandles (fc) = Total lumens (lm)/Area in square feet

1 lux (lx) = 1 footcandle (fc) × 10.76

Lux = Total lumens ÷ Area in square meters

USAGE—LEVERAGING THE INFORMATION

Lighting Schedules

Lighting is a component that is used in nearly every project, with most projects having hundreds of different lighting components. Rather than attempting to manually count the number of fixtures necessary based on square foot area or manually parsing through drawings, building information modeling allows us to create a series of schedules to count each specific fixture. Each room or area within a building may use different fixtures based on the overall aesthetic.

Creating lighting schedules will allow the architect and contractor to see exactly what types of fixtures are used in various rooms and spaces and, where the information is added, the specifics regarding its construction and usage, such as trim rings, ballast types, bulbs, and power consumption.

Above and beyond the informational abilities of schedules, a lighting schedule can give an architect or lighting designer the controls to customize each fixture based on its environment, without needing to search through the model to locate a specific fixture. Within a lighting schedule, the photometric properties, such as luminance, color temperature, efficacy, and light loss, can be quickly customized to create different lighting scenes within the project for trial and error. Information regarding the energy consumption of the fixtures can be organized and viewed to determine the types of loads that are created from different spaces within the building. This allows an engineer to study and analyze the overall demand of the building based on the amount of power consumed at different times of the day.

Lighting Studies

The more information about lighting components we add to the model, the more we may analyze the environment of the overall project. Lighting fixtures have an effect not only on the aesthetic of the building and its components, but on the surrounding environment as a whole. Both positive and negative attributes of light can be considered when lighting studies are performed. Light improves visibility within a space but also may cast undesired shadows and create reflection and glare in bad locations, detracting from the quality of the overall environment. Properly formatted lighting components along with an accurately situated project will allow artificial and natural light to be analyzed for benefits and shortcomings.

Natural light is the daylight that comes from the sun, and is affected by the weather, smog, and external forces related to the natural environment. The amount and intensity of the light differ at different times of the year and different locations in the world. Many building information modeling software platforms allow the user to control where the project is located and the time of year and time of day that are to be studied. Because windows, skylights, and doors placed within the model allow natural light to pass through them, it is possible to study where glare and shadows may be present at different times of day to improve the overall quality of the indoor environment. Modifying the locations of transparent openings will have an immediate effect on the visibility within the model, allowing for the addition or removal of openings as necessary.

Artificial light comprises all types of lighting other than that from the sun. Whether it is interior or exterior fixtures, landscape lighting, or light sources from outside of the project, artificial light can have positive and negative effects on a building and its location. As we add various types of light fixtures into the model, we can study the types of light that are cast and determine their suitability for a given location. Lighting designers can leverage the information within the model for basic calculations of the amount of light necessary in different areas. Workspaces may require a great deal more light than recreational or living spaces, and exterior or task lighting may be directed in a certain manner so that it will focus on a specific location or job.

Lighting may be studied by either static or dynamic analysis. Static analysis looks at a specific location at a specific point in time. Dynamic analysis takes into consideration a timeline, for instance, from sunrise to sunset, or a 22-hour period. Static analysis is useful for general quick studies to determine lighting averages at different points in the day. The use of a dynamic analysis is more effective when adding natural light into the equation in order to visualize shadows over a period of time.

To create an accurate static lighting study that takes into consideration both natural and artificial light, the project itself must be oriented according to due north. In addition, its location in the world, either by city or by latitude and longitude, is necessary. Orientation and location will allow light to accurately enter through daylight portals such as windows and doors to recreate the effects of the sun. This daylight study becomes the baseline for the project in determining how much natural light is available within the building and then assists in the determination of where and how much artificial light is necessary. Once

FIGURE 21.6 Lighting study

a daylight baseline has been created, it becomes a trial-and-error process of adding and removing different types of fixtures in various locations to achieve the desired results. Lighting consultants have years of experience working with different types of fixtures in different scenarios, so they can design quickly and effectively in the least amount of time.

Once a static lighting study has been created, the same settings may be leveraged to develop a dynamic study. The dynamic study takes the baseline and sets it in motion over a timeline. During the dynamic study, a video file is created, which is essentially a series of static lighting studies viewed in sequence as if it were from a flip book. Because they're created in this fashion, multiple studies may be created and stitched together using video software to turn artificial lights on at a certain point in the day and off at another.

SAMPLE LIGHTING COMPONENTS AND THEIR ATTRIBUTE SETS

FIGURE 21.7

Typical recessed light fixture object

- Diameter: 5"
- Lamping: CFL – (1) 26-watt triple twin tube
- Ballast type: electronic – 4 pin
- Reflector: reflector – clear haze Alzak
- Spacing criteria: 0.7
- Voltage: 277 VAC
- Amperage: 0.24 A
- Power consumption: 16 W
- Color temperature: 3450 K
- Intensity: 1250 lm
- Photometry file: ABCLighting123.IES

FIGURE 21.8

Typical decorative light fixture object

- Width: 14"
- Height: 10"
- Finish: bright brass
- Diffuser: glass – 65% opaque – blue
- Projection: 8½"
- Lamping: incandescent – (2) 40-watt e27 screw base
- Spacing criteria: contact manufacturer for more information
- Voltage: 120 VAC
- Amperage: 0.66 A
- Power Consumption: 80 W
- Color temperature: 2800 K
- Intensity: 1000 lm
- Photometry file: XYZLighting123.IES

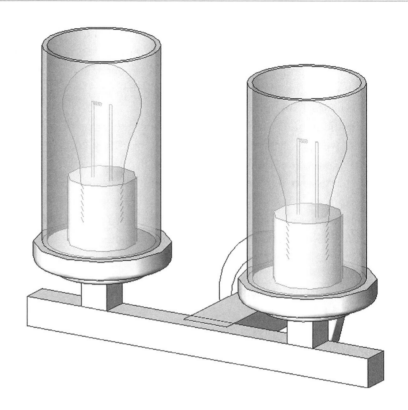

FIGURE 21.9

Typical site/exterior light fixture object

- Unit size: 12"
- Mounting height: 12'-0"
- Lamping: high-pressure sodium
- Ballast type: coil magnetic
- Diffuser: acrylic
- Photocontrol: NEMA Twistlock
- Finish: aluminum – powdercoat – bronze
- Spacing criteria: 0.4
- Voltage: 120 VAC
- Amperage: 0.7 A
- Power Consumption: 150 W
- Color Temperature: 2100 K
- Intensity: 125,000 lm
- Photometry file: XYZLighting123.IES

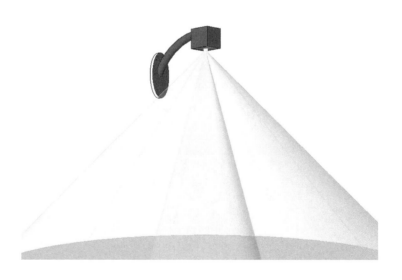

CHAPTER 22

Mechanical, Electrical, and Plumbing Components

ANATOMY

Mechanical, electrical and plumbing (MEP) components used in a building information model generally require fewer graphics and a considerable amount of information. These types of components are designed to be used within a system, and provide the ability to analyze the individual component in the system as a whole. Just as with any other component in a model, the amount of analysis possible is limited to the amount of accurate information supplied. Three basic types of systems are used within a building information model, or a building, for that matter: plumbing and piping systems provide domestic water, sanitary services, and fire suppression; heating, ventilation, and air conditioning (HVAC) and ductwork systems transport air throughout a building; and electrical and wiring systems move electricity throughout a building. If we think about how each of these systems actually works, we will have a better idea of how to create the components necessary for the systems.

Nobody looks at a catalog and says, "Gee whiz, that's a good looking hydronic pump . . . I must have that on my project!" Products like this are selected by function, not by form. We can separate MEP components into two basic categories: (1) equipment and (2) devices and fixtures. Equipment is components that are behind the scenes of a project and are never seen in the "front of the house." For all practical intents and purposes these components can be represented by simple cubes in a model, so long as they take up the appropriate amount of space. Developing components like this requires little geometry but a great deal of information. They should take up the amount of space necessary for placement and be designed for appropriate mounting. Devices and fixtures, on the other hand, are electrical components that carry an aesthetic value. The reality is that any component used in a project that has a power cord or other connection to a building system should be developed as such. Every component that uses utilities on a project should be designed with MEP connections so it may be attached to circuits. Just as cost information would be incomplete without every component being accounted for, energy usage information is just as incomplete without attaching each device.

Since we have already discussed how to develop devices and fixtures in the chapter on fixtures and fittings, the focus of this chapter is more on creating equipment objects and assigning appropriate connections so they may be used in systems. Figure 22.1 is a rudimentary example of a domestic water piping system

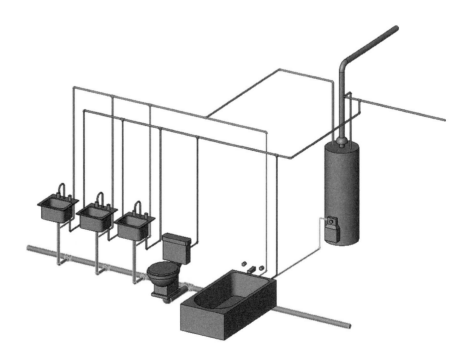

FIGURE 22.1 Typical domestic water system

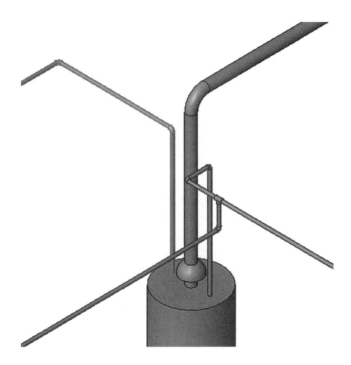

FIGURE 22.2 Basic appearance of a hot-water heater

and a few components that are attached to it. Cold water travels through the pipes into a hot-water heater and out to plumbing fixtures. From the plumbing fixtures, waste water drains into sanitary lines out to a sewer or septic system.

In this case, the hot-water heater is a piece of plumbing equipment, and the sinks, toilet, and tub are plumbing fixtures. Each component has a series of connectors that are designed to accept a certain size pipe. To assign a specific pipe size as well as a classification of the type of system, a series of connectors is added to the components. The BIM software is trained to understand the purpose of each of these connectors, as well as make corrections where necessary. Figure 22.2 shows the hot-water heater with connection points for cold water supply, hot-water output, and electrical connection for power.

CONSIDERATIONS

Water flows through supply pipes from a source to a component that heats the water, and out through a faucet or other type of fixture. From this fixture, the water needs to go somewhere, so to create an entire plumbing "circuit," drain piping is required. There are specific pipes with different materials and sizes necessary for different applications. When we create components that are used with piping systems, they generally have specific size fittings that are designed to attach to the pipes. Appropriately sizing these fittings will allow the piping to either disallow the connection or automatically create a reducer that is necessary to make the connection. If a 1-inch pipe is supplying water to a faucet with a ½-inch fitting, a mismatch can occur if the connections are not assigned correctly.

The basic types of components associated with a plumbing or piping system are the pipes, the pipe fittings, and the fixtures or equipment. Generally, the pipes themselves are a function of the software, so graphically they are simplified to represent little more than their shape. Typically, the color of the pipe is a function of its usage. Hot-water pipes are represented in red, cold water in blue, and drain/waste/vent (DWV) pipes in green. The different types of fittings that represent the connections within a model often may be simplified, as they are rarely specified based on their unique appearance. Equipment of this nature is selected based on performance and usage, not on aesthetics, so rather than spending time developing the graphics, it is better to add additional information to maximize functionality. Providing enough graphic accuracy to depict what a component is and how much space it takes up is generally an acceptable solution. Where components are selected based on their appearance, such as faucets, sinks, and toilets, their graphics should be treated as discussed in the chapter on fixtures and fittings.

The same principles apply when dealing with HVAC components. The size and shape of registers and equipment connections must be assigned appropriately; otherwise, a mismatch can occur. Whether we're dealing with a round or rectangular connection, couplers are designed to transition between the two components. They may change size, shape, or both size and shape to accommodate the difference between the component and the ductwork itself. While it may show, the up-close appearance of ductwork is generally not relevant.

With electrical systems, the voltage must be correct and the current must not exceed the rating for the circuit; otherwise, errors are generated to notify the engineer that there is a problem. Developing objects for electrical systems requires that the device being created is compatible with the electrical system of the project. If the circuit created is 120 V, and a light fixture that is 277 V is added to the circuit, notifications are given and the circuit is left as incomplete.

As we think about developing these types of components, the most important aspect to consider is the location of the connections, especially when it comes to plumbing drain locations. Unpressurized water can only flow downhill, and drain pipes are required by code to be at a specific slope, so having connections located appropriately is critical. While it is good practice to locate supply lines and electrical connections in their appropriate locations, it is not always necessary. Knowing where exact connection points are is

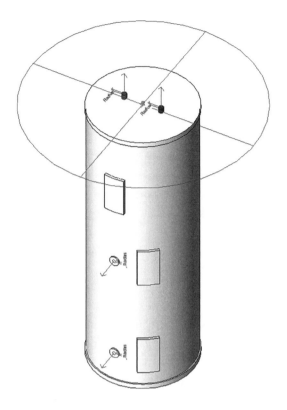

effective for determining clearances for pipe and distances for placement of adjacent components. Figure 22.3 shows a piece of equipment with each of its connections located in the appropriate spot.

Because the size and shape of the pipe will change based on the needs of the connection, the connector must be dynamic and not controlled by the object itself. Pipe connectors are sized based on the radius of the pipe rather than the diameter, and all sizes are nominal. If calculations are developed that will translate radius to diameter in order for the information to show in data sets, it is important to place the calculation within the right parameter. Since the radius is the driving force and changes based on the pipe size, the diameter itself should be calculated based on the radius. If the radius is calculated by an equation within an object, then it cannot be calculated by the size of the pipe at the same time. So if we wanted to attain the pipe diameter from the radius, which may change based on the connected pipe, the calculation would look like this:

HW pipe diameter = HW radius * 2

not

HW radius = HW pipe diameter/2

Tip

If calculations are developed that will translate radius to diameter, for the information to show in data sets, it is important to place the calculation within the right parameter.

Above and beyond establishing the size and shape of connections, they must be assigned correctly in order for the software to understand the purpose of the connection. Plumbing, for instance, may be classified as domestic water supply, sanitary, hydronic, or for use in fire protection. It may also be listed as hot water or cold water and consist of supply or return lines, depending on the type of system. Different types of components are placed into different categories. A component might be a piece of mechanical equipment, a plumbing fixture, or an electrical device, to give three examples. Within these categories, sub-categories exist that further describe what the component is and how it relates to the overall system. There are several different types of electrical equipment, each of which is designed to perform a different task, be it a panel board, transformer, junction box, switch, or something else. Mechanical and plumbing equipment is also categorized by how it behaves within the system. Is the component designed to be at the terminus of the pipe run or break into the middle of it? Is the pipe fitting a tee or an elbow? These are just a couple of subcategorizations of components that may be found in BIM objects.

One of the most important things to consider when developing BIM content for MEP objects is how the component is placed. Many engineers do not use walls, floors, ceilings, or roofs when they are developing their models. This allows the model to be dropped into an architectural model easily without overrunning existing objects, and also keeps everything in their working views visible. One of the biggest gripes that I have with BIM software, in general, is the use of host-based components. When mechanical, electrical, or plumbing components, including lighting, are created as host-based, in many cases they are unusable to engineers. Rather than components being developed based on a wall or a floor, they should be based upon a face, or better, a work plane. This allows the components to be used by both architects and engineers with no additional effort required by either party. Figure 22.4 illustrates a basic HVAC system with a series of registers that would likely being installed in the ceiling. Rather than the components being ceiling based, they are not reliant on a host for placement. In cases where a component is required to recess into a wall or floor and it is desirable to remove geometry from the host solid, this

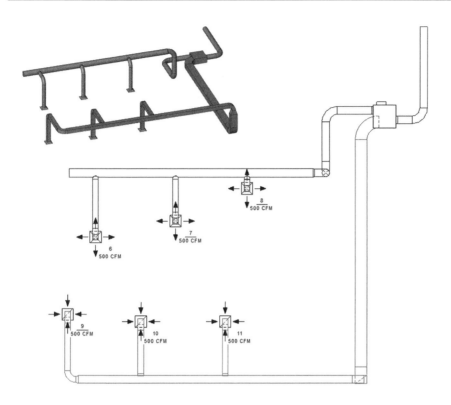

FIGURE 22.4 Typical HVAC system

can be done by adding void geometry into a face-based object that cuts out from the face.

GRAPHICS AND CONNECTIONS

Procedurally, the graphics associated with each engineering discipline are fairly similar when we're dealing with equipment. Graphics are not as relevant as the information contained within them and are limited to gross sizes and connection locations. When developing each object, create a solid or series of solids that will consider the overall size of the unit and its general appearance and shape. The venting louvers on the side of a boiler or the fins on the side of a condenser are extraneous graphics that are not generally appreciated by either the architecture or engineering communities using the components. To simplify locating and placing connectors, small solids that are similar to the shape of the connection itself should be placed in their appropriate locations. The simplest way to place a connector is on the face of a solid, then the solid that represents the connector will automatically center itself in its appropriate location. We can even simplify this process further by creating a series of very small connector graphics objects that can be nested into the host components and used over and over.

> ## Tip
>
> The simplest way to place a connector is on the face of a solid, then the solid that represents the connector will automatically center itself in its appropriate location.

Every connection is different and is used for a different purpose. HVAC connectors carry specific information that applies to HVAC, plumbing to plumbing, and electrical to electrical. In most cases, two or all three types of connections are necessary, especially when dealing with equipment. An oil-fired boiler, for instance, will have connections for electrical, water, exhaust air, and fuel supply. A gas-fired furnace will have connections for electrical, supply air, return air, exhaust air, and fuel supply. Electrical connectors are designed to be wired in series, and there is a hot, neutral, ground and, in some cases, a traveler. Based on the components that are within the circuit, the appropriate wire type is selected. Electrical systems can also be classified as data, and allow a series of computers or other devices to be networked together.

Needless to say, developing the appropriate connectors for BIM objects requires a basic understanding of the principles behind designing building systems. If the content developer does not have a clear understanding of how the component is designed to be used, the manufacturer or an engineer should oversee the development to ensure that the components are developed correctly. Even though the procedure for developing graphics for MEP objects is pretty much the same no matter what type of component we're developing, there are subtle nuances for each discipline that will help in creating better objects that are easier to use.

Plumbing Objects

Plumbing components can be broken into four basic categories: domestic water supply, sanitary, hydronic, and fire protection. Entire building water systems are developed using these four systems and when the objects used within them are developed appropriately, very effective analysis can ensure that the system is designed properly and does not interfere with adjacent building elements.

Domestic water is a low-pressure system that brings water from either the street or a well into a building. Once the water enters the building, it

Plumbing	
Flow Pressure (default)	8.000 psi
Vent Connection	☑
Waste Connection	☑
CW Connection	☑
HW Connection	☑
Mechanical	
WFU	2.000000
HWFU	3.000000
CWFU	3.000000
Dimensions	
Sanitary Radius	3/4"
Sanitary Diameter	1 1/2"
Bath Tub Width	3' 0"
Bath Tub Length	5' 6"
Bath Tub Height	1' 6"
Hot Water Radius	1/4"
Hot Water Diameter	1/2"
Cold Water Radius	1/4"
Cold Water Diameter	1/2"

FIGURE 22.5 Plumbing component attributes

needs to exit somewhere. This is the sanitary or sewer system, which is an unpressurized system that uses gravity to direct the water from drain points throughout a building to a given location. A piping system must be designed and sized accordingly to ensure that enough water can get to a fixture and that the sanitary system can accommodate the number of fixtures that drain into it. One system that is used incorporates *fixture units* to determine how large specific types should be and where drains and vents should be located in relation to adjacent components. This book teaches how to design an object not how to design a system, but it is enough to understand that plumbing fixtures such as faucets and tubs should have the information necessary to perform these types of calculations. Figure 22.5 illustrates the waste fixture units (WFU), hot-water fixture units (HWFU), cold-water fixture units (CWFU), and some commonly used attributes that take into consideration the incoming water pressure at the sizes of the connections necessary for the unit.

Most plumbing components can be categorized as fixtures, with the exception of specialized pipe fittings used within piping systems. Because of this, many of these components can be looked at as aesthetic or architectural components as well as MEP components. As components such as faucets and sinks are developed, additional care should be taken in their graphic representation in order to provide the ability to render the model. Kitchens and bathrooms are some of the most commonly rendered items in the interior of a project. To enhance the renderings and provide better realization of the project, more detail should be added to the visible aspects of the plumbing fixtures.

Electrical Objects

There are three basic types of electrical objects: equipment, devices, and lighting components. As noted before, equipment comprises the elements that are behind the scenes and make the system work. Because in most cases these types of components are embedded in walls or buried in mechanical rooms, they need be no more detailed than their overall size. While we may choose to detail the cover of a load center or breaker panel or to create slight details on an electrical disconnect, components that are not visible or graphically relevant provide no additional value to the model. Creating objects like this should focus on the information rather than the appearance.

Devices are the second type of electrical object and make up the bulk of the components used on a project. There are typically only a few or one load center on a project, but hundreds or thousands of devices. Because so many of these devices are used on the project, keeping them graphically simple allows them to be used for multiple purposes. When a single object can be used to represent all receptacles and another for all switches, the overall file size of the project can be kept manageable. These types of components should never exceed 300 KB or so, and must be able to load and regenerate quickly. Because interference checking is an important aspect of building information modeling, components that are recessed into the wall should carry a solid, which will allow it to interfere with adjacent components. If the receptacle or switch is modeled simply as a represented surface plate, hypothetically a pipe running behind it could interfere and it would never be known until the installer had placed the components in the project. While this seems like a simple fix in the field, it could cause problems if the electrical components have been installed prior to the plumbing and the electrician is no longer on the project.

Many larger components used on a project are electrical in nature, but are often overlooked in terms of their MEP functionality. Any component that is hardwired into a building should carry MEP connectors and, to a large degree, even those components that are plugged into receptacles should be considered. Any component that is plugged into a building and uses a dedicated receptacle, such as a refrigerator or dishwasher, should carry with it an electrical connector so it may be added to the electrical system within the project.

Lighting components are the third basic category of electrical objects. These are unique in that they are used for three purposes. The first and probably most important is their ability to create light. Building information into these components that allows them to render actual light within a project is critical and is discussed in depth in the chapter on lighting. The second and third aspects of a light fixture are their appearance and the fact that they use power. Which of the two is more important will likely depend on who we ask; nevertheless, both should be considered when developing lighting components.

Electricity is looked at in terms of electrical potential or *voltage*, current or *amperage*, and apparent power or *wattage*. These are the three most important attributes of any electrical device, as the electrical potential will determine the type of circuit on which the device should be placed, but current will determine the size of the circuit, and the apparent power will show the theoretical usage of the component if it is used at all times. Figure 22.6 shows basic attributes found in electrical devices. From these attributes, calculations can be generated that can derive useful information about each component. If an average daily usage index is created and applied to each object, annual power consumption can be estimated over the entire project by creating a couple simple calculations within a schedule inside the model.

HVAC Objects

There are hundreds of different HVAC components that may be used on projects, depending on the situation at hand. Whether it is heat generation equipment, air conditioning components, exhaust gas equipment, or basic ductwork with registers and diffusers, there are countless components for different situations. Because there are so many possible components, in many cases the most effective way to manage them is to keep the graphics as simple as possible. If a solid is used to represent the overall space required for the component, it can be placed such that interference checking may be performed and the component itself can be understood. The various connectors and their locations are what differentiate one type of component from the next.

Registers and diffusers are probably the most relevant components to develop graphically, as they are the only elements that are generally visible

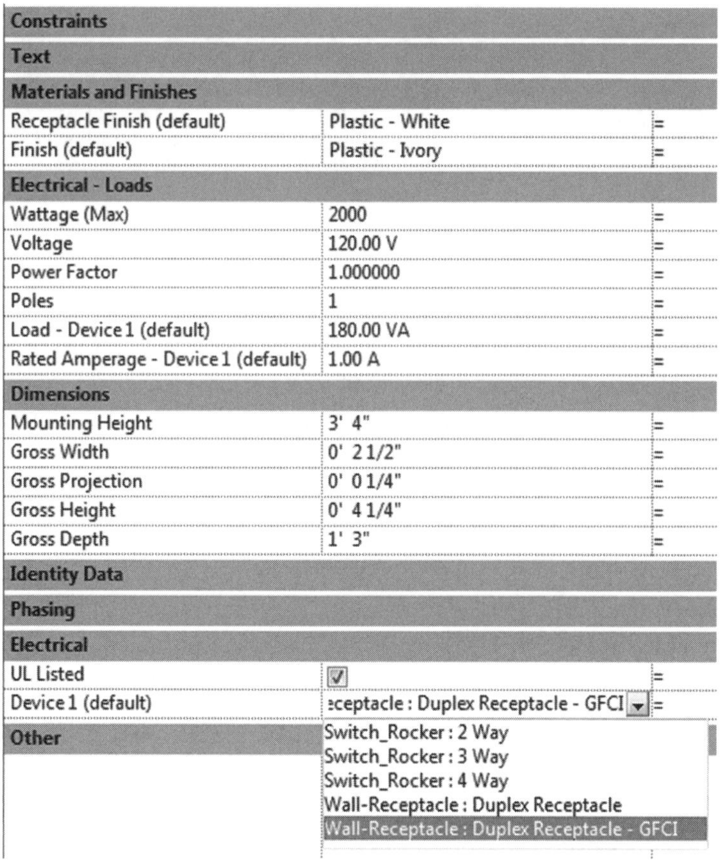

Constraints		
Text		
Materials and Finishes		
Receptacle Finish (default)	Plastic - White	=
Finish (default)	Plastic - Ivory	=
Electrical - Loads		
Wattage (Max)	2000	=
Voltage	120.00 V	=
Power Factor	1.000000	=
Poles	1	=
Load - Device 1 (default)	180.00 VA	=
Rated Amperage - Device 1 (default)	1.00 A	=
Dimensions		
Mounting Height	3' 4"	=
Gross Width	0' 2 1/2"	=
Gross Projection	0' 0 1/4"	=
Gross Height	0' 4 1/4"	=
Gross Depth	1' 3"	=
Identity Data		
Phasing		
Electrical		
UL Listed	☑	=
Device 1 (default)	eceptacle : Duplex Receptacle - GFCI ▼	=
Other	Switch_Rocker : 2 Way	
	Switch_Rocker : 3 Way	
	Switch_Rocker : 4 Way	
	Wall-Receptacle : Duplex Receptacle	
	Wall-Receptacle : Duplex Receptacle - GFCI	

FIGURE 22.6 Typical electrical component attributes

and may find themselves in a rendered view of a model. While the ductwork may have a unique spiral pattern on it, it generally is not relevant; however, if it is important to represent it accurately within the model, piping and ductwork may have a material superimposed on them or "painted," as shown in Figure 22.7.

Many registers, especially decorative ones, use perforated grilles for their aesthetic qualities. Attempting to model this level of detail using solid geometry is not effective, and is not actually important, as air never really flows through it. Rather than modeling the perforations, hatch patterns will effectively represent the surface appearance in model views, and black and white perforation patterns or image files can be used for rendered views.

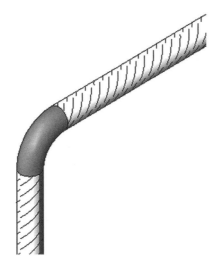

FIGURE 22.7

Assigning a material to a pipe or duct for rendering purposes

EXAMPLE FIXTURE AND FITTING COMPONENTS AND THEIR ATTRIBUTE SETS

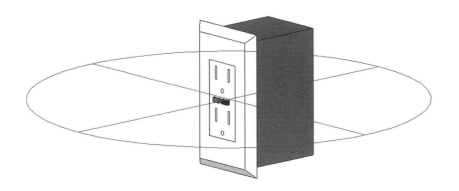

FIGURE 22.8

Typical electrical device

- Voltage: 120 VAC
- Amperage: 20 A
- Wattage or apparent load: 2000 W
- Poles: 1
- Usage: GFCI

FIGURE 22.9

Typical plumbing fixture

- Flow pressure: 8 psi
- Flow rate: 1.2 gpm
- Supply fittings – cold: ½"
- Supply fittings – hot: ½"
- Drain radius: ¾"
- Connector 1: cold-water supply
  - Direction: in
  - System: domestic water – cold
  - Radius: ¼"
  - CWFU: 3
- Connector 2: hot-water supply
  - Direction: in
  - System: domestic water – hot
  - Radius: ¼"
  - CWFU: 3
- Connector 3: sanitary drain
  - Direction: out
  - System: sanitary
  - Radius: ¾"
  - CWFU: 2

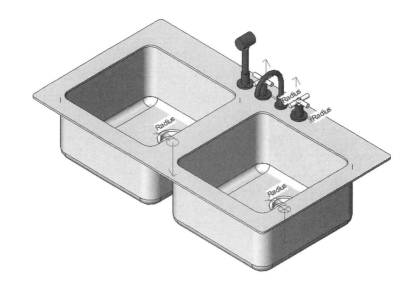

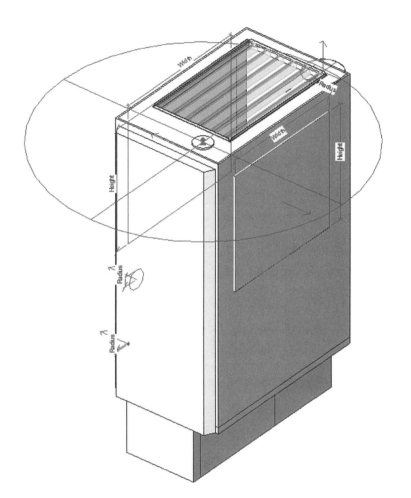

FIGURE 22.10

Typical HVAC component

- Output capacity: 38,000 Btu/h
- Air flow: 1400 cfm
- Connector 1: supply air
  - Direction: out
  - System: supply air
  - Duct shape: rectangular
  - Length: 18"
  - Width: 20"
- Connector 2: return air
  - Direction: in
  - System: return air
  - Duct shape: rectangular
  - Length: 19"
  - Width: 22"
- Connector 3: combustion air
  - Direction: out
  - System: other
  - Duct shape: round
  - Radius: 1"
- Connector 4: exhaust air
  - Direction: out
  - System: other
  - Duct shape: round
  - Radius: 1½"
- Connector 5: fuel supply
  - Direction: in
  - System: other
  - Radius: ¼"

CHAPTER 23

Site and Landscape Components

CONSIDERATIONS

Building information modeling has opened the door for the visualization of exterior settings around a construction project. For this reason, a lot of effort has been put into the creation of accurate site-based component objects, landscaping, planting, and topography. These types of components may or may not be highly detailed, depending on the distance from which rendered views are desired. The development of site-based components, such as benches, planters, and trash receptacles, can often become overly detailed when it is not necessary. In terms of scale, visualizing the exterior of a project takes into consideration views that may be 300 feet wide or larger. As we place small components in the field of view, they become obscured, so exact detail is often not necessary. Landscape and planting components are typically driven by image files that trick the eyes into thinking they are viewing a three-dimensional solid, when it is actually a flat image superimposed into the model. Topography is generally created by importing a point coordinate file, which brings into the project points that have been located by the surveyor, by importing a CAD file containing contour lines, or by manually entering points within the project model.

Site improvements such as benches and planters should contain enough graphic accuracy to be represented at about 50 feet. In many cases the surface material or color is the most important aspect, as it allows the component to stand apart from its surroundings and allows its purpose to be visually understood. Many site components actually have few graphic parametrics associated with them, as these types of units are generally unique and ornate in nature. The overall shape of a bench or planter will likely stay fixed, though perhaps the length will change, but, in a general sense, these are not complex objects. Other objects, such as tree grates, fountains, bollards, and decorative light fixtures, may have no graphic parameters due to their detailed nature. This can make the development of site-based components a long and tedious process as each object must be re-created from scratch rather cloned from an existing component and modified slightly to suit a new one.

Landscape and planting components are often created by special companies that focus on this type of BIM content. ArchVision (archvision.com) is one such company and provides not only landscape and planting components,

FIGURE 23.1
Appropriate level of detail for site components

FIGURE 23.2 ArchVision landscape component—model view and rendered

but people, vehicles, and basic clutter. When added to a visualization, these components make the model appear more realistic by adding context to the view. Rather than using model graphics to represent the rendered appearance of landscaping objects and others that are nearly impossible to model graphically, the component uses a series of images taken at different angles around a tree, flower, bush, person, or other real-world component in order to create a highly detailed, photo realistic visualization of the landscaping component.

Other types of components used in sight and landscaping include fences, retaining walls, and paving. Some of these may be created by using the existing tools within the software, while others may require a little more effort to develop. Retaining walls, for instance, may be developed the same way any other wall is created. The difficult part, which may require manual effort, is training the walls to follow the contour of the land when they are not placed on a horizontal surface. Paving is handled differently depending on whether we're dealing with a level surface or one that follows the grade of the land. A patio or basement slab is designed to be level, or slightly pitched to allow for drainage. Tools within the software similar to those for floors allow a slab to be placed on the grade, filling in topography beneath it. Driveways, on the other hand, follow the contours of the land, so rather than placing a slab that follows its path, it is more effective to create a separate topographic region to represent it, modifying the topography as necessary to smooth out high and low spots. From a construction standpoint, fences and railings use the same types of components: posts, rails, and infill. This allows fences to be created using the same tools that are used for railings. The primary issue with this is tricking the railing into thinking that it is on the topography rather than a flat surface.

No matter what type of site or landscape component we're developing, we should focus more on its ability to be quantified or counted and its specification information. Exact appearance can give way to a more basic visual in order to provide these types of tertiary components used for developing the aesthetic of the project.

FIGURE 23.3 Site topography

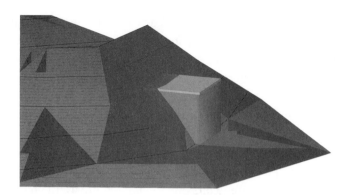

FIGURE 23.4 Slab placed within topography

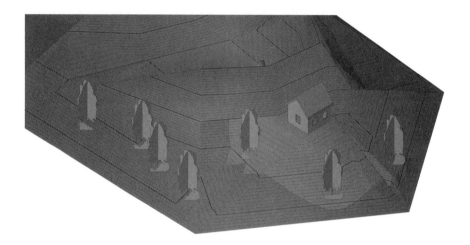

FIGURE 23.5
Topographic subregion

GRAPHICS

Site-based Components

Site-based components that are stand-alone objects should not become overly detailed. While these types of components are often highly ornate, items such as the tiny pushbutton or drain in a water fountain or the bolts that mount a bench to the ground need not be modeled. Less is more, as they say, since the less graphics we place in the model, the more useful it actually is. Surface textures and finishes are probably the most noticeable aspect of site-based components. An exposed aggregate finish may show up in the rendering, adding depth to the overall image. The benefit of putting in the effort to create appropriate materials for each facet of the component will outweigh the effort it takes to make sure that the radius of a corner is three quarters of an inch rather than 1 inch. The graphics of these components need to be carefully weighed against where in the model they will be placed and whether or not they will be visible in close-up views. If a component is designed to be placed near the entrance of the building, it will likely find itself in more closely cropped views during rendering. These types of components may merit slightly more detail in order for them to be represented accurately during rendering. If, on the other hand, the component is off in the distance in most cases, simplified geometry usually will fit the bill. Adding the appropriate finishes to these components will generally offset their appearance.

Trash receptacles, planters, bollards, and fountains are types of components that are likely to find themselves with in rendered views. Modeling these accurately to about ¼ inch is sufficient to allow them to be represented. Focus on the overall shape of the component and its surfaces rather than the detailed aspects of it. If we look at a drinking fountain, we might see a pedestal that is one foot square with a step at the base and a chrome base atop it. It likely has a faucet with a pushbutton and a drain. Focusing the model on the pedestal, the step, and the basin provides enough graphic detail to be viewed effectively in nearly any rendered view. If the file size is kept small, it is possible to even add the faucet itself, provided it is not overly detailed. As I noted earlier, items like the pushbutton and the drain are not relevant, as water will never flow through this object and nobody is really going to push that button.

Telephone poles, fire hydrants, and tree grates are examples of components that should be downplayed within the model. If considerable detail is added to these types of components, it can potentially draw the eye away from many of the components that are relevant to the overall aesthetic of the project. Nobody wants to see a telephone pole or fire hydrant from the rendered view. They should be assumed to be present, but not be detailed enough to draw the eye to them.

The answer to the question of how to create planting components is pretty easy—source them from somewhere else or use the ones from within the software. Creating these types of components really is not building information modeling but project visualization. If we spend time trying to model leaves on a bush or tree, we'll probably find that it would have been far less expensive and far more accurate to have purchased a professionally created component designed for use with the rendering engine within our software.

There are two ways to create a retaining wall, depending on the type being used. For a vertical retaining wall, using typical wall tools and assigning specific materials to them to represent the surface is the most effective method. When dealing with a retaining wall that is incrementally stepped as it becomes taller, we may want to consider creating a line-based site component that can follow the contours of the land and incrementally step back as it becomes taller. Alternatively, custom walls may be created, which can be stepped back as they become taller. This requires a considerable amount of effort when developing the wall type, and often creating complex walls like this becomes more effort than it is worth.

Topography

Topography is not exactly a BIM component but a function of the software. It is created by importing a map with coordinates in elevations or by manually placing points throughout the project in specific locations. The topography is controlled not only by its coordinates in space but by its material. We can assign different soil types to different parts of the toposurface to re-create actual conditions. This may be effective information that is useful when performing soil studies to determine whether the land will drain as necessary. We will discuss this later in the chapter as we go through both the materials and attributes of site and landscape components. Two aspects of topography are volume and surface. Volume deals with what type of soil is in question, and surface determines how it will appear in both model view and renderings. Different types of grass, sand, topsoil, crushed stone, asphalt, or any other material can be represented so long as they are attached to the topography appropriately through their materials.

When a construction project is started, rarely, if ever, is a piece of land prepared to receive a foundation. A considerable amount of site work and excavation is necessary to ready the worksite before construction can begin. This aspect of building information modeling is generally handled by an engineer prior to or concurrently with design. The building design team makes assumptions about elevations based on how excavation and grading occurs. If we think of building information modeling starting not with the design of the building, but with the selection of a plot of land, it is clear that there is a considerable amount of effort associated with site preparation. Knowing how much fill material is necessary to prepare the project site based on the amount of available soil on hand can provide a rough estimate of the amount of time and money it will take to prepare the site. As we change the topography within a building information model to simulate excavation, we can calculate how much soil is being moved and estimate how much soil is necessary. What happens in real life is rarely what happens in design, so it is important to understand that excavators run into large rocks, ledges, and drainage issues that are unforeseen prior to excavating the site.

There is specific software designed to focus on the topography and soil engineering of the project. In many cases the files may be exchanged and imported directly into the building information modeling software. This allows the architect to have an accurate starting point from which to build his project, or a complementary file he can import. Files like these may or may not consider important aspects of the project that are buried underground. Knowing where and where not to dig based on a model is an invaluable tool. The septic system and leach field, sewer pipes, gas lines, buried electrical conduits, and all critical underground elements for future facility management purposes may be quickly located in the event of an emergency and aid in making decisions about future project expansion and renovation.

Paving components within a project are best represented using the existing tools within the software. These tools can assign material surface patterns to a surface, which can represent everything from a gravel driveway to interlocking pavers. Just as nobody is going to stack each brick or concrete block into a wall, it is not practical to expect an architect to place each paver into a surface individually. To represent a specific paver that is of a specific color and has a specific pattern, it is far more effective to let the material itself to work. Colors and textures can be assigned to paving materials and even patterns can be overlaid atop them to represent a specific surface appearance, such as an ashlar or herringbone pattern.

MATERIALS

The primary focus of materials used inside site-based components is their surface appearance. Generally speaking, site components are selected based on their aesthetic qualities, and, thus, it should be possible to represent them with a reasonable amount of accuracy. Because these types of components are placed outside of the project, they're generally created using very durable materials, such as concrete and metals with specialized finishes. For each available finish of a given component there should be an associated material that represents its general appearance or color in model view, and a detailed appearance for rendering purposes. In most cases image files are used to represent the surface appearance, as textured finishes and exposed aggregates are difficult to represent using modeling means. To limit the amount of tiling that is visible in the rendering, make sure that the image file is high resolution and as large as possible. Using a sample texture that is considerably larger than the component itself can functionally eliminate tiling altogether.

Repeating patterns are another visual aspect of materials used inside site-based components. When using images to represent concrete blocks stacked to create a retaining wall or pavers that make up a patio surface, take care to align the surface pattern appropriately and crop the image so that it repeats exactly. When the repeat pattern does not align, it creates unsightly tiling lines that are very visible within renderings. These types of issues detract from a rendering's overall appearance, making the visualization look less realistic. While large-format photographs of pavers may be difficult to capture, the larger the pattern, the less tiling that occurs. Creating images to represent the patterns that are at least 4 feet in width will allow them to be superimposed on most walkways with little or no tiling. When attempting to create these types of images, lighting is essential as well. Even the most minor shading at one edge of the image becomes very visible when it is superimposed on a large area such as a patio.

Creating materials for soils and grasses is similar to creating materials used for pavers, with the difference being that they are random in nature. Repeat patterns are less important, as they are far less visible based on their nonuniform dimensions. Shading, however, is a concern. Just as with pavers or any other material used in a project, shading found on soils and grasses will create unsightly tiling lines even when the image itself is perfect. In addition to the image file, which is used more to represent color than texture, a bump map should be added to the material to give it the appearance of depth. In many cases an effective way to create this type of file is to use a photograph of the surface material and convert it to black and white. The rendering tools within the software use this type of image to offset the bottom from the top, where the regions in the image that are black are the base depth, and the regions that white are the top.

The creation of water to be represented within a building information model is primarily controlled by the tools within the software. The software vendor generally affords us the ability to create different types of water based on preset standards. We can then customize the water image slightly to increase ripples or waves, and change its color to represent a murky swamp differently than a crystal-clear swimming pool. Water is also unique in that it reflects and refracts light from both outside and within it. In a swimming pool at night, for instance, placing a pool light fixture with a green filter in the pool will illuminate the water in green. While the user does not have a lot of control when attempting to represent different types of water, this is not generally a focal point within a project anyway. Preset water types can easily be copied and modified slightly to represent the different types of water found within the project.

DATA—ATTRIBUTES AND EQUATIONS

What the attributes associated with site-based components really are depends on what the component is. Trash cans are designed to hold garbage, while a bollard is designed to withstand the impact of a vehicle or otherwise prohibit traffic. Other components, such as planters and tree grates, are aesthetic in nature but have specific weights and dimensional attributes that may prove useful during procurement and construction.

As you determine which attributes are necessary to add into a site-based BIM object, think about its intended purpose. If a trash can holds refuse, how much refuse can it hold? If a bollard can withstand the impact of a vehicle, how much force can it withstand? By looking at the performance and usage aspects of a product, you can work backward into a data set that qualifies the reasons for specifying a certain product and creates a benchmark of performance or quality that alternate products may be required to meet.

Typical Site Component Attributes

- *Surface material*: Specific material(s) used to represent the appearance of the major outer solids and faces of the object. In addition to calling out a specific material, be specific about finishes and textures as well.

- *Accent material*: Specific material(s) used to represent the appearance of the major outer solids and faces of the object. In addition to calling out a specific material, be specific about finishes and textures as well.

- *Dimensions*: Relevant length, width, height, area, and volume attributes that determine how much space is required to place the component. Minor dimensions may be made parametric for development purposes but need not be showcased within the data set.

- *Capacity*: What the is component capable of doing. If it seats people, how many? If it holds trash, how much?

- *Performance*: Many components are designed to perform a specific task. Objects such as a bollard are designed to withstand a certain amount of force, the pump within a fountain may use a certain amount of electricity, soils may have specific drainage properties, and hardscapes and paving may be porous or non-porous. Manufacturers' data sheets and information are very good resources for finding this type of information.

EXAMPLE SITE COMPONENTS AND THEIR ATTRIBUTE SETS

FIGURE 23.6

Anti-ram bollard object

- Material: concrete – 4000 psi
- Finish: paint – red enamel
- Crash rating: K-8 SB 5 T 6.5 B10-SB
- Impact resistance: 15,000 lb at 50 mph
- Operation: retractable

FIGURE 23.7

Decorative trash receptacle object

- Material: concrete – exposed aggregate – finish as selected from manufacturer's standard finish options
- Door material: stainless steel – no. 4 brushed finish
- Support post material: steel – enamel paint finish – black
- Length: 2'-4"
- Width: 2'-4"
- Height: 44"
- Capacity: (1) – 32-gal refuse container

FIGURE 23.8
Kentucky bluegrass
material

- Species: *Poa pratensis*
- Shade resistance: poor
- Planting: seed
- Mowing height:
  1½–2½"
- Seasonal zone: 4–7

CHAPTER 24

Detailing and Annotations

CONSIDERATIONS

Construction details and annotations are the core elements used within a BIM project to transform it from a three-dimensional model to a two-dimensional set of drawings. The assembly of all drawings used on a given project is referred to as the *plans*. These plans are essential to those in the field and those who do not have access to the native project file. Construction details give us a sense of how two elements affect each other, such as the connection between a wall and a floor, the transition between the roof and a parapet wall, or the termination of a suspended ceiling where it meets a wall. Annotations allow us to provide notations, or *callouts*, where specific information is required. A series of annotations may point out the various materials used in a wall assembly from a section view, note the locations of specific elements within a plan view, or provide supporting information regarding the design and construction of specific elements in elevations. Without details and annotations, the building information model would have little value outside of conceptualization, as the project would lack the appropriate documentation necessary to construct it.

Historically, both drawings and specifications made up elements of the construction documents independent of each other, but complementary. Drawings were provided to convey design intent of the overall project, while specifications provided the accurate detail information and the requirements for the performance of the project and its specific components. Building information modeling has clouded the line between drawings and specifications, in that now we have the ability to carry considerable specification information within the drawings themselves. While this goes a long way toward a fully integrated and unified project team, it also requires us to be much more careful with the way we handle information. Annotations on drawing sheets were once little more than a basic description and a keynote that referenced the specification document. As the ability and desire to add specification information into the model increases, the level of detail found in annotations should increase accordingly. Rather than requiring an individual reading the drawings to cross-reference to an entirely different document, annotations for building information modeling provide the ability to tailor the information we provide to the individual who is reading the drawings. The drawings are created by the architect, and the specifications are created by the specifier. When working on a building information modeling project where attributed information is associated with each material, assembly, and component, the specification information should be derived from the information found in the model. Therefore, the annotation information should be derived from the same information found in the model, not cross-referenced. In terms of "saying it once and saying it in the right place," the BIM project file is quickly becoming the one place to say it, as it is a relational database that allows for easy access, manipulation, and extraction of project information.

Details are often created or imported from traditional CAD software and enhance the actual appearance of connections, transitions, and terminations within section views. The three-dimensional elements used within common BIM software are not intuitive enough to relate themselves to adjacent components in terms of exact construction. Wall elements are drawn using a single line and carry the information about their construction in terms of height, width, and depth. Figure 24.1 graphically considers information such as the spacing of structural members or components, such as wall anchors, that are not found as a layer that covers the entire wall surface.

A section view that is created where a wall meets a steep slope roof will show each component from the inside of the wall to the outside and from the bottom of the roof to the top, but does not show the exact construction in terms of how the sill plate was constructed at the top of the wall, the exact location and size of the bird's mouth cut into a rafter, or the structural bracing. This type

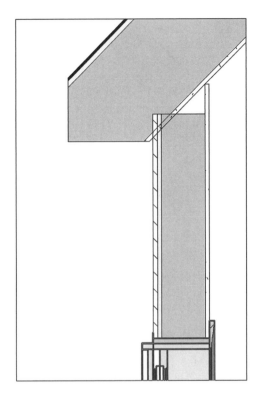

FIGURE 24.1 Section view at roof-to-wall transition

of information is generally created in two dimensions; the three-dimensional element of the project is used more for the conceptualization and design rather than the overall detailing of the project.

A section view that shows the connection between a window and the wall in which it is placed is an example of the considerable amount of manual effort necessary to convey the exact construction without two-dimensional detail. It is not practical to expect an architect to draw the membrane flashing, head flashing, nailing flange, fasteners, sealants, and other related components necessary to install a window, and the window as a BIM component is not intuitive enough to understand what type of wall it is being installed into. The detail will vary considerably, whether it is a wood-framed wall, a masonry wall, or a cavity wall. Expecting a manufacturer to provide an exact component for each possible configuration in which the window is installed is equally impractical and will bloat the overall size of the project file, since, if this is done with Windows, it should be done with doors, fixtures, fittings, casework, and every other component that is affixed to an adjacent component.

It would be nice to eventually see the software become sophisticated enough to create three-dimensional construction details intuitively. At present,

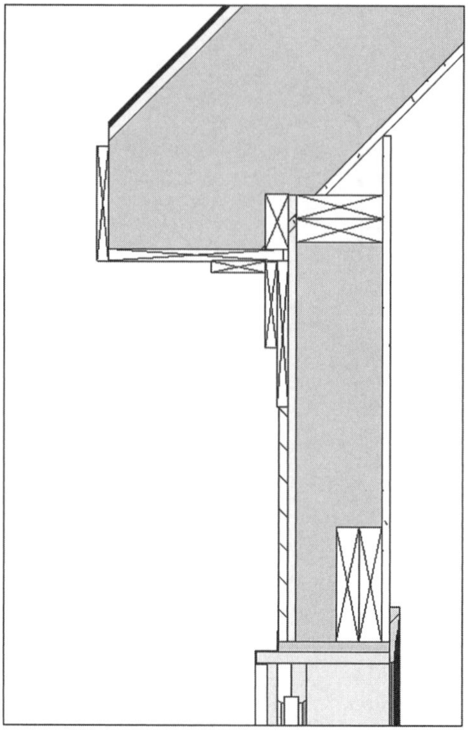

FIGURE 24.2 Section view at roof-to-wall transition with details

for BIM to create details in three dimensions such that accurate section views could be generated from at any location within the project, the modeler would be required to place a considerable number of components manually. Instead, it is more practical to create section views at specific locations to represent how a specific termination, transition, or connection between two or more elements should be made.

Annotations or callouts are used to provide specific information necessary to understand what the graphics on the drawing sheets represent. In traditional two-dimensional drawings, these callouts are created manually by typing in a specific note that applies to the material or element being focused on. The *leader* is the line used to connect the notation to the element the note applies to and can be drawn in one of several ways, depending on what the annotation is used for, and what it is pointing to. It may have an arrow at the end of it, a circle at the end of it, or neither. The uniform drawings standard (UDS) and national CAD standard (NCS) have guidelines for the use of different types of callouts, but in many cases it is user preference.

Building information modeling allows annotations to be used for more than typical description callouts. Specialized annotations can allow any information stored in the model to be conveyed in views and drawing sheets. Annotations

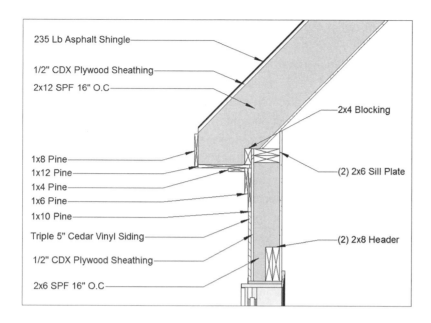

235 Lb Asphalt Shingle

1/2" CDX Plywood Sheathing

2x12 SPF 16" O.C

2x4 Blocking

1x8 Pine
1x12 Pine
1x4 Pine
1x6 Pine
1x10 Pine
Triple 5" Cedar Vinyl Siding
1/2" CDX Plywood Sheathing

2x6 SPF 16" O.C

(2) 2x6 Sill Plate

(2) 2x8 Header

FIGURE 24.3 Section view at roof-to-wall transition with details and annotations

are components of the model just like a window or door, and are equally parametric. We can toggle the appearance and information within annotations without disrupting the model graphics. Annotations have the ability to carry any piece of text information to the drawing sheets that is found in an element. If we want to convey the sound transmission classes between walls on a specific drawing sheet generated for a contractor responsible for sound attenuation, specialized annotations can be used to note these, provided the associated information is listed in the walls.

Annotations can also be bidirectional, allowing information to be not only viewed, but quickly modified where required. This allows another method of quickly inserting, confirming, and modifying project information. If the description of a component is what is used for the annotation on drawing sheet, clicking on the annotation will allow the user to change the description not only on the drawing sheet, but within the component itself.

GRAPHICS

The graphics associated with details and annotations are very simple in nature. In a general sense, they are nothing more than two-dimensional vector line work with attributed text. Parametric capabilities of building information modeling software allow us to globally modify and customize these to suit the needs of our project or office. An annotation is made up of three basic components: the annotation text, the leader line, and the leader head.

- The annotation *text* is the information being conveyed. It may be the description of a component being pointed to, a cross-reference to an additional view within another drawing sheet, or a keynote that references the specification documents. Regardless of what the information is, it is based on a set of attribute and value pairs, and carries the ability to join or concatenate multiple text strings to create the desired information.

- *Leader lines* join the notation to the location to which the note applies. It allows us to put information in locations in a view or drawing sheet that has enough space to convey the necessary information. A section view of a wall will have a series of layers, many of which are very thin. Drawing a leader line from the thin layer within a wall to a location where the text is readable allows for more information to be added and keeps the view looking clean and professional.

- *Leader heads* are used to create a more specific appearance of what the note is pointing to. Typically, a filled or hollow arrow is used, with a 15- or 30-degree angle. Additionally, a filled or hollow circle may be used. The UDS and NCS provide more information governing when to use each type.

Cross-reference annotations are used to note specific information that cannot fit in the same view or on the same drawing sheet. Section views are probably one of the more common examples of this. Where section views are located within a plan view, a cross-referenced notation will provide a quick way to locate the sheet number and detail number associated with that section.

Some things to consider about the graphics of annotations have to do with their ultimate purpose: to be read. Annotations are designed to be readable, regardless of what scale the detail graphics are in. When creating views and placing annotations, it is important to first place our view at the appropriate scale prior to placing annotations. This will save a lot of headache and time moving annotations around after finding that our view does not fit on the drawing sheet appropriately. Text fields determine how much space the annotation may take up and how it should be formatted to ensure that text will not overrun and will always look natural. This is especially important when creating annotations using multiple attributes. In many cases it may be more practical to put each attribute on its own line and justify all of them to one side, rather than attempting to size them to appear natural.

Detail drawings are a series of two-dimensional CAD or BIM files used to convey the exact conditions of a specific construction. These detail drawings

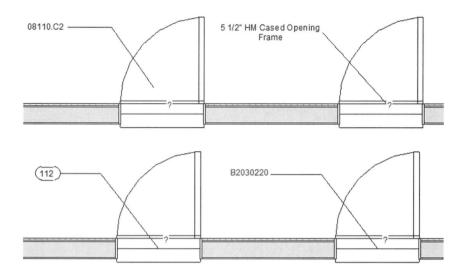

FIGURE 24.4 Common types of annotations

can be either a function of a drawing sheet or a function of a view within the model. Where they are noted as a function of a drawing sheet, they are placed directly into a specific sheet, without cross-reference. This may be practical in preliminary stages, but it is more effective to make a detail drawing a function of a view, such that the view may be duplicated and cross-references may be made. When importing two-dimensional CAD files for use as details, it is critical to note scale. Everything in building information modeling is drawn at full scale, so all files imported should reflect the same scale in order for them to look appropriate.

In many cases, two-dimensional detail drawings are overlaid onto graphics within section views to provide additional information about components that are not visible in the modeling graphics. Detail drawings are generally a representative sample of what the construction might look like, and often do not take into consideration the sizing of adjacent components, as they are not relevant to the detail at hand. The connection detail where a roof rafter joins a wall is the same regardless of whether the wall is framed with 2×4 or 2×6 studs or the roof rafters are 2×8 or 2×12. Because of this, in many cases, it can be more effective to add detail components instead of entire details. Creating a single detail component that represents a cut view of a 2×4, or even a parametric detail that represents the cut view of all dimensional lumber, will allow the individual components to be dropped into place rather than our attempting to modify an entire detail to overlay it on to the actual construction.

DATA—FROM ATTRIBUTES TO ANNOTATIONS

The method I use with BIM is to add a material with its specification section number to the annotation for vendor-neutral materials that are not specifically called out: (06 11 00_ 2 × 4 dimensional lumber – species as noted in the contract documents) or (07 54 00_TPO membrane – thickness as noted in the contract documents). I use the term "contract documents" here as there are changes happening in the industry, and while the contract documents now would be the project manual, in the future, they may not be. The descriptions are very fluid and allow for modification based on the amount of information known. For instance, a knowledge manager may handle the annotations for the roof membrane like this:

- PP – (07 00 00_roof as noted in the contract documents)
- SD – (07 50 00_roof membrane – as noted in the contract documents)
- DD – (07 54 00_roof membrane – thermoplastic – as noted in the contract documents)
- CD – (07 54 23_roof membrane –.060 TPO – tan)
- Post bid – (GAF EverGuard .060 TPO membrane – tan)

The idea is to give an appropriate description based on the amount of information known at a given time and to reference the contract documents for the next pieces of information that may be necessary. This allows the annotation to always be correct, regardless of how much effort is put into the annotations or even if they never get updated past schematics. I used phases as an example above, but I see phases as we know them disappearing to some degree with the growth of BIM. Because effort is recyclable in BIM, we can actually have detail views in schematic design that have merit. Standardized views can be moved from place to place within a template project, and only the annotations need be moved to create *progress drawings* at various phases of the project.

All in all, it's my belief that the concept of keynoting really only pertains to the drawings that are ultimately viewed by the contractor. I truly believe that requiring general contractors to cross-reference information that is located in a specification in order to obtain the *basic* information necessary do their job is just plain lazy! Models and drawings should follow the same CSI principles as specifications (clear, concise, complete, correct), and the fifth C—consistent. Keynoting makes incomplete drawings, as there is no single unified keynote structure and there is no practical way to take into consideration every possible component within a given specification section. It took over 1200 different BIM materials for a metal-framing manufacturer to represent its metal stud offerings, which consider dimension, yield strength, web depth, and spacing.

Drawings are created before specifications, and BIM is the root of both. As information goes into the model, it first becomes a function of the drawing, and the attributed information becomes a tabular specification that can be used to develop a text-based document. It is actually very simple (and beneficial) to add the attributed information into the individual materials and components, as BIM provides not only the ability to toggle between keynote and annotation globally, but to actually concatenate attributes to create an accurate callout.

The syntax for annotating a roof membrane material might look like this:

Single Attribute Only

- Syntax: [MF number]
- Example: [07 54 23]
- Actual: 07 54 23

Preplanning (PP)

- Syntax: [MF number]_[component] [type]
- Example: [07 00 00]_[roof] [as noted in the contract documents]
- Actual: 07 00 00_roof as noted in the contract documents

Schematic Design (SD)

- Syntax: [MF number]_[component] [type] – [material]
- Example: [07 50 00]_[roof] [membrane] – [as noted in the contract documents]
- Actual: 07 50 00_roof membrane – as noted in the contract documents

Design Development (DD)

- Syntax: [MF number]_[component] [type] – [material]
- Example: [07 54 00]_[roof] [membrane] – [thermoplastic]
- Actual: 07 54 00_roof membrane - thermoplastic – as noted in the contract documents

Construction Documents (CD)

- Syntax: [MF number]_[component] [type] – [size] [material] – [finish]
- Example: [07 54 23]_[roof] [membrane] – [.060] [TPO] – [tan]
- Actual: 07 54 23_roof membrane –.060 TPO – tan

Post BID

- Syntax: [type] [component] – [manufacturer]_ [trade name] – [size] [material] – [finish]
- Example: [MEMBRANE] [ROOF] – [GAF] [EverGuard] [.060] [TPO] – [tan]
- Actual: membrane roof – GAF EverGuard .060 TPO – Tan

The syntax for annotating a vinyl casement window might look like this:

Single Attribute Only

- Syntax: [model]
- Example: [Encompass 3046]
- Actual: Encompass 3046

Preplanning (PP)

- Syntax: [MF number]_[component] [type]
- Example: [08 00 00]_[window] – [type as noted in the contract documents]
- Actual: 08 00 00_window – type as noted in the contract documents

Schematic Design (SD)

- Syntax: [MF number]_[component] – [type] – [material]
- Example: [08 53 13]_[window] – [type as noted in the contract documents] – [vinyl]
- Actual: 08 53 13_window – type as noted in the contract documents – vinyl

Design Development (DD)

- Syntax: [MF number]_[component] – [type] – [material]
- Example: [08 53 13]_[window] – [30 × 46 casement] – [vinyl]
- Actual: 08 53 13_window – 30 × 46 casement – vinyl

Construction Documents (CD)

- Syntax: [MF number]_[component] [type] – [finish] [material]
- Example: [08 53 13]_[window] – [30 × 46 casement] – [white] [vinyl]
- Actual: 08 53 13_window – 30 × 46 casement – white vinyl

Post BID

- Syntax: [component] – [manufacturer] – [trade name] – [type] – [finish] [material]
- Example: [window] – [Pella]_[Encompass] – [30 × 46 casement] – [white] [vinyl]
- Actual: window – Pella Encompass – 30 × 46 casement – white vinyl

The syntax for annotating a wall assembly might look like this:

Single Attribute Only

- Syntax: [fire rating]
- Example: [90 minute]
- Actual: 90 minute

Preplanning (PP)

- Syntax: [UF number]_[component] [type]
- Example: [C1010]_[partition wall] – [type as noted in the contract documents]
- Actual: C1010_partition wall – type as noted in the contract documents

Schematic Design (SD)

- Syntax: [UF number]_[component] [type]
- Example: [C1010100]_[partition wall] – [fixed]
- Actual: C1010100_partition wall – fixed

Design Development (DD)

- Syntax: [UF number]_[component] [type] – [structure]
- Example: [C1010145]_[partition wall] – [fixed] – [gypsum wallboard w/metal stud]
- Actual: C1010100_partition wall – fixed – gypsum wallboard w/metal stud

Construction Documents (CD)

- Assembly syntax: [UF number]_[component] [type] – [structure]
- Example: [C1010145]_[partition wall] – [fixed] – [gypsum wallboard w/metal stud]

- Actual: C1010145_partition wall – fixed – gypsum wallboard w/metal stud
- Included material syntax: [mf number]_[component] [type] – [size] [material] – [finish]
  - Actual material: 09 29 00_gypsum wallboard – type X – 5⁄8" – finish as specified
  - Actual material: 05 41 00_metal stud framing – 4" × 1.625" web – knurled finish

Post BID

- Assembly syntax: [UF number]_[component] [type] – [structure]
- Example: [C1010145]_[partition wall] – [fixed] – [gypsum wallboard w/metal stud]
- Actual: C1010145_partition wall – fixed – gypsum wallboard w/metal stud
- Syntax: [type] [component] – [manufacturer]_[trade name] – [size] [material] – [finish]
  - Actual material: gypsum wall sheathing – USG SHEETROCK FIRECODE – 5⁄8" – paper facer
  - Actual material: metal stud framing – Telling Industries TRUE-STUD – 4" web × 1.25" flange – knurled finish

When dealing with assemblies, you'll notice that the preliminary levels of information are organized not by MasterFormat® numbers, but by UniFormat™ numbers as well. Generally, a wall assembly is made up of several specification sections, each of which applies to a material or layer of the assembly. As we reach the construction documents phase, the information then becomes relevant in terms of master format. The UniFormat™ number along with the information contained within the assembly that was actually created can provide enough information to develop specification sections for each of the materials or building products that were specified.

Because of this structure, I use only the six digits of MasterFormat®, with no following enumeration that corresponds to a construction or specific material. A keynote is great if a machine needs to read it, but we are not machines. We are humans who want to see the information that we need, not to have to follow a path to reference a different document. The BIM database already does this for us, and because it maps the information in such a way that it is no additional effort to create the more detailed information, there is no reason *not* to use full text callouts. We are all collaborating on a project and should consider the needs of the individuals who are actually using our deliverables.

I do understand that we can put only so much information on an E-sized plot, but with the on-screen digital world right in front of us, changing scale and creating additional sheets that apply to specific trades at a more detailed scale is a simple Duplicate w/Detailing command.

All of this information is searchable within the model and allows for analysis, so by adding a few attributes to each material, an annotation is automatically created and can be globally updated based on the status of the project or who needs the information. Whether or not keynoting is relevant and useful is no longer an issue in my estimation—that ship has sailed already. I think the idea is how detailed the annotations need to be to suit the needs of every member of the project. If BIM can automate the annotation and keynoting process by leveraging attributes from within the material, assembly, or component, then the bigger issue is the accepted taxonomy and structure for the information that needs to be managed.

Usage—Leveraging the Information

As I mentioned earlier in this chapter, the primary purpose of details and annotations is to provide a more accurate depiction of the project at specific locations. Transition, termination, and connection details are usually uniform throughout the project. The method used to create a base flashing typically does not change, so it is not necessary to create a three-dimensional representation at every location that it exists. A representative two-dimensional depiction of the base flashing is perfectly acceptable for use on drawing sheets. This is how it is done today, and historically it has been a very successful and effective method for conveying construction details.

The ability to create customized annotations opens the door for the creation of drawing sheets that can apply to individual trades working on a project. By simply changing the type of annotation used in a specific view, we can convey information that applies to different trades working on the same component. Multiple subcontractors may be working on a wall to create its structure, sheathing, accents and trim, and finishes. Each subcontractor likely needs to see different information to complete his scope of work effectively. The framer does not care what species of trim is being used at the baseboard. Conversely, the finish carpenter may want to know what type of framing components were used within the wall.

Eventually, it is likely that we will see three-dimensional components with the intelligence to be able to create two-dimensional details on the fly with little or no effort from the user. Much of this development must be driven by the intuition of the software. The software must be able to determine and understand what types of walls are used, the properties of those walls, and the essential construction techniques necessary to detail the various types of conditions found on projects. This is no small task for software vendors. Based on the countless combinations of construction coupled with constant innovation within the building products industry, the use of two-dimensional details within drawing sheets will likely be with us for some time.

CHAPTER 25

Constellations

WHAT IS A CONSTELLATION?

In terms of building information modeling, a constellation is a series of components that work together to create a single element. A single star, which is likely its own solar system in and of itself, becomes interconnected with a series of stars to become a celestial constellation. BIM objects have the ability to work the same way. A fully functioning door has a frame, door panel, hinges, a series of weatherproofing components, and a series of access components. In most cases, these components come from more than one manufacturer. It's rare to see door hardware such as handles, exit devices, and closers come standard with a specific manufacturer's door. This has created a real issue with attempting to place door hardware within building information models. Rather than placing the hardware on each door within a project, it is more practical to place it on a single door and load that door into the project, placing it in its necessary locations. The real problem with this is that there are too many combinations of door hardware associated with any given project.

Some building information modeling software platforms allow a connection between components of a given category. Just as curtain walls will automatically allow us to select from a series of curtain panels that are loaded into the project, a door object formatted as a constellation will allow us to select from a series of panels, hardware, and weatherproofing components. There are substantial benefits to developing certain types of components this way. Project elements that require additional components to be fully functional or those that have a considerable number of options can leverage constellation development to keep file size low and functionality high. If we build a single door that contains 20 different panel styles, three frame types, and four types of hinges, the single object is likely to exceed 2 MB, which is far larger than any architect would care to work with.

Generally, only a few styles of door would be required on a single project. While creating a single model that can represent each and every door is beneficial to the manufacturer, as it offers all of his options within the fewest number of components, it is a detriment to the architect, as the file size and regeneration time are too great. Rather than generating 240 options based on the panel, frame, and hinge, a single constellation object can be created that will allow the architect to load only the options he is looking for. This is just the beginning of the door development, as we have yet to consider the various access hardware options, which would easily bring the number of options into the millions if we take into consideration the sheer number of manufacturers and the number of access components they sell.

Building a constellation is more about standardization than it is about the components themselves. It is formatting components into a specific category so that they may be accessible through a drop-down menu, naming the components appropriately, and using standardized insertion points for each category of object. Formatting components so that they may be shared with

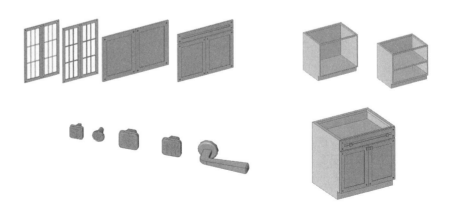

FIGURE 25.1 The
assembly of a constellation

other objects and placing them into a specific category will allow them to show up in drop-down menus within the constellation. It is likely that many components of different types will be within the same category, so naming them appropriately will minimize the risk of improperly located components, like hinges ending up where a door handle is supposed to be. Door hardware components such as exit devices, closers, handles, hinges, and kick panels are likely to be found in the same category, so they show up within door hardware schedules appropriately. The first element of the name should be that of the type of component it is. If it is an exit device, the first part of the name should start with *exit-device_* or something similar; if it is a door closer, it should start with *door-closer_* or the like. This will allow the components to be selected appropriately from a series of drop-down menus. This is important for placing the components within the data set, but to place them graphically, the most important aspect of a constellation is the point of origin of the component.

Door Hardware Options

Door closer

    Door-closer_surface mounted

    Door-closer_concealed

    None

    As specified in 08 71 00

Interior access hardware

    Exit-device_manufacturer A

    Exit-device_manufacturer B

    Exit-device_manufacturer C

    Knob_manufacturer A

    Knob_manufacturer B

    Knob_manufacturer C

    Lever_manufacturer A

    Lever_manufacturer B

    Lever_manufacturer C

    None

    As specified in 08 71 00

Exterior access hardware

    Pull_rounded_manufacturer A

    Pull_rounded_manufacturer B

Pull_rounded_manufacturer C

Knob_manufacturer B

Knob_manufacturer C

Lever_manufacturer A

Lever_manufacturer B

Lever_manufacturer C

Cover plate_manufacturer A

Cover plate_manufacturer B

Cover plate_manufacturer C

None

As specified in 08 71 00

Notice in Figure 25.2 that each type of component has two additional options that take into consideration the absence of a component in that category and the lack of decision regarding the component. Having an option for "None" is essential, as in many cases there may not be a door closer or there may not

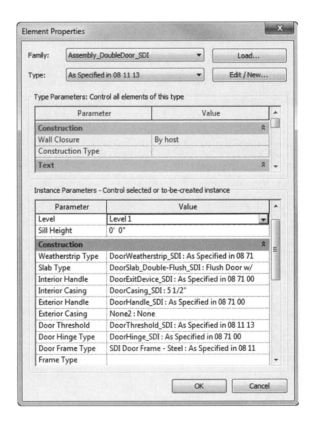

FIGURE 25.2
Constellation data set

be an exterior access hardware device. This gives the design team maximum flexibility about when and how they make decisions regarding these types of components. Adding "As specified in . . ." is not absolutely necessary, but for the sake of the data set associated with the model, it provides a visual cue to individuals who are managing the information that decisions must be made regarding specific components. Whereas "None" reflects a conscious decision that has been made to omit a component from the project, "As specified" reflects a lack of decision as to whether or not the component is to be used. When constellations are loaded into the project early, all of the options are generally listed "As specified" until the design team has made the appropriate product determinations.

Constellations also allow the model to evolve graphically as design decisions are made. During schematic design there may be a series of walls and a series of openings. An opening may become a door, the door may become a double door, then a six-panel door, and a six-panel double door may become a six-panel double door with astragal and hardware formatted, so that, finally, it is an emergency access fire door. Because each of the components associated with a related decision is loaded into the model independently, the file size stays relatively low during the early stages of design. The constellation itself may be only 250 KB, as it contains very few graphics until the decisions about specific elements of the component are made. Since most of the more noticeable and wholesale changes are made to the design early on, keeping the file size as small as possible allows the design team to work quickly to implement those changes.

The use of constellations is not for every situation and not without its drawbacks. There are certainly situations where mistakes can easily be made when using a constellation. We do not have the ability to limit selections that may not be applicable. If they are within the category and they are loaded in the project, they can be placed into the constellation. While it is my firm belief that building information modeling should never be considered a configurator that will automatically select products for us, there are some who place this level of expectation on the technology. There is no substitute for product knowledge, so when working with constellations, there should be a clear understanding of the product that has been modeled and how to appropriately specify it.

Constellations can be used anywhere multiple components rely on each other to complete their graphic appearance. Certain categories of components stick out immediately as those that see the most benefit from the creation of a constellation. Doors and cabinets are the most notable, as they generally comprise several different components, some of which may be sourced from different manufacturers. Door and cabinet manufacturers both pride themselves on a robust selection of styles that is made available to the general public. Rather than re-creating all of the geometry associated with the door, it is easier to change only the aspects that require modification. When deciding on whether to develop a component as a constellation, think about whether the object as a whole has the ability to locate embedded components. Can a door provide a reference that will locate the placement of a handle? Is the panel a uniform shape that can effectively stretch to fit a given opening? If we use enough reference planes within the component, just about anything can be created as a constellation; whether it is practical or not is another matter.

BUILDING CONSTELLATIONS

The first step to building a constellation is to develop the host object that will contain all of the embedded components. This will allow us to lay out the locations of each subcomponent and determine whether they should be fixed and be a function of the type of host component, or dynamic and be a function of the user's input. The backset of a door or the distance between the edge of the door panel and the centerline of a door access device is a good example of this. Doors will generally have a defined backset, often 2⅜" or 2¾". Because this is a fixed value, it should not be left up to the user to decide; it should be a function of the type of host object and limited to only the appropriate values. Placing references that will determine the insertion point along the X, Y, and Z planes will ensure that each component is located appropriately.

Reference planes are the most important aspect of constellations. The primary object will likely have several reference planes to create a single insertion point for each component. Each reference plane should be named accordingly so that errors do not arise when you are developing and testing the host. Setting the type of reference that each plane corresponds to is equally important, as this determines its relationship to adjacent components. This is more important when dealing with the subcomponents than with the host, but nevertheless is a good practice to maintain at all times. Setting reference planes that apply to top, bottom, left, right, front, back, and centerlines for the X, Y, and Z axes ensures that we'll always know which way is up.

The host component of a constellation should carry some type of base graphics that apply to the component as a whole. In the case of a door or window, often the frame is the most appropriate aspect, since there are typically fewer frame options than there are panel options, and the graphic aspect of the frame is generally limited. If we are developing a cabinet, the body may be the graphics that are found in the host. Developing the graphics for these components is no

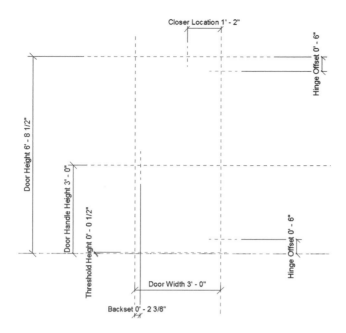

FIGURE 25.3
Constellation door object reference planes

different in principle than doing so for any other component that is to be built, except for the importance of appropriate reference planes. If we're developing a door, we follow the modeling principles found in the chapter on doors; information on cabinets is found in the chapter on fixtures and fittings. Because most of the graphics associated with the component as a whole are developed in a modular fashion and are a function of the various subcomponents, there will likely be little to do in the way of graphics within the host component.

Once the base object is created, it should be tested for functionality on its own before adding any subcomponents. This host object is the primary component from which all other components within the category can be made. This single unit can represent a whole range of manufacturers using a single component, because the data and graphics that differentiate one manufacturer from the next have not been added yet.

The subcomponents used within the primary require considerably more effort to build, as they are far more detailed and require substantially more testing to ensure that they all work. To simplify the process, it is a good idea to develop a template for each category and set the reference planes before adding any graphics. This template should be used to develop every component of that category. From the template, a good practice is to develop one component of each category, load it into the host object, and test it. If we cannot generate errors or cause the graphics to be inappropriate, then that first component can be used to develop all subsequent components of that category.

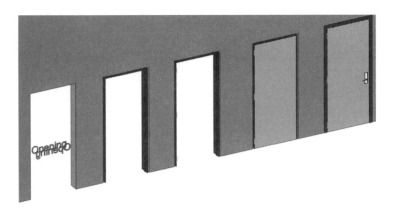

FIGURE 25.4
Constellation door object

Each component category is going to have a different, and in many cases unique, insertion point. While each category may have a different insertion point, all components of that category MUST use the same one. If we attempt to use different insertion points within a given category, as components are swapped out, there is a good chance that errors will occur and the graphics will not look correct. Not only must insertion points be the same, but the type of host that is used must be the same as well. This is another reason why working from templates for each category will ensure that they are always correct. As mentioned earlier, building constellations is more about standards than about graphics. Multiple manufacturers may be used, all of which may have developed their components in a slightly different fashion. While setting an industry standard for development of these types of components will aid in improving the overall development of BIM content, the likelihood of all components actually being developed in that fashion is fairly low.

Tip

While each category may have a different insertion point, all components of that category MUST use the same one. If we attempt to use different insertion points within a given category, then as components are swapped out, there is a good chance that errors will occur and the graphics will not look correct.

When deciding on the insertion point of the subcomponent, think in terms of how and where it is installed in the primary component, and its relationship to the insertion planes within the host. The backset of a doorknob is based on the centerline of the handle itself, so a logical insertion point would be the left/right and top/bottom centerlines of the knob. It is important to note all three planes that make up the insertion point, and it is not uncommon for one to inadvertently be forgotten. Since the knob is placed flush to the door, its back surface is a practical insertion point, rather than its centerline from front to back. Many components, especially those of doors, are handed. If we were dealing with a handle rather than a knob, we would see that a handle typically faces away from the jamb of the door, so when placing components, we must make sure they are oriented properly before locking them to their respective reference planes.

Certain subcomponents are going to have dimensions that relate to the host component and would normally be parametrically locked in order to drive their size. The height and width of a door panel, for instance, is based on the size of the door. In a door object that was created in a typical fashion, the door panel might be an embedded object that has width and height attributes that are locked to width and height attributes from the door itself. When dealing with constellations, rather than using parameters to drive the sizes, creating the door panel with dimensional parameters that are instance based will allow us to resize it by stretching it and locking it to appropriate reference planes. What this does is limit the number of parameters that must be passed back and forth, and keeps templates simplified. In the case of a door panel, it also allows us to use one door family to represent both single and double doors using the same object, as well as any other type of door that may rely on the same type of frame. Rather than creating a single- and double-door constellation, single- and double-door subcomponents may be created. It's all a matter of making sure that the reference planes for all of the components are the same.

Locking reference planes rather than passing parameters from constellations to subcomponents also allows us to use a single object that applies to an option of "None." When we pass parameters from the host component to a subcomponent, the subcomponent must contain the same parameters; otherwise, errors will occur. If no parameters are passed from constellation to subcomponent, we only need one object that is titled "None" and we can use it for all component options within a category. If you to pass parameters, make sure that the object used to represent the option of "None" contains those parameters with arbitrary values that will not cause errors. Remember that while the "None" object has no graphics, it does have reference planes, which may stretch and/or lock themselves to host reference planes; so, even though the object may not be visible, it is attempting to create graphic impossibilities. This is a common error when the values for length parameters are left at zero.

Materials are an aspect of constellations that can get a bit tricky. They can be controlled either through the subcomponent or by passing parameters from the constellation. Controlling the materials through the subcomponent itself can prove to be more effective, as adding a considerable number of material parameters to the constellation object can get confusing. If a subcomponent does not exist within the constellation and is noted in the data set as "None," there should be no material value associated with it, yet there should be a material parameter that has some value attached to it. By controlling the material through the subcomponent, we can create a series of subcomponent types that are driven by the material or, alternatively, we can make them user defined, so that the architect may select finishes when he deems it to be appropriate. Components of constellations will show up in schedules of their own merits and carry their own attributes. When materials are left unattached, they can be manipulated either through the graphics or through the schedules. In many cases, the selection of finishes is more of a last-minute item, so being able to look at them on schedules and update them en masse can make it easier for the architect. In cases such as cabinetry, the finish may be an integral part of both the constellation and the subcomponent. If so, it is more practical to pass the cabinet finish parameter down to the subcomponent in order to change its appearance all at once.

After creating a series of subcomponents that apply to the constellation, one of each category should be loaded into the host for testing and parameter assignment. One at a time, install each component in its appropriate location, orient it accurately, and lock the three reference planes from the subcomponent to the three reference planes to which they apply in the constellation. Once they are locked in place, test the constellation itself by flexing each of the parameters accordingly. If errors occur, check your reference planes and make sure that the subcomponents are locked by their reference planes rather than by a geometric face. After testing has been performed, assign a parameter to each category of subcomponent to create the drop-downs shown in Figure 25.5. In the case of a door, there will often be a need for a door panel, interior access hardware, exterior access hardware, and closer controls. There is no limit to the number of controls that can be added, but as you develop the constellation, think in terms of how much information you want from the model and how many components you want to have show up within the schedules.

At this point, the primary constellation has been completed. It should be tested within a project to ensure that it works correctly and that graphics can be swapped out accordingly. One simple test is to take the template that was used to create the component, strip out any graphics that may be contained within it, rename it as "None," and load it into the project alongside the constellation that has been created. Within a project, if we select the constellation component and select "None" as an option for all of the parametric subcomponents,

FIGURE 25.5
Constellation object with drop-down options

the graphics should disappear without causing any errors. As we change them back to their original component, or a different component that was created using our templates, there should be no errors as well.

QUALITY CONTROL—TIPS AND BEST PRACTICES

Developing constellation objects is about as complex an undertaking as we're likely to come across when developing BIM content. Because we're dealing with so many aspects of standardizing, formatting, and implementing components, quality control is essential. The first step to quality control is creating a series of templates that work for each constellation and each subcomponent of that constellation. Devise a standard that will work for your entire library so that all of the components that may be relevant to the constellation will work. This may require going back and adding or changing reference planes and insertion points of existing objects, but in the long run will save you a considerable amount of time in model development and information management.

First and foremost, test your objects often. Each time a reference plane, dimension, or new piece of geometry is added, flex the related parameters to ensure that nothing else has been affected. When geometry is added, make it a habit to lock the geometry to its related reference planes right away, rather than waiting and doing it all at once. This allows you to test more frequently and minimizes the chances of forgetting to lock something up later. With constellations, it is often more effective to test the components from within a project rather than from the development window. This will allow you to see the behavior of the various reference planes and insertion points that relate to the different subcomponents.

Certain dimensions and options associated with constellations may be user defined. The location of the pull on the cabinet door may vary based on preference. If we test these parameters from within a project, we have the ability to move and stretch them to see if and when errors may occur. Attributes that are associated with the type of constellation or the type of subcomponent are easily tested within projects as well. By loading all of the subcomponent options into the project alongside the constellation, we can quickly test both the constellation and subcomponent options together to see whether errors generated by the constellation are due to the presence of one or more subcomponents. Once all of the testing has been performed and we are comfortable with both the constellation and each of the subcomponents, loading the smallest subcomponent for each category will keep the constellation file size minimized. If the initial file size is of critical importance, the use of the "None" or the "As specified" object will eliminate the graphics altogether while still maintaining the ability to select the options later on.

Below is a checklist of eight commonly overlooked items that can cause errors or unexpected results when we're developing constellations. The bulleted lists are example names, requirements, or remedies associated with the situation.

Constellation Troubleshooting Checklist

(1) Are 9 reference planes named and assigned correctly?

- Top
- Bottom
- Left
- Right
- Front
- Back
- Center top/bottom
- Center left/right
- Center front/back

(2) Is the insertion or origin point assigned on three planes?

- X axis

- *Y* axis
- *Z* axis

(3) Is the insertion point the same on all subcomponents of a given category?

- The same three planes determine the origin of all door access components.
- The same three planes determine the origin of all drawer handles and pulls.

(4) Are parameters passed from constellation to subcomponent available within all subcomponents?

- *Parameter*—Finish passed from cabinet constellation to cabinet door subcomponent must be available within all cabinet door subcomponents, including "None."
- *Parameter*—Panel thickness passed from door constellation to door panel subcomponent must be available within all door panel subcomponents.

(5) Are parameters passed from constellation to subcomponent locked to all subcomponents?

- *Parameter*—Door finish passed from door constellation to door panel subcomponent must be locked together, else the finish will not be updated appropriately.

(6) Are all subcomponents visible as options from drop-down menus after they are loaded into a project?

- If subcomponents are not visible in the drop-down menus, check to see if the object category is the same as the category assigned to the parameter.
- If subcomponents are not visible in the drop-down menus, check to see that they are formatted to be shared among other objects within a project.

(7) Are parameters assigned appropriately as instance or type?

- All subcomponents should have their parameter types aligned.
- To pass parameters from constellation to subcomponent, the subcomponent must have an associated instance parameter.

(8) Does the "None" object have arbitrary values that work assigned to the related parameters?

- Dimensional parameters can cause errors if they are set to zero or a value that is too small to generate the subcomponent.

CONSTELLATION TYPES

While much of the discussion from this chapter is based on the development of door and cabinet objects as a constellations, it can apply to any component within the model that has multiple subcomponents that work together. Whether we are creating a door or cabinet, window, access floor, skylight, or even an entire bathroom assembly, the concept of constellations is to provide architects with components that are easier to use, smaller in size, and more dynamic in nature. Developing constellations allows us to offer templated spaces as well as easy-to-use objects. There are a few standard layouts for bathrooms, for instance. Depending on whether we have a half-bath, three-quarter bath, or full bathroom, we'll always have a toilet and sink and may or may not have a shower or bathtub. If we create a constellation component that considers the four outside walls of the space and insertion points of each relevant component, we can create a simplified block that may be used to place related components jointly.

While this may not seem overly important to an architect, plumbing engineers can create bathroom groups, kitchen groups, and other specialty plumbing component sets that will allow them to be placed together and swapped out later for actual components with minimal effort. Think of constellations not in terms of making it easier to create BIM content, but in terms of creating graphics and information to be augmented later as decisions are made, and simplifying the use of building information modeling software. Below are a series of constellation types that may help you think about other ways to approach developing components in this fashion.

Door

Example Subcomponent Options

Door panel

Double flush hollow core

Double 2-panel solid core

Double 6-panel steel

Interior access hardware

Handle

Knob

Exit device

Trim panel

Exterior access hardware

> **Handle**
>
> Knob
>
> Trim panel

Door closer

> Concealed closer
>
> Flush mounted closer
>
> **None**

Interior kick panel

> 12"
>
> 10"
>
> 8"
>
> **None**

Hinge

> **5 pin and barrel – standard**
>
> 5 pin and barrel – self-closing
>
> 5 pin and barrel – hospital
>
> 5 pin and barrel – roller

Astragal

> **2" steel**
>
> None

Threshold

> **Steel**
>
> None

Interior casing

> 2⅝" colonial casing
>
> 3½" clear pine
>
> **None**

Exterior casing/trim

> 3½" aluminum clad pine
>
> 3½" PVC trim
>
> **5½" aluminum clad pine**
>
> 2" brickmould
>
> None

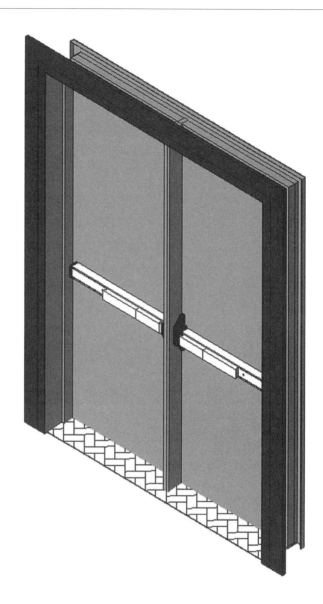

FIGURE 25.6   Door constellation

Cabinet

Example Subcomponent Options

Door

  2 door – flush panel

  2 door – Shaker

  2 door – Shaker glazed

  2 door – Shaker glazed w/prairie grids

  None

Shelf

1 shelf

2 shelves

3 shelves

None

Door hardware

Round pulls – bronze

Square pulls – satin nickel

Colonial handle

Shaker handle

None

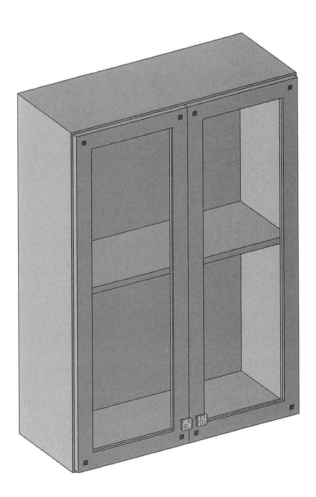

FIGURE 25.7 Cabinet constellation

Window

Configuration

Single unit

2 windows

3 windows

4 windows

6 windows

Operation/sash

Casement

Double hung

Single hung

Awning

Hopper

Rolling

Fixed

Access hardware

Turn locks – white

Turn locks – chrome

Turn locks – brass

Muntins

Colonial – 2 × 3

Colonial – 3 × 2

Prairie

None

Interior casing

2⅝" colonial casing

3½" clear pine

None

Exterior casing/trim

3½" aluminum clad pine

3½" PVC trim

None

FIGURE 25.8 Window constellation

OmniClass Table 49 – Properties

DEFINITION

Properties are characteristics of construction entities. Property definitions do not have any real meaning out of context, without reference to one or more construction entities.

DISCUSSION

Properties serve as modifiers of the objects represented by the contents of other OmniClass tables. This table is limited to properties that are common to, or shared by, multiple construction entities. The names of very specific or finely tailored properties that may be unique or specific to individual construction objects do not currently appear in this table, though the organizational structure of this table could be used to classify and organize libraries of property objects regardless of their breadth of possible application.

EXAMPLES

Common properties include color, width, length, thickness, depth, diameter, area, fire resistance, weight, strength, and moisture resistance.

TABLE USES

- To describe the characteristics of instances of objects, by indentifying a classification defined in one of the other tables and modifying it with properties selected from this table.
- To define requirements for proposed or potential construction objects.
- To describe the characteristics of products not yet incorporated into constructed objects, by adding modifiers from this table to a product name selected from Table 23.
- To compare the characteristics of any two similar objects.
- To classify information resources on subjects relating to factors and properties.
- To facilitate the arrangement of information in technical documents.
- To organize property object collections or libraries.

TABLE USERS

All persons involved in the application of any of the OmniClass tables who also need to define properties or requirements.

Technical information library managers, information providers, product manufacturers, designers, specifiers, facility managers, cost estimators, purchasing agents, construction managers, commissioning agents.

LEGACY SOURCES

- British Standards Institute. *BS 6100 Glossary of Building and Engineering Terms*. Oxford: Blackwell Science, Ltd., 1993.
- Ray-Jones, Alan. *CI/SfB Construction Indexing Manual*. London: RIBA Publishing, 1991.

- Institute of Electrical and Electronics Engineers. IEEE/ASTM SI 10-1997, *Standard for Use of the International System of Units (SI): The Modern Metric System*. Los Alamitos, CA: IEEE, 1997

- International Organization for Standardization. *ISO 12006-2 Properties and Characteristics (by type)*. Geneva: International Organization for Standardization, 2001

- International Organization for Standardization. *ISO 31-0 – Quantities and Units*. Geneva: International Organization for Standardization, 1992.

- Construction Project Information Committee. *Uniclass: Unified Classification for the Construction Industry*, Table N – Properties and Characteristics. RIBA Publications, 1997.

- Green Building XML Schema (GBXML) http://gbxml.org

- Autodesk Revit MEP 2010

- Munro, Ronald G. Data Evaluation *Theory and Practice for Materials Properties* (SP 960-11). Gaithersburg, MD: National Institute of Standards and Technology (NIST), 2003.

- Building and Fire Research Laboratory, National Institute of Standards and Technology (NIST). *Building for Environmental and Economic Sustainability (BEES)*. Gaithersburg, MD: NIST, 2007.

- National Institute of Standards and Technology (NIST). NIST Reference Fluid Thermodynamic and Transport Properties Database (REFPROP): Version 8.0. Gaithersburg, MD: NIST, 2009.

- Underwriters' Laboratories of Canada. *Standard Test Method for Determination of Long-term Thermal Resistance of Closed-Cell Thermal Insulating Foams* (CAN/ULC-S770). Toronto: Underwriters' Laboratories of Canada, 2005.

Table 49   Properties

OmniClass Number	Level 1 Title	Level 2 Title	Level 3 Title	Level 4 Title	Definitions
49-11 00 00	Identification Properties				Properties that identify objects or provide or enhance metadata about objects
49-11 11 00		Facility Identifications			Properties that identify a facility by location or other criteria. Refer to Tables 11 and 12 for Facility Types.
49-11 11 11			Site ID		
49-11 11 13			Site Type		
49-11 11 15			Landmark ID		
49-11 11 17			Facilities Group		
49-11 11 19			Facility Name		
49-11 11 21			Facility Number		
49-11 11 23			Street Address		
49-11 11 23 11				Address Suffix	Can be expressed as N, E, S, W, NE, NW, SE, SW
49-11 11 23 13				Unit Number	Can be expressed as Unit #, apartment, suite
49-11 11 23			Street Name		Refer to US Postal Service Publication 28. http://pe.usps.com/cpim/ftp/pubs/Pub28/pub28.pdf
49-11 11 25			Zip or Postal Code		
49-11 11 27			Emergency Services Information		
49-11 11 27 11				Building Data Access Policy	
49-11 11 27 13				Facility Monitoring Company	The IP Address of the Monitoring Station server that transmitted the message to the PSAP. Used to verify identity of the alarm company.
49-11 11 27 15				Public Service Answering Point (PSAP)	Can be expressed as PSAP ID, the Code identifying the PSAP as listed in the FCC PSAP registry. http://www.fcc.gov/pshs/services/911-services/enhanced911/psapregistry.html
49-11 11 27 17				Agency ID	Can be expressed as Emergency Service Agency ID
49-11 11 27 19				Master Street Address Guide (MSAG)	

OmniClass Number	Level 1 Title	Level 2 Title	Level 3 Title	Level 4 Title	Definitions
49-11 11 27 21				Emergency Service Number (ESN)	3-5 digit Emergency Service Number associated with street segment. The Service Provider, providing the E9-1-1 Selective Routing will assign ESN's. As defined by NENA.
49-11 11 27 23				Road Segment ID	Unique Road Segment ID number. As defined by NENA.
49-11 31 00		Space Identifications			Properties that identify or describe volumes enclosed by surfaces. Refer to Tables 13 and 14 for Space Types.
49-11 31 11			Floor Number		
49-11 31 13			Owner Space Name		
49-11 31 15			Standard Space Name		
49-11 31 17			Owner Space Number		
49-11 31 19			Space Number		
49-11 31 21			Means of Egress		
49-11 51 00		Occupancy Identifications			Properties that identify or describe facility occupants and user groups
49-11 51 11			Occupancy Class		
49-11 51 13			Occupant Organizational Groups		
49-11 51 15			Occupant Demographics		
49-11 51 17			Animal Occupants		
49-11 71 00		Work Result Identifications			Properties that identify or describe work results or details associated with work results
49-11 71 11			Category		
49-11 71 13			Subcategory		
49-11 71 15			Version		
49-11 71 17			Material ID Ref		ID used by a CAD/BIM program to reference its internal materials library. A GBXML defined property. http://www.gbxml.org/

(continued)

Table 49   (Continued)

OmniClass Number	Level 1 Title	Level 2 Title	Level 3 Title	Level 4 Title	Definitions
49-11 71 19			Object ID		The CADObjectId Element is used to map unique CAD object identifiers to gbXML elements. Allows CAD/BIM tools to read results from a gbXML file and map them to their CAD objects. A GBXML defined property. http://www.gbxml.org/
49-11 71 21			Industry Foundation Class		
49-11 71 23			International Framework for Dictionaries		
49-11 71 25			Label Type		
49-11 71 27			Radio Frequency ID (RFID)		
49-11 71 29			Bar Code Marking		
49-11 71 31			Tracking Number		
49-11 71 33			Source of Data		Individual or Organization that last updated the record
49-11 71 35			Seat Numbers		Seat can be expressed as desk, cubicle, workstation
49-11 71 37			Referencing Detail		A Revit MEP 2010 Sheet Property supplied property
49-11 71 39			Current Revision		A Revit MEP 2010 Sheet Property supplied property
49-11 71 41			Certified By		Example: IGMA (Refer to Product Properties), Manufacture (Installer)
49-11 71 43			Approved By		A Revit MEP 2010 Sheet Property supplied property
49-11 71 45			Designed By		A Revit MEP 2010 Sheet Property supplied property
49-11 71 47			Checked By		A Revit MEP 2010 Sheet Property supplied property
49-11 71 49			Drawn By		A Revit MEP 2010 Sheet Property supplied property
49-11 71 51			File Path		A Revit MEP 2010 Sheet Property supplied property
49-11 71 53			Issued To		
49-11 71 55			Issued By		

OmniClass Number	Level 1 Title	Level 2 Title	Level 3 Title	Level 4 Title	Definitions
49-11 81 00		Proprietary Identifications			Properties that specifically identify objects, typically products
49-11 81 11			Brand Name		
49-11 81 13			Fabricator Name		
49-11 81 15			SKU Number		
49-11 81 17			EAN Number		
49-11 81 19			Trademark		
49-11 81 21			UPC Code		
49-11 91 00		Communi-cation Identifications			Properties that identify or describe information types or exchanges
49-11 91 11			URL		A string of characters used to identify a name or a resource on the Internet.
49-11 91 13			Internet Country Code		
49-11 91 15			Telephone Number		
49-11 91 17			Fax Number		
49-11 91 19			Email Address		
49-11 91 21			IP Address		
49-21 00 00	Location Properties				Properties that provide physical location information
49-21 11 00		Geographic Locations			Properties that describe positions or points in physical space that an object occupies on the Earth's surface
49-21 11 11			Latitude		
49-21 11 13			Longitude		
49-21 11 15			Altitude		
49-21 11 17			State Plane Coordinates		
49-21 11 19			GPS position		
49-21 11 21			WGS84		GPS reference coordinate system.
49-21 11 23			Compass Orientation		
49-21 51 00		Political/ Legal Locations			Properties that describe positions in relation to nations, national subdivisions, and their relationship to the world
49-21 51 11			Country		Is expressed as a two-letter ISO 3166 code.
49-21 51 13			Region		

(continued)

Table 49   (Continued)

OmniClass Number	Level 1 Title	Level 2 Title	Level 3 Title	Level 4 Title	Definitions
49-21 51 15			State/Province		A state, commonwealth, national subdivision, region, province, prefecture, province, or other such geopolitical subdivision of a country.
49-21 51 17			County		A county, parish, or other such geopolitical subdivision of a state; district. US County Name as given in FIPS 6-4.
49-21 51 19			Municipality		Unique Community ID Number or Geocode.
49-21 51 21			Municipality Division		Can be expressed as city division, borough, district, ward, historic district.
49-21 51 23			Authority Having Jurisdiction (AHJ)		
49-21 51 25			Zoning District		
49-21 51 27			Planning District		
49-21 51 29			Legal Description		
49-21 51 31			Land Parcel		
49-21 71 00		Manufacturing and Product Locations			Properties that describe locations in relation to production and distribution of objects or resources
49-21 71 11			Manufacturer Location		
49-21 71 13			Assembly Location		
49-21 71 15			Warehouse Location		
49-21 71 17			Product Harvest Location		
49-41 00 00	Properties of Time and Money				Properties relating to scheduling, durations, and cost
49-41 31 00		Time and Scheduling Properties			Properties when combined that result in a schedule by describing sequences, delivery and cost activities, lifespans, periods of time, and other values.
49-41 31 11			Age		
49-41 31 13			Age Range		
49-41 31 15			Time Span		
49-41 31 17			Time Increment		
49-41 31 19			Elapsed Time		

OmniClass Number	Level 1 Title	Level 2 Title	Level 3 Title	Level 4 Title	Definitions
49-41 31 21			Actual Life Span		
49-41 31 23			Expected Life Span		
49-41 31 25			Purchase Date		
49-41 31 27			Extraction Date		
49-41 31 29			Harvest Date		
49-41 31 31			Manufacture Date		
49-41 31 33			Date Updated		Date of last update Format: CCYY-MM-DD
49-41 31 35			Day Type		A GBXML supplied property. http://www.gbxml.org/
49-41 31 37			Manufacturing Lead Time		
49-41 31 39				Set Up Time	
49-41 31 41				Run Time	
49-41 31 43				Process Time	
49-41 31 45				Idle Time	
49-41 31 47				Cycle Time	
49-41 31 49				Throughput Time	
49-41 31 51			Ship Date		
49-41 31 53				Shipping Time	
49-41 31 55				Delivery Time	
49-41 31 57			Delivery Date		
49-41 31 59			Installation Start Date		
49-41 31 61			Installation End Date		
49-41 31 61 11				Setting Time	
49-41 31 61 13				Pot Life	
49-41 31 61 15				Shelf Life	
49-41 31 61 17				Tack Free Time	
49-41 31 61 19				Recoat Time	
49-41 31 61 21				Cure Time	
49-41 31 63			Site Inspection Date		
49-41 31 65			Site Test Date		
49-41 31 67			Acceptance Date		

(continued)

Table 49   (Continued)

OmniClass Number	Level 1 Title	Level 2 Title	Level 3 Title	Level 4 Title	Definitions
49-41 31 69			Commissioning Date		
49-41 31 75			Project Phase		
49-41 31 75 11				Phase Created	
49-41 31 75 13				Phase Demolished	
49-41 31 77			Service Response Time		
49-41 31 79			Date Put in Storage		
49-41 31 81			Maximum Storage Time		
49-41 31 83			Operations and Maintenance		
49-41 31 83 11				Depreciation Schedule	
49-41 31 83 13				Maintenance Schedule	Sometimes called Produce Maintenance Report.
49-41 31 85			Decommissioning Date		
49-41 31 87			Demolition Date		
49-41 31 89			Disposal Date		
49-41 31 91			Recycled Date		
49-41 31 93			Removal Date		
49-41 61 00		Cost Properties			Properties that describe costs and other monetary values
49-41 61 11			Cost Value		
49-41 61 13			Currency Type		
49-41 61 15			Unit Price		
49-41 61 17			Wholesale Cost		
49-41 61 19			Retail Cost		
49-41 61 21			Manufacturer's Suggested Retail Price		
49-41 61 23			Cost Discount		
49-41 61 25			Shipping Cost		
49-41 61 27			Installation Cost		
49-41 61 29			Purchase Terms		

OmniClass Number	Level 1 Title	Level 2 Title	Level 3 Title	Level 4 Title	Definitions
49-61 00 00	Source Properties				Properties relating to the creation, distribution, or installation of objects, chiefly products or work results
49-61 11 00		Manufacturer Properties			Properties relating to the creation and distribution of objects, chiefly products
49-61 11 11			Source Limitations		
49-61 11 13			Manufacturer Name		
49-61 11 15			Manufacturer Experience		
49-61 11 17			Manufacture Production Rate		
49-61 11 17 11				Management Level	
49-61 11 17 13				Operators Level	
49-61 11 17 15				Controllers Level	
49-61 11 17 17				Field Level	
49-61 11 19			Designer Name		
49-61 11 21			Method of Manufacture		
49-61 11 23			Manufacturer's Certification		
49-61 41 00		Product Properties			Properties that describe product and manufacturer qualities
49-61 41 11			Product Name		
49-61 41 13			Stock or Custom		
49-61 41 15			In-Stock		
49-61 41 17			Pre-Assembled		
49-61 41 19			Product Certification		
49-61 41 21			Packaging		
49-61 41 23			Level of Quality		
49-61 41 25			Grade		
49-61 41 25 11				Residential	
49-61 41 25 13				Commercial	
49-61 41 25 15				Heavy-Duty	
49-61 41 25 17				Extra Heavy Duty	

(continued)

Table 49   (Continued)

OmniClass Number	Level 1 Title	Level 2 Title	Level 3 Title	Level 4 Title	Definitions
49-61 41 27			Species		
49-61 41 29			Product Construction		
49-61 41 29 11				Surface Type	
49-61 41 29 13				Backing Type	
49-61 41 31			Style		
49-61 41 33			Pattern		
49-61 41 35			Relief Pattern		Decorative design pressed onto a surface.
49-61 41 35 11				Relief Pattern Height	
49-61 41 35 13				Relief Pattern Scale	
49-61 41 37			Perforations		
49-61 41 39			Product Enclosure		
49-61 41 41			Product Modifications		
49-61 41 43			Factory Settings		
49-61 41 45			Service Access		
49-61 41 47			Product Features		Important characteristics or features relevant to product specification. As defined by Spie – J.C. Moots, Eaton Corporation.
49-61 41 49			Accessories		
49-61 41 51			Options		
49-61 41 53			Color		
49-61 41 53 11				Interior Color	
49-61 41 53 13				Exterior Color	
49-61 41 53 15				Color Coding	
49-61 41 53 17				Dye Lot	
49-61 41 53 19				Integral Color	
49-61 41 55			Orientation		NIST 960-11
49-61 41 57			Finish		
49-61 41 57 11				Finish – Applied	
49-61 41 57 13				Finish – Integral	
49–61 41 57 15				Face Finish	
49–61 41 57 17				Field Finishing Material	

OmniClass Number	Level 1 Title	Level 2 Title	Level 3 Title	Level 4 Title	Definitions
49-61 41 57 19				Field Finishing Method	
49-61 41 57 21				Texture	
49-61 41 57 23				Base Finish	Can be expressed as Cove, Straight, Butt To, Sanitary, Traditional, One-Side
49-61 41 57 25				Ceiling Finish	
49-61 41 57 27				Wall Finish	
49-61 41 57 29				Floor Finish	
49-61 41 57 31				Gloss	
49-61 41 57 33				Sheen	
49-61 41 57 35				Patina	
49-61 41 59			Treatment		
49-61 41 59 11				Anti-Microbial Treatment	
49-61 41 59 13				Pressure Treatment	
49-61 41 59 15				Fire Retardant Treatment	
49-61 41 59 17				Herbicide Treatment	
49-61 41 59 19				Pesticide Treatment	
49-61 41 59 21				Anti-Corrosive Treatment	
49-61 51 00		Warranty Properties			
49-61 51 11			Manufacturers Warranty Type		
49-61 51 13			Manufacturers Warranty Terms		
49-61 51 15			Installers Warranty Type		
49-61 51 17			Installers Warranty Terms		
49-61 51 19			Warranty Service Location		
49-61 51 21			Warranty Period		
49-61 51 21 11				Warranty Start Date	

(continued)

Table 49 (Continued)

OmniClass Number	Level 1 Title	Level 2 Title	Level 3 Title	Level 4 Title	Definitions
49-61 51 21 13				Warranty End Date	
49-61 71 00		Shipping Properties			Properties that relate to distribution
49-61 71 11			Shipping Mode		
49-61 71 13			Shipper Type		
49-61 71 15			Shipping Packaging		
49-61 71 17			Delivery Marking		
49-61 71 19			Delivery Terms		
49-61 81 00		Installation Properties			Properties that relate to the use of products in the installation and creation of work results
49-61 81 11			Installation Configuration		
49-61 81 13			Surface Preparation		
49-61 81 15			Installation Method		
49-61 81 15 11				Mechanical Attached Method	
49-61 81 15 13				Adhered Method	
49-61 81 15 15				Loose-Laid Method	
49-61 81 15 17				Ballasted Method	
49-61 81 15 19				Adhesive Type Method	
49-61 81 17			Fastening Method		
49-61 81 19			Fastener Type		
49-61 81 21			Installer Properties		
49-61 81 21 11				Installer Experience	
49-61 81 21 13				Installer Qualifications	
49-61 81 23			Application Rate		
49-61 81 23 11				Theoretical Application Rate	

OmniClass Number	Level 1 Title	Level 2 Title	Level 3 Title	Level 4 Title	Definitions
49-61 81 23 13				Actual Application Rate	
49-61 81 25			Coverage		
49-61 81 25 11				Theoretical Coverage	
49-61 81 25 13				Actual Coverage	
49-61 81 27			Mounting Method		
49-61 81 29			Joining Method		
49-61 81 29 11				Joint Type	
49-61 81 29 13				Seam Type	
49-61 81 31			Ambient Temperature during Installation		
49-61 81 33			Cleaning Method		
49-71 00 00	Physical Properties				Properties that describe the physical presentation of an object or that exist within an object by itself or as used, considered, or installed
49-71 11 00		Quantity Properties			Properties that describe the count or number of components
49-71 11 11			Unit of Measure		
49-71 11 11 11				Metric	
49-71 11 11 13				Imperial	
49-71 11 11 15			Single		
49-71 11 11 17			Set		
49-71 11 11 19			Pair		
49-71 11 11 21			Number		
49-71 11 11 23			Amount of Substance		
49-71 11 11 25			Concentration		
49-71 11 11 27			Distribution		NIST 906-11
49-71 11 11 29			Capacity		Refer to Function and Use and Facility Services for equipment capacities
49-71 11 11 31			Yield		Percentage of output from a process that passes inspection as good output
49-71 11 11 33			Mean Size		
49-71 11 11 35			Batch Size		NIST 906-11
49-71 11 11 37			Clearance Requirements		

(continued)

Table 49   (Continued)

OmniClass Number	Level 1 Title	Level 2 Title	Level 3 Title	Level 4 Title	Definitions
49-71 15 00		Shape Properties			Properties that describe the geometric shape of components
49-71 15 11			Form		
49-71 15 13			Shape		
49-71 15 15			Geometry		
49-71 15 17			Modular		
49-71 15 19			Hand – Left or Right		
49-71 15 21			Profile		
49-71 15 23			Face		
49-71 15 25			Edge		
49-71 15 27			Edge Profile		
49-71 15 29			Vertex		
49-71 15 31			Point		
49-71 19 00		Single Dimensions			Properties that quantify a specific distance or angle
49-71 19 11			Standard or Custom Size		
49-71 19 13			Length		
49-71 19 15			Width		
49-71 19 17			Distance		
49-71 19 19			Span		
49-71 19 21			Height		
49-71 19 21 11				Sill Height	
49-71 19 21 13				Head Height	
49-71 19 23			Depth		
49-71 19 25			Thickness		Thickness of cross-section.
49-71 19 25 11				Thickness of Cover	
49-71 19 25 13				Product Thickness	
49-71 19 25 15				Dry Film Thickness	
49-71 19 27			Gauge		
49-71 19 29			Radius		
49-71 19 31			Spacing		
49-71 23 00		Area Dimensions			Properties that quantify the extents of spaces with a 2-dimensional bound

OmniClass Number	Level 1 Title	Level 2 Title	Level 3 Title	Level 4 Title	Definitions
49-71 23 11			Angular Dimensions		
49-71 23 13			Arbitrary Dimension		
49-71 23 15			Net Rentable Area		
49-71 23 17			Floor Area Per Occupant		
49-71 23 19			Floor Area Ratio		
49-71 23 21			Inside Diameter		
49-71 23 23			Outside Diameter		
49-71 23 25			Circumference		
49-71 23 27			Perimeter		
49-71 23 29			Plane Angle		
49-71 23 31			Rise		
49-71 23 33			Fall		
49-71 23 35			Slope Angle		
49-71 23 37			Solid Angle		
49-71 27 00		Volumes			Properties that quantify the extents of spaces with a 3-dimensional boundary
49-71 27 11			Fluid Volume		
49-71 27 13			Dry Volume		
49-71 27 15			Specific Volume		
49-71 27 17			Volume per Unit Time		
49-71 27 19			Air Infiltration Volume		
49-71 27 21			Air Specific Volume		
49-71 27 23			Water Penetration Volume		
49-71 27 25			Section Modulus		
49-71 27 27			Second Moment of Area		
49-71 31 00		Relational Measurements			Properties that quantify one measurement in relation to another
49-71 31 11			Acceleration		
49-71 31 13			Angular Acceleration		

(continued)

Table 49   (Continued)

OmniClass Number	Level 1 Title	Level 2 Title	Level 3 Title	Level 4 Title	Definitions
49-71 31 15			Aspect Ratio		NIST 960-11
49-71 31 17			Dependent Variable		
49-71 31 19			Dependent Value		
49-71 31 21			Frequency		
49-71 31 23			Relative Age		
49-71 31 25			Relative Humidity		
49-71 31 27			Relative Power		
49-71 31 29			Relative Range		
49-71 31 31			Relative Sound		
49-71 31 33			Relative Time		
49-71 31 35			Rotational Frequency		
49-71 31 37			Speed		
49-71 31 39			Unit of Analysis		
49-71 31 41			Velocity		
49-71 31 41 11				Angular Velocity	
49-71 31 41 13				Relative Velocity	
49-71 35 00		Properties of Sustainability			
49-71 35 11			Building and Material Reuse		
49-71 35 11 11				Salvaged Materials	
49-71 35 11 13				Refurbished Materials	
49-71 35 11 15				Reused Materials	
49-71 35 11 17				Existing Walls Reuse	
49-71 35 11 19				Existing Floors Reuse	
49-71 35 11 21				Existing Roof Reuse	
49-71 35 13			Harvest Method		
49-71 35 15			Extraction Method		
49-71 35 17			Recycled Content		

OmniClass Number	Level 1 Title	Level 2 Title	Level 3 Title	Level 4 Title	Definitions
49-71 35 17 11				Recycled Content by Mass	
49-71 35 17 13				Post-industrial recycled content	
49-71 35 17 15				Pre-consumer recycled content	
49-71 35 17 17				Post-consumer recycled content	
49-71 35 19			Rapidly Renewable Materials		
49-71 35 21			Non-Renewable Materials		
49-71 35 23			Sustainable Product Certification		
49-71 35 25			Sustainable Manufacturing Certification		
49-71 35 25 11				Water Intake	NIST: BEES
49-71 35 25 13				VOC Emissions	
49-71 35 25 15				Recycled Waste	
49-71 35 25 17				Liquid Wastes	
49-71 35 25 19				Air Pollution	
49-71 35 25 21				Toxic Emissions	
49-71 35 25 23				Particulate Pollution	
49-71 35 27			Life Cycle Analysis (LCA)		Standard self-certification to be verified by an independent 3rd party
49-71 35 27 11				Life Cycle Inventory	
49-71 35 27 13				Life Cycle Cost Analysis	
49-71 35 27 15				Life Cycle Impact Assessment (LCIA)	
49-71 35 27 17				Environmental Impact	A full set of impacts includes land use, resource use, climate change, health effects, acidification, and toxicity

(continued)

Table 49 (Continued)

OmniClass Number	Level 1 Title	Level 2 Title	Level 3 Title	Level 4 Title	Definitions
49-71 35 27 19				Green House Gas Emissions	
49-71 35 29			Environmental Product Declaration (EPD)		Product may have a comprehensive LCA or an EPD for reporting
49-71 35 31			Environmental Footprint of Supply Chain		A combination of information about a building and site, environmental programs, awards, reorganization. As defined on www.greenformat.com.
49-71 35 33			Environmental Stewardship		
49-71 35 35			Relocatability		
49-71 39 00		Properties of Chemical Composition			
49-71 39 11			Alloy, Temper		
49-71 39 13			Biodegradability		
49-71 39 15			Chemical Aging		NIST 960-11
49-71 39 15 11				Corrosion Rate	NIST 960-11
49-71 39 15 13				Activation Energy	NIST 960-11
49-71 39 15 15				Hydration Rate	NIST 960-11
49-71 39 15 17				Diffusion Rate	NIST 960-11
49-71 39 17			Chemical Composition		
49-71 39 19			Compatibility		
49-71 39 21			Constituent Materials		
49-71 39 23			Ductility		
49-71 39 25			Malleability		
49-71 39 27			Solubility		
49-71 39 29			Expansion		
49-71 39 31			Shrinkage		
49-71 39 33			Dielectric Constant		
49-71 39 35			Galvanic Constant		
49-71 39 37			Raw Material		
49-71 39 39			Odor		

OmniClass Number	Level 1 Title	Level 2 Title	Level 3 Title	Level 4 Title	Definitions
49-71 45 00		Properties of Regulated Content			Properties that apply to values that are controlled or regulated by a governing body
49-71 45 11			VOC Content		
49-71 45 13			VOC Compliance		
49-71 45 15			Asbestos Content		
49-71 45 17			Formaldehyde Content		
49-71 45 19			Lead Content		
49-71 45 21			Radiation Resistance		
49-71 45 23			Ozone Depletion Content		
49-71 45 25			Persistent, Bioaccumulative, and Toxic Pollutants (PBTs)		
49-71 45 27			Chlorofluoro-carbon (CFC) Emissions		
49-71 45 29			Hydrochlo-rofluorocarbons (HCFC) Emissions		
49-71 45 31			Toxic Content		
49-71 45 33			Ecological Toxicity		NIST: BEES
49-71 51 00		Properties of Temperature			Properties that apply to temperature
49-71 51 11			Absolute Temperature		
49-71 51 13			Ambient Temperature		
49-71 51 13 11				Ambient Outdoor Temperature	
49-71 51 13 13				Ambient Temperature during Installation	
49-71 51 15			Brittleness Temperature		

(continued)

Table 49   (Continued)

OmniClass Number	Level 1 Title	Level 2 Title	Level 3 Title	Level 4 Title	Definitions
49-71 51 17			Design Temperature		
49-71 51 19			Temperature Types		
49-71 51 19 11				Condensation Temperature	
49-71 51 19 13				Deflection Temperature	
49-71 51 19 15				Ground Temperature	
49-71 51 19 17				Mean Temperature	Average of hot and cold plate temperatures corresponding to the temperature at the mid-plane of the test specimen in °C or °F. As defined by the NIST.
49-71 51 19 19				Heat Radiated Temperature	
49-71 51 19 21				Inside Air Temperature	
49-71 51 19 23				Outside Air Temperature	
49-71 51 19 25				Supply Air Temperature	
49-71 51 19 27				Surface Temperature	
49-71 51 19 29				Summer Dry Bulb Temperature	Summer ambient air temperature (not affected by humidity). Dry bulb temperature is used as an indicator of heat content. The dry bulb temperature is determined by using data that includes project location. A Revit MEP 2010 Sheet Property defined property.
49-71 51 19 31				Winter Dry Bulb Temperature	Winter ambient air temperature (not affected by humidity). Dry bulb temperature is used as an indicator of heat content. The dry bulb temperature is determined by using data that includes project location. A Revit MEP 2010 Sheet Property defined property.
49-71 51 19 33				Wet-Bulb (WB) Temperature	

OmniClass Number	Level 1 Title	Level 2 Title	Level 3 Title	Level 4 Title	Definitions
49-71 51 19 35				Summer Wet Bulb Temperature	Summer temperature of adiabatic saturation (evaporation of water on a thermometer and its cooling effect). The wet bulb temperature is always lower than the dry bulb temperature but identical to 100% relative humidity. The wet bulb temperature is determined by using data that includes project location. A Revit MEP 2010 Sheet Property defined property.
49-71 51 21			Temperature Points		
49-71 51 21 11				Minimum Temperature	
49-71 51 21 13				Maximum Temperature	
49-71 51 21 15				Boiling Point Temperature	
49-71 51 21 17				Dew Point Temperature	
49-71 51 21 19				Flash Point Temperature	
49-71 51 21 21				Freezing Point Temperature	
49-71 51 21 23				Melting Point Temperature	
49-71 51 21 25				Cooling Setpoint	Temperature at which the system will maintain the cooling for spaces in the zone. A Revit MEP 2010 Sheet Property defined property.
49-71 51 21 27				Heating Setpoint	Temperature at which the system will maintain heating for spaces in the zone. A Revit MEP 2010 Sheet Property defined property.
49-71 51 23			Temperature Ranges		
49-71 51 23 11				Acceptable Temperature Range	
49-71 51 23 13				Cycling Temperature Range	

(continued)

Table 49   (Continued)

OmniClass Number	Level 1 Title	Level 2 Title	Level 3 Title	Level 4 Title	Definitions
49-71 51 23 15				Service Temperature Range	
49-71 51 23 17				Mean Daily Range	The mean temperature range based on the project location.
49-71 51 23 19				Delta T	Difference of hot and cold plate temperatures in °C or °F. As defined by the NIST.
49-71 51 25			Phase Temperatures		NIST 960-11
49-71 51 25 11				Phase Transition Temperature	NIST 960-11
49-71 51 25 13				Phase Transition Pressure	NIST 960-11
49-71 51 25 15				Glass Transition Temperature	NIST 960-11
49-71 51 25 17				Curie Temperature	NIST 960-11
49-71 51 25 19				Neel Temperature	NIST 960-11
49-71 51 25 21				Triple Point Temperature	NIST 960-11
49-71 51 27			Temperature Rise		
49-71 51 29			Temperature Interval		
49-71 51 31			Temperature Differential		
49-71 51 33			Heat Index		
49-71 53 00		Properties of Structural Loading			Properties that pertain to external forces applied to components
49-71 53 11			Static Loads		
49-71 53 11 11				Hardness Testing Method	
49-71 53 13			Dynamic Loads		
49-71 53 13 11				Uniform Design Load	
49-71 53 13 13				Wind Load	
49-71 53 13 15				Snow Load	

OmniClass Number	Level 1 Title	Level 2 Title	Level 3 Title	Level 4 Title	Definitions
49-71 53 13 17				Horizontal Live Load	
49-71 53 13 19				Impact Load	
49-71 53 13 21				Seismic Load	
49-71 53 13 23				Moving Load	
49-71 57 00		Properties of Air and Other Gases			
49-71 57 11			Indoor Air Quality (IAQ)		NIST: BEES 4.0
49-71 57 13			Vapor Transmission		
49-71 57 15			Criteria Air Pollutants		NIST: BEES 4.0
49-71 57 17			Carbon Dioxide Level		NIST: BEES 4.0
49-71 57 19			Methane Level		NIST: BEES 4.0
49-71 57 21			Nitrous Oxide Level		NIST: BEES 4.0
49-71 57 23			Smog Level		NIST: BEES 4.0
49-71 57 25			Visibility		
49-71 63 00		Properties of Liquids			Properties that describe and qualify fluids
49-71 63 11			Liquid Concentration		
49-71 63 13			Liquid Evaporation Rate		
49-71 63 15			Liquid pH		
49-71 63 17			Hygrometric Expansion		
49-71 63 19			Hygroscopicity		
49-71 63 21			Fluid Viscosity		
49-71 63 23			Fluid Density		
49-71 69 00		Properties of Mass			Properties that apply to the weight and amount of matter
49-71 69 11			Mass		
49-71 69 11 11				Mass per unit length	

(continued)

Table 49   (Continued)

OmniClass Number	Level 1 Title	Level 2 Title	Level 3 Title	Level 4 Title	Definitions
49-71 69 11 13				Mass per unit area	
49-71 69 11 15				Mass per unit time	
49-71 69 11 17				Molar Mass	
49-71 69 13			Weight		
49-71 69 13 11				Weight Classification	
49-71 69 13 13				Shipping Weight	
49-71 69 15			Density		
49-71 69 15 11				Bulk Density	Heat Transmission Properties of Insulating and Building Materials The bulk density (including voids) of the test specimen in kg*m-3 or lb*ft-3. As defined by the NIST.
49-71 69 15 13				Specific Gravity Density	
49-71 69 15 15				Angular Momentum Density	
49-71 69 15 17				Moment of Inertia Density	
49-71 69 15 19				Momentum Density	
49-71 69 17			Specific Gravity		
49-71 69 19			Momentum		
49-71 69 19 11				Angular Momentum	
49-71 69 21			Exchange Effectiveness		
49-71 69 23			Initial Moisture Content		The amount of water (by mass) present in the test specimen at the start of a test in %. As defined by the NIST.
49-71 69 25			Final Moisture Content		The amount of water by mass present in the test specimen at the end of a test in %. As defined by the NIST.
49-71 73 00		Properties of Force			Properties which cause a mass to change velocity or direction
49-71 73 11			Force, General Properties		

OmniClass Number	Level 1 Title	Level 2 Title	Level 3 Title	Level 4 Title	Definitions
49-71 73 13			Applied Forces		
49-71 73 15			Force Per Unit Length		
49-71 73 17			Surface Tension		
49-71 73 19			Thrust to Mass Ratio		
49-71 73 21			Viscosity		
49-71 73 21 11				Dynamic Viscosity	
49-71 73 21 13				Kinematic Viscosity	
49-71 73 23			Moment of Force		
49-71 73 25			Moment of Inertia		
49-71 73 27			Torque		
49-71 73 29			Electromotive Force		
49-71 75 00		Properties of Pressure			Properties that relate to forces applied to a unit area of surface
49-71 75 11			Absolute Pressure		
49-71 75 13			Air Pressure		
49-71 75 13 11				Cyclic Static Air Pressure	
49-71 75 13 13				Uniform Static Air Pressure	
49-71 75 15			Ambient Pressure		
49-71 75 17			Applied Pressures		
49-71 75 19			Atmospheric Pressure		
49-71 75 21			Calibrated Pressure		
49-71 75 23			Design Pressure		
49-71 75 25			Gage Pressure		
49-71 75 27			Leakage Under Pressure		
49-71 75 29			Residual Pressure		
49-71 75 31			Static Pressure		

(continued)

Table 49 (Continued)

OmniClass Number	Level 1 Title	Level 2 Title	Level 3 Title	Level 4 Title	Definitions
49-71 75 33			Static Pressure Differential		
49-71 75 35			Pressure Drop		
49-71 75 37			Vacuum Pressure		
49-71 75 39			Vapor Pressure		
49-71 75 41			Wind Pressure		
49-71 81 00		Properties of Magnetism			Properties which quantify and qualify attractive and repulsive (magnetic) forces
49-71 81 11			Magnetic Flux		
49-71 81 13			Magnetic Vector Potential		
49-71 81 15			Magnetic Permeance		
49-71 81 17			Mutual Inductance		
49-71 81 19			Magnetic Potential Difference		
49-71 81 21			Magnetomotive Force		
49-71 81 23			Magnetic Induction		
49-71 91 00		Environmental Properties			Properties that relate to soil, land and troposphere
49-71 91 11			Seismic Classification		
49-71 91 13			Design Criteria		Refer to the Information Table
49-71 91 15			Wind Speed		
49-71 91 17			Weather Class		
49-71 91 19			Ozone Concentration		
49-71 91 21			Land Features		
49-71 91 23			Water Body Type		
49-81 00 00	Performance Properties				Properties that express the behavior of an object in reaction to physical properties and forces
49-81 11 00		Testing Properties			Properties that define testing methods and conditions
49-81 11 11			Test Method		

OmniClass Number	Level 1 Title	Level 2 Title	Level 3 Title	Level 4 Title	Definitions
49-81 11 13			Test Authority		A GBXML defined property. http://www.gbxml.org/
49-81 11 15			Pre-Test Conditions		Specifies the ambient conditions (temperature, humidity, time), if available, that the specimen was conditioned to prior to testing. As defined by the NIST.
49-81 11 17			Test Conditions		
49-81 11 19			Reference Standard		
49-81 11 21			Inspection Protocol		
49-81 11 23			Factory Testing		
49-81 11 23 11				Factory Inspection Method	
49-81 11 23 13				Factory Test Date	
49-81 11 23 15				Factory Test Method	
49-81 11 23 17				Factory Level of Compliance	
49-81 11 23 19				Factory Reference Grade	
49-81 11 25			Field Testing		
49-81 11 25 11				Field Inspection Method	
49-81 11 25 13				Field Test Method	
49-81 11 25 15				Field Level of Compliance	
49-81 11 25 17				Field Reference Grade	
49-81 15 00		Tolerance Properties			Properties that define permissible limits or variations in limit of dimensional and other measured properties
49-81 15 11			Deflection Tolerance		
49-81 15 13			Dimensional Tolerance		
49-81 15 13 11				Flatness Tolerance	

(continued)

Table 49 (Continued)

OmniClass Number	Level 1 Title	Level 2 Title	Level 3 Title	Level 4 Title	Definitions
49-81 15 13 13				Length Tolerance	
49-81 15 13 15				Thickness Tolerance	
49-81 15 13 17				Warp Tolerance	
49-81 15 13 19				Width Tolerance	
49-81 15 13 21				Camber	
49-81 15 15			Shape Tolerance		
49-81 15 17			Installation Tolerance		
49-81 15 19			Plumbness		
49-81 15 21			Squareness		
49-81 15 23			Levelness		
49-81 15 25			Texture Tolerance		
49-81 21 00		Function and Use Properties			Properties that define aspects of functionality and characteristics of the object for a particular service
49-81 21 11			Functional Efficiency		
49-81 21 13			Functional Limitations		
49-81 21 15			Method of Operation		
49-81 21 15 11				Manual Operation	
49-81 21 15 13				Electric Operation	
49-81 21 15 15				Pneumatic Operation	
49-81 21 17			Functional Capacity		
49-81 21 17 11				Maximum Occupancy	
49-81 21 17 13				Operational Capacity	
49-81 21 17 15				Rated Capacity	
49-81 21 17 17				Breaking Capacity	
49-81 21 17 19				Cyclic Capacity	

OmniClass Number	Level 1 Title	Level 2 Title	Level 3 Title	Level 4 Title	Definitions
49-81 21 19			Code Performance		Code Compliance issue(s) which the product satisfies. As defined by Spie – J.C. Moots, Eaton Corporation.
49-81 21 21			Coverage Rate		
49-81 21 23			Ease of		
49-81 21 23 11				Ease of adding on	
49-81 21 23 13				Ease of application	
49-81 21 23 15				Ease of assembly	
49-81 21 23 17				Ease of installation	
49-81 21 23 19				Ease of moving	
49-81 21 23 21				Ease of placing	
49-81 21 23 23				Ease of relocation	
49-81 21 23 25				Ease of removal	
49-81 21 23 27				Ease of storing	
49-81 21 25			Serviceability		
49-81 21 27			Suitability		
49-81 21 27 11				Suitable for Exterior Exposure	
49-81 21 27 13				Suitable for Continuous Immersion	
49-81 21 27 15				Suitable for Ground Contact	
49-81 21 27 17				Suitable for Marine Use	
49-81 21 29			Workability		
49-81 21 31			Weatherability		The degree of resistance when exposed to heat, moisture, cold, solar radiation, etc.
49-81 21 33			Waste Produced in Use		
49-81 31 00		Strength Properties			Properties that define ability of an object to resist applied force
49-81 31 11			Adhesion Strength		

(continued)

Table 49   (Continued)

OmniClass Number	Level 1 Title	Level 2 Title	Level 3 Title	Level 4 Title	Definitions
49-81 31 13			Bendability		
49-81 31 15			Bending Moment		
49-81 31 17			Bending Radius		
49-81 31 19			Bending Strength		
49-81 31 21			Bond Strength		
49-81 31 23			Compressibility		
49-81 31 25			Compressive Resistance		
49-81 31 27			Compressive Strength		
49-81 31 29			Creep Resistance		
49-81 31 31			Ductility		NIST 960-11
49-81 31 33			Elasticity		
49-81 31 35			Elongation		
49-81 31 35 11				Elongation at Yield	
49-81 31 35 13				Ultimate Elongation	
49-81 31 37			Fastener Pullout Resistance		
49-81 31 39			Fatigue Strength		NIST 960-11
49-81 31 41			Fiber Strength		
49-81 31 43			Flexural Strength		
49-81 31 43 11				Flexural Strength, parallel	
49-81 31 43 13				Flexural Strength, perpendicular	
49-81 31 45			Fracture Energy		NIST 960-11
49-81 31 47			Fracture Toughness		NIST 960-11
49-81 31 49			Friction		
49-81 31 51			Hardness		
49-81 31 53			Impact Strength		
49-81 31 55			Resistance to Intentional Attack		
49-81 31 55 11				Theft Resistance	

OmniClass Number	Level 1 Title	Level 2 Title	Level 3 Title	Level 4 Title	Definitions
49-81 31 55 13				Ballistic Resistance	
49-81 31 55 15				Blast Resistance	
49-81 31 55 17				Bullet Resistance	
49-81 31 57			Magnetic Field Strength		
49-81 31 59			Modulus of Elasticity		
49-81 31 61			Peel Strength		
49-81 31 63			Proportional Limit		NIST 960-11
49-81 31 65			Puncture Resistance		
49-81 31 65 11				Static Puncture Resistance	
49-81 31 65 13				Dynamic Puncture Resistance	
49-81 31 67			Release Strength		
49-81 31 69			Shear Strength		
49-81 31 71			Stiffness		
49-81 31 73			Strain		NIST 960-11
49-81 31 75			Stress		NIST 960-11
49-81 31 77			Stress Rating		
49-81 31 79			Surface Tension		
49-81 31 81			Tear Resistance		
49-81 31 83			Tear Strength		
49-81 31 85			Tensile Strength		
49-81 31 87			Ultimate Strength		NIST 960-11
49-81 31 89			Uniform Wind Load Resistance		
49-81 31 91			Vibration		
49-81 31 93			Wind Uplift Resistance		
49-81 31 95			Yield Strength		NIST 960-11
49-81 41 00		Durability Properties			Properties that define ability of an object to maintain resistance to the effects of applied force

(continued)

Table 49   (Continued)

OmniClass Number	Level 1 Title	Level 2 Title	Level 3 Title	Level 4 Title	Definitions
49-81 41 11			Abrasion Resistance		
49-81 41 13			Abuse Resistance		
49-81 41 15			Acid Resistance		
49-81 41 17			Alkali Resistance		
49-81 41 19			Animal Resistance		
49-81 41 21			Bacteria Resistance		
49-81 41 23			Chemical Resistance		
49-81 41 25			Corrosion Resistance		
49-81 41 27			Crack Resistance		
49-81 41 29			Decay Resistance		
49-81 41 31			Degradation Resistance		
49-81 41 33			Delamination Rate		NIST 960-11
49-81 41 35			Fade Resistance		
49-81 41 37			Fatigue Resistance		
49-81 41 39			Friction Coefficient		NIST 960-11
49-81 41 41			Fungus Resistance		
49-81 41 43			Impact Resistance		
49-81 41 45			Indentation Resistance		
49-81 41 47			Infrared Resistance		
49-81 41 49			Insect Resistance		
49-81 41 51			Lubricity		NIST 960-11
49-81 41 53			Maintenance Durability		
49-81 41 55			Mechanical Durability		
49-81 41 57			Microorganism Resistance		

OmniClass Number	Level 1 Title	Level 2 Title	Level 3 Title	Level 4 Title	Definitions
49-81 41 59			Mildew Resistance		
49-81 41 61			Ozone Resistance		
49-81 41 63			Plant growth Resistance		
49-81 41 65			Stain Resistance		
49-81 41 67			Termite Resistance		
49-81 41 69			Thermal Shock Resistance		
49-81 41 71			Ultraviolet (UV) Resistance		
49-81 41 73			Wear Coefficient		NIST 960-11
49-81 41 75			Wear Rate		NIST 960-11
49-81 51 00		Combustion Properties			Properties that define the burning or oxidation of a substance, in gaseous, liquid, or solid form and the results of such burn.
49-81 51 11			Artificial Heat Source		
49-81 51 13			Combustibility		
49-81 51 15			Fire Resistance Rating		
49-81 51 17			Fire Severity		
49-81 51 19			Fire Source		
49-81 51 21			Fire Type		
49-81 51 23			Flame Propagation		
49-81 51 25			Flame Spread Index		
49-81 51 27			Flammability		
49-81 51 29			Ignitibility		
49-81 51 31			Heat Release Rate		The amount of energy (fire intensity) released by burning materials
49-81 51 33			Smoke Density		
49-81 51 35			Smoke Developed Index		
49-81 51 37			Smoke Produced		
49-81 51 39			Surface Burning Characteristics		

(continued)

Table 49   (Continued)

OmniClass Number	Level 1 Title	Level 2 Title	Level 3 Title	Level 4 Title	Definitions
49-81 51 41			Explosion Resistance		
49-81 51 43			Fire Resistance		
49-81 51 45			Ignition Resistance		
49-81 51 47			Critical Radiant Flux		The numeric value assigned to a material when tested in accordance with ASTM E–648 by an independent laboratory
49-81 61 00		Properties of the Envelope			Properties Between Inside and Outside Environment. Refer to other categories for Structural, Moisture/Permeability, Combustion and Fire Resistance, Acoustics, Impact Resistance.
49-81 61 11			Absorptance		A GBXML supplied property. www.gbxml.org
49-81 61 13			Air Infiltration		
49-81 61 15			Air Tightness		
49-81 61 17			Air Leakage		
49-81 61 19			Water Penetration		
49-81 61 21			Condensation Resistance Factor (CRF)		Determined by the manufacturer and expressed in values from 0 to 100
49-81 61 23			R-Value		Related to one component, relative but not specific to an assembly. Ratio of the temperature difference across an insulator and the heat flux (heat flow per unit area) through it.
49-81 61 25			R-Value Système International (RSI)		A measure of thermal resistance in SI units
49-81 61 27			U-Value		Overall conductance. Thermal resistance of entire assembly including outside and inside, fenestration, and percentage of openings. Sometimes called U-Factor.
49-81 61 29			USI		Metric U-Value. Inverse of RSI
49-81 61 31			Insulation Density		
49-81 61 33			Insulation Profile		
49-81 61 33 11				Tapered	
49-81 61 33 13				Flat	

OmniClass Number	Level 1 Title	Level 2 Title	Level 3 Title	Level 4 Title	Definitions
49-81 61 35			Properties of Openings		
49-81 61 35 11				Opening Type	
49-81 61 35 13				Opening Number	
49-81 61 35 15				Opening Transmittance	
49-81 61 35 17				Opening Reflectance	
49-81 61 35 19				Opening Emittance	
49-81 61 35 21				Opening Conductivity	
49-81 61 37			Solar Heat Gain Coefficient (SHGC)		Visual Transmission of solar radiation (visual light admitted versus rejected) is calculated using SHGC
49-81 61 39			Shading Coefficient		The ratio of total solar transmittance for the specified glazing system to the total solar transmittance for the standard reference glazing (1/8" clear). A GBXML defined property. www.gbxml.org.
49-81 61 41			Heat Transfer Coefficient		Heat transfer coefficient is the inverse of thermal insulance. As defined by Wikipedia. http://en.wikipedia.org/wiki/Heat_transfer_coefficient.
49-81 61 43			Specific Heat		Percentage of higher or lower value based on the proportion of solid versus openings. The ratio of the amount of heat required to raise the temperature of a unit mass of a substance by one unit of temperature to the amount of heat required to raise the temperature of a similar mass of a reference material, usually water, by the same amount.
49-81 61 45			Internal Thermal Energy		
49-81 61 47			Linear Thermal Expansion Coefficient		
49-81 61 49			Long-Term Thermal Resistance (LTTR)		CAN/ULC-S770

(continued)

Table 49   (Continued)

OmniClass Number	Level 1 Title	Level 2 Title	Level 3 Title	Level 4 Title	Definitions
49-81 61 51			Specific Heat Input		
49-81 61 53			Thermal Break		
49-81 61 55			Thermal Conductance		The time rate of steady-state heat flow through a unit area of a material or construction induced by a unit temperature difference between the specimen surfaces (in W·m-2·K-1 or Btu·h-1·ft-2·°F-1). As defined by NIST.
49-81 61 57			Thermal Conductivity		The time rate of steady-state heat flow through a homogeneous material induced by a unit temperature gradient normal to the unit area (in W·m-1·K-1) or (Btu·in·h-1·ft-2·°F-1). As defined by NIST.
49-81 61 59			Thermal Diffusivity		
49-81 61 61			Thermal Insulance		
49-81 61 63			Wind Uplift Resistance		
49-81 71 00		Properties of Permeability and Moisture Resistance			Properties of objects, surfaces or membranes that define the characteristics and the degree to which it can be pervaded by a liquid or gas (as by osmosis or diffusion)
49-81 71 11			Condensation Resistance		
49-81 71 13			Freeze-Thaw Resistance		
49-81 71 15			Frost Resistance		
49-81 71 17			Gas Permeability		
49-81 71 19			Percent Perviousness		
49-81 71 21			Magnetic Permeability		
49-81 71 23			Moisture Absorption Resistance		
49-81 71 25			Moisture Content		
49-81 71 27			Pollutant Permeability		

OmniClass Number	Level 1 Title	Level 2 Title	Level 3 Title	Level 4 Title	Definitions
49-81 71 29			Porosity		The ratio of the total amount of void space in a material (due to poses, small channels, and so on) to the bulk volume occupied by the material. A GBXML defined property. http://www.gbxml.org/
49-81 71 31			Resistance to Rising Damp		
49-81 71 33			Vapor Permeability		The rate water vapor is allowed through a surface. A GBXML defined property. http://www.gbxml.org/
49-81 71 35			Vapor Resistance		
49-81 71 37			Velocity Permeability		
49-81 71 39			Water Absorption		
49-81 71 41			Water Absorption Resistance		
49-81 71 43			Water Imperviousness Resistance		
49-81 71 45			Water Permeability Resistance		
49-81 71 47			Surface Water Absorption		
49-81 81 00		Acoustic Properties			Properties that define the behavior or quality of sound in relation to an object or substance, or the response of an object to sound
49-81 81 11			Acoustic Impedance		
49-81 81 13			Reverberation Time		Only related to interior finishes
49-81 81 15			Noise Level		
49-81 81 17			Noise Reduction Coefficient (NRC)		
49-81 81 19			Acoustical Absorption		
49-81 81 21			Sound Absorption		
49-81 81 23			Sound Absorption Average (SAA)		
49-81 81 25			Sound Attenuation		

(continued)

Table 49 (Continued)

OmniClass Number	Level 1 Title	Level 2 Title	Level 3 Title	Level 4 Title	Definitions
49-81 81 27			Sound Energy Density		
49-81 81 29			Sound Energy Flux		
49-81 81 31			Sound Frequency		
49-81 81 33			Acoustical Insulation		
49-81 81 35			Sound Insulation		
49-81 81 37			Sound Intensity		
49-81 81 39			Sound Isolation		
49-81 81 41			Sound Power		
49-81 81 43			Sound Pressure		
49-81 81 45			Sound Speed		Property supplied by NIST Reference Fluid Thermodynamic and Transport Properties Database (REFPROP): Version 8.0
49-81 81 47			Sound Reflectance		
49-81 81 49			Sound Transmission Class (STC)		
49-81 81 51			Speech Intelligibility		
49-91 00 00	Properties of Facility Services				Engineering the internal environment and environmental impact of a building. Wikipedia Properties of systems used in facility services, often comprised of a number of individual component objects – these properties tend to apply to whole systems, component properties are typically classified elsewhere.
49-91 11 00		General Properties of Facility Services			General properties defining aspects of systems for Facilities Services
49-91 11 11			Accuracy		
49-91 11 13			Area Covered		
49-91 11 15			Capacity		
49-91 11 17			Components		
49-91 11 19			Connections		

OmniClass Number	Level 1 Title	Level 2 Title	Level 3 Title	Level 4 Title	Definitions
49-91 11 21			Constituents		Optional constituent features, parts or finishes. As defined by Spie – J.C. Moots, Eaton Corporation.
49-91 11 23			Parts		
49-91 11 25			System Equipment		
49-91 11 27			Equipment Type		A GBXML defined property. http://www.gbxml.org/
49-91 11 29			System Name		
49-91 11 31			Controls		
49-91 11 33			Flow Factor		
49-91 11 35			Flow Configuration		
49-91 11 37			Flow Direction		
49-91 11 39			Flow Conversion Method		
49-91 11 41			Design Flow Rate		
49-91 11 43			Instrumentation		
49-91 11 45			Inputs		
49-91 11 47			Outputs		
49-91 11 49			Loss Method		
49-91 11 51			Mode		
49-91 11 53			Number of Elements		
49-91 11 55			Service Connections		
49-91 11 57			Sensor Type		
49-91 11 59			Sensor Zone		
49-91 11 61			Sensor Detail Text		
49-91 11 63			Sensor Location		
49-91 11 65			System Type		
49-91 11 67			Service Type		
49-91 11 69			System Limitations		
49-91 11 71			Zone		
49-91 21 00		Properties of Fire Protection Systems			System or component properties uniquely found in Fire Protection Systems

(continued)

Table 49 (Continued)

OmniClass Number	Level 1 Title	Level 2 Title	Level 3 Title	Level 4 Title	Definitions
49-91 21 11			Fire Protection Class		
49-91 21 13			Sprinkler Type		
49-91 23 00		Properties of Plumbing Systems			System or component properties uniquely found in Plumbing Systems
49-91 23 11			Domestic Cold Water		
49-91 23 13			Domestic Hot Water		
49-91 23 15			Sanitary Water		
49-91 23 17			Waste Water		
49-91 23 19			Storm Water		
49-91 23 21			Fire Department Water		
49-91 23 23			Plumbing Volume		The volume of liquid contained in the system. A Revit MEP 2010 defined property.
49-91 23 25			Plumbing Fixture Units		The sum of the fixture units in the system. A Revit MEP 2010 defined property.
49-91 25 00		Properties of HVAC Systems			System or component properties uniquely found in HVAC Systems
49-91 25 11			HVAC System Type		A GBXML defined property. http://www.gbxml.org/
49-91 25 13			HVAC Efficiency		A GBXML defined property. http://www.gbxml.org/
49-91 25 15			HVAC Loads		
49-91 25 15 11				Design HVAC Load per area	Total HVAC load for the space. This value can be specified, calculated by the heating and cooling loads analysis tool, or read from a gbXML file. A Revit MEP 2010 User Guide defined property.
49-91 25 15 13				Actual HVAC Load	Total heating load for the space calculated by the integrated heating and cooling loads analysis tool. (Revit MEP 2010 User Guide)
49-91 25 15 15				Design Other HVAC Load per area	Total Other load for the space. This value can be specified, calculated by the heating and cooling loads analysis tool, or read from a gbXML file. A Revit MEP 2010 User Guide defined property.

OmniClass Number	Level 1 Title	Level 2 Title	Level 3 Title	Level 4 Title	Definitions
49-91 25 15 17				Actual Other HVAC Load	Total Other load for the space calculated by the integrated heating and cooling loads analysis tool. (Revit MEP 2010 User Guide)
49-91 25 15 19				Calculated Heating Load	Total heating load for the space. This value can be calculated by the integrated heating and cooling loads analysis tool or read from a gbXML file. "Not Computed" displays prior to the project receiving loads analysis results. A Revit MEP 2010 User Guide defined property.
49-91 25 15 21				Design Heating Load	Total heating load for the space. This value can be specified, calculated by the integrated heating and cooling loads analysis tool, or read from a gbXML file. (Revit MEP 2010 User Guide)
49-91 25 15 23				Calculated Cooling Load	Total cooling load for the space. This value can be calculated by the integrated heating and cooling loads analysis tool or read from a gbXML file. "Not Computed" displays prior to the project receiving loads analysis results. A Revit MEP 2010 User Guide defined property.
49-91 25 15 25				Design Cooling Load	Total cooling load for the space. This value can be specified, calculated by the integrated heating and cooling loads analysis tool, or read from a gbXML file. A Revit MEP 2010 User Guide defined property.
49-91 25 15 27				Zone Cooling Load	Refer to gbXML: ZoneCoolingLoad. A GBXML supplied term. www.gbxml.org.
49-91 25 17			HVAC Airflow		
49-91 25 17 11				Specified Supply Airflow	Supply airflow introduced in the space. This value can be specified, calculated by the integrated heating and cooling loads analysis tool, or read from a gbXML file. A Revit MEP 2010 User Guide defined property.
49-91 25 17 13				Calculated Supply Airflow	Total airflow required to head and cool the space. This value can be calculated by the integrated heating and cooling loads analysis tool or read from a gbXML file. (Revit MEP 2010 User Guide)

(continued)

Table 49   (Continued)

OmniClass Number	Level 1 Title	Level 2 Title	Level 3 Title	Level 4 Title	Definitions
49-91 25 17 15				Actual Supply Airflow	Total supply airflow in the space. This value is the sum of the airflow for all supply air terminals in the space. A Revit MEP 2010 User Guide defined property.
49-91 25 17 17				Return Airflow	Determines how the return airflow is calculated for the space. A Revit MEP 2010 User Guide defined property.
49-91 25 17 19				Specified Exhaust Airflow	Total exhaust airflow for the space.
49-91 25 17 21				Actual Exhaust Airflow	Total exhaust airflow for the space.
49-91 25 19			Air Volume Calculation Type		
49-91 25 21			HVAC Capacity		
49-91 25 21 11				Capacity Unit	A GBXML defined property. http://www.gbxml.org/
49-91 25 21 13				Heating Capacity	A GBXML defined property. http://www.gbxml.org/
49-91 25 21 15				Cooling Total Capacity	A GBXML defined property. http://www.gbxml.org/
49-91 25 21 17				Cooling Sensible Capacity	A GBXML defined property. http://www.gbxml.org/
49-91 25 21 19				Cooling Latent	A GBXML defined property. http://www.gbxml.org/
49-91 25 21 21				Cooling Sensible Heat Ratio (SHR)	A GBXML defined property. http://www.gbxml.org/
49-91 25 23			HVAC Conditioning		A GBXML defined property. http://www.gbxml.org/
49-91 25 23 11				Conditioning Unit	A GBXML defined property. http://www.gbxml.org/
49-91 25 23 13				Condition Heated	A GBXML defined property. http://www.gbxml.org/
49-91 25 23 15				Condition Cooled	A GBXML defined property. http://www.gbxml.org/
49-91 25 23 17				Condition Heated and Cooled	A GBXML defined property. http://www.gbxml.org/
49-91 25 23 19				Unconditioned	A GBXML defined property. http://www.gbxml.org/

OmniClass Number	Level 1 Title	Level 2 Title	Level 3 Title	Level 4 Title	Definitions
49-91 25 23 21				Vented	A GBXML defined property. http://www.gbxml.org/
49-91 25 23 23				Naturally Vented Only	A GBXML defined property. http://www.gbxml.org/
49-91 25 25			HVAC Controls		
49-91 25 25 11				HVAC Fan Control	A GBXML defined property. http://www.gbxml.org/
49-91 25 25 13				HVAC Pump Control	A GBXML defined property. http://www.gbxml.org/
49-91 25 25 15				HVAC Valve Control	A GBXML defined property. http://www.gbxml.org/
49-91 25 27			K Coefficient		
49-91 25 29			HVAC Calculated Results		
49-91 25 29 11				Peak Cooling Total Load	Total cooling load for all spaces in the building. This includes conduction, ventilation, pipe and duct gains, and sensible and latent loads. A Revit MEP 2010 User Guide defined property.
49-91 25 29 13				Peak Cooling Month and Hour	Date used to calculate peak calculations. A Revit MEP 2010 User Guide defined property.
49-91 25 29 15				Peak Cooling Sensible Load	Seasonal sensible cooling load high point for the building. A Revit MEP 2010 User Guide defined property.
49-91 25 29 17				Maximum Cooling Capacity	The maximum cooling capacity required, determined by sum of the peak cooling loads for the zones in the building. This recognizes that the peak load may occur at different times depending on conditions, such as the location of zones within the building (north-facing vs. south facing). A Revit MEP 2010 User Guide defined property.
49-91 25 29 19				Peak Cooling Airflow	Seasonal high point for cooling airflow for the building. A Revit MEP 2010 User Guide defined property.
49-91 25 29 21				Peak Heating Load	Total heating load for all spaces in the building. This includes conduction, ventilation, pipe and duct gains, and sensible and latent loads. A Revit MEP 2010 User Guide defined property.

(continued)

Table 49   (Continued)

OmniClass Number	Level 1 Title	Level 2 Title	Level 3 Title	Level 4 Title	Definitions
49-91 25 29 23				Peak Heating Airflow	Seasonal high point for heating airflow for the building. A Revit MEP 2010 User Guide defined property.
49-91 25 31			HVAC Checksums		
49-91 25 31 11				Cooling Load Density	Total Cooling Load for the building divided by the Occupied Analytical Area in the building. A Revit MEP 2010 User Guide defined property.
49-91 25 31 13				Cooling Flow Density	Cooling Airflow divided by the Occupied Analytical Area of the building. A Revit MEP 2010 User Guide defined property.
49-91 25 31 15				Cooling Flow/ Load	Cooling Airflow divided by the Total Cooling Load of the building. A Revit MEP 2010 User Guide defined property.
49-91 25 31 17				Cooling Area/ Load	Analytical Area of the zone divided by the Total Cooling of the building. A Revit MEP 2010 User Guide defined property.
49-91 25 31 19				Heating Load Density	Total Heating Load for the building divided by the Occupied Analytical Area in the building. A Revit MEP 2010 User Guide defined property.
49-91 25 31 21				Heating Flow Density	Heating Airflow divided by the Occupied Analytical Area of the building. A Revit MEP 2010 User Guide defined property.
49-91 25 33			Minimum Efficiency Reporting Value (MERV) Rating		
49-91 25 35			Manufacturer's coil bypass factor		
49-91 31 00		Properties of Integrated Automation Systems			Network and other properties of Integrated Automation Systems
49-91 31 11			Standard Network Variable Type (SNVT)		
49-91 31 13			Control Type		A GBXML defined property. http://www .gbxml.org/
49-91 31 15			Expected Engineering Units		
49-91 31 17			Node ID		

OmniClass Number	Level 1 Title	Level 2 Title	Level 3 Title	Level 4 Title	Definitions
49-91 31 19			Domain Address		
49-91 31 21			Subnet Address		
49-91 41 00		Properties of Electrical Systems			Properties defining supply, demand and characteristics of Electrical Power, features of Electrical Systems and Electrical Components
49-91 41 11			Amperage		
49-91 41 13			Voltage		
49-91 41 13 11				Voltage Drop	The difference between the voltage applied and the voltage consumed on the circuit. A Revit MEP 2010 User Guide defined property.
49-91 41 15			Electrical Source		
49-91 41 17			Electrical Power Factor		The difference between Apparent Load and True Load, expressed as a decimal.
49-91 41 19			Electrical Power Factor State		Lagging or Leading, depending on whether the load is inductive or capacitive.
49-91 41 21			Properties of Electrical Currents		NIST 906-11
49-91 41 21 11				Current Draw	
49-91 41 21 13				Electrical Current Density	
49-91 41 21 15				True Current	
49-91 41 21 17				True Current and Phase	
49-91 41 23			Properties of Electrical Loads		
49-91 41 23 11				Load Classification	
49-91 41 23 13				True Load	
49-91 41 23 15				Balanced Load	Indicates whether the load is distributed evenly between the phases. A Revit MEP 2010 User Guide defined property.
49-91 41 25			Properties of Electrical Panels		
49-91 41 25 11				Panel Name	
49-91 41 25 13				Panel Number	
49-91 41 25 15				Number of Poles	

(continued)

Table 49   (Continued)

OmniClass Number	Level 1 Title	Level 2 Title	Level 3 Title	Level 4 Title	Definitions
49-91 41 25 17				Maximum Number of Pole Breakers	
49-91 41 25 19				Main Ratings	
49-91 41 25 21				Apparent Load and Phase	
49-91 41 27			Properties of Circuits		
49-91 41 27 11				Circuit Name	
49-91 41 27 13				Circuit Number	
49-91 41 27 15				Circuit Load Name	
49-91 41 27 17				Dedicated Circuit	
49-91 41 27 19				Wire Type	
49-91 41 27 21				Wire Size	
49-91 41 27 23				Number of Runs	The number of parallel conductors required to supply the circuit. A Revit MEP 2010 User Guide defined property.
49-91 41 27 25				Number of Hot Conductors	
49-91 41 27 27				Number of Neutral Conductors	
49-91 41 27 29				Number of Ground Conductors	
49-91 41 29			Estimated and Connected Demands		
49-91 41 29 11				HVAC Total Estimated Demand	
49-91 41 29 13				HVAC Total Connected	
49-91 41 29 15				Lighting Total Estimated Demand	
49-91 41 29 17				Lighting Total Connected	

OmniClass Number	Level 1 Title	Level 2 Title	Level 3 Title	Level 4 Title	Definitions
49-91 41 29 19				Power Total Estimated Demand	
49-91 41 29 21				Power Total Connected	
49-91 41 29 23				Other Total Estimated Demand	
49-91 41 29 25				Other Total Connected	
49-91 41 29 27				Total Estimated Demand	
49-91 41 29 29				Total Connected	
49-91 41 31			Dielectric Constant		
49-91 41 33			Earth Ground Resistance		
49-91 41 35			Electrical Admittance		
49-91 41 37			Electrical Capacitance		
49-91 41 39			Electrical Charge		
49-91 41 41			Electrical Charge Density		
49-91 41 43			Electrical Conductance		
49-91 41 45			Electrical Conductivity		
49-91 41 47			Electrical Field Strength		
49-91 41 49			Electrical Flux Density		
49-91 41 51			Electrical Frequency		
49-91 41 53			Electrical Inductance		
49-91 41 55			Electrical Insulation		
49-91 41 57			Electrical Potential Difference		

(continued)

Table 49   (Continued)

OmniClass Number	Level 1 Title	Level 2 Title	Level 3 Title	Level 4 Title	Definitions
49-91 41 59			Electrical Reluctance		
49-91 41 61			Electrical Resistance		
49-91 41 63			Electrical Susceptance		
49-91 41 65			Electrical Permittivity		
49-91 41 67			Electrical Phase		
49-91 41 69			Input Impedance		
49-91 41 71			Output Impedance		
49-91 41 73			Self Inductance		
49-91 41 75			Solid State		
49-91 41 77			Surge Content		
49-91 51 00		Properties of Lighting Systems			Properties defining Lighting Systems or Lighting Components
49-91 51 11			IEEE Illumination Levels		
49-91 51 13			Average Estimated Illumination		
49-91 51 15			Footcandles		
49-91 51 17			Glare		Minimum amount of glare to trigger the shades to close. A GBXML defined property. http://www.gbxml.org/
49-91 51 19			Glare Index		
49-91 51 21			Index of Refraction		Measurement of how much a ray of light bends
49-91 51 23			Illuminance		Illuminance level that the lights are maintained if daylighting controls present. A GBXML defined property. http://www.gbxml.org/
49-91 51 25			Light Absorption		
49-91 51 27			Light Brightness		
49-91 51 29			Lighting Calculation Workplane		The level used as the base for calculating Illumination.
49-91 51 31			Light Emission		

OmniClass Number	Level 1 Title	Level 2 Title	Level 3 Title	Level 4 Title	Definitions
49-91 51 33			Light Exposure		
49-91 51 35			Light Illuminance		
49-91 51 37			Light Polarization		
49-91 51 39			Light Reflectance		
49-91 51 41			Light Refractive Index		Measurement of how much a ray of light bends
49-91 51 43			Light Source		
49-91 51 45			Light Transmission		
49-91 51 47			Lighting Controls		
49-91 51 47 11				Light Control ID	
49-91 51 49			Luminance		
49-91 51 49 11				Lumens Per Lamp	
49-91 51 49 13				Luminous Efficacy	
49-91 51 49 15				Luminous Flux	
49-91 51 49 17				Luminous Intensity	
49-91 51 51			Reflectance		
49-91 51 51 11				Ceiling Reflectance	
49-91 51 51 13				Wall Reflectance	
49-91 51 51 15				Floor Reflectance	
49-91 51 51 17				Solar Reflectance	
49-91 51 51 19				Solar Reflectance Index (SRI)	
49-91 51 53			Room Cavity Ratio		This parameter is automatically calculated based on room dimensions to determine illumination calculations. Room Cavity Ratio = 5 x height (length + width)/(length x width), where height is the difference between the Lighting Calculation Workplane and the either the Limit Offset or level of an upper room bounding component, whichever is lower. A Revit MEP defined term.
49-91 51 55			Translucence		

(continued)

Table 49 (Continued)

OmniClass Number	Level 1 Title	Level 2 Title	Level 3 Title	Level 4 Title	Definitions
49-91 51 57			Transparency		
49-91 51 59			Opacity		
49-91 51 61			Ultraviolet Light		
49-91 51 63			Visible Light		
49-91 51 65			Visible Light Transmittance		
49-91 61 00		Properties of Communication Systems			Properties defining the performance and attributes of Communication Systems or Communication Systems Components
49-91 61 11			Cable Category		
49-91 61 13			Cable Classification		
49-91 61 15			Cable Listing		
49-91 61 17			Cable Material		
49-91 61 19			Cable Rating		
49-91 61 21			Cable Terminations		
49-91 61 23			Cable Type		
49-91 61 23 11				Unshielded Twisted Pair (UTP)	
49-91 61 23 13				Twisted Pair	
49-91 61 25			Fiber Count		
49-91 61 27			Fiber Type		
49-91 61 27 11				Fiber Optic	
49-91 61 27 13				Nonconductive	
49-91 61 27 15				General Purpose	
49-91 61 27 17				Communications Plenum	
49-91 61 27 19				Communications Riser	
49-91 61 29			Shielding		
49-91 61 31			Signal Set Choice		
49-91 61 33			Signal Type		
49-91 61 33 11				Broadband	
49-91 61 33 13				Modulated	

OmniClass Number	Level 1 Title	Level 2 Title	Level 3 Title	Level 4 Title	Definitions
49-91 61 35			Signal-to-Noise Ratio		
49-91 61 37			Transmission Performance Rating		
49-91 71 00		Properties of Safety and Security Systems			Properties describing the performance and features of Safety and Security Systems and their components
49-91 71 11			Alarm Type		
49-91 71 13			Status Code		
49-91 71 15			Audit Trail		
49-91 71 17			System Status		
49-91 71 19			Backup Battery Capacity		
49-91 71 21			Control Point		
49-91 71 23			Display Type		
49-91 71 25			Fail-Safe Capability		
49-91 71 27			Logic Points		
49-91 71 29			Report Type		
49-91 71 31			Reporting Area		
49-91 71 33			Termination Point		
49-91 71 35			Time Stamp		
49-91 81 00		Properties of Energy Systems			Properties describing the supply, demand and flow of Energy and other characteristics of Energy Systems
49-91 81 11			Energy Consumption		
49-91 81 13			Energy Demand		
49-91 81 15			Energy Unit		A GBXML defined property. http://www.gbxml.org/
49-91 81 17			Energy Per Unit Area Time		
49-91 81 19			Energy Density		
49-91 81 21			Energy Efficiency		
49-91 81 21 11				Energy Efficiency Measurement	

(continued)

Table 49   (Continued)

OmniClass Number	Level 1 Title	Level 2 Title	Level 3 Title	Level 4 Title	Definitions
49-91 81 21 13				Energy Efficiency Verification	
49-91 81 21 15				Water Efficiency	
49-91 81 21 17				Fuel Efficiency	
49-91 81 23			Heat Flux Density		The amount of power or heat flow that is exchanged across a unit area of a system
49-91 81 25			Impact Energy Absorption		
49-91 81 27			Potential Energy		
49-91 81 29			Power Output		
49-91 81 31			Radiance		
49-91 81 33			Radiant Intensity		
49-91 81 35			Irradiance		Total quantity of solar energy that hits a surface during a specific time period. A Wikipedia defined property. http://en.wikipedia.org/wiki/Irradiance
49-91 81 37			Specific Energy		
49-91 81 39			Total Solar Energy		
49-91 81 41			Total Solar Energy Reflectance		

Index